# INTERNET BANKING AND THE LAW IN EUROPE

The European Union has long sought to create a single financial area across Europe where consumers in one country benefit from financial markets and activities in other countries. With the emergence of the Internet as a platform for the provision of online banking services, the creation of a pan-European market for banking services appeared a realistic proposition. In practice, however, this has not happened. This book asks why and argues that the creation of banking markets via the Internet relies on both available technologies and appropriate laws and regulations. The institutional and legal framework for online banking services in the single European market are examined, as is the level of legal harmonization achieved in the UK, France and Germany under the influence of the EU Directives pertaining to online banking activities.

APOSTOLOS ATH. GKOUTZINIS is an Associate in the Capital Markets Group of the London office of the international law firm Shearman & Sterling LLP. His practice includes providing legal advice to investment banks and major corporate clients regarding equity and debt securities offerings and other complex capital market transactions, exchange listings, corporate governance and other corporate matters. Prior to joining the firm, he was Lecturer in Financial Law and Joint Academic Director of the MSc Programme in Finance and Financial Law at the School of Oriental and African Studies (SOAS), University of London. He also held a Teaching and Research Fellowship at the Centre for Commercial Law Studies at Queen Mary, University of London. He is admitted to practise law in the State of New York, England and Wales, and Greece.

# INTERNET BANKING AND THE LAW IN EUROPE

Regulation, Financial Integration and
Electronic Commerce

APOSTOLOS ATH. GKOUTZINIS

CAMBRIDGE UNIVERSITY PRESS
Cambridge, New York, Melbourne, Madrid, Cape Town, Singapore,
São Paulo, Delhi, Dubai, Tokyo, Mexico City

Cambridge University Press
The Edinburgh Building, Cambridge CB2 8RU, UK

Published in the United States of America by Cambridge University Press, New York

www.cambridge.org
Information on this title: www.cambridge.org/9780521860710

© Apostolos Gkoutzinis 2006

This publication is in copyright. Subject to statutory exception
and to the provisions of relevant collective licensing agreements,
no reproduction of any part may take place without the written
permission of Cambridge University Press.

First published 2006

*A catalogue record for this publication is available from the British Library*

ISBN 978-0-521-86071-0 Hardback
ISBN 978-0-521-15323-2 Paperback

Cambridge University Press has no responsibility for the persistence or
accuracy of URLs for external or third-party internet websites referred to in
this publication, and does not guarantee that any content on such websites is,
or will remain, accurate or appropriate. Information regarding prices, travel
timetables, and other factual information given in this work are correct at
the time of first printing but Cambridge University Press does not guarantee
the accuracy of such information thereafter.

Στη Δέσποινα,
Για τις ώρες που δεν ήμουν εκεί

CONTENTS

*Tables*  *page* xiii
*Preface*  xv
*Tables of legislation*  xix
*Table of EU legislation*  xxvii
*Table of international conventions*  xxxvi
*Table of cases*  xxxvii
*Abbreviations*  xliii

Introduction  1

PART I **Introduction to electronic finance and Internet banking**  5

1 Internet banking in Europe: basic concepts and recent trends  7

    The Internet as catalyst of international financial integration  7

    Internet banking in Europe  20

2 The legal foundations of electronic banking activities  29

    The banker–customer relationship  29

Electronic finance and credit    40

Online securities trading    42

PART II **Online banking and international market access: The causes of incomplete financial integration and what to do about them**    49

3    Legal barriers and necessary regulatory reforms    51

The causes of incomplete European integration in online financial services    51

International governance of cross-border electronic commerce and finance    63

EU policies affecting electronic commerce in financial services    73

4    The governance of the European market in cross-border electronic banking activities    82

Introduction    82

Institutional foundations of the single European market in financial services    84

Mutual recognition of national laws as institutional principle    86

Mutual recognition beyond the EC Treaty: 'home country' control in various forms as institutional anchor of the single financial market    99

Minimum harmonization of national laws and enforcement practices as prerequisites of mutual recognition of national laws and 'home country' control    123

PART III  **EU harmonization and convergence of national laws relating to electronic banking activities**    135

5  Risks and regulatory concerns relating to electronic banking activities and the convergence of national prudential regulatory standards    137

Convergence of national laws and the notion of 'general good' in the single European market    137

Risks and prudential regulatory concerns caused by electronic banking activities    148

Non-EU international initiatives of legal harmonization concerning electronic banking activities    150

EU harmonization measures in the field of prudential banking regulation    154

The prudential regulation of electronic banking activities in key European countries    156

6  EU measures of legal harmonization concerning electronic commerce and distance marketing of financial services, data protection, banking contracts and investor protection    165

E-commerce and distance marketing of financial services    165

Privacy and data protection    179

The harmonization of national laws of
banking contracts 183
Online bank loans and the Consumer
Credit Directive 205
Convergence of national laws regulating the provision of
online investment services 213
Assessing the level of convergence of national
laws regulating Internet banking 226

PART IV **Applicable law and allocation of regulatory responsibility in cross-border electronic banking activities** 229

7 Cross-border Internet banking and the principle of 'home country' control in the EU Financial Services Directives 231

Introduction 231

Cross-border Internet banking without the benefit of 'home country' regulation and supervision 232

Mutual recognition of national laws on the basis of 'home country' control in the Banking and Investment Services Directives 237

The notion of 'general good' in the Banking Consolidation Directive 242

'Host country' powers to apply domestic laws in non-prudential matters 243

8    Mutual recognition of national laws under the principle of 'country of origin' of the Electronic Commerce Directive    262

    Scope of application of the 'country of origin' rule    262

    The 'coordinated field'    266

    The implementation of the 'country of origin' principle    278

    The case-by-case derogation of Article 3(4)–(6)    281

    The normative impact of the principle of 'country of origin'    286

9    Applicable law and jurisdiction in cross-border electronic banking contracts    289

    International contracts, conflicts of laws and European financial integration    290

    Choice of law and choice of jurisdiction in cross-border banking contracts    292

    Choice of law and forum in consumer contracts    296

    Choice of law and the impact of mandatory rules    305

Conclusions    310

*Select bibliography*    319

*Index*    339

TABLES

1.1 Penetration of Internet banking and brokerage
    (end of 2000)      *page* 21
1.2 Internet banking in the United Kingdom,
    France and Germany      23
6.1 Information requirements under ECD and DMD      180
6.2 Coverage of Unfair Contract Terms Regulation in key
    EU countries      197
6.3 Coverage of Consumer Credit Regulation in key
    EU countries      208
6.4 National laws limiting party autonomy in consumer
    credit contracts      211

# PREFACE

This book is the culmination of a five-year long research project, which was carried out initially at the Centre for Commercial Law Studies, Queen Mary, University of London, then at Harvard Law School and, at the final stages, during my sparse spare time as an attorney at the London office of Shearman and Sterling (London) LLP. The book encapsulates my fascination with the Internet and my interest in how the powers of electronic networks, information technology, advanced telecommunications and financial innovation are transforming national and international financial markets in Europe and elsewhere. It is also a book about international financial integration and cross-border trade in financial services and how the Internet can facilitate consumers' access to financial services and firms' access to markets across national borders.

Artificial legal and structural barriers to cross-border financial services seem so unreasonable when one realizes the human and economic cost of policies and actions which purport to eliminate physical barriers. At the time when we spend astronomical amounts of money to improve our communications and systems of transportation by air, land or sea – thus diminishing time and distance in the circulation of goods and services – at the same time we are keen to maintain (or at least we tolerate) artificial barriers which are no less effective than distance and rough terrain in disturbing trade in goods and services, particularly financial services. Thus the failure of the single European market project to abolish all direct and indirect legal restrictions on the free movement of financial services – which are suitable for circulating over computer networks – in the era of the Internet was a reason for reflection and research.

I would never have completed this project had it not been for the influence, support, encouragement, assistance and advice of a large number of people.

Chris Reed, Professor of Electronic Commerce Law and my research supervisor during my formative years, guided me through this process magnificently. To the best of my knowledge, Professor Chris Reed is unique in his achievement to be an e-commerce expert and a financial services expert. It was my privilege to work under his supervision. Dr Rosa Maria Lastra, Senior Lecturer at the Centre for Commercial Law Studies was my second doctoral supervisor and has now become a close personal and family friend. She was immensely influential in many respects. She contributed her world-class expertise in the law and economics of financial regulation and provided inspiration for key parts of the thesis. She has offered me unconditional support on various academic fronts and assisted in the development of this book with her guidance and accuracy. I will always remain deeply indebted for the opportunity to test my ideas teaching in her LLM course Regulation of Financial Markets at the University of London in the academic year 2003–4.

The Greek government and the director and staff of the State Scholarships Foundation (Athens) enabled me to pursue my graduate studies with the generous funding that I received as a Banking Law Scholar 1999–2003. Professor Dr Aristidis Chiotellis of the University of Athens was my supervisor appointed by the State Scholarship Foundation and supported me throughout this project. I must also thank the Central Research Fund of the University of London for funding my research expedition to Bonn, Paris and Brussels in the summer of 2002.

Professor Laurence Harris, Director of the Centre for Financial and Management Studies, School of Oriental and African Studies, University of London offered me a unique working environment and unlimited support to progress with this book as I was teaching and working as Lecturer in Financial Law at the Centre. I also sincerely thank Professor Joseph Norton for offering me the opportunity to teach as a Fellow at the International Financial Law Unit of the Centre for Commercial Law Studies. Last but not least, I would like to thank the partners, lawyers and support staff of Shearman and Sterling (London) LLP for providing such a stimulating and resourceful working environment at the very last stages of this project. The reader should kindly note, however, that I wrote the book in a personal capacity and no views or arguments held should be attributed to Shearman and Sterling LLP, its partners and lawyers in any way whatsoever.

I owe deep gratitude to Eric Ducoulombier (European Commission), Alain Duchateau (Commission Bancaire & Electronic Banking Group), Peter Snowdon and Peter Parker (FSA), Stefan Czekay (Bundesanstalt für Finanzdienstleistungsaufsicht), Sven Jongebloed and Magdalen Heid

(Deutsche Bundesbank) for sharing their views with me; the library staff at the Institute of Advanced Legal Studies, Harvard Law School, Queen Mary College, British Library, London School of Economics, University of Bonn, University of Paris (Paris II) and Free University of Brussels for their professionalism and quality of services.

I thank all my friends and family for their strong encouragement and support, particularly Manolis and Christina Michaelidis, Kalliopi and Vaggelis Spanos, Kostas Georgiadis, Athanasios Stogiannidis, Rosanna M. Annan, Nikolaos Skoulas, Alexis and Niki Lappas, Marinos and Eleni Kyriakopoulos, Antonios Patrikios, Nikolaos Koutsoupias and Georgia Filitsopoulou. I owe special thanks and gratitude to Akis and Maria Ioannidis for their love, support and warm hospitality in London over the recent years.

I am extremely grateful to my editor Jane O'Regan, the production editor Wendy Phillips and their dedicated teams at Cambridge University Press for turning my ideas into a book. Words cannot describe my pride in publishing my first book with this prestigious institution.

My spiritual fathers in the Greek Orthodox Church, in Kavala, Mount Athos and London I thank from my heart for praying for me, particularly the Very Revs. Father Constantinos, Father Myron, Father Anthimos, Father Georgios and Father Demetrius.

God blessed me with a caring family where no one is left to carry a burden alone and everybody shares his joy with others. My beloved brother the Very Reverend Arch. Father Sophronios Gkoutzinis has been supporting me all my life. I thank him for his prayers, love and respect. My parents, Athanassios and Maria, have always carried all the burdens that I could not. This book is theirs more than it is mine. Maria, Athanassios and Konstantinos, my lovely children, are supporting their daddy in their own way.

My wife Despina is what makes all that interesting. She has been my strongest supporter and a resourceful supplier of hope. She alone deserves all the credit. This work is dedicated to her.

# TABLES OF LEGISLATION

## France

Code Civil (Civil Code)
    art. 1108(1) 187
    arts. 1156–61 199
    art. 1163 199
    art. 1164 199
    art. 1316(4) 187
    art. 1369(1) 184
    art. 1369(2) 188
    art. 1382 173
    art. 1383 173
    arts. 1984–2010 46
    art. 1991 221
Code de la Consommation (Consumer Code)
    art. 311(1) 207
    art. 311(2) 207
    art. 311(3) 207
    art. D 311(1) 207
    art. D 311(2) 207
    art. L 3(4) 260
    art. L 121(1) 174, 260
    arts. L 121 174
    art. L 121(8) 174
    arts. L 121(20)(8)–(16) 170
    art. L 121(20)(12) 190
    art. L 132(1) 199
    art. L 133(2) 193
    art. L 213(1) 174
    art. L 311(2) 207
    art. L 311(3) 42, 207
    art. L 311(4) 207
    art. L 311(8) 209

**France** (*Continued*)
  art. L 311(15) 209
  art. L 311(16) 209
  art. L 311(29) 210
  art. L 312(1) 196
  art. L 311(8) 209
  art. L 311(9) 209
  art. L 311(10) 209
  art. R 311(6) 209
Code de la Procédure Pénale (Code of Criminal Procedure)
  art. 689 260
Code du Commerce (Commercial Code)
  art. L 132(1) 46
Code Monétaire et Financier (Monetary and Financial Code) 160
  art. L 133(1) 202
  art. L 311(1) 32, 41, 236
  art. L 311(3) 32
  art. L 312(1) 204
  art. L 312(1)(1) 188
  art. L 312(1)(2) 204
  art. L 312(2) 31
  art. L 312(3) 204
  art. L 313(1) 41
  art. L 321(1) 46, 236
  art. L 341 174
  art. L 342 174
  art. L 343 174
  art. L 351(1) 188
  art. L 511(1) 32, 41, 236
  art. L 511(9) 236
  art. L 511(22) 238
  art. L 511(33) 133
  art. L 511(41) 161
  art. L 531(1) 236
  art. L 532(1) 236
  art. L 532(18) 238, 256
  art. L 533(1) 220
  art. L 533(4) 221, 256
  art. L 533(6) 220
  art. L 533(7) 221, 222
  art. L 533(8) 221

art. L 561(1) 133
art. L 562(1) 239
art. L 563(1) 189
art. L 611(1) 160
art. L 612(1) 160
art. L 612(2) 160
art. L 613(1) 161
art. L 621(1) 160
art. L 632(1) 133
art. R 312(3) 204
Code Pénal (Penal Code)
art. L 113(2) 260
Déclaration des Droits de l'Homme et du Citoyen 1789
art. 1 14
art. 4 14
Loi 2003-706 (Financial Security Act), 1 August 2003 160
Loi 2004-575 pour la Confiance dans L'Economie Numérique, 2004-575 281
art. 14 168, 281
arts. 14–28 168
art. 16(1) 281
art. 17(1) 281
art. 17(2)(1) 281
art. 18 286
art. 19 177
art. 20 177
art. 21 177
art. 22 174
art. 25 184
Loi 2004-801 (Data Protection Act) 182
art. 5 182, 184

## Secondary legislation

Décret 84-708
art. 7 193
Décret 96-880
art. 7 241
art. 15 241
Ordonnance 2000-1223, 14 December 2000 160
Ordonnance 2005-648, 6 June 2005 171
Règlement 86–13
Règlement 97–02

**France** (*Continued*)
    art. 5 161
    art. 11 161
    art. 14 161

# Germany

Bundesdatenschutzgesetz (Data Protection Act) 182
    § 1 Abs.5 182
Bürgerliches Gesetzbuch (BGB) (Civil Code)
    § 126 Abs.3 187
    § 126a 187
    § 242 34
    § 276 225
    § 305 Abs. 2 193
    § 305 Abs.1 196
    § 309 198
    § 312 170
    § 312e 184, 188
    § 312s 190
    § 355 190
    § 488 41
    § 488–498 41
    § 489 210
    § 491 207
    § 492 209
    § 492 Abs.1 209
    § 493 209, 210
    § 507 207
    § 667 45
    § 675 45
    § 676a 33
    § 676a–676c 202
    § 676f 31
    § 823(3) 226
Elektronischer Geschäftsverkehr Gesetz (EGG) (E-Commerce Act) 167
Finanzdienstleistungaufsichtsgesetz (FinDAG) (Integrated Financial Services Supervision Act) 162
Gesetz gegen den Unlauteren Wettbewerb (UWG) (Unfair Competition Act) 176
    § 1 176
    § 3 176
    § 23 177

Gesetz über das Aufspüren von Gewinnen aus Schweren Straftaten (GwG) (Money Laundering Act)
  § 1 189
  § 1 Abs.3 239
  § 8 189
Gesetz über die Nutzung von Telediensten (TDG) (Teleservices Act)
  § 4 Abs.1 280
  § 4 Abs.2 280
  § 5 286
Gesetz zur Änderung der Verschriften über Fernabsatzverträge bei Finanzdienstleistungen (Distance Marketing Act) 170
Gesetz zur Regehung des Rechts der Allgemeinen Geschäftsbedingungen (Act on the Regulation of the Law of General Business Conditions) 198
Grundgesetz (Constitution)
  § 12(1) 14
Handelsgesetzbuch (HGB) (Commercial Code)
  § 384 45
Kreditwesengesetz (KWG) (Banking Act)
  § 1 31, 41, 238
  § 1(1) 45
  § 3 248
  § 7 162
  § 8 133
  § 9 133
  § 23a 248
  § 24a 241
  § 27 133
  § 32 31, 41, 235
  § 37 248
  § 44 133
  § 44c 248
  § 49 248
  § 50 248
  § 53b 241
  § 53b Abs. 3 248
  § 53b Abs.2a 239
  § 53b Abs.3 239
Strafgesetzbuch (StGB) (Criminal Code)
  § 3 260
  § 9 260
Teledienstengesetz (TDG) (Teleservices Act) 167

**Germany** (*Continued*)
   § 1 168
   § 2 Abs.1 168
   § 2 Abs.2(1) 168
   § 2 Abs.2(5) 168
   § 3 Abs.3 168
   § 3 Abs.4 168
   § 6 177
Wertpapier-Handelgesetz (WpHG) (Securities Trading Act) 224
   § 31 Abs.1(i) 225
   § 31 Abs.1(ii) 225
   § 31 Abs.2 225
   § 31 Abs.2(ii) 226
   § 31(3) 255
   § 32(3) 255
   § 33 224
   § 34 224

## Secondary Legislation
Abgabeordnung
   § 154 189
Preisangabenverordnung (Disclosure of Price Information Regulation)
   § 1 207
   § 6 207

# United Kingdom

Consumer Credit Act 1974
   s. 8 207
   ss. 8–20 207
   s. 44 207
   s. 46 174, 257
   s. 61 208
   s. 63 208
   s. 65 208
   s. 74 210
   s. 94 210
   s. 95 210
   s. 189 207
Consumer Protection Act 1987 257
   s. 20 175

Data Protection Act 1998 182
    s. 5(1) 182
Electronic Communications Act 2000
    s. 15(1) 209
Financial Services and Markets Act 2000 30, 156
    s. 2(3) 156
    s. 5(2) 156
    s. 19 30, 232, 235
    s. 21(8)(a) 175
    s. 22 233
    s. 150 220
    s. 165(1) 133
    s. 169 133
    s. 175(5) 133
    s. 274(8) 133
    ss. 348–354 133
    s. 418 235
    s. 418(5) 232
    sch. 2(2) 46
    sch. 2(3) 46
    sch. 3 238
    sch. 3 para 14 241
    sch. 3 para 20 241
    sch. 6 219
Interpretation Act 1978
    sch. 1 186
Private International Law (Miscellaneous Provisions) Act 1995
    s. 11(2)(c) 257
Supply of Goods and Services Act 1982
    s. 13 34
Trade Descriptions Act 1968
    s. 4 174, 257
Unfair Contract Terms Act 1977
    s. 11(1) 197

## Secondary Legislation

Consumer Credit Act (Electronic Communications) Order 2004 (SI 2004/3236) 208
Consumer Credit (Advertisements) Regulations 2004 (SI 2004/1484)
    regs. 2-9 207
    reg. 4 210
    reg. 8 210
    sch. 2 210

Consumer Credit (Agreements) Regulations 1983 (SI 1983/1553) 208
  reg. 6(1) 208
  sch. 6 208
Consumer Credit (Cancellation Notices and Copies of Documents) Regulations 1983 (SI 1983/1557) 208
Consumer Credit (Rebate on Early Settlement) Regulations 2004 (SI 2004/1483) 210
Control of Misleading Advertisements Regulations 1988 (SI 1988/915) 174, 257
Cross-Border Transfers Regulations 1999 (SI 1999/1876) 202
Electronic Commerce Directive (Financial Services and Markets) Regulations 2002 (SI 2002/1775) 167, 278
  reg. 3(4) 278
  reg. 3(6) 278
  reg. 6(1) 285
Electronic Commerce (EC Directive) Regulations 2002 (SI 2002/2013) 167, 278
  reg. 5 286
  reg. 5(2) 286
  reg. 9 184
  reg. 10 177
  reg. 11 188
Financial Services and Markets Act 2000 (Financial Promotion) Order 2001 (SI 2001/1335)
  art. 2(1) 175
  art. 6(b) 175
  art. 6(c) 175
  art. 7(3) 175
Financial Services and Markets Act 2000 (Regulated Activities) (Amendment) (No 2) Order 2002 (SI 2002/1776) 279
Financial Services (Distance Marketing) Regulations 2004 (SI 2004/2095) 170
  reg. 9(1) 190
  reg. 9(2) 190
Money Laundering Regulations 2003 (SI 2003/3075) 189
Unfair Contract Terms in Consumer Contracts Regulations 1999 (SI 1999/2083) 196

# TABLE OF EU LEGISLATION

## Treaties

Amsterdam Treaty 1997
    art. 6(54), 88

Brussels Convention on Jurisdiction and the Enforcement of Judgments in Civil and Commercial Matters 1968, 293
Brussels Convention on Jurisdiction and the Enforcement of Judgments in Civil and Commercial Matters 1998, 249
    art. 5(1), 249
    art. 5(1)(b), 249

EC Treaty, 2
    art. 3(1)(c), 11
    art. 4, 86
    art. 5, 85, 124
    art. 7, 85
    art. 8b, 88
    art. 10, 131
    art. 14, 85, 88
    art. 14(2), 2, 84
    art. 15, 86
    art. 43, 2
    art. 47(1), 88
    art. 47(2), 85, 154
    art. 49, 14, 84, 85, 270
    art. 50, 263, 265
    art. 56, 84
    art. 67, 56
    art. 95, 75, 85, 86, 125
    art. 100b, 88, 126
    art. 153, 75, 86, 102, 143

**Treaties** (*Continued*)
  art. 220, 85
  art. 293, 88

Rome Convention on the Law Applicable to Contractual Obligations 1998, 116, 249, 272, 276, 289, 291, 292–3
  art. 3(1), 293
  art. 4(1), 249, 294
  art. 4(2), 294
  art. 4(5), 295
  art. 5, 293, 305, 306, 309
  art. 5(1), 298
  art. 5(2), 114, 302, 297, 299, 314, 316
  art. 5(4)(b), 302
  art. 7(2), 305, 306, 309, 314

Single European Act 1986, 88
  art. 19, 88

# Directives

84/450 Misleading and Comparative Advertising Directive [1984] OJ L250, 171
  art. 1, 171
86/635 Bank Accounts Directive [1986] OJ L372, 155, 239
87/102/EEC Consumer Credit Directive [1987] OJ L42, 169
  recital 3, 205
  recital 5, 205
  recital 6, 205
  recital 7, 205
  recital 9, 205
  art. 1(2)(a), 145
  art. 1(2)(c), 205
  art. 1(a)(2), 206
  art. 2(1)(e), 205
  art. 2(1)(f), 205
  art. 2(1)(g), 205
  art. 3, 206
  art. 4(1), 186, 206
  art. 4(2), 206
  art. 4(3), 206
  art. 6(1), 206
  art. 6(2), 206

art. 6(3), 207
art. 8, 206
art. 15, 207
Annex I, para. 2, 206
Annex I, para. 4, 206
88/361/EEC Directive for the implementation of Article 67 of the Treaty [1988] OJ L178, 56
91/308/EC Money Laundering Directive [1991] OJ L166, 155–6
  art. 3(1), 155
  art. 3(2), 156
  art. 3(8), 156
  art. 3(11), 156
  art. 6, 156
  art. 8, 156
  art. 9, 156
  art. 11, 156
  art. 15, 156
93/12/EEC Unfair Contract Terms Directive [1993] OJ L95, 194–9
  recital 3, 194
  recital 4, 194
  recital 5, 194
  recital 12, 195
  recital 15, 195
  recital 16, 194
  recital 17, 195
  recital 18, 195
  art. 1(1), 194
  art. 1(2), 194
  art. 2(1), 214
  art. 3(1), 194
  art. 3(2), 194
  art. 3(3), 194
  art. 4(1), 195
  art. 4(2), 195
  art. 5, 195
  art. 8, 196
93/13/EEC Unfair Terms in Consumer Contracts Directive [1993] OJ L95
  art. 2, 298
93/22/EEC Investment Services Directive [1993] OJ L141, 169, 254
  art. 11, 218, 216, 254
  art. 15(4), 44
94/19/EC Deposit Guarantee Schemes Directive [1994] OJ L135, 139, 155

95/46/EC Data Protection Directive [1995] OJ L281, 179–82
    recital 7, 179
    recital 19, 182
    art. 4(1)(b), 182
    art. 6, 181
    art. 7, 179
    art. 10, 182
    art. 11, 182
    art. 12, 182
    art. 14, 182
    art. 15, 182
    art. 17, 182
97/5/EC Cross-border Credit Transfers Directive [1997] OJ L43, 169, 200
    recital 8, 201
    art. 1, 200
    art. 2(f), 200
    art. 3, 201
    art. 3(g), 201
    art. 4, 201
    art. 5, 201
    art. 6(1), 201
    art. 6(3), 201
    art. 8(1), 201
    art. 8(3), 201
    art. 9, 201
97/9/EC Investor Compensation Directive [1997] OJ L84, 155, 239
98/34/EC
    art. 1(2), 263
98/48/EC Amending Directive 98/34/EC, 263
    art. 1(2)(1), 265
    Annex V para. 1, 265
    Annex V para. 2, 265
2000/12/EC Banking Directive [2000] OJ L126, 154–5, 237
    recital 1, 154
    recital 3, 154
    recital 7, 154, 240
    recital 9, 237
    recital 12, 155
    recital 16, 242
    recital 17, 155, 239, 240, 242
    recital 22, 155
    recital 34, 155

TABLE OF EU LEGISLATION  xxxi

   recital 35, 155
   art. 1(6), 237
   art. 1(a), 237
   art. 4, 154
   art. 5, 154
   art. 5(1), 155
   art. 6(1), 154
   art. 6(2), 154, 237
   art. 7, 154
   art. 9, 154
   art. 10, 154
   art. 13, 154
   art. 14, 154
   art. 15, 154
   art. 16, 154
   art. 17, 154, 155
   art. 18, 237, 238, 251
   art. 21, 251
   art. 21(1), 241, 244
   art. 21(2), 241
   art. 22(2)–(5), 241, 242
   art. 22(5), 242
   art. 22(9), 241
   art. 22(11), 242, 257
   art. 26, 239
   art. 26(1), 240
   art. 27, 241
   art. 28, 154, 241
   arts. 28–33, 133
   art. 30, 154
   art. 30(2), 154
   art. 31, 154, 155
   arts. 34–47, 154
   art. 47, 155
   arts. 48–50, 154
   art. 49(4), 155
   art. 51, 154
   Annex I(7), 253
2000/31/EC E-Commerce Directive [2000] OJ L178, 76–7, 79–81, 106, 165–8, 172
   recital 5, 262, 271
   recital 6, 263, 264
   recital 11, 166, 177, 206, 275

**Directives** (*Continued*)
  recital 18, 166, 263, 264, 266
  recital 19, 276, 277
  recital 21, 267, 275
  recital 22, 270, 271
  recital 23, 269
  recital 26, 284
  recital 27, 81, 264
  recital 34, 185
  recital 35, 186
  recital 38, 186
  recital 55, 276
  recital 56, 276
  recital 60, 185
  recital 63, 263
  art. 1, 165
  art. 1(1), 80
  art. 1(3), 166, 177
  art. 1(4), 271, 269
  art. 1(5), 263
  art. 1(6), 263
  art. 2(a), 166, 263
  art. 2(f), 172
  art. 2(h), 266
  art. 2(h)(i), 266
  art. 2(h)(ii), 267
  art. 3, 272, 286–7
  art. 3(1), 166, 262, 273, 274
  art. 3(2), 166, 262, 269, 273, 274, 287
  art. 3(4), 270, 274, 309
  arts. 3(4)–(6), 281–6
  art. 3(4)(a)(i), 282, 286
  art. 3(4)(a)(iii), 283
  art. 3(4)(b), 284
  art. 5(1), 177
  art. 6, 166, 172, 177
  art. 7, 166
  art. 7(1), 172
  art. 9(1), 185
  art. 9(2), 185
  art. 10, 182, 184
  art. 10(3), 193

TABLE OF EU LEGISLATION xxxiii

art. 11, 188
art. 19(3), 283
art. 22(1), 167
Annex, 270
2001/24/EC Directive on Reorganization and Winding Up of Credit Institutions [2001] OJ L125, 155, 239
2002/58/EC Directive on Privacy and Electronic Communications [2002] OJ L201, 173, 274
   art. 13(1), 172
2002/65/EC Distance Marketing Directive [2002] OJ L271, 78–81, 105, 168–71
   recital 6, 80, 170
   recital 12, 169
   recital 14, 169
   recital 16, 169
   recital 17, 169
   recital 20, 179
   recital 22, 169
   recital 29, 169
   art. 1(1), 80
   art. 1(2), 169
   art. 2(b), 168
   art. 2(d), 145
   art. 2(e), 169
   art. 2(f), 179
   art. 3, 169
   art. 3(1), 178
   art. 3(2), 178
   art. 3(4), 177
   art. 4, 177
   art. 4(1), 169, 177
   art. 4(3), 169
   art. 5, 179, 193
   art. 5(2), 178
   art. 6(1), 190
   art. 6(2)(a), 191
   art. 6(2)(b), 191
   art. 7, 191
   art. 9(1), 172
   art. 13, 169
   art. 16, 80
   art. 21, 170
2002/87 Financial Conglomerates Directive [2002] OJ L35, 155

2004/39/EC Directive on Markets in Financial Instruments [2004] OJ L145, 214–18
    art. 1(2), 215
    art. 13, 215
    art. 13(2), 215
    art. 13(3), 215
    art. 13(4), 215
    art. 13(5), 216
    art. 13(6), 216
    art. 13(7), 216
    art. 13(8), 216
    art. 13(10), 216
    art. 18(2), 215
    art. 19(2), 216
    art. 19(3), 216
    art. 19(4), 216
    art. 19(5), 216
    art. 19(6), 217
    art. 19(7), 217
    art. 19(8), 217
    art. 19(10), 217
    arts. 19–30, 216
    art. 21(1), 217
    art. 22(1), 217
    art. 25(2), 217
    art. 25(3), 218
    art. 28(1), 218
    art. 31(1), 218, 242
    art. 70, 214
    art. 71, 214
2005/29 Unfair Commercial Practices Directive [2005] OJ L149, 173

# Regulations

Regulation 44/2001/EC on jurisdiction and the recognition of judgments in civil and commercial matters (Brussels Regulation) OJ 2001 No. L12/1 249, 289, 293–4
    recital 13, 297
    art. 2, 293
    art. 2(1), 296
    art. 5(1)(a), 296
    art. 5(1)(b), 296
    art. 5(3), 258

art. 15, 303
art. 15(1)(c), 299, 304
art. 16, 303
art. 16(1), 304
art. 16(2), 304
art. 17, 303
art. 23, 293
art. 23(1), 294
art. 23(2), 294
Regulation 2560/2001/EC on Cross-Border Payments in Euro 2001 OJ No. L344/34, 200, 202–3
art. 3(2), 203
art. 4, 203
art. 5, 203
Regulation No 2006/2004/EC on Consumer Cooperation 2004 OJ No. L364/1, 133
art. 6, 134
art. 7, 134
art. 8, 134

# TABLE OF INTERNATIONAL CONVENTIONS

European Convention for the Protection of Human Rights and Fundamental
    Freedoms 1950
  art. 8 179
General Agreement on Trade in Services (GATS)
  2nd Annex on Financial Services
    art. 2(a) 101
    art. 5 1
Mine Ban Treaty 1997 130
Paris Convention for the Protection of Industrial Property 1883 171
  art. 10*bis* 172

# TABLE OF CASES

## Australia

Dow Jones Inc. *v.* Joseph Gutnick [2002] HCA 56, 259

## EC cases – numerical order

C-26/62 Van Gend en Loos *v.* Nederlandse Administratie der Belastingen [1963] ECR 1, 85
C-6/64 Costa *v.* ENEL [1964] ECR 585, 85
C-2/74 Reyners *v.* Belgium [1974] ECR 631, 89
C-33/74 Van Binsbergen *v.* Bestuur Vande Bedrijfsvereniging voor de Metaalnijverheid [1974] ECR 1299, 89
C-24/76 Estasis Salotti di Colanzi Aimo e Gianmario Colzani *v.* RUWA Postereimaschinen GmbH [1976] ECR 1831, 293, 294
C-150/77 Bertrand *v.* Ott [1978] ECR 1431, 299
C-33/78 Somafer SA *v.* Saar-Ferngas AG [1978] ECR 2183, 277
Joined Cases C-110/78 and 111/78 Ministère public *v.* Van Wesemael [1979] ECR 35, 140
C-120/78 Rewe-Zentral AG *v.* Bundesmonopolverwaltung für Branntwein (the 'Cassis de Dijon' case) [1979] ECR 649, 90, 140, 143
C-130/78 Salumificio di Cornuda SpA *v.* Amministrazione delle Finanze dello Stato [1979] ECR 867, 131
C-34/79 R *v.* Henn and Derby [1979] ECR 3795, 97
C-279/80 Webb (Criminal proceedings) [1981] ECR 3305, 241
C-53/81 Levin *v.* Staatsecretaris van Justitie [1981] ECR 1035, 199
C-96/81 Commission *v.* Netherlands [1982] ECR 1791, 273
Joined Cases C-115/81 and 116/81 Adoui *v.* Belgium [1982] ECR 1665, 282
C-286/81 Osthoek's Uitgeversmaatschappij [1982] ECR 4575, 146
Joined Cases C-286/82 and 26/83 Luisi and Carbonne *v.* Ministero del Tesoro [1984] ECR 377, 238
C-15/83 Denkavit Nederland BV *v.* Hoofproduktschap Voor Akkerbouqprodukten [1984] ECR 2171, 125

C-71/83 Partenreederei ms Tilly Russ v. NV Haven- & Vervoerbedrijf Nova and NV Goeminne Hout [1984] ECR 2417, 294
C-220/83 Commission v. France [1986] ECR 2663, 140, 251
C-54/84 Paul v. Emmerich [1985] ECR 915, 251
C-205/84 Commission v. Germany [1986] ECR 3755, 141, 277
C-89/85 Ahlstrom Osakeyhtio v. Commission [1988] ECR 5193, 58
C-352/85 Bond van Adverteerders v. The Netherlands [1988] ECR 2085, 264
C-407/85 Drei Glocken v. Kritzinger [1988] ECR 4233, 146
C-263/86 Belgium v. Humbel [1988] ECR 5365, 264
C-186/87 Cowan v. Tresor Public [1989] ECR 195, 94
C-382/87 Buet and EBS [1989] ECR 1235, 307
C-25/88 Ministère Public v. Buchara [1989] ECR I-1105, 128
C-362/88 GB-INNO-BM v. CCL [1990] I-667, 143, 192
C-198/89 EC Commission v. Greece (the 'Tourist Guides Greece' case [1991] ECR I-727, 94
C-288/89 Stichting Collectieve Antennevoorziening Gouda v. Commissariaat voor de Media (the 'Mediawet I' case) [1991] ECR I-4007, 140, 143
C-294/89 Commission v. France [1991] ECR I-3591, 144
C-76/90 Säger v. Dennemeyer & Co. Ltd [1991] ECR I-4221, 90, 115, 138
C-2/91 Opinion of the ECJ [1993] ECR I-1061, 131
Joined Cases C-267/91 and C-268/91 Keck and Mithouard (Criminal proceedings) [1993] ECR 1-6097, 71
C-275/92 HM Customs and Excise v. Schindler [1994] ECR I-1039, 140
C-288/92 Customs Made Commercial Ltd v. Stawa Metallbau GmbH [1994] ECR I-2913, 250
C-68/93 Shevill v. Press Alliance [1995] ECR I-415, 258–9
C-364/93 Antonio Marinari v. Lloyds Bank [1995] ECR I-2719, 258
C-384/93 Alpine Investments BV v. Minister van Financiën [1995] ECR I-1141, 2, 93, 140, 144, 240
C-412/93 Société d'Importation Edouard Leclerc-Siplec v. TFI Publicité SA [1995] ECR 179, 240
C-484/93 Svensson and Gustavsson v. Ministre du Logement et de l'Urbanisme [1995] ECR I-3955, 2, 93, 264, 298
C-55/94 Gebhard v. Consiglio dell'Ordine degli Avvocati e Procuratori di Milano [1995] ECR I-4165, 138
C-101/94 Commission v. Italy [1996] ECR I-2691, 140
C-193/94 Skanavi and Chrissanthakopoulos (Criminal proceedings) [1996] ECR I-929, 126, 241
C-233/94 Germany v. Parliament and Council [1997] ECR I-2405, 98, 139, 141, 240
C-238/94 Garcia v. Mutuelle de Prevoyance Sociale d'Aquitaine [1996] ECR I-1673, 240
C-3/95 Reisebüro Broede v. Sandker [1996] ECR I-6511, 139, 140
C-57/95 France v. Commission [1997] ECR I-1627, 246

C-222/95 Société Parodi v. Banque H. Albert de Bary et Cie [1997] ECR I-3899, 2, 91–3, 141–2, 264
C-315/95 Commission v. Italy [1996] ECR 5743, 131
C-210/96 Gut Springenheide GmbH and Tusky v. Oberkreisdirektor des Kreises Steinfurt [1998] ECR I-4657, 146

## France

Cour d'Appel (Appeal Court)
    Colmar, 24.02.1999, 1999 ZIP 1210–1211, 298
    Paris, 15th Ch. 05.10.1999, 35
    Paris, D.2002, 259
    Rennes 31.03.2000 JCP E 2000, no 48, 174
Cour de Cassation (Chambres Civiles)
    08.01.1991 Schimmel Pianoforte D v. M. Bion (1991) IR 37, 258
    09.10.1992, JCP 1993, II, 22024, 210
    14.01.1997, 86 RCDIP 504–505, 259
    09.02.1999, 44 RTD civ 836, 193
    19.10.1999, 89 RCDIP [2000] 29–34, 298
    19.10.1999, D. 2000 jur. 765, 307
    19.10.1999, Dalloz Cahier Droit des Affaires [2000] 8–9, 297
    15.05.2001, JDI 2001, 1121, 295
Cour de Cassation (Chambres Commerciales)
    05.09.1991, RTD com 1992, 436, 222
Tribunal de Grande Instance (Court of First Instance)
    Paris, 12 February 1999, 260
    Paris, 26 February 2002, 260
    Strasbourg, 02.04.2001, Recueil Dalloz Sirey, Cahier Droit des Affaires [2002] 2935, 298

## Germany

Pinneberg (16 February 2001) AZ: 64 C 376/00, 225
Bundesgerichthof (Federal Court)
    NJW 1962, 37, 259
    NJW 1964, 2058, 34
    WM 1976, 904, 35
    NJW 1981, 1140, 35
    NJW 1983, 1779, 33
    NJW 1985, 2699, 31
    WM 1989, 128, 31

**Germany** (*Continued*)
  XI ZR 275/89, 209
  XI ZR 119/91, 209
  ZIP 1991, 1413, 35
  NJW 1992, 1232, 193
  WM 1993, 2095, 31
  WM 1994, 14, 1, 307
  DtZ 1996, 51, 295
  WM 1996, 906, 225
  NJW 1997, 1697, 298, 306
  RIW 1997, 875, 309
  NJW 1998, 3114, 198
  ZIP 1999, 103, 309
  AZ:XI ZR 138/00 (12 December 2000), 198
  NJW 2000, 3496, 209
  XI ZR 164/00 (24 July 2001), 225
  XI ZR 197/00 (13 February 2001), 199
  XI ZR 329/00 (24 July 2001), 226
Landesgericht
  Berlin, MDR 2001, 391, 259
  Braunschweig, MMR 1998, 272, 259
  Hamburg, MMR 1999, 612, 259
  Itzehoe (10 July 2001) AZ: 1 S 92/01, 225
  Köln (1 December 1999) 26 O 79-1998, 198
  Nürnberg-Fürth (19 May 1999) AZ: 14 O 9971/98, 225
  Nürnberg-Fürth NJW/RR 2000, 1650, 224
  Paderborn, MMR 2001, 710, 259
Oberlandesgericht (Court of Appeal)
  Coblence WRP 1997, 874, 176
  Düsseldorf NJW/RR 1997, 374, 47
  Frankfurt MMR 1999, 427, 259
  Köln RIW 1993, 1025, 295
  Köln AZ: 6 U: 135/199 (14-4-2000), 198
  München NJW-RR 1994, 190, 258
  München RIW 1996, 330, 295
  München ZIP 1998, 1954, 226
  München CR 2000, 464, 259
  Schleswig ZIP 2000, 1721, 224

# Permanent Court of International Justice

Case Lotus (1927) PCIJ Rep Series A No. 10, 58

## United Kingdom

1-800 Flowers Inc. *v.* Phonenames Ltd [2000] ETMR 369, 257
Adamson *v.* Jarvis (1827) 4 Bing 66, 46
AIG Group (UK) Ltd *v.* The Ethniki [1988] 4 All ER 301, 295
Armstrong *v.* Stokes [1872] LR 7 QB 698, 46
Bank of New South Wales *v.* Laing [1954] AC 135, 33
Brooke *v.* Bool [1928] 2 KB 578, 46
Brown *v.* KMR Services Ltd [1995] 4 All ER 598 CA, 46
Compania Naveria Vascongado *v.* SS Cristina [1938] AC 485, 58
Clark Boyce *v.* Mouat [1994] 1 AC 428, 46
Cronos *v.* Palatin [2002] EWHC 2819 (Comm), 258
Director General of Fair Trading *v.* First National Bank Plc [2002] 1 AC 481 (HL), 197, 199, 297, 299
Euromarket Designs Inc. *v.* Peters [2000] ETMR 1025 (Ch D), 257
Foley *v.* Hill (1848) 2 HL Cas 28, 7
Greenwood *v.* Martins Bank [1933] AC 51 HL, 34
Huntpast Ltd *v.* Leadbeater [1993] CCLR 15, 307
Iran Continental Shelf Oil Co. and Others *v.* IRI International Corporation [2002] EWCA Civ 1024, 296
Joachimson *v.* Swiss Bank Corpn [1921] 3 KB 110, 30
Libyan Arab Bank *v.* Bankers Trust Co. [1989] QB 728, 34
Lloyds Bank plc *v.* Lampert [1999] 1 All ER (Comm) 161, 41
London Joint Stock Bank Ltd *v.* Macmillan and Arthur [1918] AC 777, 34
Merrill Lynch Futures Inc. *v.* York House Trading Ltd, *The Times* 24 May 1984, 45
Morgans *v.* Launchbury [1973] AC 127, 188
Olley *v.* Marlborough Court Ltd [1949] I KB 532, 193
Parker *v.* McKenna [1874] LR 10 Ch App 96, 46
R *v.* Munton (1793) 1 Esp 62, 257
R *v.* Oliphant [1905] 2 KB 67, 257
Raiffeisen Zentralbank Osterreich AG *v.* National Bank of Greece SA [1999] 1 Lloyd's Rep 408, 295
Rayner (Andrew) *v.* Richard Davies [2002] EWCA Civ 1880, 300
Rothschild Ltd (N. M.) *v.* Equitable Life Assurance Society [2002] EWHC 1022, 298
Royal Products Ltd *v.* Midland Bank [1981] 2 Lloyd's Rep 194, 33, 34
Samcrete Egypt *v.* Land Rover Exports Ltd [2001] EWCA Civ 2019, 296
Sierra Leone Telecommunications Co. Ltd *v.* Barclays Bank plc [1998] 2 All ER 821, 295
Thornton *v.* Shoe Lane Parking [1971] 2 QB 163, 193
Turner *v.* Reeve (1901) 17 TLR 592, 46
Victor Chandler International *v.* Customs and Excise Commissioners [2001] 1 WLR 1296, 177
Westminster Bank Ltd *v.* Hilton [1926] 43 TLR 124, 34

## US Cases

Bank of British North America *v.* Cooper, 137 US 473 (1890), 7
Zippo Manufacturing Co. *v.* Zippo.com., 952 F Supp 1119 (W.D.Pa. 1997) 64

# ABBREVIATIONS

| | |
|---|---|
| AGBG | Gesetz zur Regelung des Rechts der Allgemeinen Geschäftsbedingungen (Act on the Regulation of the Law of General Business Conditions) |
| Am J Comp L | American Journal of Comparative Law |
| AMF | Autorité des Marchés Financiers (Financial Markets Authority) |
| APR | annual percentage rate |
| ATM | automated teller machine |
| AUTH (FSA) | (FSA Handbook) Authorisation |
| BAFIN | Bundesanstalt für Finanzdienstleistungsaufsicht (Federal Financial Supervisory Authority) |
| BAKRED | Bundesaufsichtsamt für das Kreditwesen (Federal Banking Supervisory Office) |
| BAWe | Bundesaufsichtsamt für den Wertpapierhandel (Federal Securities Supervisory Office) |
| BGB | Bürgerliches Gesetzbuch (German Civil Code) |
| BGB-InfoV | Verordnung über Informations- und Nachweispflichten nach bürgerlichem Recht, BGBl I 2002, 342, 2 January 2002 |
| BGH | Bundesgerichtshof (Federal Court) |
| BGHZ | Entscheidungen des Bundesgerichtshofes in Zivilsachen |
| BIC | Bank Identifier Code |
| BIS | Bank for International Settlements |
| BJIBFL | Butterworths Journal of International Banking and Financial Law |
| BSI | Bundesamt für Sicherheit in der Informationstechnik (Federal Agency for Security in Information Technology) |
| BusLaw | Business Lawyer |
| CA | Court of Appeal (English); Cour d'Appel (French Court of Appeal) |

| | |
|---|---|
| Cass.civ. | Arrêts des Chambres Civiles de la Cour de Cassation (Rulings of the French Court of Cassation in civil matters) |
| Cass.com. | *Arrêts des Chambres Commerciales de la Cour de Cassation* (Rulings of the French Court of Cassation in commercial matters) |
| C.civ. | Code Civil (French Civil Code) |
| C.com. | Code du Commerce (French Commercial Code) |
| C.consom. | Code de la Consommation (French Consumer Code) |
| CDGF | Conseil de Discipline de la Gestion Financière |
| CECEI | Comité des Etablissements de Crédit et des Entreprises d'Investissement |
| CLSR | Computer Law and Security Report |
| CMF | Code Monétaire et Financier ([French] Monetary and Financial Code) |
| CML Rev | Common Market Law Review |
| C.monét.fin. | Code Monétaire et Financier ([French] Monetary and Financial Code) |
| COB | Commission des Operations de Bourse |
| COB (FSA) | Conduct of Business Sourcebook |
| C.pen. | Code Penal (French Criminal Code) |
| C.proc.pen. | Code de la Procedure Penal (French Code of Criminal Procedure) |
| CPSS | Committee on Payment and Settlement Systems |
| CR | Computer und Recht |
| CRBF | Comité de la Réglementation Bancaire et Financière |
| CSFI | Centre for the Study of Financial Innovation |
| D. | Recueil Dalloz Sirey |
| DtZ | Deutsch-Deutsche Rechtstzeitschrift |
| EBLR | European Business Law Review |
| EBOL Rev | European Business Organization Law Review |
| ECB | European Central Bank |
| ECJ | European Court of Justice |
| ECO (FSA) | FSA Electronic Commerce Directive |
| Ecofin | Economic and Financial Affairs Council of the European Union |
| EEA | European Economic Area |
| EFM | European Financial Management |
| EFSL | European Financial Services Law |
| EFT | electronic funds transfers |

| | |
|---|---|
| EGG | Gesetz über Rechtliche Rahmenbedingungen für den Elektronischer Geschäftsverkehr (German Electronic Commerce Act) |
| EL Rev | European Law Review |
| ENF (FSA) | Handbook Enforcement (FSA) |
| EP | European Parliament |
| FATF (OECD) | Financial Action Task Force on Money Laundering of the OECD |
| FBF | Fédération Bancaire Française (French Banking Federation) |
| FinDAG | Finanzdienstleistungsaufsichtgesetz |
| FIN-NET | Consumer Complaints Network for Financial Services |
| FiSMA 2000 | Financial Services and Markets Act 2000 |
| FSA | Financial Services Authority |
| GATS | General Agreement on Trade in Services |
| ERPL | European Review of Private Law |
| GG | Grundgesetz (German Constitution) |
| GwG | Gesetz über das Aufspüren von Gewinnen aus Schweren Straftaten (German Money Laundering Act) |
| HGB | Handelsgesetzbuch (German Commercial Code) |
| IBAN | International Bank Account Number |
| IBFL | International Banking and Financial Law |
| ICC | International Chamber of Commerce |
| ICLQ | International and Comparative Law Quarterly |
| ILM | International Legal Materials |
| IMF | International Monetary Fund |
| Int'l Rev L & Econ | International Review of Law and Economics |
| IOSCO | International Organization of Securities Commission |
| IPRax | Praxis des Internationalen Privat- und Verfahrensrechts |
| ISS | information society services |
| IT | information technology |
| JDI | Journal du Droit International |
| JIBLR | Journal of International Banking Law and Regulation |
| JL & Econ | Journal of Law and Economics |
| JLEcon & Org | Journal of Law Economics and Organization |
| JCMS | Journal of Common Market Studies |
| JFRC | Journal of Financial Regulation and Compliance |
| JFSR | Journal of Financial Services Research |

| | |
|---|---|
| JIBL | Journal of International Banking Law |
| KWG | Kreditwesengesetz (German Banking Act) |
| LG | Landesgericht (Court of First Instance) |
| MCOB | (FSA Handbook) Mortgages Conduct of Business |
| MiFiD | Directive on Markets in Financial Instruments 2004 |
| MJ | Maastricht Journal |
| ML (FSA) | (FSA Handbook) Money Laundering |
| MMR | Multimedia und Recht |
| MoU | Memorandum of Understanding |
| NJW | Neues Juristisches Wochenschrift |
| NWUL Rev | Northwestern University Law Review |
| NYSE | New York Stock Exchange |
| OECD | Organization for Economic Cooperation and Development |
| OJLS | Oxford Journal of Legal Studies |
| OLG | Oberlandesgericht (Court of Appeal) |
| PCIJ | Permanent Court of International Justice |
| PIN | Personal Identification Number |
| PRU (FSA) | Integrated Prudential Sourcebook |
| RabelsZ | Rabels Zeitschrift für ausländisches und internationales Privatrecht |
| RCDIP | Revue Critique de Droit International Privé |
| Règl. du CRBF | Règlement du Comité de la Réglementation Bancaire et Financière |
| RIW | Recht der Internationalen Wirtschaft |
| RTD civ | Revue Trimestrielle de Droit Civil |
| RTD com | Revue Trimestrielle de Droit Commercial |
| SEA | Single European Act |
| StGB | Strafgesetzbuch (German Criminal Code) |
| SUP (FSA) | (FSA Handbook) Supervision |
| TDG | Gesetz über die Nutzung von Telediensten (Teleservices Act) |
| Texas Int'lL.J | Texas International Law Journal |
| TGI | Tribunal de Grand Instance (French Court of First Instance) |
| ULB | Université Libre de Bruxelles |
| UNICTRAL | United Nations Commission on International Trade Law |
| UNIDROIT | International Institute for the Unification of Private Law |

| | |
|---|---|
| UNTS | United Nations Treaty Series |
| UWG | Gesetz gegen den Unlauteren Wettbewerb (Unfair Competition Act) |
| WM | Zeitschrift für Wirtschafts- und Bankrecht |
| WpHG | Wertpapier-Handelsgesetz (German Securities Trading Act) |
| WTO | World Trade Organization |
| ZBB | Zeitschrift für Bankrecht und Bankwirtschaft |
| ZEW | Zebtrum für Europäische Wirtschaftforschung |
| ZfRV | Zeitschrift für Rechtsvergleichung |
| ZHR | Zeitschrift für das gesamte Handelsrecht und Wirtschaftsrecht |
| ZIP | Zeitschrift für Wirtschaftsrecht |
| ZvglRWiss | Zeitschrift für Vergleichende Rechtswissenschaft |

# Introduction

The liberalization of international trade in financial services is a significant component of global and regional economic cooperation. Modern economies depend on well-functioning financial markets and financial markets benefit from the flow of financial services across borders. Financial institutions may engage in transactions with non-residents either directly from their headquarters or by establishing branches and subsidiaries overseas. This book focuses on services provided via the Internet by commercial banks (or 'credit institutions' in the EC terminology) and explores the potential contribution of electronic finance to meeting the objectives of financial integration in the single European market.

The notion of 'financial services' essentially refers to the full array of functions performed by financial institutions, including but not limited to the acceptance of deposits, lending, payment services, securities underwriting and trading, asset management, financial advice, settlement and clearing services.[1] In conducting these activities with *non-residents*, a financial institution engages in international trade in financial services. The modes of providing financial services across borders are basically four: first, the financial institution remains outside the territory of the client and the client remains inside his territory of residence and the service is supplied with the help of information and telecommunications technology (cross-border services). Second, the client physically moves from his country and receives the service in the location of the financial institution (consumption abroad). Third, the financial institution supplies the service to non-residents through a foreign affiliate, branch or subsidiary located in the country of the client (commercial presence). Finally, the financial service is provided by natural persons (as opposed to corporate entities) that move to the country of the client (presence of natural persons).

---

[1] See General Agreement on Trade in Services (GATS) (Marrakesh, April 1994) OJ 1994 No. L336/190, 23 December 1994, 2nd Annex on financial services, art. 5.

At the European level, the marriage of e-commerce and trade in financial services is a primary objective of policy reforms pursuant to the Financial Services Action Plan. With regard to international trade in the context of the World Trade Organization (WTO), one key factor driving the interest in the services component of the international trade negotiations is the increasing number of services that can be traded electronically without having to establish a physical presence in the importing country.

The EC Treaty[2] requires the establishment of a single European market comprising an area without internal frontiers in which the free movement of financial services and capital are guaranteed.[3] The legal and institutional framework must safeguard the elimination of direct or indirect trade restrictions in a diverse set of circumstances, including market entry through the permanent establishment of an agency, branch or subsidiary in the territory of another Member State;[4] the temporary presence of the bank's agents and staff in another Member State;[5] the temporary movement of the customer to the territory where the bank is established;[6] and the provision of the service at a distance, via the Internet or otherwise, with the bank and the customer being located in different Member States.[7] This last mode of providing banking services electronically is the subject of this book.

In chapter 1, the reader is introduced to the basic concepts and services relating to electronic finance and Internet banking. We will also discuss the importance of electronic finance for financial integration in Europe and recent market developments in this sector. I will also discuss my own survey of online banking activities in key European markets, which demonstrates that the actual contribution of the Internet to stimulating cross-border services has so far been limited, in contrast with the substantial growth of purely domestic Internet banking.

In chapter 2, I will examine the legal concepts and foundations of electronic banking activities in the three countries examined in the present book, namely the United Kingdom, France and Germany. In

---

[2] See Treaty Establishing the European Community (Rome, 25 March 1957); consolidated text at OJ 2002 No. C325, 24 December 2002.
[3] *Ibid.*, art. 14(2).
[4] *Ibid.*, art. 43.
[5] See Case C-222/95 *Parodi* v. *Banque H. Albert de Bary et Cie* [1997] ECR I-3899.
[6] See Case C-484/93 *Svensson and Gustavsson* v. *Ministre du Logement et de L'Urbanisme* [1995] ECR I-3955.
[7] See Case C-384/93 *Alpine Investments BV* v. *Minister van Financien* [1995] ECR I-1141.

chapter 3, I will explain how excessive regulation and legal uncertainty affect the cross-border provision of banking services via the Internet. There is a brief comparative survey of different regulatory models internationally and an introduction to EU policies affecting e-commerce in financial services in the single European market.

My normative arguments in favour of mutual recognition and 'home country' control as the overarching institutional framework for e-commerce in financial services are fully discussed in chapter 4. There I will outline the ongoing policy debate regarding the virtues of various alternative models of governance and I will explain why the model of 'home country' control is more functional and efficient than the alternatives and which conditions must be met before those benefits can be enjoyed.

The ensuing chapters 5 and 6 are descriptive of the multifaceted process of legal convergence in the single European market. To the extent that mutual recognition of national laws and 'home country' control cannot operate without the prior minimum convergence of national laws around commonly accepted standards, it is expedient to examine the attained level of legal convergence of national laws relating to electronic banking activities. Chapter 5 discusses the convergence of prudential regulatory and supervisory standards, while chapter 6 examines the attained harmonization in the non-prudential legal requirements relating to marketing and advertising, consumer and investor protection and certain key types of banking and financial contracts.

Moving from the question of harmonization of national laws, the final chapters, 7, 8 and 9, examine in depth the applicable law and allocation of regulatory responsibility in cross-border electronic banking activities. More specifically, chapter 7 focuses on the implementation of the principle of 'home country' control in prudential and investor protection matters and examines the remaining regulatory, supervisory and enforcement powers of the 'host country', which continue to disturb cross-border financial services in Europe. The ensuing chapter 8 takes a closer look at the implementation of the principle of 'country of origin' of the E-Commerce Directive[8] and the extent to which this recent institutional reform safeguards the mutual recognition of non-prudential national laws on the basis of 'home country' control. Finally, chapter 9

---

[8] Council and EP Directive 2000/31/EC of 8 June 2000 on certain legal aspects of information society services, in particular electronic commerce, in the internal market, OJ 2000 No. L178/1, 17 July 2000.

will examine the applicable law and jurisdiction in the contractual aspect of cross-border electronic banking activities, which remains unaffected by EU reforms in the field of financial services and electronic commerce and still subject to the general law established under the Rome Convention[9] and the Brussels Regulation on jurisdiction and enforcement of judgments in commercial and civil matters.[10]

It should be noted that legal barriers in the single European market are primarily imposed by national measures, while the effectiveness of liberalization and integration policies is measured by the extent to which legal restrictions embedded in national law are removed, particularly if market integration is pursued by means of Directives whose effectiveness relies on the quality of national implementation. For that reason, existing legal barriers and the political, economic and legal forces operating in the single financial market cannot be understood outside the context of applicable national laws. The book attempts to discuss and explain the law of Internet banking in the single European market in direct and constant dialogue with applicable national laws in England and Wales, Germany and France. This was not a random choice. The three countries are traditionally at the forefront of developments of new integration policies and institutional reforms. Their special economic, financial and political weight influences significantly the outcome of internal market negotiations. They often represent competing views on markets, regulation and free trade. They belong to different legal traditions. I concluded that a fair understanding of the interaction between EU law and the national laws of the three jurisdictions is the appropriate method of examining this still evolving area of financial law. The law is stated on the basis of materials available to me at 15 October 2005.

---

[9] Convention on the Law Applicable to Contractual Obligations (Rome, 19 June 1980); consolidated version at OJ 1998 No. C27/34, 26 January 1998.
[10] Council Regulation 44/2001/EC of 22 December 2000 on jurisdiction and the recognition and enforcement of judgments in civil and commercial matters, OJ 201 No. L12/1, 16 January 2001.

# PART I

Introduction to electronic finance and
Internet banking

# 1

# Internet banking in Europe: basic concepts and recent trends

Since the late 1990s the Internet and other technological advances in telecommunications, information technology and computer software and hardware have transformed the provision of financial services and the structure of financial markets. By the end of the 1990s, electronic finance applications had influenced most aspects of the business of banking, with the exception perhaps of large-value corporate lending. Similarly in the field of capital markets, the Internet has transformed the financial landscape by enabling the seamless interaction among issuers, investors and securities firms.

### The Internet as catalyst of international financial integration

The concept of electronic finance may broadly be defined as the provision of financial services and the creation of financial markets using information technology, telecommunications and computer networks. Although the advent of electronic finance has rightly been associated with the most recent application of advanced technologies in the financial services industry, in strictly technical terms e-finance predates the era of the Internet by several decades: the first era of electronic banking in the form of telegraphic fund transfers in the late 19th century gave rise to legal problems that would appear familiar to electronic banking lawyers today.[1]

### *The Internet and the banker–customer relationship*

Electronic banking can be defined as the provision of banking services and the initiation and performance of payments through the banking system by electronic means and other advanced technologies. Electronic

---

[1] See *Bank of British North America v. Cooper*, 137 US 473 (1890) (liability for negligent performance of a transatlantic wire funds transfer).

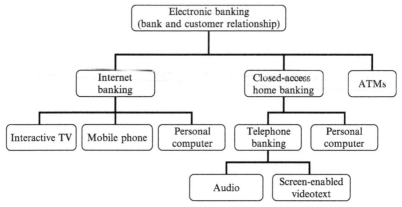

Figure 1.1. Communication methods and access devices in electronic banking.

banking is a conceptually generic term, which denotes banking services provided through a variety of access devices and links of communication (see figure 1.1).

Internet banking refers to the provision of electronic banking services via the Internet, commonly through a personal computer (PC) or other access devices with Internet capabilities. The concept of telephone banking refers to services provided via the ordinary telephone or more advanced screen-enabled terminals. Other terms are less technical. Online banking and Internet banking are often used interchangeably. Home banking would include any remote delivery channel, including telephone banking.

Internet banking gives customers the ability to access virtually any type of banking services (except cash) in any place and at any time. From an economic perspective, information technology and computer networks have enhanced the automation, speed and standardization in communications and internal administration, increasing customer convenience and functionality and reducing costs in back-office and front-desk banking functions.[2]

The same technological advances have stimulated financial innovation and improved efficiency in financial markets by enabling the seamless communication among issuers, investors, intermediaries and organized

---

[2] See Allen Berger, 'The Economic Effects of Technological Progress: Evidence from the Banking Industry' (2003) 35 *Journal of Money, Credit and Banking* 141.

markets.[3] Electronic trading, whether in organized markets or in alternative trading systems, can reduce costs, attract new investors and remove the physical limitations on how prices are discovered and trades are performed, thus improving the functionality, transparency and trading capacity of organized markets.[4]

Openly accessible and globally connected computer networks enable the two-way transportation of information between the bank and the customer. The basic function of the Internet Protocol (IP)[5] is to receive and transmit any information, which may take digital form. The primary Internet code enables the transmission of data from one computer unit to another, without it being necessary that the originator and the recipient of information share a direct network connection. Transmitted data are transported through a sequence of available connections and routes between otherwise unrelated servers and host computers. Crucially, no particular server or local network is an essential component of that chain. Although individual computers may be connected to the network or disconnected, at the will of their administrators or because of disruptive events, data transmitted over the Internet always discover open network routes through the remainder of available networks and servers. As a result, the Internet enables the unimpeded circulation of data, which may be retrieved by or transmitted to computers located anywhere in the world, without the process being affected by the territorial proximity, or the lack thereof, between the initial originator and the final recipient of data.[6]

In the context of the banker–customer relationship, data transmitted from the bank to the customer and vice versa may result in the establishment, alteration, exercise or termination of legal rights and obligations in accordance with the contract between the bank and the customer. In that respect, the Internet enables the initial establishment of the banker–customer relationship and the electronic delivery and performance of services thereafter, within the boundaries set by available technical and legal mechanisms of authorization and access control.

---

[3] See International Organization of Securities Commissions (IOSCO), *Second Report on Securities Activity on the Internet* (Madrid, 2001).

[4] See Committee on the Global Financial System, *The Implications of Electronic Trading in Financial Markets* (Basel: BIS, 2001).

[5] The Internet Protocol is the method or code by which data is sent from one computer to another on the Internet.

[6] See Preston Gralla, *How the Internet Works* (Indianapolis: Que, 2004), ch. 1.

*Electronic commerce and international financial integration*

The archenemy of market integration is geography, not law. Historically, the most important causes of incomplete economic integration and partition of local markets have been geography, distance and poor networks of transportation and communications. Legal and regulatory obstacles to the circulation of goods, services and capital became apparent only after the improvement of means of transportation, shipment and communication provided a realistic setting for the expansion of international trade. In a similar way, the Internet eradicates the constraints of geography and distance in the movement of digital data which do not require storage facilities, packages, docks, motorways or airports to circulate. It provides an affordable medium for the circulation of any type of content or speech which can take digital form, thus facilitating communication and commercial relations across national borders. It was rightly observed that the single European market for goods and services could have been invented for electronic commerce and vice versa because they share a common point: the Internet brings down physical barriers, while the single market programme brings down legal barriers.[7] Although the production, distribution, marketing, sale or delivery of goods and services by electronic means are hardly new, on certain conditions the contribution of electronic commerce to international economic integration could be substantial. This is particularly true for European and international financial integration, because the intangible nature and effortless convertibility into digital data of cross-border capital flows and financial services are especially suitable for exploiting the potential of computer networks to break national boundaries in the circulation of any content that may take digital form.

*Financial integration in Europe and beyond*

According to the *Oxford English Dictionary*, integration is the action or process of integrating; the making up or composition of a whole by adding together or combining the separate parts or elements; and, crucially, the organization of economic activities so that national boundaries do not matter.[8] It is the process or state of affairs which involves the

---

[7] See E. Crabit, 'La Directive sur le Commerce Electronique. Le Projet Méditerranée' (2002) *Revue du Droit de l'Union Européenne* 749, at 753.

[8] See *Oxford English Dictionary* (2nd edn, 1989).

amalgamation of separate economies into larger free trading regions.[9] In Europe, the integration of national economies is described by the term 'internal market', which is characterized by the abolition, as between Member States, of obstacles to the free movement of goods, persons, services and capital.[10]

The global process of economic integration comes close to the popular notion of economic globalization. 'Globalization' can be defined as the free movement of goods, services, labour and capital, thereby creating a single market in inputs and outputs; and full national treatment for foreign investors (and nationals working abroad) so that, economically speaking, there are no foreigners.[11] Lindsey makes a crucial distinction between globalization as a political process, whereby government policies eliminate barriers to free economic movement, and globalization as an economic process, fuelled by developments in information technology and telecommunications. The political process of globalization through the reduction of legal barriers is the essential precondition for setting in motion the economic process of globalization.[12]

The core elements of economic integration, whether global, regional or bilateral, are two: first, the operation of economic and technological forces that facilitate the flow of goods, services, capital and persons; second, the operation of political forces that lead to elimination of legal barriers and liberalization of capital flows, trade in goods and services through internal reform and international legal agreements. In the long run, the gradual elimination of economic and legal frontiers is expected to result in the economies of independent states functioning as one entity.[13]

Financial integration is a species of 'economic integration'. It denotes the economic integration of financial markets and activities, in other words, *first*, the elimination of legal obstacles in the movement of capital, financial services and financial institutions across borders and, *second*,

---

[9] See generally Ali M. El-Agraa, 'General Introduction' in Ali M. El-Agraa (ed.), *Economic Integration Worldwide* (London: Palgrave Macmillan, 1997).
[10] See EC Treaty (Rome, 25 March 1957); consolidated Text at OJ 2002 No. C325, 24 December 2002, art. 3(1)(c).
[11] See Martin Wolf, *Why Globalization Works* (New Haven: Yale University Press, 2004), p. 14.
[12] See Brink Lindsey, *Against the Dead Hand: The Uncertain Struggle for Global Capitalism* (New York: Wiley, 2002), p. 275.
[13] See Willem Molle, *The Economics of European Integration: Theory, Practice and Policy* (4th edn, Aldershot: Ashgate, 2001), at p. 8.

the economic and technological forces that facilitate cross-border financial activities so that, with respect to finance, there are no 'foreigners' within the integrated area. The political component, i.e. the elimination of artificial legal barriers obstructing financial flows, services and institutions, is an essential but not sufficient condition of international financial integration. Advances in information processing, transportation and telecommunications and, of course, commercial and economic justifications and competitive forces are all significant determinants of international financial integration.

In the perfect form of international integration, national financial markets are entirely fused into a truly global market, thus rendering the distinction between residents and non-residents with regard to financial flows and services meaningless. For example, in perfectly integrated markets, the transfer of capital in exchange for primary securities is unrelated to the residence of the parties. Moreover, trading of marketable securities in secondary markets is also unconnected to the location of the market and the residence of parties and their intermediaries. In addition, financial intermediaries may receive funds from savers, transfer funds to borrowers and provide other financial services across national borders, or set up a physical presence in another country facilitating financial flows overseas. In short, financial institutions and their customers are able to engage in financial activities with non-residents without impediments, delays, higher risk and cost when compared to the same transaction executed domestically.

## The Internet and the single European market for financial services

The diffusion of personal computers to large segments of the population, the creation of innovative software and the availability of dial-up modems connected to a global telephone network were technological breakthroughs that all came together in the late 1980s and early 1990s to create the basic infrastructure for the emerging digital economy. Thomas Friedman sees in that process the genesis of a flat global order, a truly 'flat world', where the digitization of content and the ability to access this content via an inexpensive Internet browser from any location in the world have connected people, businesses and governments, within and across borders, as never before.[14] People and businesses suddenly

---

[14] See Thomas L. Friedman, *The World Is Flat, A Brief History of the Twenty-First Century* (New York: Farrar, Straus and Giroux, 2005).

realized that in a market place flattened by advanced technologies all analogue content and processes – everything from photography to entertainment to communication to bank accounts to financial information – can be digitized and therefore can be shaped, stored, processed and transmitted over computers, the Internet, satellites or fibre-optic cable, at high speed, with total convenience and ease and very high standards of security. The net result of that process was the creation of a global, Internet-enabled market place that allows for multiple forms of exchanging information and content in real time, without regard to geography and distance.

If one takes a hard look at the various subsectors of the services economy as classified by international standards, the majority of those services could be traded electronically without a commercial presence in the recipient country; and that class of services is constantly increasing due to technological developments and institutional reform. Whereas certain services are more amenable to electronic delivery than others, the distinction between the two is diminishing and what was non-tradeable yesterday without a commercial presence will not be tomorrow.[15]

Because in their basic form financial transactions involve the creation, transfer and settlement of claims which, being intangible in nature, do not rely on paper to circulate, the power of the Internet to create an integrated global market for financial services and financial flows is substantial. Most financial transactions and services can be reduced to a sequence of contractual claims, which can be stored, processed, transmitted and distributed in the form of data, which are initially accounted in computer-based and electronically administered databases and subsequently transferred or settled by appropriate book entries, in response to messages transmitted electronically. In a perfectly integrated global market based on the power of computer networks, national financial markets may interconnect. Intermediaries connect with other intermediaries. They also connect with any financial market. Investors, depositors or borrowers acquire direct access to any financial service and market. Financial services and capital are distributed at the point of demand. Demand is directed straight into the ultimate source of capital. This is done at a distance, regardless of physical location or time zones, at an unprecedented speed, from unlimited sources of demand towards unlimited sources of supply.

---

[15] See generally Sacha Wunsch-Vincent and Joanna McIntosh, *WTO, E-Commerce and Information Technologies* (New York: Markle Foundation, 2005), p. 123.

This vision of electronic finance as catalyst of international financial integration does not portray the current state of the world. Strong mechanisms of social, legal and technical control still affect the electronic circulation of content across national borders. National legal institutions and regulatory standards, cultural differences, technical mechanisms of access control, are all potential impediments of cross-border financial activities over the Internet. An essential condition for converting the potential for market integration into real opportunities for financial institutions and their customers is to settle the inherent antagonism between 'free movement' (i.e. the unimpeded flow of financial data, capital and services) and 'control' (i.e. the many layers of legal, regulatory and technical control aiming to promote plausible societal values).

In addition, the success of the Internet as a widely-used technology for delivering financial services depends on the broader acceptance and use of the Internet by a sizeable portion of the population. In that respect, the signs are encouraging. Electronic commerce has already grown at a steady pace, which is likely to accelerate.[16] The volume and value of transactions increases in tandem with lower computer prices, lower cost of Internet access, more Internet access opportunities per inhabitant and improvement in information technology (IT) skills.[17]

In Europe, electronic commerce in financial services could be a driving force towards deeper and better financial market integration. The benefits of electronic financial markets and services at a distance are symmetrical and correlated to the benefits of the single European market for financial services in general. The former cannot be seen in isolation from the latter. The end objective is the emergence of open and transparent financial markets where the cost and supply of capital and the quality of financial services will be unrelated to restrictions posed by geography, distance, politics or law. Internet banking in its widest sense is simply one of many routes to achieve the overriding objective.

One of the fundamental values of political and economic liberalism, enshrined in national constitutional traditions[18] and the EC Treaty[19] is the individual liberty to engage in economic activities and the

---

[16] See Organization for Economic Cooperation and Development, *Measuring the Information Economy* (Paris, 2002).
[17] *Ibid.*, pp. 27–40.
[18] See the German Constitution (*Grundgesetz*), art. 12(1); see also the French *Déclaration des Droits de l'Homme et du Citoyen de 1789* (Declaration of the Rights of Man 1789), arts. 1 and 4.
[19] See EC Treaty, art. 49.

requirement that legal and institutional impediments to economic liberties, including restrictions on international trade, be justified on worthy grounds relating to the public interest. Notwithstanding the constitutional foundations of economic liberalism in Europe, the project of creating a single European market sought to reverse a deeply-rooted tradition of economic protectionism and pervasive legal barriers to international trade in goods and services. It is therefore appropriate to remind the reader of the benefits of financial liberalization so as to place the discussion regarding cross-border electronic banking against its proper socio-economic context.

The basic idea is that the Internet may function as a potential catalyst, alongside other macroeconomic and legal developments, towards 'freer' and more vibrant financial markets and a better performing single financial area in Europe. For financial institutions, computer networks provide access to new markets and, for customers, access to new services and capital. For efficient firms it creates vital market opportunities. For savers, borrowers and investors it enlarges the pool of available capital and increases choice in diverse and innovative services not available in less efficient markets. The need for those services, particularly in the area of pensions, savings and life assurance is likely to increase in the light of demographic developments which will probably erode the generosity of the welfare state.

Services at a distance enable customers to spread their risk and diversify their credit, savings and investment portfolios with potential gains for performance and growth. It empowers the active recipient of services to seek better financial solutions in other, probably more efficient, financial markets from the comfort of her desk. Further, the elimination of structural barriers to cross-border electronic transfers of funds will be beneficial for merchants and suppliers of services by lowering the cost and improving the quality of cross-border payments.

To date, consumers have enjoyed the benefits of the single financial market only when they have travelled abroad to sign up for services overseas or when a foreign financial institution has established a commercial presence in their country. The Internet renders the single market more approachable and useful for consumers by enabling individuals who are less likely to travel abroad and residents in Member States which fail to attract foreign financial firms to sign up electronically for financial services in another EU country.

Furthermore, legal protectionism is in effect a subsidy to local firms, at the expense of foreign firms competing in the same market segment.

Although the attempted protection of national financial institutions from foreign competition may help to create a relatively stable financial market, there is often a substantial price to pay: lack of foreign competition often results in complacency and concentration of power in a handful of local market leaders at the expense of innovation and quality of service for local borrowers, savers and investors. Vibrant financial markets and open borders place domestic institutions under the pressure of international competition, destroy complacency and unleash dormant forces. As a result, inefficient financial centres or individual firms are forced to undertake reform or decline, and efficient ones are obliged to prove themselves again and again by raising the quality of service and spreading finance opportunities to larger segments of the population. By offering a ubiquitous access point and raising awareness of products and services available abroad, the Internet forces inefficient local banks to improve the quality of their services or perish.

On the Internet, the high volume, quality and convenience in the discovery of available information about financial institutions, services and prices improve the transparency of the market. The size of the market precludes any particular player from dominating. Automation, standardization of services and the metamorphosis of the customer into the bank's data entry clerk trim down the costs of market entry for new ventures. The ability to provide services from within a single location to many different markets creates economies of scale and reduces costs. In that respect, the adoption of the single European currency eliminated duplication in bank internal and front-desk operations, enhanced transparency of prices of financial services and products and stimulated consumer interest and confidence in cross-border financial services. Evidence now suggests that in markets less susceptible to legal barriers, notably the inter-bank money and debt markets, the contribution of the euro to full integration has been substantial.[20]

Taken together, the foregoing qualities may potentially level the playing field of financial competition with potential gains for customers, including lower commissions for online securities trading, more competitive rates of interest for credit and savings and innovative electronic financial services and products.[21]

---

[20] See Jean Dermine, 'European Banking: Past, Present and Future' (paper presented at the 2nd ECB Central Banking Conference, Frankfurt, October 2002), pp. 3–19.

[21] See T. Granier and C. Jaffeux, *Internet et Transactions Financières* (Paris: Economica, 2002), ch. 3; see also www.halifax.co.uk (last visited 3 August 2005) where Halifax, a UK

For customers and banks in smaller Member States the benefits may go even further. Imported competition will unleash dormant domestic forces towards reform and modernization. Local savers, borrowers or investors will benefit from a far greater supply and a better quality of services than domestic institutions are able to offer. Perhaps they may enjoy for the first time the convenience of Internet banking which poorly performing domestic firms have failed to provide.

Furthermore, Internet banking may contribute to economic growth and development. It may enlarge the pool of affordable credit for entrepreneurs living in remote and isolated communities by facilitating access to liquid but distant financial centres. It may provide investors with direct access to overseas financial markets and dynamic local businesses with access to wider pools of capital and better performing or innovative financial services. It may offer an alternative strategy to those financial institutions that have been reluctant to take advantage of the single European market deterred by the high cost of entry by way of establishment. It may encourage businesses from wealthier Member States to invest in less developed Member States, creating jobs and tax revenue, in the assurance that the trusted services of banks in their home country are available electronically. A similar argument can be made with regard to the movement of natural persons for purposes of employment, education or retirement to a country other than their own. They can now enjoy their new lifestyle in the country of their choice without forgoing the long and trusted relationship with their financial adviser, bank or investment firm.

## The challenge for policy makers

The network architecture of the Internet is deliberately minimalist. Its protocols are indifferent to the geographical origins or destination of the data, their content, the purpose of their transportation or whether the originator or the recipient of data has a legitimate claim upon them. It was originally intended for research, not regulated commercial and financial activities, and therefore its technical specifications reflect the conscious decision to disable control and stimulate speed and efficiency in the circulation of digital data. To the server, where the bank website is

bank, offers lower rates of interest for online personal loans, not available in branch-based transactions.

hosted and towards which the customer transmits her request for the delivery of data, the Internet Protocol reveals only the Internet Protocol address of the customer's computer and nothing else. On that information alone, the Internet Protocol ensures that sensitive financial and account data will be delivered.

Although ingenious for facilitating the free circulation of content, this minimalism is useless for purposes of social control and a major source of risk in the business of banking. For that reason, users and financial institutions impose control of access or content peripherally, without the core Internet Protocol being otherwise affected. Having been disabled for the sake of simplicity and speed, barriers to the free flow of information may easily be reinstated in the form of access control and authentication procedures.

Clearly the romantic description of the Internet as a *sui generis* social environment, the *cyberspace*, where availability and exchange of information is unimpeded, anonymity is guaranteed, identities do not matter and the location of data does not affect their accessibility, refers solely to the properties of the core Internet Protocol. It does not accurately reflect the tiered layers of control that the decentralized network may permit over transportable data of different content, value and economic purpose. Those mechanisms of control lend a new shape to the open-source Internet structure and redefine the actual (as opposed to the potential) value of network technology for breaking the boundaries of distance, geography or time.

Banking lies at the heart of the tension between 'free flow of data' and 'control' in a paradoxical way. Few data-intensive activities could benefit more from the open-source structure of the Internet architecture; and hardly any other activity is subject to so many layers of control which must be implemented by public regulatory authorities and the banks themselves through self-imposed mechanisms of access control and network security. The normative argument on how best to reconcile the two competing claims is not easy to settle. For the single European market in financial services, this key question lies at the heart of the controversies and antithetical claims which have burdened the single market project from its inception.

The properties of the core Internet Protocol facilitate economic integration but cannot conceal the many political, institutional and legal forces that point towards the opposite direction. The gap between the promising qualities of network technology and the essential technical and legal infrastructure required to actually deliver financial services across national borders can be wide. To date, customer acceptance and industry investment have primarily been driven by claims of efficiency, lower prices and rates of interest and convenience.[22] Less attention has been given to the potential scope for increased profitability or customer choice, let alone cross-border market expansion. To reverse this trend, particularly at the consumer end of the market, difficult battles must be won on various fronts. The legal front is one of them.

Olson demonstrated that when sound legal institutions such as contract laws and enforcement mechanisms are lacking, commercial transactions tend to concentrate in spot markets (e.g. oriental bazaars) where personal trust and confidence replace law enforcement in safeguarding that the undertaken obligations will be honoured.[23] Conversely, the absence of personal relationships in transactions at a distance, between parties in different countries or cities, leaves a gap which must be filled by the parties' confidence in the quality of the legal framework or (perhaps) by the high benefits of the project which render high legal risks worth taking.

Cross-border Internet banking upsets the international legal framework in two respects. First, online banking as a form of international trade in financial services is inherently different from the traditional mode of entering foreign markets by way of establishment of commercial presence locally and therefore it is not fully compatible with the prevailing principle of territoriality which determines the application of national law to cross-border transactions and activities. Second, as a form of banking service, online banking relies upon a delivery channel that presents a new range of risks. Unless these issues are fully understood and financial institutions and their customers are assured that the departure from the familiar local markets will not be penalized by unacceptable levels of legal risk, the prospects of using the Internet as a means for engaging in financial activities across borders are unpromising.

Regardless of the unique legal and operational risks associated with online banking, the objective of improving the institutional framework of the single European market for the benefit of financial institutions and users of financial services is subject to the dynamics of European

---

[22] See Laura Bradley and Kate Stewart, 'A Delphi Study on the Drivers and Inhibitors of Internet Banking' (2002) 20 *International Journal of Bank Marketing* 250.
[23] See Mancur Olson, *Power and Prosperity: Outgrowing Communist and Capitalist Dictatorships* (New York: Basic Books, 2000), at p. 186.

political and economic integration. For example, the debate concerning the optimal institutional framework for online financial activities raises the same old antagonism between 'de-regulation' in the form of elimination of restrictive layers of legal control and 'regulation' as a means of addressing unacceptable risks and achieving worthy social, economic and political objectives. EU countries do not hold identical views and preferences regarding the objectives of European integration and how the tension between 'liberalization' and 'regulation' should be reconciled. Moreover, electronic commerce in financial services is subject to further uncertainty and institutional transition because national policies are likely to be in tentative mode and subject to frequent revision insofar as the legal and regulatory implications of electronic commerce in financial services have just begun to emerge.

## Internet banking in Europe

Internet banking and online securities brokerage have achieved significant market penetration in most developed countries and key emerging markets and demonstrate potential for further growth (see table 1.1).

It appears that higher income and higher market acceptance of electronic finance are strongly correlated. This probably reflects the link between high income and good IT resources and skills. According to the directory of European banks maintained by Qualisteam,[24] over nine hundred depository institutions across Europe perform services over the Internet. Customer acceptance of the business model is also high and still rising. One in five bank customers performs transactions over the Internet and the figure rises to one in four among Internet users.[25] The growth of Internet brokerage has also been considerable, with over five million investors already trading online as of the end of 2001. The service is particularly popular in the Scandinavian and Nordic countries.[26] In the Mediterranean countries, the market is less developed but grows rapidly. The annual growth of the market in Spain is in excess of 10 per cent[27] and all major financial institutions in Greece have launched

---

[24] See http://www.qualisteam.com/Banks/Europe/index.html (last visited 23 May 2005).
[25] See Centre for the Study of Financial Innovation (CSFI) (ed.), *The New World of European E-Finance* (London, 2002), p. 47.
[26] *Ibid.*, pp. 129–33.
[27] *Ibid.*, pp. 146–50.

Table 1.1. *Penetration of Internet banking and brokerage (end of 2000)*

| Income group/economy | Internet banking (% of total bank customers) | Internet brokerage (% of total bank customers) |
|---|---|---|
| **Industrial country average** | 8 | 27 |
| Australia | 4 | 22 |
| Belgium | 4 | 20 |
| Denmark | 6 | 38 |
| Finland | 20 | |
| France | 2 | 18 |
| Germany | 12 | 32 |
| Italy | 1 | 16 |
| Japan | | 32 |
| Netherlands | 15 | 40 |
| Norway | 8 | 25 |
| Portugal | 2 | 7 |
| Singapore | 5 | 10 |
| Spain | 2 | 8 |
| Sweden | 31 | 55 |
| United Kingdom | 6 | 26 |
| United States | 6 | 56 |
| **Emerging markets average** | 5 | 30 |
| Brazil | 5 | 6 |
| India | 11 | 2 |
| S. Korea | 13 | 65 |
| Mexico | 3 | 41 |

Source: S. Claessens et al., *Electronic Finance: A New Approach to Development* (Washington, DC: World Bank, 2002)

fully interactive and transactional services.[28] It appears that education, age and profession are the most influential demographic variables, alongside income, of customer acceptance:[29] the typical user is profiled as a degree holder, aged between twenty-three and forty-six, urban, professional and with a relatively high income.

[28] See Hellenic Bankers' Association, *E-Banking: New Horizons in Banking Enterprise* (Athens, 2001).
[29] See Hans Christiansen, *Electronic Finance: Economics and Institutional Factors* (Paris: OECD Financial Affairs Division, 2001), pp. 8–9.

## Market trends in key European countries

In the United Kingdom, it is estimated that eight million bank customers perform their financial transactions on the Internet.[30] The acceptance of the Internet as a channel for delivering banking services is high in France as well. The number of customers is estimated at ten million, whereas one in four transactions in the Paris Stock Exchange is initiated by market orders routed via the Internet.[31] The size of the German market is even larger. With nearly sixteen million bank account holders and over four million investors, Germany accounts for one half of all bank customers in Europe who perform banking transactions over the Internet.[32]

To identify and understand business practices and, primarily, to check whether the Internet has facilitated the process of European financial integration, I surveyed 148 banks operating in the United Kingdom, France and Germany. This survey examined the available online services of commercial banks that satisfied the definition of 'credit institution'. To confirm the regulatory status of 'credit institution', I relied on the supervisory records maintained by national supervisory authorities. I aimed to classify the services available, the method of accepting new customers and the content of standard form contracts. Last but not least, I checked whether services were made available to customers in other Member States, thus indicating the extent to which online financial services have facilitated further financial integration in Europe. A summary of the survey is made available in table 1.2, which indicates that the Internet has yet to emerge as a dominant medium for the delivery of banking services across national borders. Not many firms are prepared to accept non-resident customers and even fewer seem actively to solicit opportunities abroad.

Available services and transactions in most Internet banking applications fall into three broad categories:

(a) core banking activities which include the acceptance of deposits, the performance of fund transfers, which may be sole or perpetual by way of a standing order, and the availability of statements of account and transaction history;

---

[30] See CSFI, European E-Finance, p. 96.
[31] See Commission des Operations de Bourse (COB), *Les Courtiers en Ligne* (Bulletin COB No. 348 July/August 2000), pp. 13–46.
[32] See CSFI European E-Finance, pp. 139–46.

Table 1.2. *Internet banking in the United Kingdom, France and Germany*

|         | Banks surveyed | Cross-border services | Core Internet banking | Online trading | Online credit | Core Internet banking & online trading | All three types of services |
|---------|---------------|----------------------|----------------------|---------------|--------------|---------------------------------------|----------------------------|
| UK      | 48            | 2.08%                | 75%                  | 31.25%        | 45.8%        | 31.25%                                | 23%                        |
| France  | 50            | 12%                  | 84%                  | 64%           | 18%          | 62%                                   | 8%                         |
| Germany | 50            | 2%                   | 86%                  | 72%           | 30%          | 70%                                   | 24%                        |
| Total   | 148           | 5.4%                 | 81.1%                | 56.1%         | 31.1%        | 54.05%                                | 18.24%                     |

(b) the use of the Internet to accept customer applications for loans and credit for consumer or business purposes by way of a direct loan or an overdraft credit facility linked to a current account; and

(c) online brokerage and securities trading whereby the customer transmits and the bank receives via the Internet orders for the purchase or sale of securities for the account of the customer.

In some cases, only interest-bearing savings accounts are offered, with very little potential for interactivity and performance of electronic banking functions. The customer may view statements, pay funds in and withdraw funds out of the account through a 'linked' current account kept with another institution. But the service cannot be used for making electronic funds transfers to third parties.

Online securities trading is a service which many banks advertise but the service is occasionally performed by a separate legal entity, which is typically admitted to the organized securities markets where the trades are agreed upon and executed. This entity is either an affiliated member of the banking group or a third party operating in joint venture with the bank.

The granting of consumer credit via the Internet is often conditional upon the applicant holding a bank account with the same institution. In some cases, new customers are also encouraged to apply. The application process is completed at a distance but not entirely via the Internet. An application form is submitted electronically and, upon reception, the bank decides whether to make an offer or reject the application. If satisfied, the bank sends by post a copy of the credit agreement which the customer must sign and return. The funds are released by cheque or by way of a funds transfer to a designated bank account.

A number of ancillary facilities and functions are also available: access to statements of account and information on individual transactions; access to current valuations of investment portfolios and online information on index, individual stock and corporate performance; and purely administrative functions, such as management of personal security devices, for example, Personal Identification Numbers (PINs) and passwords and ordering cheque books and similar consumables.

From a business organization perspective, Internet banking services are typically offered by either (a) established banks providing services to existing customers; or (b) established banks using a separate brand for Internet banking but without creating a separately incorporated and authorized entity; or (c) new business ventures, duly incorporated and authorized, which provide services via the Internet without maintaining branch networks (Internet-only banks). This last model is rarely used. From a technical standpoint, the service requires the real-time availability of data. The data are stored on secure operational systems and special software applied by the bank enables customers to obtain access through an ordinary web browser.

### *Measuring the impact of the Internet on cross-border banking services*

According to Schüler and Heinemann, there are a variety of direct and indirect methods to measure the level of integration between two or more national financial markets.[33] Under the direct method, measuring financial integration is limited to identifying barriers to cross-border activities such as the existence of capital controls, regulatory impediments and information and transaction costs. It is an assessment of the extent to which financial integration as a political process creates the potential for cross-border financial operations. The effects of eliminating the various barriers are not examined.

In contrast, the indirect methodologies aim to examine the actual effects of opening up national borders to cross-border financial flows. The earlier literature on the process of international financial integration looked at the actual links between national financial markets and measured the actual flows of funds from savers in one country to

---

[33] See Martin Schüler and Friedrich Heinemann, *How Integrated Are the European Retail Financial Markets? A Cointegration Analysis* (ZEW Discussion Papers, Mannheim: ZEW, 2003), available at http://opus.zbw-kiel.de/volltexte/2003/875/pdf/dp0222.pdf (last visited 10 August 2005).

borrowers in another. The underlying hypothesis of that method is intuitive: the elimination of barriers would no doubt result in higher volumes of cross-border flows. The key objection to that hypothesis, however, is that if perfect integration among different nations means that all opportunities for cross-border financial flows have been exhausted, it is conceivable in theory that even a small flow of funds would signal complete integration when all opportunities for gainful transactions among residents and non-residents have been used. For that reason, more sophisticated approaches tend to disregard the actual flow of funds focusing instead on the flow of information as reflected in market expectations, reactions and asset prices and the relationship between domestic savings and investment.[34]

The relationship between savings and investment is methodologically based on the assumption that in perfectly integrated markets A and B, the sum of total investment in country A is not limited by the sum total of savings in that country. Country A should be able to raise the level of domestic investment regardless of the low level of savings by simply borrowing from country B. Studies usually find evidence that the level of domestic savings is very close to the level of domestic investment and therefore indicate a low degree of financial market integration.[35] A variation of this approach measures the relationship between domestic savings and domestic consumption (as opposed to investment) with similar results.[36]

Arguably the most popular criterion for measuring the actual state of financial integration is the law of one price or one rate of interest of equivalent financial assets which are both mobile and perfectly substitutable for one another. The basic idea behind price measurement as a proxy for financial integration is that in a perfectly integrated financial market the prices or rates of interest of identical financial assets traded in different national markets should be equal.[37] It therefore suffices to examine the prices of perfectly substitutable assets as an indirect indication of the level of financial integration.

---

[34] See generally Lars Oxelheim, *International Financial Integration* (New York: Springer, 1990), p. 2.
[35] See Schüler and Heinemann, *Retail Financial Markets*.
[36] See generally Giovanni P. Olivei, 'Consumption Risk-Sharing Across G-7 Countries' (2001) *New England Economic Review* (March/April) 3.
[37] See generally Peter B. Kenen, *Capital Mobility and Financial Integration: A Survey* (Princeton Studies in International Finance 39, 1976); Schüler and Heinemann, *Retail Financial Markets*.

For our purposes, it suffices to note that the various quantitative methods assume that, when national borders do not matter, the volume of cross-border transactions rises. On that premise, quantitative methods endeavour to measure the frequency and volume of cross-border services. Economists convincingly argue that in measuring financial integration the distinction between wholesale and retail banking and financial markets becomes crucial. Price-related methods are generally difficult to apply in the retail sector where fully substitutable financial services and products do not exist across different countries, primarily because differences in taxation, consumer protection rules and customer preferences preclude the development of identical financial products. The quantity-related approach was employed by the 2002 Gyllenhammar Report,[38] the first comprehensive account of the benefits of a functioning European retail market for financial services. My own survey of Internet banking in Europe sought to examine the extent to which financial services are provided across borders via the Internet. In that respect, I focused on the logically prior question of whether European banks are prepared to provide online services to non-residents in the first place.

In summary, I found that most surveyed firms expressly disclaim directing services or addressing customers in other countries. In cases where the contract between the bank and the customer may be concluded at a distance, the residence of the applicant within the jurisdiction is expressly elevated into a necessary precondition. A limited number of banks do not expressly preclude the provision of cross-border services to non-residents but in practice the number of those actually performing these services may be even lower. In some cases, non-residents are encouraged to apply only if they are prepared to travel to the 'home country' of the bank and open an account in one of the local branches. Some other banks indicate that any applications submitted by non-residents are to be assessed on their merits unless the service would break the law in the country of the overseas applicant. Those banks are also keen to disclaim the active solicitation of customers domiciled in other jurisdictions. First-e, an earlier project to create a transnational banking service via the Internet on the premise of a single banking licence and physical establishment, no longer operates. ING Direct (UK) NV, a credit institution incorporated and authorized in the Netherlands,

---

[38] See Friedrich Heinemann and Matthias Jopp, *The Benefits of a Working European Retail Market for Financial Services* (Report to European Financial Services Round Table – the 'Gyllenhammer Report') (Berlin: EU Verlag, 2002), pp. 45–55.

has set up a branch in the United Kingdom in exercise of the EU passport rights to serve UK residents only.[39]

A genuine case of cross-border Internet banking used to be the online service of Cortal Consors SA, trading as Cortal. Cortal is a credit institution authorized in France. The bank used to accept deposits and provide online securities trading services to customers in three European countries, namely the United Kingdom, France and Spain without maintaining a place of business outside France. Services to UK customers were provided on a cross-border basis under the passport rights established under the Banking Consolidation Directive.[40] Each national market was targeted and served by a different website set up in the relevant national language. On the basis of a single nominee trading account, investors could trade in securities listed in nine different recognized investment exchanges, including New York Stock Exchange (NYSE) and Nasdaq, London Stock Exchange, Paris, Frankfurt, Madrid, Amsterdam, Zurich and Milan, regardless of location. The cross-border Internet service is no longer available but the bank continues to provide online services in six European countries from local branches and subsidiaries within those countries.

Generally, retail-banking activities are rarely conducted across borders. Put simply, most consumers and small businesses appreciate proximity and convenience and would rather establish relationships with local financial institutions than seek financial services in a distant location, domestically or abroad. A recent study by the Federal Reserve has found that 92.4 per cent of small businesses in America use a depository institution that is within a distance of thirty miles.[41] Similarly in the European Union, for all the regulatory measures to encourage the establishment of a single market in retail financial services, cross-border loans to the private sector make up less than 5 per cent of the total loan book of European banks.[42] Similar observations can be made for the

---

[39] See Financial Services Authority (FSA) Register number 223156.
[40] Council and EP Directive 2001/12/EC of 20 March 2000 relating to the taking up and pursuit of the business of credit institutions, OJ 2000 No. L126/1, 26 May 2000. See Interview with Leon Burt, Monitoring and Notification Department, *Financial Services Authority* (London, 4 July 2003, on file with author).
[41] See Kenneth P. Brevoort and Timothy H. Hannan, *Commercial Lending and Distance: Evidence from Community Reinvestment Act Data* (Board of Governors of the Federal Reserve System, Finance and Economics Discussion Series 5, 2004).
[42] See European Central Bank (ECB), *Report on EU Banking Structure*, (Frankfurt, 2004), p. 10; Lieven Baele and others, *Measuring Financial Integration in the Euro Area* (Frankfurt: European Central Bank, 2004), p. 64.

market for bank deposits, savings accounts and residential mortgages.[43] In July 2005, a European Commission staff working paper on the progress of financial integration in Europe observed that retail financial services are still delivered locally through local establishments or intermediaries. The channels available to European banks and consumers to distribute or purchase financial services across borders, primarily via Internet, are barely used to date.[44] With regard to customer demand, the consumer does not seem to distinguish between buying from a foreign-owned or national service provider, as long as the service is available locally. With regard to product segments, one area where the Commission expresses a mild optimism is the market for savings products. Given the actual and verified convergence of interest rates and banks margins across the Euro area, it is at least arguable that aggressive pricing by overseas banks, unrestricted entry of new competitors and an increase of alternative distribution channels could conceivably trigger a meaningful integration of the retail sector in savings products. But this has yet to materialize in practice. Despite a far-reaching legislative programme and the emergence of a single European currency, retail financial markets in Europe remain fragmented.

In short, the contribution of the Internet to further financial integration in Europe, particularly at the retail end of the market, is poor, insofar as one can tell from the low volume and frequency of services provided across national borders. This is demonstrated by my research into the practices of nearly one hundred and fifty European banks operating in three leading financial centres. It also accords with the conclusions of empirical research on the state of financial integration in Europe[45] and further confirmed by national regulators and EC officials in a series of interviews with the present author.[46]

---

[43] *Ibid.*
[44] European Commission, *Commission Staff Working Paper: Financial Integration Monitor 2005*, SEC (2005) 927, June 2005, p. 10.
[45] See Martin Schüler, 'Integration of the European Market for E-Finance – Evidence from Online Brokerage' in Paolo Cecchini, Friedriech Heinemann and Matthias Jopp (eds.), *The Incomplete European Market for Financial Services* (Heidelberg: Physica Verlag, 2003).
[46] See Interview with Eric Ducoulombier, *Principal Administrator Commission of the European Communities* (Brussels, 11 February 2002); Interview with Mr A. Duchateau, General Secretary *Commission Bancaire* and *Electronic Banking Group*, Basel Committee on Banking Supervision (Paris, 19 June 2002); Interview with Peter Snowdon, Office of the Legal Counsel and Peter Parker, The Internet Unit, *Financial Services Authority* (London, 11 December 2002); Interview with Stefan Czekay, Bank Supervision *Bundesanstalt für Finanzdienstleistungsaufsicht* (via e-mail August 2002); Interview with Sven Jongebloed and Magdalen Heid, Bank Supervision, *Deutsche Bundesbank* (via e-mail August 2002).

# 2

# The legal foundations of electronic banking activities

The European law governing the contractual aspects of electronic banking activities is an amalgamation of the law of contracts, the law of the banker–customer relationship and, depending on the particular aspect of the service, the law governing distinct banking contracts and services, normally found in English common law and equity and, in the rest of Europe, in civilian codifications, such as the civil and the commercial codes of jurisdictions like France and Germany.[1] A vast corpus of case law has further adapted these rules and principles to the special requirements of banking and financial practice. Moreover, specialist statutes, secondary statutory instruments and administrative regulations superimpose restrictions, rights and obligations in the pre-contractual and contractual stage, mainly for purposes of consumer, depositor and investor protection, transparency, disclosure and fairness in banking practice or, less frequently, economic and monetary policy. Finally, EU policies in the area of financial services and consumer protection are now firmly established as constant sources of national legal rules and institutions.

## The banker–customer relationship

The relationship between the online bank and the customer is based on contract. It consists of a general contract, which comes into being upon the establishment of the banker–customer relationship, and special contracts, which arise only by specific agreement of the parties.

---

[1] See generally Ross Cranston, *Principles of Banking Law* (2nd edn, Oxford: Oxford University Press, 2002); C. Gavalda and J. Stoufflet, *Droit Bancaire* (5th edn, Paris: Litec, 2002); Norbert Horn (ed.), *German Banking Law and Practice in International Perspective* (New York: Walter de Gruyter, 1999).

## The bank account

The bank account is the foundation of separate and distinct contracts that come into being during the life of the banker–customer relationship. The bank account is legally a commercial book where the inward and outward movements of funds are recorded in chronological order as credits and debits of monetary value and automatically fuse into a net balance which represents a single claim against the bank or the customer (if the account is overdrawn). The bank agrees to accept the customer's deposits made either by the customer or by a third party by means of payment or collection from another bank account and repay a sum of equivalent value, in total or in part, on demand or at a specified date, with or without interest, to the customer or to a third party at the customer's order.[2]

In English law, the operation of a current account in which sums of money are from time to time paid in or withdrawn by the customer is an essential element of the business of banking. The facilities afforded to the account holder for depositing funds and making account-based payments lie at the heart of the legal relationship. Deposits may be withdrawn on demand or on a specified notice. It was established in *Foley* v. *Hill*[3] that between the bank and the customer the current account establishes a pure relationship of debtor and creditor. All money coming to the banker's hands for the credit of a bank account is to be taken as lent to the banker who, in turn, undertakes to repay an equivalent sum of money subject to a few additional obligations and limitations relating to the practicalities of the banking practice and the fact that the banker acts as the customer's agent on many occasions.[4] From a regulatory perspective, the activity that triggers the application of the regulatory regime established under the Financial Services and Markets Act 2000 (FiSMA 2000) is the acceptance of deposits. Accepting deposits by way of business constitutes *regulated activity* and, under the 'general prohibition' of section 19 of the FiSMA 2000, no person may carry on a regulated activity unless it is authorized by the Financial Services Authority (FSA) or it is within the scope of available exemptions.

---

[2] See *Joachimson* v. *Swiss Bank Corpn* [1921] 3 KB 110; S. Kümpel, *Bank- und Kapitalmarktrecht* (2nd edn, Cologne: Verlag Dr Otto Schmidt, 2000), pp. 297–319; Gavalda and Stoufflet, *Droit Bancaire*, pp. 147–70.

[3] See *Foley* v. *Hill* (1848) 2 HL Cas 28.

[4] See *Joachimson* v. *Swiss Bank Corpn* [1921] 3 KB 110, at 127.

In Germany, the acceptance of funds from others as deposits (*Einlagengeschäft*) and/or the execution of cashless payment and clearing operations, including electronic funds transfers (giro transactions or *Girogeschäft*), for commercial purposes constitute regulated *banking business* for the purposes of the German Banking Act.[5] From a contractual perspective, the acceptance of deposits establishes a relationship of debtor and creditor.[6] Deposits can be claimed at any time without notice (on-sight deposits or *Sichteinlagen*) or at a specified date (fixed-term deposits or *befristete Einlagen*).[7]

On-sight deposits are invariably complemented by a separate contract establishing the customer's right to use the funds deposited in the account for making cashless payments by way of giro transfers of funds.[8] This giro contract (*Girovertrag*) is a contract for the performance of duties for the account of others akin to a contract for the provision of services (*Geschäftsbesorgungsvertrag mit Dienstvertragscharakter*) subject to the law of agency and mandate.[9] The bank undertakes to operate the bank account in the name of the customer accepting payments in credit of the account and carry out transfers of funds to third parties at the customer's mandate debiting the bank account as appropriate.[10]

In France, funds received from the public in the form of bank deposits entitle the bank to make use of them for its own account subject to an obligation of repayment on demand or at a specified date.[11] The contract establishes a relationship of debtor and creditor.[12] Deposits are repayable on demand (on-sight deposits) or at a specified date (fixed-term deposits) and are normally complemented by the conceptually distinct contract of deposit in the form of a current account (*compte courant*). Repayment may be in cash to the depositor or to third parties at the customer's request in the form of electronic transfers of funds.[13] The bank agrees to honour the customer's mandate to use the deposit

---

[5] See *Kreditwesengesetz* (KWG) (German Banking Act), arts. 1 and 32.
[6] See H.-P. Schwintowski and F. A. Schäfer, *Bankrecht: Commercial Banking, Investment Banking* (Cologne: Carl Heymanns, 1997), pp. 161–3.
[7] See Kümpel, *Bank- und Kapitalmarktrecht*, pp. 297–319.
[8] See BGH WM 1989, 128, 129.
[9] See BGH, NJW 1985, 2699; BGHZ 93, 315; BGH WM 1995, 2095.
[10] See *Bürgerliches Gesetzbuch* (BGB) (German Civil Code), art. 676f.
[11] See *Code monétaire et financier* (C.monét.fin.) (French Monetary and Financial Code), art. L 312(2).
[12] See F. Grua, *Les Contrats de Base de la Pratique Bancaire* (Paris: Litec, 2000), pp. 123–4.
[13] See Gavalda and Stoufflet, *Droit Bancaire*, pp. 168–70.

account for making cashless payments to third parties.[14] For regulatory purposes, the acceptance of deposits by way of regular business and the supply and administration of means of payment, defined as all instruments which, irrespective of the medium or technical procedure used, enable any person to transfer funds,[15] constitute regulated banking operations subject to prior regulatory authorization in accordance with the provisions of the Monetary and Financial Code (*Code Monétaire et Financier*).[16]

## Internet services and electronic transfers of funds

The use of the Internet as an alternative means of initiating and transmitting customer instructions to the customer's bank for the performance of electronic transfers of funds is one of the most visible aspects of Internet banking. Electronic transfers of funds, initiated via the Internet, are members of the extended family of electronic banking applications and electronic funds transfers (EFT), which encompass any type of payment order, initiated through an electronic device, telephonic instrument or computer or magnetic tape so as to order, instruct or authorize a financial institution to debit or credit an account.

## The law of electronic funds transfers

In a typical Internet banking application, funds are transferred from the bank account of the account holder and Internet user ('originator') to the bank account of a third person ('beneficiary'), in which case the Internet serves as a convenient means of communicating the originator's mandate to the originator's bank. The bank will then realize the transfer of funds to the beneficiary by carrying out a giro transfer acting as the originator's agent. In particular, upon receipt of the electronically transmitted mandate, the bank verifies the authority of the originator, the legal status of the account and the availability of funds. On the basis of that information the bank initiates the internal process of the transaction by debiting the originator's account with the relevant amount. In the event that the originator's bank is also the beneficiary's bank, the electronic transfer of funds is an entirely in-house transaction performed

---

[14] See Grua, *Contrats de Base*, pp. 124, 149–59.
[15] See C.monét.fin., art. L 311(3).
[16] *Ibid.*, arts. L 511(1) and 311 (1).

by adjusting the balances of the originator's and beneficiary's accounts. For transfers to a different bank, the instruction to credit the beneficiary's account must be communicated by the originator's bank to the beneficiary's bank. The beneficiary's bank receives the instruction and credits the beneficiary's account, thus completing the transfer of value from the originator's to the beneficiary's account.

In English law, the electronically transmitted mandate to the originator's bank is an *authority* and *instruction* from the customer to his bank, within the framework of the banker–customer relationship, to transfer funds to bank accounts held with the same or another bank, that other bank being impliedly authorized to accept credit by its own customer and beneficiary of the transfer by virtue of their own relationship.[17] The relationship remains one between a debtor and creditor with the additional obligation imposed on the bank to obey the customer's mandate if the account is in credit or the customer has been granted an overdraft facility.[18]

In Germany, a credit funds transfer (*Überweisung*) is a specified type of giro contract whereby the originator's bank makes available to whomever the originator indicates a sum of money by way of transfer of funds to the beneficiary's bank account in exchange for a fee.[19]

The customer may instruct the performance of a single transfer or regular transfers of a fixed amount to a specified beneficiary (standing order). After receiving the instruction, the originator's bank debits the originator's account. Subsequently, the originator's bank forwards the instructions to the beneficiary's bank which duly credits the beneficiary's account with the sum designated in the originator's instructions. Essentially, Internet-based transfers of funds constitute *credit transfers* because the first account entry is a debit in the originator's account followed by the 'pushing' of funds to the beneficiary's account. The transfer of funds is essentially the adjustment of balances on the bank accounts of the originator and the beneficiary. The debt owed to the originator by her bank is extinguished or reduced *pro tanto* by the amount of the transfer. The debt owed to the beneficiary by her bank is increased (or the debt owed by the beneficiary is reduced if the account is overdrawn). No assignment of claims or novation takes place. Rather than

---

[17] See *Royal Products Ltd* v. *Midland Bank Ltd* [1981] 2 Lloyd's Rep 194 at 198.
[18] See *Bank of New South Wales* v. *Laing* [1954] AC 135, at 154.
[19] See BGB, art. 676a; BGH NJW 83, 1779.

a transfer of funds proper, the process should be better understood as a transfer of value initiated by the originator's mandate, which is transmitted via the Internet, and completed by the reciprocal adjustment of the debts between the two pairs, namely originator/originator's bank and beneficiary/beneficiary's bank.[20]

The electronic transmission of the customer's mandate is the first step of a highly standardized process of determining the reciprocal debit and credit positions of the originator's and beneficiary's banks (clearing) and the transfer of value from the originator's bank to the beneficiary's bank in final settlement of the debt owed by the former to the latter (settlement). The Internet is used as medium of transmission of the customer's mandate and communication of legally significant transactional information in digital form between the bank and the customer. From an operational standpoint, Internet services are fully integrated to and rely on banking and payment networks and institutions which are not Internet-specific such as the bank account, clearing systems and inter-bank settlements of payment instructions.

From a contractual perspective, the bank must carry out the customer's mandate with reasonable care and skill.[21] The required standard of skill and care is what is reasonably expected of persons of similar standing and competence.[22] The duty extends to selecting reliable intermediaries to carry out part of the service in appropriate circumstances. The duty of the customer is to exercise care and skill in transmitting instructions to avoid misleading the bank or facilitating fraud[23] and notify the bank of known unauthorized payments.[24]

Banks performing account services in Germany must demonstrate good faith, care and diligence in running the account and handling the customer's affairs.[25] More specifically, the bank must treat the customer fairly, must provide information pertaining to the customer's affairs, the state of the account and the performance of the customer's instructions[26] and disclose instances of conflict between the bank's and the customer's

---

[20] See *Libyan Arab Bank* v. *Bankers Trust Co.* [1989] QB 728 at 750 per Staughton J.
[21] See *Royal Products* v. *Midland Bank* [1981] 3 Lloyd's Rep 194, 198 (QB); Supply of Goods and Services Act 1982, s. 13.
[22] See *Westminster Bank Ltd* v. *Hilton* [1926] 43 TLR 124.
[23] See *London Joint Stock Bank Ltd* v. *Macmillan and Arthur* [1918] AC 777.
[24] See *Greenwood* v. *Martins Bank* [1933] AC 51 (HL).
[25] See BGB, art. 242; Norbert Horn, 'Germany' in Ross Cranston (ed.) *Banking Law – The Banker–Customer Relationship* (London: Lloyd's of London Press, 1998), pp. 72–3.
[26] See BGH NJW 64, 2058.

interests.[27] The standard of care, disclosure and information required varies depending on the circumstances of the case, the representations made by the bank, the express terms of the contract and the actual experience and sophistication of the customer.[28] In performing electronic transfers of funds, via the Internet or otherwise, the bank must carry out the mandate without delay, in accordance with the instructions and supply the originator with all relevant information and documents upon completion.[29] The customer must exercise care to provide correct information in transmitting the order leaving no doubt as to the beneficiary's identity, amount and account information.[30]

French law establishes a similar overriding duty of care in providing banking services. The bank must operate the customer account and perform electronic transfers of funds with care, being subject to liability for negligence or non-performance of contractual obligations.[31]

### The 'Internet service' agreement

The availability of Internet access to bank account information and services and the execution of the customer's instructions transmitted over the Internet are not ordinary elements of the banker–customer relationship which banks are legally bound to perform if asked. Internet access and services must be the subject of a separate 'Internet service' contract establishing special rights and obligations with regard to the availability and use of online Internet services. This conceptually distinct contract integrates the terms of use of the Internet to the overarching banker–customer contract. The 'Internet service' contract establishes the Internet as an alternative means of communicating the originator's mandate for carrying out transfers of funds, remotely accessing account information and enjoying certain ancillary services. Standard form contracts for the provision of Internet services contain terms regulating issues relating to access rights, the identification and authentication of account holders, the application and use of security procedures and devices, contingency procedures in the event of disruption

---

[27] See Horn, 'Germany', p. 73.
[28] See BGH NJW 81, 1140.
[29] See BGH WM 1976, 904.
[30] See BGH, ZIP 1991, 1413.
[31] See CA Paris, 15th Ch., 05.10.1999: (2000) *Revue du Droit Bancaire et Financier* (May/June) 150, at p. 171.

of service and the allocation of liability in the event of unauthorized use or fraud.

The contractual terms of use of the 'Internet service' exist side by side with the contractual rights and obligations implied by the banker–customer relationship and any specific contracts coming into existence by special agreement of the parties during the life of the relationship. Under the contract, the online bank is required to establish and maintain Internet-accessible online networks for the transmission and reception of the customer's mandate and the availability of access to account information and other ancillary account functions in accordance with the terms of use of the Internet service but always subject to the rights and obligations arising out of the underlying banker–customer relationship and account agreement.

From a policy perspective, the acceptance and widespread use of Internet services require a high level of automation and standardization of operations, efficiency and speed in processing a large volume of transactions, certainty and predictability in the rights and obligations of the parties, security of networks and communications and low cost. While the Internet scores high in most of these qualities, the question of security and integrity of networks, systems and communications has always been a crucial determinant of customer acceptance and institutional promotion of Internet services. A wide range of security systems, controls and devices have been tried and implemented to prevent unauthorized access to available Internet services (access control), to verify the identity of the actual user and originator of legally significant electronic instructions (identification) and ensure that whoever uses the service is legally entitled to initiate transactions (authentication) and finally to prevent the rightful account holder from repudiating transactions which were duly authorized via the Internet by the rightful account holder (non-repudiation of transactions). From a legal standpoint, the implementation of robust security measures is required by law, either implicitly or explicitly, in a diversity of legal contexts such as the banker's duty of care, the duty of confidentiality, the law of data protection and by regulatory standards promoting the systemic and individual safety and soundness of bank practices and operations.

With regard to the 'Internet service' contract, a key aspect of the bank's general duty of care and skill is arguably the implied obligation to install and maintain a reasonably efficient and reliable network and exercise reasonable care in maintaining robust operational systems which are fit for purpose.[32] The applicable standard of reliability depends on what is reasonably expected in view of available technology and prevailing industry practices. Online banks in the United Kingdom expressly promise to 'operate secure and reliable banking and payment systems'.[33] The duty is limited to technical standards within the bank's immediate control and does not extend to failures in public networks, unless the bank has unwisely accepted responsibility. The *Fédération Bancaire Française* (FBF) (French Banking Federation) has also assumed self-regulatory standards of good practice concerning online services.[34]

A key aspect of the bank's duty of care relates to access control. Access control denotes simultaneously a negative and a positive obligation. In its negative form, access control prevents the disclosure of account information to unauthorized third parties in breach of the duty of confidentiality and applicable privacy rules. In its positive form it aims to ensure that the Internet service is used by the person entitled thereto, thus preventing the performance of unauthorized transactions. Access control is carried out by means of security devices agreed between the bank and the customer subject to the banker's implied duty to install and operate reasonably efficient and safe security systems.[35] The terms of use of the Internet service invariably prescribe the customer's duty to use the security devices such as PINs and passwords in accordance with standards of good practice setting out the customer's liability for breach of contract in the event of violation of those standards. The UK Banking Code epitomizes a number of broadly accepted principles of good practice and security precautions regarding the use of Internet services.[36]

## Internet services across borders

The conceptual link between the single European market in financial services and Internet banking is the opportunity to use computer

---

[32] See also Chris Reed, *Electronic Finance Law* (Cambridge: Woodhead-Faulkner, 1991), pp. 20–1; Anu Arora, *Electronic Banking and the Law* (2nd edn, London: Banking Technology, 1993), at p. 146.
[33] See British Bankers Association, *The UK Banking Code*, March 2005, s. 2.
[34] See Féderation Bancaire Française, *Banque en Ligne: Guide des Bonnes Pratiques* (Paris, 2003).
[35] See Robert Pennington, 'Fraud, Error and System Malfunction' in Roy M. Goode (ed.), *Electronic Banking: The Legal Implications* (London: Institute of Bankers, 1985), p. 77.
[36] See UK Banking Code, s. 12(9).

networks to provide banking services via the Internet across national borders. In practice, as far as bank account services and electronic transfers of funds are concerned, the institutional and operational structure of national banking and payment systems does not guarantee that cross-border banking operations enjoy the same level of automation, standardization and low cost as purely domestic transactions.

Let us assume that a customer in country A (country of destination of services) opens an account and signs up to the Internet service of a bank established and operating in country B (country of origin of services). The customer may use the account and Internet service to pay for goods and services in country B (where the account is maintained) or in country A (where the customer lives) or in a third country C. It can be observed that, although the bank and the customer are located in different countries, the electronic transfer of funds from the customer's account in country B to a beneficiary's account in country B would be a domestic credit transfer for clearing and settlement purposes notwithstanding the cross-border nature of the banker–customer relationship. On the other hand, a transfer of funds to a beneficiary's account in country A will require an international credit transfer from the bank account in country B to the bank account in country A, even though the originator and the beneficiary would be residents in country A. Moreover, an electronic transfer of funds via the Internet service to a bank account in a third country C would also be an international credit transfer.

Whenever the relationship between the online bank and the customer generates cross-border transfers of funds, the limitations of the Internet as potential facilitator of international financial integration become visible. Notwithstanding the properties of the online environment, which facilitate the banker–customer communication and the transmission of legally significant instructions to the bank without constraints imposed by time, distance and geography, the institutional and operational structure of national banking and payment systems still raises significant obstacles to clearing and settlement of international banking transactions.

Historically, the structure and institutional membership of national clearing and settlement systems have been developed for currency areas within national boundaries in view of performing domestic bank payments.[37] In multilateral clearing systems, participating banks present and

---

[37] See generally European Central Bank, *The Blue Book: Payment and Securities Settlement Systems in the European Union* (Frankfurt, 2001).

exchange data or documents relating to transfers of funds under a common set of rules and standards through the clearing facilities operated by a central clearing house, which collects, matches, sorts, aggregates and transmits payment instructions from the originator's to the beneficiary's bank and calculates the net inter-bank claims to be settled at the end of business. Thereafter, settlement balances are routed electronically to a trusted settlement bank, typically the country's central bank, where the net inter-bank claims are discharged by means of fund transfers between accounts held by participating clearing banks with the settlement bank.[38] Because of the domestic bias of national banking and payment systems, the clearing and settlement of cross-border transactions are subject to direct and indirect operational and legal impediments which hold back the potential contribution of the Internet to convenient cross-border banking. For example, the technical standards used in different EU countries by the originator's bank to collect essential information concerning the payment instruction, such as the names of the originator and beneficiary, their account numbers and sorting codes, differ substantially from country to country and fall below the level of compatibility required for the performance of cross-border account transactions as efficiently and conveniently as entirely domestic ones.[39] Lack of compatibility of applicable standards prevents data relating to international transactions from being seamlessly integrated into the highly standardized process of collecting and processing domestic cheques, credit and debit card payments and domestic online transactions, thus raising considerably the cost of international transfers of funds and obstructing the European integration of national retail banking and payment systems.

Moreover, the institutional membership of national clearing and settlement systems is often restricted by law or custom to certain key financial institutions, at the exclusion of smaller domestic banks and non-resident credit institutions.[40] For lack of cross-border clearing and settlement privileges in their own right, most financial institutions clear and settle their customers' cross-border transactions through bilateral correspondent banking arrangements or multilateral facilities formed

---

[38] See generally Committee on Payment and Settlement Systems (CPSS), *Clearing and Settlement Arrangements for Retail Payments in Selected Countries* (Basel: BIS, 2000).
[39] See European Central Bank, *Improving Cross-Border Retail Payment Services: The Eurosystem's View* (Frankfurt, 1999).
[40] See ECB, *The Blue Book*.

privately by a small number of participating institutions.[41] In these cases, the cost and delay of processing cross-border electronic transfers of funds far exceeds the cost of comparable domestic transactions, thus undermining the feasibility and development of a single European market in retail banking and payment services via the Internet or otherwise.

## Electronic finance and credit

Online banks use the Internet for communicating information on credit and loan services and collecting customer applications for a wide range of consumer, business or residential loans and credit. From the perspective of financial policy, the Internet facilitates access to sources of finance regardless of distance and physical location, thus spreading finance opportunities to businesses and consumers that may be poorly served by traditional 'brick and mortar' lenders. From the perspective of European financial integration, borrowers applying online for credit facilities across borders may potentially find greater liquidity, better rates of interest, repayment terms and financial practices than those available in the domestic market, thus realizing the tangible benefits of the single European market in financial services and often revitalizing dormant competitive forces in the domestic market.

Notwithstanding the contribution of the Internet to more transparent and accessible domestic and cross-border credit opportunities for lenders and borrowers, the integration of national credit markets will remain a largely theoretical proposition in the absence of legal and market institutions such as credit reference services capable of sustaining the collection, processing and exchange of credit information on a cross-border basis. Insofar as the scope of coverage of applicable standards and protocols of automated straight-through processing of credit scores and references remains largely domestic, the ability of European borrowers to enjoy the benefits of electronic commerce in financial services on a pan-European basis will be severely curtailed.

The law governing bank loans and overdrawn credit facilities is settled. Under English law a loan contract is an agreement by which a lender agrees to pay money to a borrower or to a third party at the borrower's request, on terms that the borrower will repay the money with the agreed interest. In banking practice, an overdraft facility involves the

---

[41] See CPSS, *Clearing and Settlement*, pp. 17–20.

extension of credit to an account holder for a relatively short period of time. It is in law a loan granted by the bank to the customer pursuant to an express or implied contract. The customer may overdraw on the current account up to a specified limit for a specified period of time, although the bank may retain the right to call for repayment on demand.[42] Finally, the Consumer Credit Act 1974 has established a special regulatory framework for consumer credit agreements for purposes of debtor protection.

In Germany, the granting of money loans commercially or on a scale that requires a commercially organized business constitutes lending activity (*Kreditgeschäft*) and requires a banking licence under the *Kreditwesengesetz* (German Banking Act).[43] The general law governing bank loans and consumer credit is found in the *Bürgerliches Gesetzbuch* (German Civil Code).[44] In a loan contract (*Darlehensvertrag*) the lender is bound to place at the disposal of the borrower a sum of money of the agreed amount and the borrower is bound to return it with interest at the due date.[45] The disposal may be in cash, through a cashless payment in a bank account or simply through an extended credit facility, including a funds transfer, in the form of an overdraft facility by way of a current account credit.[46] A consumer loan contract (*Verbraucherdarlehensvertrag*) is a specific type of loan contract entered into by the borrower for purposes falling outside her trade or profession.[47] Consumer loans are subject to special consumer protection rules.

In France, credit transactions (*opérations de crédit*) by way of business are regulated banking services subject to prior authorization in accordance with the provisions of the Monetary and Financial Code.[48] The concept encompasses any transaction by which a person, for valuable consideration, places or promises to place funds at the disposal of another person or assumes a commitment in favour of the latter in the form of commitments under signature, guarantees or the like.[49] Loans of money are the most common credit transactions. Overdraft facilities

---

[42] See *Lloyds Bank plc* v. *Lampert* [1999] 1 All ER (Comm) 161.
[43] See KWG, arts. 1 and 32.
[44] See BGB, arts. 488–98.
[45] See BGB, art. 488.
[46] See P. Müllbert, 'Die Auswirkungen des Schuldrechtsmodernisierung im Recht des Bürgerlichen Darlehensvertrags' (2002) 56 WM 465–76 at 468.
[47] *Ibid.*, at p. 465.
[48] See C.monét.fin., arts. L 311(1) and 511(1).
[49] See art. L 313(1).

linked to a current account to draw funds by debiting the account up to a specified limit constitute loans of money.[50] Like the rest of Europe, consumer credit activities are subject to special regulatory protection.[51] Consumer credit is defined negatively as any contract for the provision of credit regardless of legal form or nature, unless it purports to finance projects relating to professional activity.[52]

## Online securities trading

Online providers of securities trading services via the Internet have not fundamentally changed the trading process in organized securities markets. The Internet is used at the front-end of the agent banker–customer relationship, namely the initial transmission of trading orders from the investor to the bank. It also improves the efficiency of the agent bank's internal systems of collecting, aggregating and transmitting orders for execution. It does not, however, enable investors to execute trading orders in their own name and account, at least for securities traded in organized securities markets, and does not affect the ways in which orders are executed, cleared and settled.

### The process of securities trading via the Internet

The process begins with the electronic transmission of the order to the bank's trading system.[53] The system automatically verifies the investor's right of access established under the 'Internet service' contract and generates an electronic message which informs the customer of the quoted financial particulars of the trade, including price and quantity, requesting confirmation of the trade. Provided that confirmation is promptly received and the customer's account is not subject to trading limitations or lacks sufficient credit, the order is routed to the market where the instrument is traded for execution in accordance with the customer's instructions and the terms of the contract. No advice on the merits of the transaction is generally offered. Online trading is

---

[50] See Gavalda and Stoufflet, *Droit Bancaire*, p. 308.
[51] *Ibid.*, pp. 321–31.
[52] See C.consom., art. L 311(3).
[53] For a comprehensive description of the process, see Office of New York State Attorney General, Investor Protection and Securities Bureau, *A Report on the Problems and Promise of the Online Brokerage Industry*, November 1999, pp. 16–123.

predominantly, if not invariably, 'execution-only' service. Upon execution, the customer receives confirmation of the transaction, which marks the end of the bilateral banker–customer interaction. Now the transaction must be settled through the delivery of securities in exchange for payment by way of funds transfer in a designated bank account. It will depend on the terms of the banker–customer contract whether the customer is the registered holder of legal title over the securities or, more commonly in retail services, the beneficiary of interests in securities held by the bank in its own name in a pooled nominee account along with securities held for the benefit of other investors.

Well-functioning systems for post-trade clearing and settlement of securities transactions are essential conditions for developing trading services via the Internet, domestically or across borders. The process starts with the execution of the trade and involves four distinct stages: the confirmation of the terms of the trade, the clearing of transactions to establish the performance expected of the parties, the delivery of the securities from the seller to the buyer and, finally, payment by way of transfer of funds from the buyer's to the seller's bank account.[54] Securities traded in European and international markets are either immobilized in physical form and held in collective safe custody or, more commonly, fully dematerialized existing only as electronic records in the books of domestic or international central securities depositories.[55] In both cases, securities transactions are settled by book entry and not the physical delivery of securities.

## Online securities trading across borders

Whenever the online bank and the customer are located in different EU countries, the customer may trade in securities markets either in the bank's home country, the customer's home country or a third country within or outside the single European market. In any case, the bank cannot provide trading services unless it has access to vital market institutions. First, the bank must be a member of the market with the right to execute trades or, alternatively, engage the execution services of a duly admitted third party. Second, it must have direct access to clearing and

---

[54] See generally Group of Thirty, *Global Clearing and Settlement: A Plan of Action* (Washington DC, 2003).
[55] See generally Joanna Benjamin, *Interests in Securities* (London: Sweet and Maxwell, 2000), chs. 1 and 2.

settlement facilities in the market whose securities are covered by the Internet service or alternatively clear and settle its trades through the books of another participant in those systems.

Regardless of the location of the customer, the transmission via the Internet of trading orders for execution in securities markets located in the bank's 'home country' combines the benefits of electronic communication with the convenience and efficiency of executing, clearing and settling trades domestically. Even if the online broker and the customer are located in different countries, the Internet enhances investment opportunities by enabling the efficient transmission of trading orders for execution in the broker's home country, thus taking advantage of established and reliable domestic networks for executing, clearing and settling securities transactions.

On the other hand, the online provision of trading services for securities traded in securities markets located outside the broker's 'home country' is far more complicated a process. Although the physical establishment of securities firms in the country where the market is located is not a legal precondition of market membership following the implementation of the Investment Services Directive,[56] securities firms wishing to provide trading services in several EU countries from within their home country must still overcome the considerable economic and regulatory cost of establishing and maintaining execution, clearing and settlement facilities in each national market whose securities are covered by the firm's trading services. Moreover, practical impediments are often imposed by local rules concerning market structure which place non-resident firms at a competitive disadvantage vis-à-vis local firms or render remote electronic access inconvenient or excessively expensive.[57] The structural impediments caused by the fragmentation of essential market components and institutions along national lines are therefore considerable and restrain the potential advantages of the Internet for enabling cross-border securities trading in the single European market, notwithstanding the structural benefits generated by the ongoing trend of cross-border market consolidation through alliances, networks and mergers of exchanges, intermediaries, clearing houses and settlement systems.

---

[56] See Council Directive 93/22/EEC of 10 May 1993 on investment services in the securities field, OJ 1993, No. L141/27, 11 June 1993, art. 15(4); ECB, *The Blue Book*, at pp. 246–53 (France), 508–14 (United Kingdom) and 152 (Germany).
[57] See Giovannini Group, *Cross-border Clearing and Settlement Arrangements in the European Union* (Brussels, 2001), pp. 38–44.

## Legal aspects of the contract for providing trading services

The contract for providing securities trading services via the Internet (or otherwise) is one of agency.[58] It establishes the legal authority of the agent bank to bind the customer in transactions entered into within the scope of that authority.

In German law, the contract for purchase and sale of securities in the agent bank's own name for the account of others (principal broking service or *Finanzkommissionsgeschäft*) is a specified regulated activity under the Banking Act.[59] It establishes the agent's obligation to receive the customer's mandate via the Internet and execute the trade for the customer's account. From a contractual standpoint, the contract is subject to the law of contracts, the law of commercial agency and special duties of proper professional conduct imposed by financial regulatory statutes and administrative regulations.[60] From a contract law perspective the contract is for the performance of duties for the account of others with elements of a contract for the provision of services (*Geschäftsbesorgungsvertrag mit Dienstvertragscharakter*) falling within the general law of agency and mandate.[61] From a commercial law perspective, the contract is one of *commission agency* (*Kommissionsvertrag*).[62] In providing the investment services the agent bank must comply with the customer's instructions and carry out the mandate with the standard of care required of a prudent merchant[63] avoiding conflicts of interest.[64] The agent is entitled to receive commission and be reimbursed for expenses reasonably incurred in the course of the transaction.[65]

In France, the regulated investment service of 'executing orders for the account of others' may take several forms, which correspond to one of three types of commercial contracts, namely carrying out transactions in securities either as broker (*courtier*) or agent (*mandataire*) or

---

[58] See *Merrill Lynch Futures Inc. v. York House Trading Ltd*, The Times, 24 May 1984.
[59] See KWG, art. 1(1).
[60] See Stefanie Tetz, 'The German System of Securities and Stock Exchanges' in Norbert Horn (ed.) *German Banking Law and Practice in International Perspective* (Berlin: Walter de Gruyter, 1999), pp. 59–67.
[61] See BGB, art. 675; G. Mai, 'Wertpapierhandel im Internet' (2002) CR 200, at 201.
[62] See U. Florian, *Rechtsfragen des Wertpapierhandels im Internet* (Munich: C. H. Beck, 2001), pp. 48–9.
[63] See K. Hopt and A. Baumbach, *Handelsgesetzbuch* (29th edn, Munich: C. H. Beck, 1995), pp. 953–6.
[64] See BGB, art. 667; HGB, art. 384.
[65] See Mai, 'Wertpapierhandel', at p. 203.

commission agent (*commissionaire*).[66] Contracts for the provision of trading services via the Internet invariably take the form of *agency on commission* in which the agent bank receives and executes the trading order in its own name for the account of the customer.[67] The contract is governed by the law of agency on commission as set out in the French Commercial and Civil Codes[68] subject to additional financial regulatory standards of business conduct. The bank must carry out the order in accordance with the customer's instructions[69] with care and loyalty in the customer's best interests and is entitled to receive commission.[70]

In the United Kingdom, *dealing in investments* as agent and *arranging deals in investments* are regulated activities under the FiSMA 2000.[71] In receiving and executing the customer's orders via the Internet for the sale or purchase of securities, online banks are engaged in the business of *dealing in investments* which is defined as: 'buying, selling, subscribing for or underwriting investments or offering or agreeing to do so as an agent'.[72] The contract is one of agency.[73] In particular, the agent bank is a *commission agent* acting in its own name for the account of the customer in exchange for commission or reward.[74] The agent bank is subject to well-established duties of contractual and fiduciary nature as well as investor protection requirements established by the FiSMA 2000 and the FSA Handbook. The agent must carry out the mandate with reasonable care and skill.[75] The fiduciary character of the relationship precludes the agent bank from making secret profits[76] or having own interests conflicting with the interests of the principal.[77] The agent bank is entitled to receive remuneration[78] and be reimbursed for all expenses reasonably incurred in the execution of the duties.[79]

---

[66] See C.monét.fin., art. 321(1); Règlement Général AMF, art. 312(2).
[67] See C.com., art. L 132(1); T. Garnier and C. Jaffeux, *Internet et Transactions Financières* (Paris: Economica, 2002), pp. 18–19.
[68] See Code du Commerce (C.com.), art. L 132(1); Code Civil (C. civ.), arts. 1984–2010.
[69] See Gavalda and Stoufflet, *Droit Bancaire*, p. 541.
[70] See T. Bonneau and F. Drummond, *Droit des Marchés Financiers* (Paris: Economica, 2001), pp. 334–6.
[71] See FiSMA 2000, sch. II (2) and (3).
[72] *Ibid.*; FSA Handbook AUTH 2.6.7 R.
[73] See e.g. *Brooke* v. *Bool* [1928] 2 KB 578.
[74] See *Armstrong* v. *Stokes* [1872] LR 7 QB 698.
[75] See *Brown* v. *KMR Services Ltd* [1995] 4 All ER 598 (CA).
[76] See *Parker* v. *McKenna* (1874) LR 10 Ch App 96.
[77] See *Clark Boyce* v. *Mouat* [1994] 1 AC 428.
[78] See *Turner* v. *Reeve* (1901) 17 TLR 592.
[79] See *Adamson* v. *Jarvis* (1827) 4 Bing 6.

## The 'Internet service' agreement

The contractual framework for providing trading services via the Internet consists of three components:

(a) the agency contract establishing the customer's right to instruct the agent bank, the bank's authority to trade in securities for the customer and the right to receive commission for services rendered and reimbursement for expenses incurred;
(b) the contractual aspects relating to the special nature of the contract as contract for the provision of investment services, for example terms defining the markets and securities covered by the contract and the terms of operation of the customer's trading and cash accounts;
(c) the 'Internet service' element which regulates the use of the Internet service and the electronic transmission and reception of trading instructions, the process of identifying the customer and authenticating the customer's mandate and ancillary information regarding the use of the agent's website.

The hybrid nature of the contract can be observed in the nature of the agent bank's duties. For example, the duty to carry out the customer's instruction with reasonable care and skill mainly relates to the quality of performance of investment services but it also affects the 'Internet service' element of the contract by implying the online agent's special duty to establish and maintain a reliable and secure electronic environment for receiving and processing the customer's mandate.[80]

---

[80] See OLG Düsseldorf NJW/RR 1997, 374 (378).

# PART II

Online banking and international market access: The causes of incomplete financial integration and what to do about them

# 3

# Legal barriers and necessary regulatory reforms

The rather poor contribution of electronic commerce to further liberalization of financial services in Europe, especially at the retail level, is neither surprising nor incidental. It is yet another instance of gaps in the legal and institutional framework of the single European market and symptomatic of the ongoing antagonism between legal and regulatory control – which is inherently national and local – and the provision of financial services across national borders.

## The causes of incomplete European integration in online financial services

Although physical barriers at the border and tariffs do not obstruct the cross-border flow of capital and financial services, certain types of laws and regulations raise significant obstacles to international finance.

### Legal barriers and international banking

Legal barriers to international economic integration can be express and intentional (direct or discriminatory barriers) or indirect and inadvertent (non-discriminatory or indirect barriers).[1] Direct or discriminatory measures draw an explicit distinction between resident and non-resident financial institutions, investors or borrowers to the disadvantage of the non-residents (overt discrimination) or result in disadvantageous treatment of non-residents without stating so explicitly (covert discrimination). At one extreme, direct barriers can take the form of complete prohibition of cross-border capital flows and international banking by way of branches and subsidiaries. In practice, more common are less draconian operating restrictions such as exchange controls on

---

[1] See Sydney J. Key and Hal S. Scott, *International Trade in Banking Services: A Conceptual Framework* (Washington DC Group of Thirty, 1991).

movements of capital, limiting the presence of foreign firms to a single city or region or limiting their assets and market share to a fixed percentage of the total value of the local market.[2]

With the liberalization of financial markets and national banking systems in many countries over the last twenty years, direct legal barriers have become less frequent, and a different and more obscure set of legal impediments has attracted considerable attention: the coexistence and conflict of diverse national laws and regulatory standards. It is arguable that compliance with multiple and diverse national systems of law entails economic costs which burden the flow of capital and the provision of financial services across borders.[3] The notion of regulatory diversity refers to the coexistence of national legal systems which have developed different laws, regulations and practices to suit diverse national and local preferences, objectives and resources.

The economic effects of legal diversity on international finance are diffused and indirect. The cause of incomplete integration is not the discriminatory treatment of foreign financial institutions but the very coexistence of diverse national laws and regulatory institutions. Although non-financial international transactions are also subject to the economic effects of conflicting national regulations, legal diversity is a significant cause of incomplete financial regulation. Financial activities are subject to comprehensive regulation relating to systemic safety and soundness, consumer and investor protection, privacy, market integrity and corporate governance. Because of the density and wide scope of financial laws and regulations, which render legal diversity more likely across nations, the economic cost of regulatory compliance with multiple systems of law is considerable.

## Direct barriers

Legal barriers to international banking may potentially affect all three modes of providing services internationally. They may obstruct, discourage or prevent financial institutions from operating in another country, consumers from accessing financial services abroad or services from

---

[2] See Ingo Walter and Peter Grady, 'Protectionism and International Banking: Sectorial Efficiency, Competitive Structure and National Policy' (1983) 7 *Journal of Banking and Finance* 597.
[3] See Albert Breton and Pierre Salmon, 'External Effects of Domestic Regulations: Comparing Internal and International Barriers to Trade' (2001) 21 *International Review of Law and Economics* 135.

being delivered at a distance without the parties being simultaneously present. Moreover, discriminatory barriers may relate to the firm providing the service (e.g. a prohibition of establishing commercial presence in the local market), the customer receiving the service (e.g. a prohibition of depositing funds with foreign banks) or the cross-border flow of capital which is often the subject-matter of the financial service.

Historically the most commonly used measures have been restrictions obstructing or prohibiting the entry by way of local branches, agencies and subsidiaries of financial institutions in foreign markets.[4] Foreign entry can be restricted by administrative measures that aim to reduce or completely eradicate the number of foreign firms entering the national market or the ability of local customers to access foreign financial institutions. At one extreme, foreign entry may be completely prohibited. More common, however, are rules that make foreign entry conditional on various limitations, for example, on the permissible legal form of the local entity or its legal powers to engage in financial activities. Common are also restrictions on the total number of foreign firms which are permitted to operate in the country as well as occasional and temporary suspensions of issuance of new charters. When foreign entry takes the form of equity investment in an existing local firm, local rules have often specified the maximum percentage of equity that could be taken up by foreign investors. An equally effective means of discrimination is introduced by national measures that restrict the ability of local residents to receive services from foreign banks and other financial institutions.

In addition to direct restrictions on foreign entry, the hostility of local authorities towards foreign financial institutions may take the form of *operating restrictions* which aim to impede foreign firms after their initial market entry has been achieved. These measures have the effect of limiting the size of the domestic market available to foreign firms either directly or indirectly, for example by increasing the cost of their operations, limiting the number of branches that a foreign bank may establish, discouraging local customers from doing business with them or affording discriminatory benefits to domestic competitors. Common practices include: rules that directly limit the size of the market available to foreign firms; administrative quotas which impose ceilings on the value of local assets that foreign firms may acquire; regulations which

---

[4] See Walter and Grady, 'Protectionism and International Banking'.

increase the cost of capital of foreign firms by prohibiting the acceptance of local deposits (or certain types of deposits or deposits from certain types of customers); regulations limiting the geographic range of foreign banks' local operations; 'nuisance' measures that are designed to increase the cost of doing business locally or compromise the quality of financial services, for example limitations on acquiring real estate, limitations on staff and management recruitment or exclusion from essential clearing and settlement networks and other forms of discriminatory treatment with regard to taxes, benefits and subsidies that have the effect of reinforcing the competitive advantage of domestic financial institutions.

Indirect barriers and the cost of doing business internationally

The elimination of direct legal barriers and the establishment of a level playing field between domestic and foreign financial institutions do not necessarily lead to full contestability and integration of international markets. In fact, the liberalization of the financial sector often reveals a second and more elusive layer of legal impediments which are simultaneously more pervasive and more difficult to eliminate. The so-called 'structural barriers' to international economic activities are natural products of the international economic and legal order and the conflict between transnational markets and local regulatory control: legal plurality (the fact that international banks operate in more than one legal system) and legal diversity (the fact that legal systems adopt different rules to deal with similar issues) raise considerable obstacles to international financial integration.

Given that different individuals and groups have different preferences, experiences and objectives, legal diversity across different nations is inevitable and desirable. Legal rules constitute essential instruments of political and economic organization. They ought to adapt to and cater for local preferences, needs, resources and objectives. Different nations seldom hold identical views concerning the content of their laws. The political philosopher Charles de Montesquieu accepted the inevitable diversity of national laws which 'should be adapted in such a manner to the people for whom they are framed that it should be a great chance if those of one nation suit another.'[5] Voltaire, on the other hand, did not quite share Montesquieu's views and portrayed the evils of legal diversity

---

[5] See Charles de Montesquieu, *The Spirit of Laws*, Book I Of Laws in General (Amherst, NY: Prometheus Books, 2002).

(and implicitly the virtues of legal harmonization) in the following terms: 'Is it not an absurd and terrible thing that what is true in one village is false in another? What kind of barbarism is it that citizens must live under different laws? When you travel in this kingdom you change legal systems as often as you change horses'.[6]

The classic articulation of the disturbing effects of regulatory diversity on economic integration is rather simple: regulatory differences across countries can increase the cost of transactions consummated and firms operating across national boundaries.[7] More specifically, the legal and regulatory framework can potentially increase the costs of non-resident firms engaging in cross-border economic activities more than it increases costs for resident firms inside the regulating country, thus conferring a competitive advantage on domestic firms against their foreign competitors, or merely rendering international activities costly and unappealing. Moreover, the lack of coordination of domestic regulatory policies is often viewed as a source of competitive inequality in international markets. By exercising their regulatory autonomy and tailoring their domestic regulatory framework, countries are able to confer competitive advantages to local firms. The drastic reduction in the regulatory burden generated by domestic rules reduces the operating costs of regulated entities and thereby strengthens their competitive position internationally.

The concept of regulatory diversity refers to the coexistence of more than one national legal systems (and financial regulatory structures) that have developed different traditions, rules and standards. This diversity of legal systems raises the cost of international financial activities which are subject to many different sets of rules. And the more national authorities legislate and regulate within their own borders, the more likely it is that these domestic rules will indirectly affect international transactions and economic integration. Obviously this is neither new nor extraordinary. Financial institutions, investors and borrowers venturing outside their home countries have always been subject to foreign laws and regulatory procedures. What, however, makes the current experience remarkable is not so much regulatory diversity *per se* but the acute tension between, on the one hand, the unprecedented opportunities

---

[6] See Voltaire, *Oeuvres de Voltaire VIII* (1838) 8. I found this quotation in Philip R. Wood, *Maps of World Financial Law* (University Edition, London: Allen and Overy, 2005), p. 4.
[7] See Alan Sykes, 'The (Limited) Role of Regulatory Harmonization in International Goods and Services Markets' (1999) 2 *Journal of International Economic Law* 49.

afforded by the technological and commercial forces of economic globalization and, on the other hand, the less accommodating reality of an international legal order that still comprises hundreds of sovereign sources of law. It is the economic and technological capacity to fully integrate national markets perhaps for the first time in history that places the remaining legal impediments into a whole new perspective.

## Reducing legal barriers in the single European market – the 1992 reforms

The flat distinction between direct and indirect barriers does not fairly represent the current state of affairs in the single European market for financial services. Following an extended period of stagnation and slow progress in building the single market during the 1970s and early 1980s, European leaders decided to revitalize the single market with an ambitious mix of policies which significantly reduced trade barriers and transformed the European economic landscape. Set out by the European Commission in 1985, the policy plan envisioned the completion of a fully integrated market in goods and services by 1992.[8] Following the liberalization of capital movements in 1988,[9] the single European market in financial services was intended to emerge after the implementation of a three-prong set of institutional reforms: the minimum harmonization of national regulatory and supervisory standards; the mutual recognition by Member States of one another's rules and supervision; and the allocation of legislative, supervisory and enforcement jurisdiction in prudential matters to the authorities of the bank's 'home state' in relation to activities carried on at home and services provided in other Member States. The policies were intended to achieve only the harmonization which was necessary and sufficient to secure the mutual recognition of regulatory standards and supervisory practices, for the purpose of establishing a single banking licence recognized throughout the Community on the basis of 'home country' control.

Despite the genuine expectation of success, the 1992 programme of reforms did not fully deliver on its promises. The excitement surrounding the gradual implementation of the relevant financial services

---

[8] See European Commission, *Completing the Internal Market*, COM(85) 310 final (White Paper).
[9] See Council Directive 88/361/EEC of 24 June 1988 for the implementation of Article 67 of the Treaty, OJ 1988, No. L 178/5, 8 July 1988.

Directives during the 1990s distracted attention from the gaps that the programme was leaving behind. In particular, the cornerstone of the reforms, the concept of mutual recognition, was 'imperfect', with EU countries retaining substantial powers to regulate cross-border services in their capacity as 'host countries', thus diluting the intended effectiveness of the 'single passport'.

It would still be unfair to dismiss the significance of the reforms. Notwithstanding the remaining weaknesses, the European internal market has made considerable progress since the inception of the single market project several decades ago. For example, restrictions on capital movements have been abolished and overtly discriminatory measures are nowadays scarce and systemically unimportant. However, the gradual elimination of direct legal impediments has exposed the hostile effects of seemingly 'innocent' national laws and the economic cost associated with legal and regulatory diversity — which were both previously concealed by more troublesome discriminatory rules. The long process of building the internal market resembles the draining of a lake that reveals new types of legal obstacles like mountain peaks formerly concealed as more and more water recedes to lower levels.[10]

The painful reality of European financial integration being incomplete was brought officially to light in 1998 by the European Commission's Proposed Framework for Action[11] and more emphatically by the subsequent Communication on the Financial Services Action Plan.[12] With regard to legal obstacles, academic research and influential studies such as the Lamfalussy[13] and Gyllenhammar[14] reports also suggested that in the then existing model of 'imperfect' mutual recognition, which tolerated the application of local laws and standards by the country in which cross-border services were provided, *legal plurality* (the mere fact that the internal market consisted of more than one legal system) and *legal diversity* (the fact that those legal systems adopted different rules to

---

[10] See Miles Kahler, 'Trade and Domestic Differences' in Suzanne Berger and Ronald Dore (eds.), *National Diversity and Global Capitalism* (New York: Cornell University Press, 1996), p. 299.
[11] See European Commission, *Financial Services: Building a Framework for Action*, COM (98) 625, 28 October 1998.
[12] See European Commission, *Financial Services: Implementing the Framework for Financial Markets: Action Plan*, COM(99) 232, 11 May 1999.
[13] See Committee of Wise Men, *Final Report on the Regulation of European Securities Markets* (the 'Lamfalussy Report') (15 February 2001).
[14] See Heinemann and Jopp, 'Retail Market for Financial Services'.

deal with the same issues) are indirect barriers to financial integration in general and cross-border electronic banking activities in particular.

### Legal diversity and conflicting national laws as causes of incomplete financial integration

In the absence of international coordination, the scope of spatial application of national law is determined unilaterally by sovereign states. Public international law sets the territorial boundaries beyond which national law must not apply in economic transactions having cross-border elements. In principle, states may apply national law over activities which may cause harm or have other substantial effects within their territory regardless of the location where the activity originates or occurs.[15] Because the 'effects doctrine' is a drastic departure from strict territoriality, cross-border activities may fall within the scope of territorial application of laws and economic regulations of more than one jurisdiction, that jurisdiction having no international obligation to concede priority to others in the event of conflict except in cases of international agreement or if dictated by the rules of private international law (or conflict of laws).

Economic regulations and laws regulating the relationship between public authorities and private parties do not benefit from the conflicts process. The territorial scope of application of economic regulatory law is determined unilaterally by national authorities in the absence of multilateral agreements, such as the EC Treaty,[16] which fetter the regulatory autonomy of sovereign states.

With regard to international banking activities via the Internet or otherwise, regulatory law adopted in the interest of financial stability, consumer protection or monetary and economic policy is a major source of legal obligations and standards of behaviour. As far as questions of private law are concerned, the conflict of laws coordinates the application of national law to cross-border contracts and torts arising out of the conduct of electronic banking activities. The process of conflict of laws aims to designate the applicable law in particular

---

[15] See *Case Lotus* (1927) PCIJ Rep Series A No. 10; *Compania Naviera Vascongad* v. SS *Cristina* [1938] AC 485, at 496–7; BGHZ 74, 322; Case C-89/85 *Ahlstrom Osakeyhtio* v. *Commission* [1988] ECR 5193.
[16] Treaty Establishing the European Community (Rome, 25 March 1957); consolidated text at OJ 2002 No. C325, 24 December 2002.

transactions and legal issues. It does not, however, guarantee that contracts entered into by the same financial institution in different countries will necessarily be subject to a single set of rules so as to achieve legal certainty and economies of scale in compliance costs. As a result, a fair summary of the economic costs of regulatory diversity in a world of international transactions and conflicting domestic regulations would include information costs, uncertainty, duplication and lost economies of scale.

Finding out and understanding unfamiliar foreign laws is expensive and often discourages cross-border ventures. Internationally active banks incur significant expenses and loss of time in their attempts to become familiar with foreign laws and regulatory practices. Furthermore, they often incur 'surprise costs' when new rules are adopted in foreign markets, over which local firms have been consulted and therefore gained competitive advantage. Even more worryingly, domestic legal reform may result in seemingly non-discriminatory rules, which are nevertheless fully adapted to the structure and traditional operations of local firms but pose significant compliance challenges for foreign banks operating locally.

The coexistence of many national sources of law and regulation may cause uncertainty as to the circumstances which trigger the application of foreign laws and the involvement of national supervisory authorities, law enforcement agencies and courts.[17] The cross-border provision of financial services via the Internet departs from the usual mode of market entry by way of local establishment. This new model for obtaining market entry stretches the traditional link between the reach of prescriptive and enforcement jurisdiction and the boundaries of territorial sovereignty. Hence, the criteria for applying and enforcing domestic regulatory standards to online services provided from within another country are not well-settled and likely to depend on unilateral policy considerations that tend to vary from country to country. In the domain of economic regulation, different countries may hold different views on what the subject-matter of regulation and how long the arm of domestic regulation and supervision should be, with online financial activities being particularly vulnerable to this type of uncertainty.[18] Is the service

---

[17] See International Chamber of Commerce (ICC), *Report on Jurisdiction and Applicable Law in Electronic Commerce* (Paris, 2001); Stephen Choi, 'Assessing Regulatory Responses to Securities Market Globalization' (2001) 2 *Theoretical Inquiries in Law* 613, pp. 641–3.
[18] See Bank for International Settlements, *Electronic Finance: A New Perspective and Challenges* (Basel: BIS, 2001); Basel Committee on Banking Supervision, *Management and Supervision of Cross-Border Electronic Banking Activities* (Basel: BIS, 2003).

a regulated activity in the host country? Is cross-border electronic banking permissible without the establishment of local branches or subsidiaries? Does solicitation of customers via the Internet constitute regulated advertising and financial promotion? Will it attract local regulation? When would local authorities be likely to extend the arm of local control?

In the absence of coordination, different views in different jurisdictions are likely to cause confusion, uncertainty, perhaps overregulation. Although national authorities apply several criteria to decide whether to regulate providers of online financial services established overseas, such as the language used in the website, the actual provision of services to local residents, and the currency of the transaction, there is still scope for discretion in regulating Internet services.[19] In other cases, national approaches have been entirely inconsistent. For example, the Swiss Federal Banking Commission does not regulate foreign banks and securities firms advertising and providing online services to Swiss residents, provided that they are established overseas and have no employees and no physical presence in the country.[20] On the opposite extreme, the Indian supervisory authority strictly prohibits the provision of electronic banking services to Indian residents unless the online bank is locally incorporated, authorized and regulated.[21] Between the two positions, other national authorities accept that cross-border services may be supplied to local residents subject to local regulation and supervision.[22] Arguably, uncertainty as to the circumstances which trigger the application of foreign regulations increases the cost of doing business via the Internet and discourages cross-border electronic banking activities.[23]

---

[19] See Securities and Exchange Commission, *Use of Internet Web Sites To Offer Securities, Solicit Securities Transactions, or Advertise Investment Services Offshore* (Release No. 1125, 1998); Australian Securities and Investments Commission, *Offers of Securities on the Internet*, (Policy Statement 141, 1999); Basel Committee, *Supervision of Electronic Banking*; IOSCO, Second Internet Report.

[20] See Swiss Federal Banking Commission, *E-Finance*, available at http://www.ebk.admin.ch/e/faq/faq4.html#4P (10 August 2005).

[21] See Reserve Bank of India, *Report on Internet Banking*, 2001, para. 8.3.4, available at http://www.rbi.org.in/sec21/21595.pdf (10 August 2005).

[22] See Hong Kong Monetary Authority, *Authorization of Virtual Banks*, Regulatory Guideline, May 2000, available at http://www.info.gov.hk/hkma/eng/guide/guide_no/20000505e.htm (10 August 2005).

[23] See International Chamber of Commerce, *Survey on Jurisdictional Certainty for International Contracts* (Paris, 2001).

Regulatory diversity often results in the cumulative application of multiple, inconsistent or plainly different national rules and regulatory procedures. The most characteristic obstacles in that group are domestic rules in the form of licensing procedures that regulate the *entry* of foreign institutions in the local market. Internationally active banks must obtain regulatory authorization in their 'home country' and, additionally, in every other country where services are provided, unlike domestic firms which are subject to a single licensing procedure. Moreover, having complied with multiple sets of regulatory standards, banks offering cross-border services are subject to the distinct supervisory process of demonstrating compliance to each one of the competent national authorities by filing reports and being subject to audits and inspections. As a result of the operation of conflict of laws or the extra-territorial application of economic regulatory law, it is conceivable that two or more sets of incompatible national rules are applicable to the same situation, for example the regulation of the bank's internal affairs and corporate governance simultaneously by the 'home' and 'host' countries. If the applicable rules are inconsistent, compliance with one set of rules is a necessary violation of another, thus rendering cross-border services impossible.

It is theoretically possible that one set of national rules is more stringent than another. If compliance with the more stringent rules automatically ensures compliance with the more relaxed ones, cross-border services may be subject to a single set of stringent rules avoiding the cost of conflicting regulations. This situation would, however, be extremely rare. Moreover, financial institutions operating in the more relaxed regulatory environment would be reluctant to comply with more stringent standards for the sake of cross-border market access, placing themselves in a position of competitive disadvantage in their domestic market.

In most cases, internationally active banks are subject to a single system of law in the countries where services are provided. For example, the website of the local branch of a US bank in Greece operates almost exclusively under Greek law.[24] In this case, the bank is subject to a single set of rules and operates under conditions of competitive equality vis-à-vis domestic financial institutions. The problem here is the need to adapt the services, corporate literature, market conduct, trading practices or

---

[24] See http://www.citibank.com/greece/homepage/index.htm.

advertising information to the requirements of each national market where online services are performed. This requirement destroys the economies of scale that financial integration and the accessibility and ubiquity of the Internet promise to deliver.

With regard to cross-border contracts and torts, the conflict of laws does not always provide the best solution. Applicable connecting factors may differ from country to country, which may result in different applicable laws for the same contract depending on the forum of litigation. Although this problem is usually solved by means of international harmonization of conflict of laws, the internationally harmonized rules are often ambiguous and ripe for inconsistent implementation from country to country. The historical anchor of conflict of laws has been the location of firms, persons, 'things' and transactions.[25] With the exception of the place where the firm is established, the remainder of territorial elements raises ambiguity in transactions performed via the cross-border flow of digital data.

Financial services are products of law and contract. The quality of the service is determined to a great extent by the contract and the applicable legal framework. Financial services are often subject to mandatory rules adopted in the interest of consumer protection and economic or monetary policy such as mandatory rules of repayment, rates of interest, account transactions and contractual form. Essentially, these so-called 'product rules' determine the end value of the service which is packaged in the form of a bundle of rights and obligations relating to the structure and performance of financial and legal terms. The mandatory application of different 'product' rules in each national market precludes financial 'products' structured in accordance with one system of law from being available in other countries where the relevant legal framework does not allow certain financial and legal terms. As a result, economies of scale are lost and the level of competition is impaired to the extent that customers are more likely to choose local banks when foreign banks are precluded by law from offering products or services with different legal and financial terms.[26]

Finally, it should be noted that the causes of incomplete international integration are not limited to legal and institutional impediments. With

---

[25] See Hessel Yntema, 'The Historic Bases of Private International Law' (1953) 2 *American Journal of Comparative Law* 297.

[26] See ECJ Case C-442/02 *Caixa-Bank France v. Ministère de l'Economie des Finances et de l'Industrie* [2004] ECR I–8961, paras. 11–17.

regard to customer demand, differences in language, the poor understanding of overseas financial services and products, an embedded trust in domestic financial institutions, inertia and the reluctance to change, distance and the desire for personal contact, remaining differences in national currencies, the poor understanding of foreign financial services and consumer protection, redress and enforcement mechanisms pose substantial obstacles to customer demand for cross-border services. Moreover, lack of customer confidence in the security of transactions over the Internet and a diminishing but still sizeable lack of IT skills in the general population, which hold back the full acceptance of Internet banking in the domestic arena, undermine confidence in cross-border services as well.[27]

On the supply side, online banks may be reluctant to expand internationally discouraged by the economic cost of legal and regulatory compliance and the poor understanding of local consumer habits, preferences and market conditions. They are also discouraged by the small and unappealing size of certain national markets, which does not justify the required entry costs; and remaining privileges of domestic competitors in Member States where state-owned banks dominate the market. Finally, the high cost required for participating in local clearing and settlement systems and credit reference facilities is an additional structural barrier.

The economic effects of legal and non-legal barriers are cumulative and mutually reinforcing. For example, the small size of certain national markets would probably not discourage cross-border ventures, if the remaining legal obstacles were eliminated.

### International governance of cross-border electronic commerce and finance

Encouraging the success of electronic finance could be the missing link in stimulating greater cross-border mobility of financial institutions, services and capital. For the single European market, cross-border banking without branches, subsidiaries and representative offices is now feasible for the first time since the inception of the internal market. The slow process of dismantling legal barriers has been irreversibly

---

[27] See Z. Liao and M. T. Cheung, 'Internet-Based E-Banking and Consumer Attitudes: An Empirical Study' 2002 *Information and Management* 283.

exposed to comparison with this unprecedented opportunity for international market access which has rendered the remaining legal and institutional barriers more obvious and less justifiable.

### International regulatory policies for electronic commerce

From the early stages of development of electronic commerce it became apparent that online activities would be subject to established notions of legal and regulatory control. In sharp contrast with the romantic views of Internet modernists, which used various metaphors to describe cyberspace as an unregulated area beyond the reach of national governments,[28] online communications, speech and economic transactions were duly brought within the scope of national regulations – often in several countries simultaneously. It is certainly ironic that the global accessibility of Internet content has been one of its major weaknesses for certain types of heavily regulated activities, exposing online transactions to unprecedented legal risks and elevating the question of jurisdiction into one of the most troublesome issues for financial institutions and regulatory authorities.

In the absence of international coordination, the regulatory policies of national authorities were instinctively influenced by the global availability of online content which, while stored on a single location, may be retrieved by Internet users world wide. On that basis, the legitimate national interest to apply domestic laws to Internet transactions entailing local effects led to regulatory policies which attempted to internalize the globalization of online information. In several notable cases of unilateralism, the mere fact that online information was publicly available within the country triggered the application of national law.[29] Although not widely adopted, this approach severs the connection between state control and the territory in which relevant regulated activities are carried on, thus creating unprecedented risks of global liability. It also results in local standards of conduct being exported overseas.[30]

---

[28] See J. T. Delacourt, 'The International Impact of Internet Regulation' (1997) 38 *Harvard International Law Journal* 207–35; D. R Johnson and D. Post, 'Law and Borders: The Rise of Law in Cyberspace' (1996) 48 *Stanford Law Review* 1367.
[29] See Ray August, 'International Cyber-Jurisdiction: A Comparative Analysis' (2002) 39 *American Business Law Journal* 531.
[30] See *Zippo Manufacturing Co. v. Zippo.com.* 952 F Supp 1119, 1127, (WD. Pa. 1997).

The alternative model of regulatory jurisdiction requires a closer territorial connection than mere availability of online content. It uses the concepts of 'targeting' or 'effects' to distinguish between legitimate and tenuous claims for regulatory control based on the impact of online activities within the country in question.[31] The application of national law is limited to information and services explicitly or tacitly directed at local residents or in cases where local interests may be objectively affected. The 'effects test' has much in common with the notion of 'targeting' but they are not identical. The concept of 'targeting' describes a specific effort to reach persons in the country, whereas effects may be produced by activities that, at least on their face, are not aimed there.

The territoriality of regulated activities as the connecting factor between banking services and domestic regulation was never intended to apply to services provided at a distance and simultaneously addressed to customers located in different countries. But neither were national authorities in their capacity as recipients of services willing to cede regulatory control and refrain from regulating in the absence of specific multilateral binding commitments. In practice, national regulators have required compliance with local rules as soon as online content and services have affected local markets in a broad range of legal contexts, including standards of advertising and financial promotion,[32] banking regulation,[33] consumer protection[34] and conduct of investment business.[35]

In March 1998, the US Securities and Exchange Commission was the first major regulator to confirm that securities activities in the United States or with US persons via the Internet were within the scope of its regulatory authority regardless of the location of the regulated entity.[36] The Commission sent a strong signal that its concerns were best

---

[31] See American Bar Association, 'Achieving Legal and Business Order in Cyberspace: A Report on Global Jurisdiction Issues Created by the Internet' (2000) 55 *Business Lawyer* 1801.

[32] See Apostolos Gkoutzinis, 'The Promotion of Financial Services via the Internet – A Comparative Study of the Regulatory Framework' (2002) 17 *BJIBFL* 29–36; Chris Reed, 'Managing Regulatory Jurisdiction: Cross-Border Online Financial Services and the European Union Single Market for Information Society Services' (2001) 38 *Houston Law Review* 1003–35.

[33] See Financial Law Panel, *Report on Jurisdiction and the Regulation of Financial Services over the Internet* (London, 1998).

[34] See Norbert Reich and Alex Helfmeier, 'Consumer Protection in the Global Village' (2001) 106 *Dickinson Law Review* 111–137.

[35] See IOSCO Second Internet report.

[36] See Securities and Exchange Commission, *Securities on the Internet*.

addressed through the implementation by issuers and financial institutions of precautionary measures reasonably designed to ensure that offshore Internet offers were not targeted to persons in the United States. It reserved the right to have regard to the overall circumstances of the case but recommended the use of prominent disclaimers coupled with technical measures capable of identifying US persons prior to the conclusion of the contract.

In September 1998, the Technical Committee of the International Organization of Securities Commission (IOSCO) reviewed the policies of key securities regulators and recommended common international standards of good regulatory practice concerning jurisdiction over cross-border securities activities on the Internet.[37] The report recommended that local regulations apply whenever an offer of securities or investment services takes place or generates effects locally. Factors that may support assertion of regulatory authority include indications of targeting residents such as local advertising, prices denominated in local currency or the use of local language or indications of offers being 'pushed' to local residents. Factors supporting the opposite conclusion include listing the countries at which the website is addressed or the countries in which the provider is regulated and technical measures taken to preclude providing services to customers in certain countries. In June 2001, the second IOSCO Report reiterated the position and confirmed that the major securities regulators had all adopted the 'effects principle' as basis for local supervisory responsibility.[38]

With regard to banking supervision, the Basel Committee on Banking Supervision (the 'Basle Committee') released its recommendations in October 2000.[39] The Committee emphasized the importance of placing electronic banking activities against the backdrop of the general regulatory and supervisory framework, including the Committee's key recommendations regarding cross-border activities.[40] The Committee identified the problem of asserting regulatory jurisdiction over banking services provided electronically to customers in countries where the online bank was not physically established. It also acknowledged the

---

[37] See International Organization of Securities Commissions (IOSCO), *First Report on Securities Activity on the Internet* (Madrid, 1998), at pp. 34–6.
[38] See IOSCO Second Internet Report at p. 5 and Annex I.
[39] See Basel Committee, 'Cross-Border Electronic Banking Issues for Bank Supervisors' in *Electronic Banking Group Initiatives and White Papers* (Basel: BIS, 2000).
[40] *Ibid.* pp. 3–5.

practical limitations of cross-border enforcement and rightly emphasized the significance of cooperation between 'home' and 'host' authorities.[41]

The Committee divided the supervisory responsibilities of national authorities depending on whether local banks offer services abroad (the *in-out scenario*) or banks based outside the country provided services to parties within the country (the *out-in scenario*).[42] The thrust of the Committee's recommendations was the importance of minimizing 'jurisdictional ambiguities' and performing adequate supervision of cross-border services, at all times, with clearly defined responsibilities between 'home' and 'host' authorities.[43]

In July 2003 the Committee published its final position.[44] It emphasized the essential role of effective 'home country' banking supervision as the most appropriate model of regulation and stressed that the 'host country' should retain an auxiliary role through cooperation and consultation.[45] Of course the proposed 'home country' model still requires some indicators as to the circumstances which justify this restrained regulatory intervention of the 'host' authorities. In that respect, the Committee has adopted the 'directed at' test and listed a number of non-exhaustive indicators useful in determining whether e-banking activities are directed at the residents of a foreign country, including language, currency, domain name linked to the local market, other designs suggesting a local connection and local advertisements.[46]

### Introducing an alternative model of governance

It has been suggested that the application of national law to online transactions on the basis of 'local effects' or 'local targeting' is an unexceptional phenomenon.[47] Cross-border electronic commerce being functionally identical to traditional cross-border activity is unworthy of special treatment. It is also argued that the fear of globalization of jurisdiction in the online world may be partially attributable to the poor understanding of the fundamental distinction between the claim

---

[41] *Ibid.*   [42] *Ibid.*, pp. 7–8.   [43] *Ibid.*, p. 9.
[44] See Basel Committee, *Supervision of Electronic Banking*
[45] *Ibid.*, pp. 3–4.
[46] *Ibid.*, Annex I.
[47] See Jack L. Goldsmith, 'Against Cyberanarchy' (1998) 65 *University of Chicago Law Review* 1199; Joel P. Trachtman, 'Cyberspace, Sovereignty, Jurisdiction, and Modernism' (1998) 5 *Indiana Journal of Global Legal Studies* 561.

to apply national law and the ability to enforce it.[48] It is still difficult to enforce local laws across borders to the extent that the exercise of coercive power is strictly confined within the boundaries of the sovereign state. In the absence of bilateral agreements, the enforcement of national public law by foreign authorities is still out of the question.[49] Hence, it is argued that that the alleged risk of global or regional liability does not reflect accurately the realities of enforcement jurisdiction and may not be that pressing a problem after all: the alleged multiple claims of *prescriptive* or *legislative* jurisdiction will fail for lack of enforcement jurisdiction, unless the firm maintains local assets or an established place of business in the relevant country. Even in the case of private law claims, the lack of physical establishment or local assets will force potential claimants to resort to the country of origin of the firm, the cost of which is likely to be a major deterrence. Ironically, then, for all the talk about how the Internet transcends territorial borders and triggers multiple regulatory claims, it is the same borders which impose formidable constraints upon excessive regulation and enforcement.

I respectfully disagree. In practice, online banks, particularly in the single European market, would be unlikely to take advantage of the legal and institutional limitations of cross-border enforcement authority, ignoring official demands to comply with local regulations. To the extent that the violation of the law of the country in which offers of services are addressed creates a deficit in market and consumer confidence, the bank has sufficient incentives to comply.

Moreover, the very impracticality of international enforcement is questionable. Few bank managers would relish the prospect of having enforcement orders pending against them in other Member States. Outstanding legal actions and judgments overseas may damage the bank's reputation at home. The case of Yahoo is a strong example. When a French court sought to limit Yahoo's right to publish information on the direct sale of racist and Nazi memorabilia on its websites that were illegal in France, Yahoo decided to litigate with intensity, for more than three years, on both sides of the Atlantic in order to dismiss the case on both procedural and substantive grounds.[50] Yahoo is a

---

[48] *Ibid.*
[49] See William Dodge, 'Breaking the Public Law Taboo' (2002) 43 *Harvard International Law Journal* 161.
[50] See M. Rove, 'International Jurisdiction over the Internet: A Case Analysis of Yahoo! Inc. v. La Ligue Contre Le Racisme et l'Antisemitisme' (2003) *Temple International and Comparative Law Journal* 261.

Delaware company and could probably afford to ignore the order of a lower French court which was extremely difficult to enforce. Its decisive stance probably demonstrates the importance attached by large multinationals to domestic and international reputation. To be perceived by the public as ignoring the applicable law is simply not an option. The argument applies *a fortiori* to internationally active banks because they are subject to more rules than a relatively unregulated commercial entity like Yahoo, and primarily because reputation in banking is simultaneously more important, and inherently more vulnerable, than the reputation of non-bank commercial enterprises. It should be noted that adverse publicity initiated by supervisory authorities as official penalty against uncooperative Internet banks has already been added to the enforcement arsenal of the German bank supervisor.[51] Moreover, truly international banks would probably have assets in most EU countries. Furthermore, the threat of national authorities to exclude non-compliant entities from vital participation in local payment, clearing and settlement facilities could be sufficient enforcement remedy. Ultimately, cooperation and coordination between the 'home' and the 'host' Member States at the supervisory and law enforcement levels would ensure that the pertinent enforcement issues were adequately addressed.

The same commentators also argue that self-restraint in cross-border activities is an effective remedy to excessive jurisdictional claims.[52] I share this view. It is commonplace that a carefully implemented strategy of voluntarily avoiding cross-border effects with appropriate technical precautions insulates financial institutions from cross-border legal and regulatory risks. The voluntary avoidance, however, of international markets is certainly not a serious policy response in the single financial market which purports to achieve precisely the opposite.

It is therefore not disputed that Internet services are 'functionally equivalent' to other economic activities. They are, since they involve transactions between real entities, which are located in real places. Hence they are within the full reach of national coercive mechanisms. Our quest, however, is to choose the best among realistic models of governance for the single financial area. This perspective seldom goes down to a question of whether national intervention accords with public

---

[51] See A. Steck and K. Landegren, 'Cross-Border Services into Germany' (2003) 11 *Journal of Financial Regulation and Compliance* 21.
[52] See Goldsmith, 'Against Cyberanarchy' pp. 201–2.

international law – which is the essence of the argument that the 'effects' doctrine is legal from an international law standpoint.

In his revolutionary work on the evolution of scientific knowledge, Kuhn demonstrated that general theories were constructed in the light of presuppositions, which set the boundaries for the academic discourse.[53] New findings are assigned in their 'right place' with the assistance of these boundaries, also known as 'paradigms'. The lapse of time brings to light more and more findings, which do not fit neatly into the boundaries of the established framework, and at some point in time the collapse of the presuppositions is inevitable. At that stage, new paradigms are born and a new conceptual framework for analysis is needed. Trachtman, though an Internet realist himself, identified the scope and scale of cross-border contacts as a new paradigm in the study of the legal implications of online activities. In his view, the Internet has not raised new problems but it has forced us to think more clearly about the political and distributional choices involved in the conflict of laws and the allocation of regulatory jurisdiction between sovereign states.[54] The Internet has simply released an unprecedented amount of information and content, which is difficult to control on the basis of territorial principles, thus repackaging an old problem in a new context and exposing the 'incompleteness' of current legal and regulatory institutions to address the challenges of a global financial market. It is also arguable that the opportunities unleashed by the global accessibility of online content compel an entirely fresh approach to international economic regulation in order to ensure that the institutional framework does not obstruct market innovation and international economic integration.

The advantages of online communications coupled with the high economic and regulatory cost of 'imperfect' mutual recognition and duplication of legal control call for a careful analysis of the governance model of the single financial market. The elimination of physical boundaries by electronic networks, which unleash an unprecedented opportunity for international trade and market integration, and the failure of regulatory policy to facilitate this process, even within the relatively controlled environment of the single European market, offers the conceptual framework within which integration policies must be revisited.

---

[53] See T. Kuhn, *The Structure of Scientific Revolutions* (3rd edn, Chicago: University of Chicago Press, 1996).
[54] See Trachtman, 'Cyberspace and Sovereignty' p. 574.

Policy makers have conceded that the legal and regulatory framework of electronic commerce should be proportionate, transparent, consistent and predictable.[55] If there was ever a time for a new approach of international regulation, it is now that computer networks attain in real life the objectives of market integration that legal initiatives in the European Union or the World Trade Organization (WTO) strive to achieve.

It now appears that the European Court of Justice ('the Court') supports this view. In December 2003 the Court confirmed that the contribution of the Internet to 'freer' cross-border trade in goods and services exceeded considerably the value added by other means of delivering goods or services at a distance and potentially entailed structural changes that the institutional framework of the single market could not ignore. In *Deutscher Apothekerverband*[56] the German government and local competitors argued that the sale by DocMorris, a Dutch retailer, via the Internet of medicines for human consumption in Germany was prohibited by German legislation which limited the sale of medicinal products to pharmacies and disallowing online orders by consumers over the Internet. The Dutch online retailer argued that such a prohibition was contrary to Article 28 EC regarding the free movement of goods.

It will be recalled that national rules which regulate the ways in which products are marketed, such as advertising rules or the specific prohibition to sell medicines outside pharmacies, fall outside the scope of the EC provisions on the free movement of goods *provided* that they apply in the same way both in law and in fact to the marketing of domestic products and products from other EU countries.[57] In plain terms, marketing legislation which applies without discrimination to domestic and imported goods alike does not restrict the cross-border movement of goods even when the legislation may have an impact on sales. In the litigated case it was clear that the prohibition did not discriminate against non-German retailers and products. German and Dutch retailers were prohibited from selling medicines on the Internet to German residents. Despite the prima facie application of the *Keck* doctrine, the Court emphasized the broader implications of electronic commerce to international trade in goods:

---

[55] See e.g. OECD Ministerial Conference, *A Borderless World: Releasing the Potential of Global Electronic Commerce* (Ottawa, 1998), Conclusions.
[56] See Case C-322/01 *Deutscher Apothekerverband eV v. 0800 DocMorris NV and Jacques Waterval* [2005] 1 CMLR 46.
[57] See Joined Cases C-267/91, and C-268/91 *Keck and Mithouard* (Criminal Proceedings) [1993] ECR I-6097, paras. 15–17.

[T]he emergence of the Internet as a method of cross-border sales means that the scope and, by the same token, the effect of the prohibition must be looked at on a broader scale . . .; for pharmacies not established in Germany, the Internet provides a more significant way to gain direct access to the German market. A prohibition which has a greater impact on pharmacies established outside German territory could impede access to the market for products from other Member States more than it impedes access for domestic products.[58]

The pertinent criterion for assessing the compatibility of similar restrictions on cross-border electronic commerce is now offered by the market access opportunities created by the Internet and the trade implications of not exploiting those opportunities. Whether resident and non-resident retailers are subject to identical treatment is no longer determinative. In the language used in the *Keck* jurisprudence, electronic commerce creates systemically important 'differences in fact' between cross-border and domestic trade in goods, which bring marketing rules of the recipient country within the scope of the free movement provisions. This principle must now inform descriptive and normative arguments regarding the model of governance of e-commerce in general and e-finance in particular within the single European market. With regard to cross-border electronic banking the issue at stake is summarized by John D. Hawke, the former Chairman of the Electronic Banking Group of the Basel Committee:

In some ways, electronic banking epitomizes the supervisory challenge that the Basel Committee was created to address. The technology on which it is based is inherently transnational. One of its very purposes is to give the banks that employ it the ability to offer products and services to customers wherever they might be located, without regard to national borders. The issue that's presented for supervisors and policy makers is how such offerings can or should be regulated in this transnational environment. It should be obvious that if every jurisdiction into which an e-banking offering was broadcast attempted to regulate the offering, or the offeror, the major benefit of the new technology could very quickly be lost. One is tempted to say that if no mechanism existed for coordinating bank supervision internationally, one would have to be invented to deal with the challenge that e-banking presents.[59]

[58] See Case C-322/01 *Deutscher Apothekerverband*, para. 73.
[59] See John D. Hawke, 'Electronic Banking' (paper presented at the International Monetary Seminar, Paris, February 2001), available at http://www.occ.treas.gov/ftp/release/2001-14a.doc (10 August 2005).

The European Union would be unwise to encourage the exercise of regulatory, supervisory and enforcement control against non-established banks on grounds that online services are directed at or affect local residents or other interests. Were such a strategy to be enforced within a single financial market of 'imperfect' mutual recognition, it would become a prime example of the global regulatory 'incompleteness' towards the advantages of e-finance and would probably be fatal for the project of creating an integrated financial market with the assistance of computer networks. It has now emerged that the Court is prepared to scrutinize the readiness of national authorities to invoke outdated concepts of market control so as to obstruct the development of cross-border electronic commerce as a significant pillar of the single market in goods and services.

In short, a poorly adjusted governance model, particularly the reliance on 'imperfect' mutual recognition with residual 'host country' regulatory powers is likely to render redundant a key instrument for the completion of the internal market through uncertainty and over-regulation; to destroy the great potential for economies of scale; to deprive customers of choice in meeting their financial needs; and finally to restrict the cross-border flow of innovative online services, which enhance consumer choice, speed and convenience, reduce costs for firms and customers, trim down entry costs of new ventures, stimulate competition and ensure remote market access regardless of distance and geography. The ability to offer online financial services across borders is so beneficial for firms and consumers and the model of 'imperfect' mutual recognition in the single European market is so inadequate that the calls by several policy makers for a revised model of governance have been emphatic.[60]

## EU policies affecting electronic commerce in financial services

The institutional and legal framework for carrying on electronic banking activities in the single European market is affected by a range of policies

---

[60] From a long list of papers and speeches see European Commission, *E-Commerce and Financial Services*, Communication to the Council and the European Parliament, COM (2001) 66 final; HM Treasury, *Completing a Dynamic Single European Financial Services Market: The UK Strategy*, London, July 2000, and statement by the Chancellor of the Exchequer, Gordon Brown, 17 July 2000, available at http://www.hm-treasury.gov.uk/newsroom_and_speeches/press/2000/press_91_00.cfm

and legal reforms which are conceived and pursued by different Directorates-General of the European Commission, including measures relating to financial services, consumer protection and electronic commerce.

## Financial services

Following the national implementation of the first generation of financial services Directives in the late 1990s, the discontent with the lack of progress in the integration of European markets came officially to the forefront of the political agenda in June 1998. Meeting in Cardiff, the European Council invited the Commission to propose a framework for action by the end of the year '. . . to improve the single market in financial services, in particular examining the effectiveness of implementation of current legislation and identifying weaknesses which may require amending legislation.'[61]

In May 1999, the Commission published the Financial Services Action Plan[62] which was politically endorsed by the Lisbon European Council in March 2000. The Action Plan proposed a series of policy objectives and specific measures to improve the single financial market in the next five years. The proposed measures aimed to achieve three strategic objectives, namely ensuring an integrated market for wholesale financial services, open and secure retail markets and state-of-the-art prudential rules and supervision.

The Action Plan attributed the resuscitated political interest in reforming the legal framework of the single financial market to 'fresh priorities' caused by significant developments including the adoption of the single currency,[63] the increasing awareness of the power of efficient financial markets to stimulate growth and prosperity[64] and the ongoing advances in IT and network technology.[65] E-commerce in financial services, on the retail side, was expressly recognized as a potential driver for choice and market openness.[66]

Strategically, the Action Plan marked a radical shift in the direction of integration policies. Emphasis was put on the model of 'perfect'

---

[61] See European Council, *Presidency Conclusions* (Cardiff, 15 June 1998) para. 17.
[62] See European Commission, Financial Services Action Plan.
[63] See *ibid.*, p. 5. [64] *Ibid.*
[65] *Ibid.*, pp. 6–7. [66] *Ibid.*, p. 11.

mutual recognition and one-stop home country control[67] premised on common rules at the EC level which were intended to depart, more often than not, from the earlier model of only minimum and restrained harmonization.[68]

A turning point in the recent history of European financial law was the publication of the Lamfalussy Report in March 2001. In contrast with the Action Plan, which deals with the subject-matter of financial regulation – 'what' needs to be regulated – the Lamfalussy Committee reviewed the law-making process – 'how' common EC rules are adopted. It concluded that the law-making process was slow, unable to respond to changing market conditions, too often producing unclear and ambiguous rules and failing to distinguish between essential principles and detailed implementing rules. Hence, despite the satisfactory level of consensus on the need to deliver the Action Plan, the chances of doing so speedily were 'close to zero'.[69]

In response, the Committee emphasized the need for more transparency and openness during the legislative process. More pertinently, it proposed structural reforms on how common rules were adopted: the traditional procedure must be limited to the core political principles and ideas, leaving the details to be agreed at a non-ministerial and more technical level. The Ecofin promptly approved plans for bringing the entire corpus of financial services legislation, including banking, within the scope of the Lamfalussy process.

## Consumer protection

The original Treaty of Rome made no reference to consumers and 'consumer interests' and there was no explicit competence conferred on the EC in the consumer field.[70] Many years later, Articles 95 EC and 153 EC, inserted by the Single European Act 1986 (SEA)[71] and the Treaty of Maastricht[72] respectively, linked the internal market project with the attainment of a 'high level' of consumer protection.

---

[67] See ibid., pp. 10 and 22.
[68] Ibid., pp. 9–11.
[69] See Committee of Wise Men, *European Securities Markets*, p. 12.
[70] See Stephen Weatherill, 'Consumer Policy', in Paul Craig and Grain de Burca (eds.), *The Evolution of EU Law* (Oxford: Oxford University Press, 1999), at pp. 693–5.
[71] OJ 1987 No. L169, 29 June 1987.
[72] Treaty on European Union (consolidated text) OJ 2002 No. C325, 24 December 2002.

The current 2002–06 consumer protection strategy has three core objectives:[73] to achieve a high common level of protection as a means of stimulating confidence in cross-border transactions and act as a 'post-integration' safeguard against risks and deficits of cross-border trade; to enforce consumer protection rules effectively; and finally to achieve greater involvement of consumer organizations in EU policies. E-commerce in financial services is expressly recognized as a key driving force of the new consumer strategy.[74] The objective is to achieve *maximum harmonization* towards a more consistent environment for consumer protection across the EU.[75] The updated consumer protection strategy for 2007–13 consolidates and expands the action areas of the existing programme, with a particular emphasis on consolidating the legal provisions developed under the current strategy and the completion of the review of the community *acquis*.[76]

## E-commerce and information society

Policies in the field of electronic commerce were introduced in 1997 with the release of the Commission Communication on Electronic Commerce.[77] A framework of action was proposed in the hope of encouraging electronic commerce in the single market. To that end, the coordination of national policies and the creation of a favourable legal environment were identified as essential conditions.[78] The project was endorsed by the European Council in 1999[79] and reaffirmed on many occasions thereafter. The cornerstone of the programme was the 2000 E-Commerce Directive.[80]

The Directive was premised on the belief that e-commerce was hampered by a number of legal obstacles arising from existing divergences in

---

[73] See European Commission, *Consumer Policy Strategy 2002–2006* OJ 2002, No. C137/2.
[74] See *ibid.*, pp. 4–8.
[75] *Ibid.*, p. 5.
[76] See European Commission, *Healthier, Safer, More Confident Citizens: a Health and Consumer Protection Strategy*, COM(2005) 115 final.
[77] See European Commission, *A European Initiative on Electronic Commerce*, COM(97) 157 15 April 1997.
[78] See *ibid.*, pp. 12–19.
[79] See European Council, *Presidency Conclusions* (Cologne, 4 June 1999) para. 16.
[80] See Council and EP Directive 2000/31/EC of 8 June 2000 on certain legal aspects of information society services, in particular electronic commerce, in the internal market, OJ 2000, No. L1781, 17 July 2000.

legislation and from the legal uncertainty as to which national rules apply and under which circumstances.[81] The improvement of the legal environment was seen as a means of strengthening e-commerce which in turn would stimulate economic growth and the competitiveness of European economies. To that end, the Directive proposed two familiar policies: the harmonization of key aspects of the law relating to e-commerce in order to eliminate the economic cost of legal diversity; and the principle of country of origin as a mandatory model for coordinating the exercise of legislative and enforcement jurisdiction between Member States.

## E-Commerce in financial services

It was not too long before the separate policies on financial services and e-commerce were brought together. In February 2001, the Commission released its view on the contribution of the Internet to the objectives of the single financial market.[82] The Communication on E-Commerce and Financial Services proposed the development of three main policies: first, convergence in contractual and non-contractual rules; second, consumer confidence in cross-border redress and Internet payments; and third, cooperation among national authorities. The Commission did not leave any doubt as to its preference for a governance model of mutual recognition and 'home country' control. It was keen to emphasize the importance of the E-Commerce Directive for financial services for the reason that:

> [I]t would be unjustifiably burdensome if a financial service provider had to comply with fifteen different sets of rules and regulations. If that were the case, service providers would be forced to design different services in order to comply with different Member State requirements, discouraging the use and take up of e-commerce throughout the European Union. Customer choice would be limited. Worse still, providers may tend to concentrate on the major markets, to the detriment of the smaller Member States. And EU consumers would look elsewhere in the world to trade electronically.[83]

---

[81] See *ibid.*, recitals 5, 6 and 8.
[82] See European Commission, *E-Commerce and Financial Services*.
[83] *Ibid.*, p. 7.

The 2002 Distance Marketing Directive[84] is the second basic component of the e-finance agenda. The Commission had released the Green Paper on Financial Services and Consumers' Expectations in 1996.[85] In that text, distance selling of financial services was dealt with as a 'future challenge'.[86] At the time, the earlier single market reforms were still in the phase of implementation and there was no clear indication on how the internal market would develop. The Commission, however, recognized that e-finance was expanding rapidly.[87] Special attention was needed and the Commission felt that the properties of financial services merited an *ad hoc* examination outside the general Distance Marketing Directive. As early as in 1996 – one year before the launch of the e-commerce action plan – the Commission identified the synergies between online communications and cross-border banking:

> In remote banking, the trend is increasingly towards computer banking, with cyber-money and electronic purses already available. In the securities sector computerised trading, the creation of wholly electronic markets with electronic clearing and settlement and remote market access may ultimately revolutionise securities trading. The use of distance selling of financial services is currently offered and concluded primarily at domestic level. However, it is anticipated that cross-border business could expand rapidly, making use of the new opportunities offered by the Information Society.[88]

In 1997 the Commission released the Communication on Financial Services: Enhancing Consumer Confidence.[89] The Commission emphasized again the opportunities offered by open computer networks[90] and expressed its confidence that 'the "virtual" bank is becoming a distribution channel that is highly attractive for both consumers and, given the expected efficiency gains, the providers of financial products'.[91] It also observed that the opportunities were likely to go hand-in-hand with

---

[84] See Council and EP Directive 2002/65/EC of 23 September 2002 concerning the distance marketing of consumer financial services, OJ 2002, No. L 271/16, 9 October 2002.
[85] See European Commission, *Financial Services: Meeting Consumers' Expectations*, COM (96)209.
[86] See *ibid.*, pp. 12–14.
[87] *Ibid.*, p. 13.
[88] *Ibid.*, p. 14.
[89] See European Commission, *Financial Services Enhancing Consumer Confidence*, COM (97)309 final.
[90] See *ibid.*, p. 5.   [91] *Ibid.*

risks. National responses were likely to differ substantially, thus fragmenting the single market.[92] On that basis, the Commission took the decision to propose the Distance Marketing Directive in order to raise consumer confidence and facilitate cross-border marketing of financial services at a distance.

The first Proposal for the Distance Marketing Directive was published in October 1998[93] and after discussions in the Parliament and the Council, an amended Proposal was submitted.[94] In the meantime, the measure was brought within the framework of the second strategic objective of the Financial Services Action Plan, that of 'open and secure retail markets'.[95] The common position was agreed in December 2001 and the Distance Marketing Directive was finally adopted in September 2002.

Epigrammatically, the Distance Marketing Directive is an instrument of legal harmonization. What the Directive aims to achieve is a common level of consumer protection and greater harmonization of national laws. The Directive facilitates the free movement of services, but only indirectly, through the approximation of national rules. A special right to provide financial services at a distance subject to a single set of rules – that of the 'home' Member State – is not expressly recognized.

This observation brings me to one of the key ideas of this book: despite the contribution of legal harmonization to eliminating legal restrictions on free trade, I will argue that the principal and most effective policy of market integration is the model of mutual recognition. Mutual recognition obviously presupposes that a minimum level of convergence of the laws of participating jurisdictions has been achieved. Hence, legal harmonization is an essential but still auxiliary process. This subtle hierarchy among different models of market integration is perhaps reflected in the statutory objectives of the E-Commerce and Distance Marketing Directives. The former, which establishes the principle of perfect mutual recognition, 'seeks to contribute to the proper functioning of the internal market by ensuring the free movement of

---

[92] Ibid.
[93] See European Commission, *Proposal for a Directive of the European Parliament and of the Council Concerning the Distance Marketing of Consumer Financial Services*, COM(98) 468 final.
[94] See European Commission, *Amended Proposal for a Directive of the European Parliament and of the Council Concerning the Distance Marketing of Consumer Financial Services*, COM(99) 285 final.
[95] See European Commission, Financial Services Action Plan, p. 26.

information society services'.[96] The latter, which is confined to the establishment of common rules of consumer protection, purports 'to approximate the laws, regulations and administrative provisions of the Member States concerning the distance marketing of consumer financial services'[97] but there is no express reference to free economic movement. One may question whether this difference in the tone is accidental or reflects the qualitative superiority of mutual recognition over harmonization in achieving full market openness.

Insofar as electronic commerce is one of many ways to provide financial services at a distance, the E-Commerce Directive and the Distance Marketing Directive play complementary roles in facilitating the single European market for retail online financial services. Technically, the Distance Marketing Directive is a consumer protection measure which aims to introduce harmonized standards of consumer protection in the provision of financial services via the Internet, over the phone, through the mail or other means of distant communication. In contrast with the E-Commerce Directive, the Distance Marketing Directive makes no explicit attempt to allocate regulatory responsibility to the authorities of the 'country of origin' in the event of cross-border services or otherwise coordinate the conflict of national laws in one form or another. Nevertheless, the Distance Marketing Directive has always been regarded as an integral part of the institutional reforms towards a pure model of country of origin in the single financial market. First, the Directive itself makes clear that it should apply in conformity with the E-Commerce Directive, including the principle of country of origin.[98] Second, according to Article 16, national measures adopted in implementation of the Distance Marketing Directive may be imposed by the 'host country' on firms established overseas but only insofar as the 'home country' has not transposed the Directive. One may conclude *a contrario* that as soon as the Directive is transposed in the laws of the Member States, services provided at a distance, by electronic means or otherwise, are intended to circulate within a model of 'perfect' mutual recognition and 'home country' control.[99]

---

[96] See E-Commerce Directive, art. 1(1).
[97] See Distance Marketing Directive, art. 1 (1).
[98] See Distance Marketing Directive, recital 6.
[99] See HM Treasury, *Implementation of the Distance Marketing of Consumer Financial Services Directive* (London, 2003), paras. 21–5.

Furthermore, according to the Financial Services Action Plan, insofar as Member States have the same basic level of protection in place, national authorities should be more ready to allow financial services providers authorized in other Member States to deal with their clients without setting additional requirements on those providers.[100] And the Action Plan continues: 'proposals for E-Commerce and Distance Marketing Directives are on the table, which will facilitate the emergence of these activities'.[101] The Commission's Communication on Electronic Commerce and Financial Services has also confirmed that the two policies are complementary pillars of the same broader strategy premised on mutual recognition and 'home country' control. The Distance Marketing Directive was part of the Commission's strategy to secure increased levels of convergence in respect of consumer and investor protection rules leading to a high level of harmonization of marketing rules, financial contracts and the remaining corpus of law governing the provision of financial services so as 'to pave the way for a country of origin approach to work in practice covering all financial sectors and distance trading modes.'[102] Finally, the E-Commerce Directive clarifies that the policies in the field of electronic commerce, 'together with the future Directive of the European Parliament and of the Council concerning the distance marketing of consumer financial services, contributes to the creating of a legal framework for the online provision of financial services.'[103]

---

[100] See European Commission, Financial Services Action Plan, p. 11.
[101] *Ibid.*
[102] See European Commission, E-Commerce in Financial Services, p. 10.
[103] See E-Commerce Directive, recital 27.

# 4

# The governance of the European market in cross-border electronic banking activities

## Introduction

In the previous chapter I argued that banks providing online services across borders are exposed to unacceptable risks of legal uncertainty and overregulation because the institutional model of 'mutual recognition' and 'home country' control in its imperfect current form has not quite eradicated the residual regulatory and enforcement role of the administrative and judicial authorities of the 'host country'. I also argued that the benefits generated by cross-border electronic commerce in financial services justify bold institutional reforms with the overarching objective to achieve legal certainty, less but more efficient regulation and regulatory competition. In this chapter, I examine the benefits and disadvantages of several competing models of financial market integration in Europe and note my strong preference for a model of perfect mutual recognition and 'managed' regulatory competition based on sufficient harmonization of prudential and consumer protection standards and enforcement practices across Europe.

The most common liberalization policies and institutional reforms towards the integration of financial markets are *de-regulatory* and, often, *re*-regulatory in character. They are *de-regulatory*, because the reforms entail the elimination of legal and institutional barriers to trade in financial services and movements of capital. Existing 'de-regulating' mechanisms amount essentially to an allocation of regulatory responsibility among different countries, whatever the details of the various models. In other words, participating countries in areas of financial integration must decide whether the country of origin of financial activities may alone regulate, the recipient state may alone regulate, they may both regulate subject to limitations or a central supranational authority may alone regulate. Furthermore, the process of financial integration is often *re-regulatory* if the undertaken legal commitments of financial liberalization are complemented by or premised upon the harmonization of national laws.

# INTRODUCTION

All available models of financial integration entail some degree of coordination and cooperation among participating countries but, otherwise, there are many types of structural reforms towards financial integration: international agreements which prohibit discriminatory national measures; supranational institutions which produce total, partial or minimum harmonization of national rules and centralization of supervisory and enforcement functions; mutual recognition of national standards and practices and 'home country' regulatory control; in contractual matters, harmonization of conflict of laws and freedom of choice of applicable law; and an infinite number of hybrid solutions, including the current 'imperfect' model of mutual recognition with residual 'host country' powers.

This is a broad range of policies, which allow for creativity in tailoring the best possible structure. Of course there is no undisputed wisdom relating to the best model. In proposing reforms towards better rules for the single financial market, it is unrealistic to expect the creation of optimal symmetry whereby all classes of interests are fully satisfied. Hence, the pragmatic discussion should shift towards the negotiation of the second best solution, namely the realistic imperfect model which operates appreciably better than the remainder of realistic imperfect policies. The applicable criteria in this assessment are not chosen arbitrarily. In our case, they must reflect the set objective and respect the legal and institutional setting of the single financial area with specific reference to the operational and economic benefits of electronic finance. Predictably, the values of a genuine single market, where services circulate freely across national borders, within a certain and efficient legal and regulatory framework are given intellectual priority. The realistic achievability of the proposed policies is also a pertinent factor. The value of achievability has both a procedural and a substantive element. The procedural element concerns the realistic expectation that the proposed model of governance can be negotiated, agreed and administered efficiently and on time. Substantive achievability means that a theoretical model, which can deliver full market openness, is nonetheless ineligible insofar as it scores low on the regulatory aspect of financial 'safety and soundness' and 'consumer protection'.

Other criteria may also inform the ensuing debate: achieving a balance between centralization and decentralization of law making and supervisory functions; the value of having local regulatory interests being served by tailored regulatory structures; the practicability and achievability of coordination among national authorities and the need for good government and regulation. This is an extraordinary mix of ingredients which all define the final taste of the stew. I will begin my argument by briefly examining the institutional foundations of the single financial market so as to provide the best possible context for the ensuing normative discussion.

## Institutional foundations of the single European market in financial services

The internal market is the backbone of European integration which is founded upon laws and institutions established under the EC Treaty and the remainder of primary Community law. Drafted in succinct and laconic terms, the EC Treaty establishes the legal foundations of the internal market without mandating specific policies, which must be specified by secondary Community law. The overarching objective is the creation of a single financial area without internal frontiers in which the free movement of firms, consumers, services and capital is ensured.[1]

The most characteristic form of *deregulation* is negative economic integration, which is usually defined as a process of elimination of national rules restricting market integration. It is a form of negative integration in the sense that it refers to measures, which Member States shall abolish, and actions, which they shall refrain from taking. No *de novo* rule-making and standard setting is involved. In the EC Treaty, negative integration is established by the principle of non-discrimination and the fundamental economic freedoms as specific aspects thereof. Member States are prohibited from restricting movements of capital across borders[2] and the freedom of natural and legal persons established in one Member State to provide services to persons in another Member State.[3]

The notion of positive integration refers to the transfer of legislative powers from the national level to the level of the European Union. It involves the coordination of national legal orders through centralized law making. This process unfolds necessarily under the quasi-constitutional framework provided by the EC Treaty, which dictates the outer limits of valid Community action.

---

[1] See Treaty Establishing the European Community (Rome, 25 March 1957); consolidated text at OJ 2002 No. C325, 24 December 2002, art. 14 (2).
[2] See art. 56.     [3] See art. 49.

In overseeing the validity of EU actions, the EC Treaty establishes binding constitutional boundaries: first, a set of fundamental principles defining the outer limits of Community action,[4] including the lack on the part of the Community of inherent legislative powers beyond those expressly conferred upon it (*principle of conferred powers*), the obligation to act only if and insofar as the objectives of the proposed action cannot be sufficiently achieved by the Member States (*subsidiarity*), and the obligation not to go beyond what is necessary to achieve the objectives of the Treaty (*proportionality*); second, legislative institutions with competences which, while strictly designated, are autonomous from the national arena,[5] a formal process for making secondary law and a *numerus clausus* of available legal instruments;[6] third a Court to ensure the consistent implementation of Community law[7] and finally a pair of overarching general principles developed by the Court despite the admittedly thin textual Treaty basis, namely the direct effect of Community law in the internal legal sphere[8] and its supremacy in the event of conflict with national law, regardless of the latter's position in the national hierarchy of legal norms.[9]

The EU legislature is not restricted by the Treaty in designing the precise content of policies towards financial integration. There is only a broad reference to convergence of national laws in Article 3(1), which prescribes that the activities of the Community shall include the approximation of the laws of Member States to the extent required for the functioning of the common market. The main Treaty basis of the single market, namely Article 14, empowers the Community to adopt measures with the aim of progressively establishing the internal market. These measures may take the form of liberalization Directives as defined in Article 47(2) or harmonization Directives as defined in Article 95 of the Treaty.

Article 47(2) is symbolically placed in the free movement chapter. It provides that in order to make it easier for *companies or firms* to take-up (initial access) and pursue (exercise) activities *by way of establishment or the freedom to provide services*, the Council shall issue Directives for the coordination of the provisions laid down by law, regulation or

---

[4] See art. 5.    [5] See art. 7.
[6] See art. 49.    [7] See art. 220.
[8] See Case 26/62 *Van Gend en Loos* v. *Nederlandse Administratie der Belastinger* [1963] ECR 1.
[9] See Case 6/64 *Costa* v. *ENEL* [1964] ECR 585.

administrative action in Member States concerning the taking-up and pursuit of these activities. Article 95 EC, set out in the chapter on the approximation of laws, empowers the Council to adopt, in accordance with the specified procedure, measures for the approximation of the provisions laid down by law, regulation or administrative action in Member States which have as their object the establishment and functioning of the internal market. The mandate is not concerned with the elimination of direct trade barriers but with legal diversity and plurality as deficits in themselves. It empowers the Council to adopt harmonization instruments for the purpose of improving the legal framework of the single market.

Provided that these boundaries are not overstepped, the European Union may freely select and pursue the appropriate integration policies having regard to a limited number of binding principles. First, all policies must respect the principle of open market economy with free competition.[10] The provision does not impose direct obligations and cannot be relied upon by individuals before national or European courts.[11] Second, in proposing secondary measures the Commission shall take into account the difficulties facing less developed EU countries during the establishment of the internal market and propose derogations where necessary.[12] Third, in proposing harmonization measures under Article 95 EC the Commission shall take as a base a high level of consumer protection and within their respective powers the European Parliament and Council '. . . shall also seek to achieve this objective . . .' particularly through the protection of consumers' economic interests and the promotion of their right to information and education.[13]

### Mutual recognition of national laws as institutional principle

Despite the remaining gaps, the legacy of the 1992 programme, namely mutual recognition of national laws on the basis of minimum harmonization, is an ingenious policy towards the creation of a single European market.

---

[10] See EC Treaty, art. 4.
[11] See Case C-9/99 *Echirolles Distribution* v. *Association du Dauphine* [2000] ECR I-8207, para. 25.
[12] See EC Treaty, art. 15.
[13] See art. 153.

## The general concept

Mutual recognition of national laws refers to the agreement between sovereign states whereby they agree to the transfer of regulatory authority from the host country where a transaction takes place to the home country from which a product, person, service or firm originates. It reflects the general principle that if a service can be provided lawfully in one country, it can circulate freely in any other participating country. The term 'mutual' denotes the parity and reciprocity of the undertaken obligations. The 'recognition' is of the equivalence, similarity, compatibility or at least acceptability of another state's legal and regulatory framework and represents the scope *rationae materiae* and scale of the reciprocal obligations.

The equivalence of national norms is conceptually static because it reflects a 'fact' and a situation that exists, whereas the 'recognition' is conceptually normative and dynamic because it mandates a certain action and leads to a new arrangement between participating Member States. Member States take stock of the equivalence and convergence of national laws, evaluate and accept the remaining differences and undertake reciprocal obligations to open up national borders to banks and services originating in the 'mutual recognition' area.

Mutual recognition is a hybrid of negative and positive integration. It goes beyond the mere elimination of barriers in that it pursues liberalization through the equivalence of national regulatory perspectives and the measured and safe allocation of regulatory responsibility. In parallel, it is not a typical model of positive integration in that the replacement of national rules by common European standards is not strictly required. It is an instrument of regulation, because the division of responsibility among participating jurisdictions has a clear normative element; it is also a means of deregulation, because a disturbing layer of national control is abolished.

Ideally, services lawfully provided in one Member State may freely circulate across national borders. Hence, mutual recognition secures market openness and promotes the values of the single financial area while simultaneously avoiding the excessive policy and transaction costs of full harmonization and centralization. It thereby preserves local regulatory choices and preferences, respects the principle of 'subsidiarity' and stimulates regulatory competition. On the other hand, prior legal convergence of formerly diverse laws and regulatory practices serves as the necessary foundation upon which mutual recognition may be premised.

To create the necessary equivalence in the substantive rules of different legal systems, a coordinated process of legal harmonization is normally required. Harmonization purports to bring about consonance or accord in the legal institutions of the Member States, in other words to reduce the disturbances caused by legal plurality and diversity. Legal harmonization is a dynamic process in that it changes the *status quo* and induces a new legal environment into being. Equivalence is a descriptive concept and denotes an existing state of affairs whereby legal institutions are corresponding or virtually identical in value, effect or function. In any case, the correlation between mutual recognition and the establishment of common rules is strong and the policy of minimum harmonization as basis for mutual recognition sound.

Paradoxically, the concept of mutual recognition is only marginally referred to in the EC Treaty.[14] On closer inspection, however, this statement does not fairly represent the treatment afforded to mutual recognition by primary Community law. By virtue of the SEA,[15] mutual recognition received 'Treaty status' and was elevated into a basic component of the institutional apparatus leading to the completion of the 1992 internal market project. More specifically, Article 19 of the SEA introduced a new Article 100b in the Treaty of Rome establishing the European Economic Community according to which 'the Council, acting in accordance with the provisions of Article 100a, may decide that the provisions in force in a Member State must be recognized as being equivalent to those applied by another Member State'. In parallel, the SEA 1986 introduced the pivotal Article 8b of the EEC Treaty (the precursor of Article 14 EC) whereby the aim of progressively establishing the internal market over a period expiring on 31 December 1992 was expressly to be attained through the process of mutual recognition regulated by Article 100b EEC. After the completion of the 1992 project, the provision of Article 100b was thought to be redundant and was eventually repealed by Article 6(54) of the Treaty of Amsterdam in 1997.[16]

---

[14] See arts. 47(1) and 293.
[15] Single European Act 1986, OJ 1987 No. L169, 29 June 1987.
[16] See Treaty of Amsterdam amending the Treaty on European Union, the Treaties Establishing the European Communities and Related Acts, OJ 1997, No. C340/1, 10 November 1997.

## Free economic movement, mutual recognition and banking services under the EC Treaty

Mutual recognition is probably one of the most celebrated instances of the so-called 'activism' of the European Court of Justice ('the Court'), which in the early days of the European project turned to the four economic freedoms guaranteed by the EC Treaty and took it upon itself to give shape to the Community legal order, bring down trade barriers and, in effect, salvage an otherwise ailing process.

### Freedom to provide services and mutual recognition

Although the basic economic freedoms were established in the founding Treaty of Rome in 1957, their full normative impact was felt in the summer of 1974 when the Court recognized their so-called 'direct effect'. It held that the Treaty imposed a direct obligation to attain a precise result, namely the prohibition of restrictions against free economic movement, the fulfilment of which had to be made easier by, but not made dependent on, the implementation of a programme of progressive secondary measures, typically in the form of Directives.[17] The Treaty freedoms were held to be directly applicable and capable of being invoked by nationals in all Member States, with the exception of the free movement of capital for which an express derogation existed. With particular regard to the free movement of services, the principle of direct effect was confirmed a few months later in the landmark *Van Binsbergen* case.[18]

The judicial recognition of the direct effect of the fundamental economic freedoms was a clear signal that a binding economic constitution emerged out of the founding Treaty, which the Court was reluctant to allow to atrophy because political agreement to adopt secondary law was difficult to achieve. A new form of negative economic integration was therefore launched with the recognition of the private parties' right to invoke the Treaty provisions before any national court and eventually before the European Court of Justice through the process of preliminary rulings. The purported elimination of trade barriers could now accelerate under the pressure of diffused and decentralized judicial control at multiple levels.

---

[17] See Case C-2/74 *Reyners* v. *Belgium* [1974] ECR 631, para. 26.
[18] See Case C-33/74 *Van Binsbergen* v. *Best uur Vande Bedrijfsvereniging voor de Metaalnijverheid* [1974] ECR 1299.

From the direct effect of the basic economic freedoms it was only a short intellectual walk to the formulation of the concept of mutual recognition. This leap forward took place in the *Cassis de Dijon* Case,[19] where mutual recognition emerged as the joint outcome of three basic regulatory principles formulated by the Court: first, the regulatory independence of Member States whereby in the absence of common EC rules, it is up to national authorities to regulate intra-Community trade;[20] second, the superiority of overriding national policy objectives in the sense that if national measures disturb free trade for some worthy reason, the relevant domestic interest is superior to the claim for trade liberalization; in other words, obstacles to free movement resulting from disparities in national laws are acceptable insofar as the disturbing provisions are necessary in order to justify mandatory requirements relating to the protection of public health, fiscal supervision, consumer protection and so forth;[21] but third, and more crucially, the objective of trade liberalization takes precedence over national regulatory interests when the relevant restrictions lack an acceptable public policy rationale or the rules in the country of origin are an adequate safeguard thereof: the German laws in *Cassis* did not serve a purpose which was in the general interest and such as to take precedence over the free movement of goods and therefore there was no valid reason why products lawfully produced and marketed in one country should not be introduced into any other EU country.[22] The conceptual analysis of the Court in *Cassis* was heavily relied upon by the Commission in drafting the 1985 White Paper and was explicitly applied with regard to the free movement of services for the first time in 1991.[23]

It is now settled law that the free movement of services requires not only the elimination of all discrimination against a person providing services on the ground of his nationality but also the abolition of any restriction, even if it applies without distinction to national providers of services and to those of other Member States, when it is liable to prohibit or otherwise impede the activities of a provider of services established in another Member State where he lawfully provides similar

---

[19] See Case 120/78 *Rewe-Zentral AG* v. *Bundesmonopolverwaltung für Branntwein* (the '*Cassis de Dijon*' case) [1979] ECR 649.
[20] *Ibid.*, para. 8.
[21] *Ibid.*
[22] See para. 14.
[23] See Case C-76/90 *Säger* v. *Dennemeyer & Co. Ltd* [1991] ECR I-4221.

services.[24] The country of destination must recognize the equivalence of the law of the country of origin and should not impose national measures, the effect of which is equivalent to the effect of the legislative and administrative action in the country of origin. Compliance with the rules in the 'home country' suffices to secure market access in the country of destination without being subject to 'prohibiting' or 'impeding' measures applicable therein. This normative element of mutual recognition retreats in cases where the disturbing measures are 'justified by imperative reasons relating to the public interest'[25] but only if that interest 'is not protected by the rules to which the person providing the services is subject in the Member State in which he is established'[26] in which case mutual recognition revives.

This highlights the dual function of the law of the country of origin as the external aspect of mutual recognition. First, this function is normative, because in principle it suffices to provide a passport to unimpeded provision of services across national borders. Second, when the normative element fails for eligible 'imperative reasons', the law of the country of origin is transformed into a 'fact', which is assessed in the light of the 'public interest' in question. If an acceptable element of legal equivalence and harmonization has been achieved, the original mandate for mutual recognition is restored. Both the normative and the descriptive elements of mutual recognition are linked to the principle of proportionality. The Court regards the two principles as conceptually complementary and symmetrical. To the extent that the rules in the country of origin and 'host country' are equivalent, the country of destination must recognize them and refrain from regulating; to the extent that equivalence is lacking in view of the pertinent reasons relating to the public interest, the country of destination may regulate but only in the dosage which is necessary to fill in the gap. In the language of the Court, the disturbing national measures must be objectively necessary to ensure the attainment of the set objective and they must not exceed what is necessary to achieve it.[27]

With regard to providing banking services, the judicial implementation of mutual recognition was attempted in *Parodi*.[28] Because the

---

[24] *Ibid.*
[25] *Ibid.*, para. 15.
[26] *Ibid.*
[27] See Case C-58/98 *Corsten* [2000] ECR I-7919, para 35.
[28] Case C-222/95 *Societé Parodi* v. *Banque H. Albert de Bary et Cie* [1997] ECR I-3899.

Second Banking Directive[29] had not yet been adopted, the Court had to decide on the basis of Treaty freedom to provide services whether a Dutch mortgage lender could provide services to French borrowers without obtaining additional regulatory authorization in France. The Court accepted the principle of mutual recognition and the right of the lender, which lawfully carried on activities in its country of origin, to provide similar services across borders.[30] It also confirmed that the requirement to obtain authorization by the supervisory authorities in the country of destination restricted the free movement of services.[31] And then it went on to decide whether the initial normative element of mutual recognition would function or fail and, in the latter case, whether it would eventually revive through the test of equivalence or proportionality. The dynamic element of mutual recognition failed. The Court recognized that the banking sector 'is a particularly sensitive area from the point of view of consumer protection . . .'[32] and therefore the imposition by the Member State of destination of conditions regarding access to the activity of credit institutions and their supervision satisfied imperative reasons relating to the public interest.[33]

The second test of equivalence and proportionality was more complicated. The Court pointed to the early First Banking Directive,[34] which imposed a number of minimum prudential standards, but it recognized that there was still scope for national regulation beyond that point. It was therefore a matter of *ad hoc* analysis of the litigated facts. The Court made clear that the outcome of this process depended on precise information about the prudential standards in the country of destination. Had the French rules been a mere restatement of the rules set out in the First Banking Directive, mutual recognition would revive given the existing equivalence of national laws. Alternatively, in the most likely case that the French legislation contained standards well beyond the modest level of European harmonization, it was still a matter of actual

---

[29] Council Directive 89/646/EEC of 15 December 1989 on the coordination of laws, regulations and administrative provisions relating to the taking up and pursuit of the business of credit institutions, OJ No. L386/1, 30 December 1989.
[30] *Ibid.* para. 18.
[31] See para. 19.
[32] See para. 22.
[33] See para. 26.
[34] Council Directive 77/780/EEC of 12 December 1977 on the coordination of laws, regulations and administrative provisions relating to the taking up and pursuit of the business of credit institutions, OJ No. L322/30, 17 December 1977.

equivalence, necessity and proportionality. The Court observed the nature of the banking activity in question and the relevant risks. In particular, it held that obtaining a mortgage presents the consumer with risks that differ from those associated with the deposit of funds with a bank. In this regard, the need to protect the borrower will vary according to the nature of the mortgage and there may be cases where, precisely because of the nature of the loan granted and the status of the borrower, there is no need to protect the latter through the application of the mandatory rules of his national law. Regardless of whether the French rules were pre-empted by common European standards, they might have been either an unnecessary or a disproportionate response to the actual risks of the litigated activity for which the law of the country of origin would have provided adequate protection. In the absence of precise information about the content and the objective of the disturbing measures, the Court eventually referred the matter to the national court with specific instructions: the restriction was to be abolished unless the French authorization was based on prudential requirements (a) which went beyond the European common standards, (b) which were necessary for protection against the specific risks generated by the litigated contract, and (c) and which did not go beyond what was necessary to achieve that objective in the light of the possible adequacy of the regulatory framework in the country of origin. This assessment was a matter for the national court.

In recent years, the normative element of mutual recognition as a form of negative integration has expanded dramatically. With the exception of situations confined in all respects within a single country, the Treaty provisions on the free movement of services apply to all types of cross-border situations, including circumstances where (a) the bank moves temporarily to another Member State,[35] (b) the customer moves to the bank's 'home country',[36] (c) neither the bank nor the customer moves to another country but the service is provided at a distance, via the internet or otherwise[37] and (d) the bank and the customer move temporarily to the same Member State, other than their own. The free movement of services is guaranteed even if the provider and the recipient

---

[35] See C–222/95 *Parodi*, above note 28.
[36] See Case C-484/93 *Svensson and Gustavsson v. Ministre du Logement et de l'Urbanisme* [1995] ECR I-3955.
[37] See Case C-384/93 *Alpine Investments BV v. Minister van Financiën* [1995] ECR I-1141.

are established in the same country[38] and when the customer goes to another country to receive services.[39] The definition of legal restrictions which are 'liable to prohibit or otherwise impede' the free movement of services is also subject to ongoing review and development. It currently encompasses any rules that 'involve expenses and additional administrative and economic burdens for service providers established in other Member States, where they lawfully carry on their activities'.[40]

### The influence of the Treaty freedoms on financial integration in Europe

The process of negative integration has been instrumental in the creation of the internal market. It has allowed private parties' voices to be heard and their actions to further the internal market project. No one knows better what restricts cross-border trade than those actually pursuing it. Equipped with a binding Treaty text and encouraged by the purposive method of interpretation employed by the Court, firms and consumers have found an additional route to ensure that the binding promises for an area without internal frontiers are kept. In parallel, the increasing participation and confidence of firms and consumers in the process enhances the visibility and, why not, the political legitimacy of the Court, creating a sort of virtuous cycle: the Court is empowered to scrutinize national measures more rigorously and, in response, private parties' expectations and confidence are likely to grow larger.

Further, negative integration renders Member States more proactive in pursuing market integration. Despite the apparent legal formalism in the reasoning of the Court, its rulings entail policy implications for important conflicting values. Each time the Court reviews a national measure it must decide essentially whether there should be regulation, and if so, who will have the power to regulate. The scope given to the four freedoms defines largely the scope of national autonomy in the satisfaction of domestic regulatory interests. The Court must draw the line between the limits of public intervention in the market and free trade, centralization and decentralization within the EU and allocation of competences between the home and the host country. These are considerations that Member States want to keep for themselves.

---

[38] See Case C-198/89 *Commission Tourist Guides Greece* v. *Greece* (the case) [1991] ECR I-727.
[39] See Case C-186/87 *Cowan* v. *Tresor Public* [1989] ECR 195.
[40] See Case C-165/98 *Mazzoleni* (Criminal proceedings) *and ISA* [2001] ECR I-2189.

Negative integration is likely to have disciplinary effects of the type 'you either sort it out or we, the Court, will have to step in'. It therefore provides incentives for domestic reform in accordance with the Treaty provisions.

Furthermore, the economic freedoms are a cushion against political gridlock. Had it not been for the general Treaty prohibition, there would have been an enormous amount of pressure on political negotiators to agree on each and every detail of positive measures. Negative integration wards off this pressure and saves the political process from the impossibility and impracticability associated with full agreement. In the words of Lord Mackenzie Stuart, 'it has been known for those who sought to negotiate a text and who have been unable to agree to settle for an ambiguous expression in the hope that the court would one day be able to resolve the ambiguity'.[41]

Obviously the Treaty economic freedoms are not a panacea. The creation of a fully functioning internal market requires more than a negative covenant to abolish restrictions in intra-Community trade. Mutual recognition as a form of negative integration is predominantly integration through the courts. It is therefore burdened by the disadvantages associated with regulatory reform through litigation.

First, it diffuses through national legal systems in a piecemeal manner, initiated by the prior *ad hoc* submission of individual complaints and delayed by the inherent constraints in the functioning of national and European judicial resources. Its effectiveness is conditional upon the rigorous enforcement at national level since the Court lacks its own coercive mechanism. The Court articulates its binding opinion and refers back to the national court, which retains full powers to appraise the national measure in question. There is a real danger that national courts and authorities, either intentionally or inadvertently, may succumb to the temptation to implement the opinion of the Court in their own way, thus frustrating the purpose of having a supranational judicial authority as guardian of uniformity in the application of Community law.

Second, the process of judicial control is biased against individual consumers and small firms, which do not possess the resources to litigate against national authorities at the international level. Even firms capable of litigating may be reluctant to take up the single market cause and

---

[41] See Mackenzie Stuart (Lord), *The European Communities and the Rule of Law* (London: Stevens, 1977), p. 81.

collide with national authorities over the compatibility of domestic public policy, since a climate of animosity between firms and local regulators does not exactly promote the interests of international business.

Third, the quality of the *de-regulatory* rulings of the Court is increasingly put under pressure by the complexity and highly technical nature of many national measures. Even if a national measure is a clear restriction of cross-border trade – which is by no means certain in relation to less outspoken non-discriminatory measures – the examination of *suitability, necessity* and *proportionality* of regulation during the 'general good' evaluation, in a wide range of issues spanning from financial regulation to beer purity laws, is likely to be obstructed by lack of information and expertise. The deficiency is partly corrected by the technical input of the litigating parties but an overall risk assessment may require a wider range of views and interests not necessarily present in the judicial process. This applies *a fortiori* to online financial services.

The fiercest criticism of bold negative integration has been the lack of legitimacy and accountability of unelected judges. In so far as the Court strikes a balance between competing 'liberalization' and 'regulatory' perspectives, the process is naturally prone to being politically sensitive and controversial. In the event that national measures reflect genuine public policy concerns, the examination of 'fluid' concepts such as equivalence of regulatory values and proportionality is likely to raise some eyebrows, be doctrinally resisted and bluntly rejected at the national level. Because no supranational court would consciously produce a line of jurisprudence, which, while doctrinally correct, was likely to be disregarded in the national arena, one would expect the rigour of judicial control to be watered down under the pressure of political considerations of that sort. This is a sensible approach but detrimental for the objective of free trade in banking services. Maduro observes that in the early years of the single market a subtle coordination between the Commission and the Court emerged whereby if the two guardians of the Community objectives were not convinced that Member States would comply with the Court's decision, the violation would not be brought before its bench.[42] The Court is understandably reluctant to replace national legislatures and administrative agencies as the constant arbitrator of competing interests that are primarily a matter for national consideration.

---

[42] See Miguel P. Maduro, *We the Court: The European Court of Justice and the European Economic Constitution* (Oxford: Hart Publishing, 1998), pp. 9–10.

In Ancient Greek drama, the Gods often dictated that 'ο τρώσας και ιάσεται' ('he who has wounded others will also provide the remedy') which means that the eventual 'solution' in the tragedy often comes from the original source of evil seeking forgiveness and moral redemption. The remaining legal impediments to cross-border services generate antagonisms between plausible regulatory objectives and the values of open financial markets that must be addressed by policy makers and legislators, who created the impediments in the first place – not judges. Lawmakers at the national and European levels are better placed than the supranational judge to voice their views on the settlement of rival regulatory values due 'to their direct and constant contact with the various forces operating in their countries.'[43]

From a strictly legal perspective, the limited normative impact of judicial mutual recognition reduces the audacity of judicial regulatory reform towards freer markets. According to the jurisprudence of the Court, the initial dynamic element of mutual recognition is immediately blocked by an open-ended list of imperative reasons relating to the 'general good'. Regardless of whether the national measure entails even the most brutal disturbance of free economic movement, the confirmation of a genuine public policy concern and the absence of equivalence in the country of origin preclude any further scrutiny. Only positive integration by way of legislative reform can go beyond this point. Furthermore, judicial integration fails to address the elusive effects of legal plurality and diversity. It may ensure the parity of overseas and domestic banks vis-à-vis domestic competitors through a wide concept of non-discrimination. In the presence of equivalence, it may also eliminate duplication in supervisory and regulatory control by lifting the second layer of regulation. It is nevertheless a mere de-regulatory mechanism. It entails the *ad hoc* judicial control of specific national measures and their abolition if legal convergence has been found. When the most troubling law-based restrictions have been dismantled, it becomes increasingly problematic to fit the remainder of subtle and less obvious obstacles within the limits of the judicial process. It should be noted that, although at the early instances of free movement jurisprudence the typical question was whether the blatantly restrictive measure could be justified in the light of the 'general good', with the lapse of time and the gradual abolition of the most problematic elements, the Court has

---

[43] See AG Werner in Case 34/79 *RV. Henn and Derby* [1979] ECR 3795, para. 15.

found it extremely difficult to establish whether the national rule each time in question falls within the scope of the Treaty provisions in the first place.[44] This uncertainty marks the boundaries of the *effet utile* of the Treaty-based economic freedoms as an integration mechanism.

Take as an example the legal uncertainty regarding the applicable law and the economic cost of mandatory compliance with financial regulatory standards in each national market. Those impediments are almost impossible to eliminate through the judicial process. While the EC Treaty free movement provisions require a specific measure to be identified and abolished, the most subtle obstacles posed by legal plurality and uncertainty relate to the existence and application of more than one set of rules as a problem in itself, rather than the placement of undue burdens on the incoming firm as compared to domestic competitors. *Ex ante* legal certainty and full mutual recognition can only be secured by positive integration measures which allocate exclusive regulatory control and jurisdiction to the country of origin of the services. Mutual recognition as a form of negative integration does not function as a conflicts rule and a pure principle of country of origin or 'home country' control is not part of the economic constitution established by primary Community law.[45]

Judicial scrutiny of national rules on the basis of the Treaty economic freedoms does not purport to exclude the application of one set of national rules to the benefit of the other. It merely aims to coordinate their effects in order to avoid the most disturbing nuisances associated with their unavoidable coexistence. It imposes effectively the recognition of their coexistence as a fact that has to be considered rather than the recognition of the precedence of the one over the other which always fails in the absence of equivalence. In short, negative integration is more like a model of 'policed decentralization' or 'coordinated unilateralism', which introduces an overriding level of control in the exercise of national competence but does not correct fully the deficiencies associated with the separate claims of participating states to regulate activities with local connections. It is of course insufficient to correct non-legal impediments. A positive, standard-setting strategy is needed beyond this point.

In any case, the Court's contribution to the integration process has been instrumental. Its jurisprudence has supplied policy makers with

---

[44] See Stephen Weatherill, 'Recent Case Law Concerning the Free Movement of Goods: Mapping the Frontiers of Market Deregulation' (1999) 36 CML Rev 51.

[45] See Case C-233/94 *Germany* v. *Parliament and Council* [1997] ECR I-2405, para. 64.

precious integration concepts and ideas, which they would not easily identify in the laconic Treaty provisions. The concept of mutual recognition and the right to regulate in the interest of the 'general good' when trust is broken down are all spiritual children of the Court and constitute its valuable legacy in the policy and legal efforts towards a single financial area.

### Mutual recognition beyond the EC Treaty: 'home country' control in various forms as institutional anchor of the single financial market

The principle of 'country of origin' or 'home country' control is the most advanced form of mutual recognition. Member States are bound to recognize the substantive rules of countries where cross-border services originate as the sole applicable law, which presupposes that they have accepted the institutional quality of the legal and regulatory systems of their fellow partners. Although this model of governance is the most effective policy towards financial integration, its de-regulatory effects should respect worthy regulatory objectives within the wider context of the single financial market and the public debate regarding the limits of European integration.

*The political economy of the single financial market*

National regulatory interests are an integral part of policies towards market integration. The successful negotiation of a functional integration model presupposes that the effects of national regulatory requirements on market integration have been carefully assessed and taken into account in the final arrangement. The perspectives of 'financial liberalization' and 'financial regulation' must have regard to one another. Negotiators of liberalization policies cannot afford to disregard national regulatory preferences and national legislatures and regulators must not forget that domestic regulatory activities affect the legal framework of the single financial market by generating regulatory costs for financial institutions established in other Member States.

Different national laws and supervisory practices reflect the objective and subjective dissimilarities of Member States. Objective dissimilarities are different national needs, problems and resources. Subjective dissimilarities are different choices, preferences and perceptions with regard to similar needs, problems and resources. Hence, the optimal settlement of the rivalry between 'regulation' and 'market liberalization' is a dynamic process affected by often competing interests.

First, there is the notional collision between optimal and actual regulatory perspectives. Different national perceptions of regulation are not necessarily premised on different views of economic efficiency. The conflicting views to be reconciled are not always consistent with their textbook economic rationale. They are often shaped by less virtuous forces, including sheer protectionism, a doctrinal attachment to redistributive socialism, paternalistic intervention in the market, antagonistic interests lobbying for favourable regulatory arrangements, or simply shortage of high quality information about better alternatives, lack of resources and poor regulatory sophistication and expertise or a combination thereof.

This painful reality suffices to underscore the political gymnastics required if a workable balance between mutual recognition and legal convergence is to be achieved. On the one hand, proponents of international financial integration would be reluctant to accept *any* common standards for the sake of open and competitive financial markets. They want to see *good* common standards.[46] Conversely, countries with a stronger preference for the broader concepts of 'fairness' and 'social protection' will not easily subscribe to the neo-liberal notion of market integration for the sake of the common market.[47] The content of common rules matters and it matters a lot. In the eyes of negotiating Member States, the aim of financial market integration cannot alone purify rules and policies, which have been considered and dismissed at national level.

Second, the coordination of national regulatory perspectives in the context of market integration entails necessarily a certain loss of national sovereignty for the benefit of more centralization, the level of which will be the subject of rigorous debate and competition between different political ideas.

Third, despite the emphasis on different attitudes towards financial regulation, it is questionable whether Member States share identical liberalization objectives. On paper, the internal market brings benefits for all and enhanced opportunities within an atmosphere of competition.

---

[46] See Corporation of London, *Creating a Single European Market for Financial Services* (London, 2003), paras. v, vi, and ix.

[47] See French Banking Federation, *Five Principles for a Unified Banking and Financial Services Market* (Paris: FBF, 2003).

In practice, it creates positive trade possibilities for countries with efficient financial systems, while less competitive Member States fear the prospect of domestic firms being displaced by more competitive foreign ones. Policy makers in less competitive markets are likely to regard financial liberalization as an opportunity for domestic reform and modernization at best or, at worst, as a direct threat to national interests, which justifies in their view a less enthusiastic attitude towards financial integration shown at every opportunity. National attitudes towards financial liberalization arguably affect how proactive individual Member States are in negotiating and implementing integration policies, with protectionists being naturally less inclined to support policies that bring decisive blows to legal barriers.

Fourth, the task of reconciling competing regulatory perspectives with the overarching aim of financial liberalization amounts occasionally to attempting to square the circle. It is difficult to pursue policies aiming at both economic efficiency and fairness, the creation of a liberal market order and redistributive policies, market openness and corrective intervention. Take prudential banking regulation for example: policies strengthening the stability of the banking system restrain financial activities, whereas financial liberalization seeks to eliminate legal obstacles. Widely used supervisory techniques limit market entry, the scope of permissible activities and the levels of risk that individual banks may lawfully assume while other types of prudential measures may have collateral effects on market integration. It is difficult to achieve the optimal balance. This antagonism explains why the attainment of a certain degree of convergence of prudential regulatory standards was seen as an essential precondition of the single European 'passport' established by the Second Banking Directive. It also explains why the Court almost invariably justified restrictions on the free movement of banking services on grounds of systemic financial stability and depositor protection before the implementation of the financial services Directives in the early 1990s. Finally, at the WTO level, this subtle antagonism between regulation and financial liberalization explains the so-called 'prudential carve-out' in paragraph 2(a) of the Annex on Financial Services to the General Agreement on Trade in Services (GATS) which allows WTO Members to take prudential measures to ensure the integrity and stability of the financial system or to protect recipients of financial services regardless of any other obligation or commitment towards financial liberalization under the GATS. Similarly with regard to the interests of investors and depositors, the de-regulatory effects of financial liberalization through the elimination of legal impediments are not always compatible with high standards of investor, depositor and consumer protection. Even if the scale of the rivalry is exaggerated, the distrust between proponents of liberalization and advocates of social protection is real. The former want to limit the use of regulations as barriers to international economic integration, while the latter want to prevent market openness from serving as a barrier to domestic and international regulation.

And yet, this paradoxical marriage of potentially competing claims has been endorsed by the EC Treaty and influences the negotiations towards the most appropriate integration policies. According to the EC Treaty, a wide range of social policies constitute independent EU competences, most notably the attainment of a 'high level of consumer protection',[48] which interface with but do not necessarily promote deeper financial integration. The true proportions of the task are revealed when one realizes that the process of reconciling financial liberalization and regulation is constantly evolving. First, in view of the global dimension of financial integration, EU policies must be compatible with international regulatory initiatives and sufficiently flexible to address global and regional challenges. Second, the regulatory aspects of systemic 'safety and soundness' and social protection are evolving in the light of emerging new risks and enhanced consumer expectations. Hence the institutional framework underpinning liberalization policies must closely monitor regulatory reforms at the international and national levels. This is crucial for electronic commerce in financial services that generates new risks and regulatory concerns given the reliance on computer networks and information technology.

The elimination of restrictions on cross-border electronic banking activities is subject to the same complex issues and competing interests as any other aspect of European integration. The ideal integration policies must achieve full market openness without compromising sound regulatory objectives. The risks associated with the 'information technology' aspect of electronic finance must be addressed with measures which are compatible with a broad range of EU laws in the area of consumer protection and financial services. The international dimension of banking regulation must also be considered in view of achieving consistency with international regulatory and supervisory initiatives. And the national sensitivities regarding the appropriate content or level of common rules must be respected.

---

[48] See EC Treaty, art. 153.

## The futility of total legal harmonization and centralization of supervisory powers

The complex political economy of the single financial market exposes the poor normative value of total legal harmonization as an integration policy. In principle, the harmonization of rules reflecting objective national differences is undesirable, whereas the harmonization of rules reflecting subjective differences of opinion is difficult to achieve.

Despite the theoretical effectiveness of legal uniformity in eliminating legal barriers generated by legal diversity, legal harmonization entails significant 'policy costs' that cannot be ignored: questionable 'one size fits all' regulation; deep erosion of sovereignty and loss of valuable power to set local standards for local needs and local choices; questionable legitimacy and accountability of the promoters of uniform standards in the eyes of implementing national authorities; complex, time-consuming and institutionally exhausting procedures, long delays from inception to implementation of policies and even poor implementation or none at all; and poor adjustability and lack of flexibility for the purposes of reform in response to the constantly changing conditions of financial markets. In cases where unanimous agreement is required, the chances of promptly achieving political consensus are slim.

Regardless of achievability, there are no assurances that a centralized process of full harmonization guarantees the high quality of common standards. The reciprocal concessions and compromises, which are necessary to secure agreement, may water down the optimal textbook solutions. Special interests groups may lobby at the EU level and dictate self-serving policies. The harmonization process itself may be bureaucratic and self-serving and therefore not necessarily conducive to creating better policy, rules and government. A recent empirical study on the quality of US federal regulation has shown that the regulatory analysis conducted at the centralized level is often poor and the efficiency of centralized regulatory agencies varies considerably.[49] In Europe, similar concerns are not unknown.[50]

The question of quality in harmonized legal standards relates to the broader issue of whether the claim for sweeping harmonization

---

[49] See Robert Hahn, *Reviving Regulatory Reform: A Global Perspective*, Washington DC: (AEI-Brookings Joint Center for Regulatory Studies, 2000).
[50] See Frank E. Easterbrook, 'Federalism and European Business Law' (1994) 14 Int'l Rev L & Econ 125 at 132.

discounts and underestimates the importance of competition among states towards the creation of better rules. The competitive features of governments (competition among central and local government, federal and state government, different departments of the central government, central government and independent administrative authorities etc.) in the domestic or international arena serve a crucial function in revealing preferences for standard setting and contribute to better rules at the national level, a process which full harmonization suppresses.[51]

The prospect of regulatory competition is particularly appealing in countries with efficient financial centres.[52] Conversely, opponents of financial liberalization have every reason to support an integration policy of full harmonization resisting mutual recognition. The reason is that full harmonization consumes time. Before the measures are agreed and implemented, those profiting from a poorly competitive environment will exploit trade barriers. An institutional setting of full harmonization strengthens the position of protectionist Member States which will predictably advance their own views on market regulation through the harmonization process at the EU level in the hope to delay market integration or shape the final EU rules in accordance with less liberal a regulatory model.

Hertig and Lee have controversially argued that continental financial centres will try to promote an extensive programme of EU harmonization in order to keep the Anglo–American tradition from being imposed on European markets through the regulatory competition that mutual recognition encourages.[53] I would also suggest that rendering mutual recognition conditional upon the completion of a programme of extensive legal harmonization is a good recipe for delay of effective financial liberalization. Furthermore, it should be noted that the stronger advocates of perfect mutual recognition are found in the City of London,[54] while elsewhere in continental Europe a high level of legal harmonization is advocated on grounds of systemic stability, investor and depositor protection and fair competition.[55]

---

[51] See Albert Breton, *Competitive Governments: An Economic Theory of Politics and Public Finance* (Cambridge: Cambridge University Press, 1996).
[52] See HM Treasury, *Completing a dynamic single market*.
[53] See Gerard Hertig and Ruben Lee, 'Four Predictions about the Future of EU Securities Regulation' (2003) 3 *Journal of Corporate Law Studies* 359–77.
[54] See Corporation of London, *Creating a single market*; HM Treasury, *Completing a dynamic single market*.
[55] See French Banking Federation, *Five principles*; Bundesverband Deutscher Banken, *Banken und Verbraucher: Das verbraucherpolitische Gesamtkonzept der privaten Banken* (Berlin 2003).

In my view, even opponents of market-oriented policies should prefer minimum to total harmonization. Because of different national preferences and opinions, common EU standards of consumer and investor protection are often set, as a natural compromise, somewhere between the most protective and most liberal rules currently used in national legal orders. This raises the standards in less protective jurisdictions but lowers the standards of protection in those countries where the national choice has always been above average. In other words, full harmonization removes the power to respond to national preferences at the national level and denies more rigorous social protection in those willing Member States unless agreed at the supranational level.

As the single market project painfully experienced during the political sclerosis of the late 1970s and early 1980s, the diversity in national perspectives, the hostility towards the replacement of national policies by common EU standards and the practical limitations of negotiating and implementing sensitive policies in a timely manner are strong arguments that total harmonization is impossible, probably undesirable, and too slow and rigid a process to respond efficiently through reform to fast moving market conditions. On the institutional front, the principles of subsidiarity and proportionality of Community action provide strong normative constraints against the wholesale transfer of law-making powers to the union level. Although improvements in the law-making process – similar to those implemented under the Lamfalussy proposals – are welcome, there is a point beyond which the added value of procedural efficiency in reconciling competing interests is questionable.

### The futility of full decentralization and unlimited regulatory competition

The disadvantages of total harmonization do not imply that less ambitious harmonization programmes are easy to implement. Leaving aside the open debate about the substantive quality of EU laws and turning to the measurable values of flexibility and time efficiency, the European experience to date has been rather disappointing. It suffices to note that it took six years from the inception (1992) to the proposal (1998) of the Distance Marketing Directive[56] and another six, perhaps more, to its

---

[56] Council and EP Directive 2002/65/EC of 23 September 2002 concerning distance marketing of consumer financial services, OJ 2002 No. L271/16, 9 October 2002.

actual implementation that had yet to be completed by October 2005. The E-Commerce Directive[57] had just been fully implemented in October 2005, more than eight years after the first proposal was released in April 1997. The contrast between the pace of legal harmonization and the dramatic transformation of both electronic commerce and financial services in the same period is stark. I find it difficult to see how the poor procedural performance would not adversely affect the substantive quality and dynamism of the end result.

Equipped with empirical arguments of that sort, it is conceivable to doubt the value of legal convergence and harmonization as essential preconditions of mutual recognition. In particular, it may be argued that a model of 'uncoordinated' mutual recognition would satisfy the values of the single financial area and simultaneously trigger competition among Member States towards better and, eventually, equivalent rules.

The starting point in the studies of regulatory competition has been Tiebout's classic model on choice, preference and competition.[58] Like individuals, firms will locate their operations in countries that are more attentive to their preferences and offer the best regulatory framework. Member States will in turn strive to tailor and adapt the applicable legal framework in order to satisfy business preferences and attract investment and tax revenues or even repel undesirable firms. This is the essence of *regulatory competition* among Member States. In response, private parties will engage in *regulatory arbitrage* selecting the best regulatory environment for their activities, which in turn may lead to *regulatory emulation* by states and regulators, in other words a change in regulatory policy as a result of observing that policies pursued by others achieve better results. Hence, the quality of regulation goes up and individual preferences are satisfied.

For the purposes of market integration, the model implies that, as soon as the arbitrage on the part of firms and consumers results in a short list of efficient rules, competition among Member States will ensure that national laws will converge around the golden rulebook. In contrast with structured harmonization by bureaucrats, harmonization is achieved from the bottom up and expensive convergence exercises

---

[57] Council and EP Directive 2000/31/EC of 8 June 2000 on certain legal aspects of information society services, in particular electronic commerce, in the internal market, OJ 2000 No. L178/1, 17 July 2000.
[58] See Charles M. Tiebout, 'A Pure Theory of Local Expenditures', (1956) 64 *Journal of Political Economy* 416.

through centralized institutions become redundant. Member States retain the autonomy to make decisions at national level and market integration is achieved through political, economic and regulatory competition.

The theoretical benefits are symmetrical to the costs of full centralization:[59] preservation of national sovereignty; local rules tailored to local preferences and needs; proximity between regulating authorities and regulated entities; simplification and avoidance of bureaucratic centralization; flexibility and timely regulatory response; scope for regulatory arbitrage and choice for firms and customers; disciplinary effect on government's natural tendency to disregard the 'general good' for the sake of special interests with political leverage; avoidance of weak common rules caused by shortage in regulatory expertise, compromise or capture by special interests at the EU level; better regulation through innovation, experimentation and observation of one another's successes and failures.

A perfect model of mutual recognition is conducive to regulatory competition. The latter relies on firms and customers being subject to the laws of the country in which they choose to establish their operations. It is the choice and the certainty of law that trigger the competitive forces. Mutual recognition guarantees just that.

The value of regulatory competition as a stimulus towards harmonization or better law has been challenged, primarily on grounds that it is based on hypotheses which are extremely difficult to exist in real life (full mobility of firms, full information, political will to experiment and change the law through observation and learning, successful emulation of successful policies etc.).[60] Nevertheless, from the perspective of 'financial liberalization', uncoordinated mutual recognition would still generate high levels of cross-border mobility, market access and legal certainty with zero 'transaction costs'. At that point, a realist negotiator would have a different obstacle to overcome.

In my view, the principle of equivalence of national standards as a necessary precondition of mutual recognition reflects the inextricable connection and reciprocity between the 'liberalization' and the

---

[59] See Roger Van den Bergh, 'Regulatory Competition or Harmonization of Laws? Guidelines for the European Regulator' in Alain Marciano and Jean-Michel Josselin (eds.), *The Economics of Harmonizing European Law* (Cheltenham: Edward Elgar, 2002).

[60] See e.g. Jean-Mey Sun and Jacques Pelkmans, 'Regulatory Competition in the Single Market' (1995) 33 JCMS 67.

'regulatory' perspectives. 'Uncoordinated' and unconditional mutual recognition puts into question the very rationale of national regulatory policy and produces high policy costs in the form of deep compromise of national regulatory perspectives. Hence, it must be resisted and dismissed out of hand as a perilous concession of market access and an implausible waiver of local control vis-à-vis firms and services, towards which the essential trust and confidence are lacking.

Given the diverse national views on what constitutes a market failure and how this should be corrected, the model of 'uncoordinated' mutual recognition leads to the situation in which services lawfully provided in the country of origin may upset public policy objectives in the country of destination and produce effects which are unacceptable for the 'host' jurisdiction. In the absence of a certain minimum degree of legal convergence, Member States are likely to regard the respective regulatory framework of fellow Member States as being of poor quality and low economic efficiency; or too liberal and insufficient to meet their own standards of social protection, fairness and financial stability; or both.

Further, the model of uncoordinated mutual recognition may induce firms pursuing a policy of 'lowest cost' location to set up operations in poorly regulated Member States without losing access to profitable markets elsewhere. Critics of decentralization have argued that competing for the attraction of firms provides incentives for deregulation to the detriment of safety and protection of consumer and other societal interests.[61] The theory argues that the 'race to the bottom' accelerates under the pressure of powerful business interests, which may employ concerted actions to signal their preferences and the unhappy consequences for those countries that fail to respond. Countries will receive the message and for fear of being penalized by the business community will go down the road to regulatory laxity to the further detriment of optimal regulatory standards. Eventually, negative externalities will occur whereby the cost of failure of the lax regime will also be borne by private parties located elsewhere.

Within a 'mutual recognition' area, countries that decline to enter this 'race to the bottom' will necessarily place local institutions at a competitive disadvantage towards firms established in 'regulatory havens' and create risks for the protection of local customers from genuine

---

[61] See Chris Bradley, 'Competitive Deregulation of Financial Services Activity in Europe After 1992' (1997) 11 OJLS 545 at 554–6.

market failures. The relevant discussion is informed by a similar debate in the United States where regulatory competition seems to be working in the market for corporate laws giving rise to the so-called 'Delaware phenomenon'. This school of thought attributes the success of Delaware in attracting a sizeable number of US corporations to the laxity of its corporate laws and the preference to the interests of directors at the expense of shareholders.[62]

Others have thought differently.[63] In the absence of empirical evidence, they have questioned whether, in the case of Delaware, shareholders are so naïve as to trust their capital to firms incorporated under rules so detrimental for their own interests. This latter analysis implies that rather than winning a 'race to the bottom', Delaware has won a race to the top by enacting efficient rules which are appreciated by both the business community and investors. Romano argues in particular that Delaware may have won the market for incorporation, not necessarily because its rules are superior but because it has gained a reputation for specialization, with lawyers and judges specifically trained on corporate law, offering legal certainty and predictability to the investor and business communities.[64]

In any case, it appears that the prospect of mutual recognition without legal convergence is unpromising regardless of whether the risk of 'regulatory laxity' is fanciful or real. As long as the risk is perceived to be real, it suffices to destroy political consensus regardless of whether it actually is. Further, if regulatory competition leads to a race in excellence, less efficient financial centres would still run the risk of responding poorly and would no doubt be reluctant to grant unfettered market access in the absence of some degree of harmonization. Furthermore, cross-border market access in the absence of legal convergence would result in the provision of services formulated under completely different rules, which the recipient of these services would largely ignore. This would exacerbate the inherent problem of information asymmetry between the firm and the customer and would not enhance confidence in cross-border services within the single financial area.

---

[62] See William Cary, 'Federalism and Corporate Law: Reflections upon Delaware' (1974) 83 Yale LJ 63.
[63] See Daniel Fischel, 'The "Race to the Bottom" Revisited: Reflections on Recent Developments in Delaware's Corporation Law' (1982) 76 NWUL Rev 913.
[64] See Roberta Romano, 'Law as a Product: Some Pieces of the Incorporation Puzzle' (1985) 1 JLEcon & Org 225.

*The qualities of the principle of 'country of origin' based on minimum harmonization and efficient regulation and enforcement*

The principle of 'country of origin' on the basis of prior legal convergence and trust among national authorities is the most effective integration policy when negative integration is insufficient and full centralization is unachievable or undesirable. Legal plurality and diversity no longer pose obstacles to market openness. Firms are subject to one set of familiar rules. They avoid adaptation costs and therefore may achieve desirable economies of scale through the launch of a single website as the sole platform for outgoing cross-border services and a sole point of reference for domestic and non-resident consumers, competitors and supervisors.

'One-stop' home country supervision eradicates regulatory repetition and additional costs. Further, it deprives the 'host country' of the opportunity to use regulation as a covert form of protecting local interests through rules that may look innocent but carefully conceal the favourable treatment of domestic institutions. An almost invincible argument, which is often missed, is that in the absence of a federal supervisor, a pure model of 'country of origin' is the only arrangement that secures non-duplicative supervisory control. Even total uniformity of substantive rules cannot correct the problem of duplicative supervision if a supranational supervisory agency does not exist.

Further, the applicable legal framework consists of the regulated entity's familiar domestic rules. It thereby becomes predictable, certain and transparent, conflict of laws is circumvented and surprises caused by regulatory reform and inconsistent enforcement policies in the 'host country' are avoided. The accountability of policy makers or supervisory authorities to those affected by regulation is strengthened because the voice of local firms contributing employment opportunities and tax revenue is likely to be heard.

The model performs a plausible and realistic settlement of the rivalry between financial liberalization and local control on the condition that national regulatory values and supervisory practices have converged to a mutually agreed level. Mutual recognition renders extensive programmes of harmonization unnecessary, thus enabling policy makers to concentrate on the essential points of legal convergence. Hence, free economic movement is secured without the excessive 'policy' and 'transaction' costs of total harmonization.

The attained legal convergence strengthens mutual trust and prevents the unacceptable subordination of vital national regulatory preferences to the one-dimensional claim for financial liberalization. It also ensures that domestic and overseas firms are at competitive parity and that consumers are confident that incoming services and firms are subject to equivalent rights and duties as domestic firms in the 'host country'. This will significantly reduce the risk of confusion and enhance consumer confidence in the predictability of underlying substantive standards.

An optimal level of legal and supervisory convergence is beneficial in addressing 'post-integration' risks that transcend national borders and are better dealt with at the international level. The growth of international financial markets makes apparent that some form of international standardization and common approach is desirable. Other values promoted by appropriate levels of legal convergence may also be identified: the creation of a level playing field for firms which lack mobility and cannot reap the benefits of regulatory arbitrage; an opportunity and a forum for domestic reform and a fresh review of national rules; an improvement in the quality of regulation through collaboration of pooled national expertise, especially for less developed Member States; the adoption of rules after serious consideration, induced by the disciplinary effects of the expensive and inflexible amendment process and the collective sense of compromise; finally, the creation of a single point of reference for national legal education and professional training with obvious advantages for the mobility of legal skills.

Still in the realm of efficient regulation, it is expedient to examine the decision to vest the responsibility for consolidated supervisory control in the country of origin of financial services. In particular, it is questionable whether 'home country' authorities have sufficient incentives to commit resources for the protection of non-voting overseas customers and whether for that reason it would appear rational to allocate responsibility to the 'host country' which has a clear mandate and interest to protect domestic customers. I do not subscribe to this view. The obvious reason is that we thereby return to the full pathology of 'imperfect' mutual recognition, but there are also strong regulatory incentives.

When the bank providing cross-border online services is solely established in the 'home country', this is the first place where regulatory failure will probably cause systemic instability. Further, in all likelihood a sizeable portion of depositors of the online bank will always be resident in the country of origin, which obviously creates incentives for rigorous supervision. I cannot see how the country of origin would prevent the benefits of supervision from being enjoyed by non-residents even if I conceded that no such intention existed. The allocation of responsibility for the operation of deposit guarantee schemes in the country of origin will also provide incentives for rigorous supervision in the knowledge that the local taxpayers will bail out supervisory failure towards domestic and overseas depositors alike. Furthermore, competitive forces create enough incentives for rigorous supervision to the benefit of both resident and non-resident customers: a claim for reciprocity not necessarily in the same field; comity and a noble sense of performance of international obligations; the protection of reputation of the quality of local supervision and banking system; and finally, the self-interest to facilitate the competitiveness of domestic banks abroad, which will no doubt suffer if international markets receive a signal of underperforming supervision at the bank's home country.

The country of origin is better placed to perform quality supervision given the importance of territorial proximity between regulating authorities and regulated entities for the successful formulation and implementation of public policy objectives. This is the thrust of subsidiarity in federal or quasi-federal structures, namely that public affairs shall be managed by authorities which are as close to the subject-matter as possible. The jurisprudence of the Court is also pointing to that direction. In *Alpine Investments*,[65] the country of origin of the investment firm prohibited the promotion of financial services by way of unsolicited calls to potential clients. The prohibition applied even in cases where the firm was 'cold calling' potential customers established in other Member States. When the firm contended that the 'home country' should not regulate outgoing activities that were adequately regulated by the 'host country', the Court dismissed the claim on grounds that:

> [T]he Member State from which the telephone call is made is best placed to regulate cold calling. Even if the receiving State wishes to prohibit cold calling or to make it subject to certain conditions, it is not in a position to prevent or control telephone calls from another Member State without the cooperation of the competent authorities of that State.[66]

The question of practicability of supervision is indeed significant and applies *a fortiori* to services provided via the Internet. Even more urgent is however the question of quality of supervision. A deterrence-based enforcement policy, through punitive measures and penalties in cases of

---

[65] See Case C-384/93 *Alpine Investments BV* v. *Minister van Financiën* [1995] ECR I-1141.
[66] *Ibid.*, paras. 47–8.

harmful and non-compliant conduct, whereby failure to comply is followed by enforcement proceedings, may indeed suffer from the barriers posed by national borders. But the lack of territorial proximity is potentially fatal in a compliance-based system of supervision and enforcement, whereby the overarching aim of the regulator is to reduce the likelihood of breach through the creation of mutual trust, qualitative monitoring and close cooperation. An effective system of qualitative compliance-based enforcement presupposes a good understanding of the regulated entity: what are the causes of breach in each particular case? Is it calculated and purposeful? Or is it due to sheer indifference, incompetence, poor understanding of the law, mismanagement, breakdown of internal control systems and organization? This approach relies on mutual trust, incentives to comply, frequency in personal contacts, interactive participation, ongoing educational initiatives on the part of the supervisor and ability to learn and adapt on the part of the firm and, last but not least, quality information. These are largely conditional upon the existence of physical proximity between the regulated entity and the supervisory authority, which non-established banks cannot enjoy. In relation to conduct of business rules, the failures in market confidence caused by lack of integrity and conflict of interests are directly linked to underperforming internal control structures and a failing corporate culture, which a distant, non-established regulator will find difficult to bring to light. The 'home country' is familiar with the organization, management structure and personnel and has accumulated valuable information for supervisory purposes. Provided that a line of communication, ongoing cooperation and coordination among 'home' and 'host' country authorities is established, the argument for 'home country' control of cross-border Internet banking activities is compelling.

The question whether to vest full supervisory responsibilities in 'home country' authorities is relevant for the current debate regarding a reformed governance structure for financial supervision in Europe and the eventual centralization of supervisory functions at the European level with a creation of a European supervisory agency. The basic argument in favour of moving to a European structure is that it might be difficult to achieve simultaneously a single financial market and stability in the financial system, while preserving a high degree of national based supervision with only minimum harmonization efforts at the Union level. It seems that this argument for centralization is driven by possible efficiency gains in dealing with 'post-integration' risks and not so much by its contribution to further financial liberalization.

I am not certain whether the efficiency gains from the creation of a 'European FSA' will be sufficiently proportionate to the high 'transaction' and 'policy' costs associated with full centralization. I certainly cannot detect deficiencies in the proposed model of 'home country' control regarding Internet services, which would exert decisive leverage on the broader discourse. In principle, it is rightly observed that comparative lessons can be learned from the United States where a fully functioning single market is successfully premised upon common rules but not a federal supervisor.[67] It is also questionable how a federal authority can function within a framework of minimum harmonization, unless of course full harmonization is regarded as the inevitable by-product of a central supervisory structure. Given the substantial controversy in principle, the remaining unresolved practical issues, such as structure, terms of competence and resources, and the absence of a clear Treaty basis, the prospect for a pan-European financial supervisor is, at best, distant. To work towards improving the current regime through closer cooperation among national agencies is a realistic and better solution.

### *The normative value of party autonomy in contractual matters*

Turning to the contractual aspects of the banker–customer relationship, the superiority of freedom of choice over mandatory models of governance is not seriously disputed. Hence, the real debate is about the exceptions, most notably the protection of consumers through the mandatory application of the law of their country of residence.[68]

In full symmetry with the principle of country of origin, the free choice of governing law in contractual relationships promotes the values of the single financial area in many respects. First, it strengthens the certainty and predictability of applicable law. Further, it avoids the application of conflict of laws rules which are poorly adjusted to cross-border electronic contracts, particularly territorial concepts and fluid criteria such as 'targeting services at' a given Member State. Second, it eliminates inefficient rules through choice that promotes government discipline and healthy regulatory competition. Third, it promotes economies of scale in cross-border standard contracts by enabling financial

---

[67] See Rosa M. Lastra, 'The Governance Structure for Financial Regulation and Supervision in Europe' 10 *Columbia Journal of European Law* 41–68, at 52.
[68] See Rome Convention on the law applicable to contractual obligations, (Rome, 19 June 1980): Consolidated version at/ 34, 26 OJ 1998, No. C27 January 1998, art. 5(2).

institutions to provide services in different countries on the basis of a single standard form contract. Given the superiority of free choice of law from the perspective of international market openness, the policy arguments for dismissing free choice of law and requiring the mandatory application of regulatory standards and consumer protection rules of the customer's country of residence would have to be solid and unquestionable. They are not.

Historically, the consumer's residence alone has never been sufficient to establish mandatory protection in cross-border contracts. To pick up an obvious example, contracts concluded when the consumer is temporarily abroad, for example on holiday, are beyond the protective reach of the consumer's home country. To take advantage of consumer protection rules of one's own country, additional territorial connections are required. This additional connection is normally present when the provider of goods or services is actively targeting consumers in their own territory. As the Court has observed, the requirement to target consumers in their country of residence before the local protective mechanism is invoked, is designed to ensure that there are close connections between the contract in issue and the State in which the consumer is domiciled.[69]

Internet services are not typical of this genuine territorial connection. To export the local standards of protection when the consumer actively seeks a better deal abroad is dismissed in the case of physical movement and the same principle should apply when the active search, facilitated by modern technology, is carried out at a distance, especially when to suggest otherwise would substantially obstruct cross-border activities. In the language of the Court, a restriction of free economic movement by the country of destination

> is all the less permissible where unlike the temporary movement towards the country of destination the service is supplied without it being necessary for the person providing it to visit the territory of the Member State where it is provided.[70]

Let me hypothetically question the foregoing conclusion: can we not identify a strong normative argument in favour of mandatory protection afforded by the consumer's country of residence? It is doubtful, at best.

---

[69] See Case C-96/00 *Rudolf Gabriel* v. *Schlank & Schick GmbH* [2002] ECR I-6367, paras. 40–1.
[70] See Case C–76/90 *Säger*, above note 23, paras. 12–13.

In principle, private parties enter into contractual relationships to maximize their wealth. They know better than their governments what is best for their interests. Hence, unless this pursuit of private wealth entails adverse effects on third parties, in which case state intervention is economically justified, there is no reason why the state should correct contractual relationships, including the choice of governing law. The conclusion fails only if the underlying assumption is invalid, namely that private parties know what is best for them. In the national arena, protective intervention in consumer contracts is justified precisely because the consumer lacks the information that is required to make a rational decision. Occasionally, state intervention purports to correct the asymmetry in bargaining power, particularly when the pertinent goods and services are vital and market competition is less than optimal. In my view, the question of the governing law of cross-border contracts, particularly financial contracts, does not seem to entail similar concerns.

The original drafters of the Rome Convention justify the mandatory application of consumer protection rules of the country where the consumer is domiciled by the laconic, almost axiomatic, proposition that 'the law of the weaker party shall normally prevail over that of the seller'.[71] Almost thirty years later, the European Commission in the Green Paper on the Modernization of the Rome Convention offered a more rational explanation: '. . . the need to reassure consumers, who have a vital role to play in an internal market which has no hope of success without their active participation . . .'[72] This view is shared by leading academics who regard the natural familiarity towards one's own rules as a booster of confidence in cross-border consumer purchases of goods or services.[73]

It must be said that vulnerable consumers, who have difficulty in making an informed choice of what is best for their economic welfare, are rarely active in international financial markets.[74] They are certainly

---

[71] See Mario Giuliano and Paul Lagarde, *Report on the Convention on the Law Applicable to Contractual Obligations* ('Official Report'), OJ 1980, No. C282, pp. 1–50, at pp. 23–4.
[72] See European Commission, *The Conversion of the Rome Convention of 1980 on the Law Applicable to Contractual Obligations into a Community Instrument and its Modernization* COM(2002) 654 final, at p. 28.
[73] See Norbert Reich, *Europäisches Verbraucherschutzrecht* (Baden-Baden: Nomos, 1993), p. 243.
[74] See empirical evidence in Director General of Fair Trading, *Vulnerable Consumers and Financial Services* (London, 1999), p. 255.

not the typical users of Internet banking domestically and it is unwise to design integration policies on the assumption that they will be keen on taking up cross-border Internet banking. The average bank customer trusts familiar high street firms. Confidence in overseas banks is difficult to build and comes naturally only after the rational assessment of financial benefits and security assurances. The lack of proximity and personal contact, the security risks and the requirement for a fair competence in IT are additional barriers to overcome. This is not the natural habitat of vulnerable social groups, who are unlikely to opt for services of that nature even if the application of their domestic law was guaranteed. This is the realm of well-informed individuals who shop around to secure the best deal for their debt, savings or securities transactions. The value of e-commerce in financial services lies precisely in the power that it affords to consumers, particularly less mobile individuals, formerly tied to local firms, to seek a better solution in the single market if they think that they are not getting a fair deal at home. Those opting for an overseas firm indicate by their very choice that they know what is best for them because they overcome the natural inclination to prefer familiar local firms in order to maximize their wealth. In the absence of compelling benefits in choice and financial returns, I very much doubt whether the mandatory application of 'host country' rules will increase demand for cross-border services. Conversely, in the presence of a convincing financial argument and an acceptable level of protection guaranteed by minimum harmonization at the EU level, I doubt whether the application of the law of the bank's home country will have dissuasive effects. 'Imperfect' mutual recognition will certainly disturb the circulation of services, with detrimental effects for consumer choice and financial diversification. It is notable that consumer activists themselves raise the issue of the reluctance of credit institutions to serve non-resident customers.[75] I find most interesting that 'imperfect' mutual recognition, intended to increase consumer confidence, results in consumer detriments lamented by consumer groups. It is also unrealistic to expect growth in the cross-border supply of services in a fragmented and overregulated financial market.

---

[75] See John Mitchell, 'Response to the Commission Green Paper: Financial Services: Meeting Consumers' Expectations' (1997) *Journal of Consumer Policy* 379.

## Competition and choice as policy criteria in the single financial market

The opposition to the principle of country of origin and full party autonomy in the choice of law underestimates the importance of market competition. Insofar as the level of legal convergence is good and the equivalent standards are properly implemented and rigorously enforced, competition in laxity is unlikely to occur. Even when loopholes start to emerge, I do not detect scope for harmful abuse of the system at the expense of customers located in Member States that decline to water down their own standards.

First, there is always the last resort of emergency resumption of powers by the country of destination, when trust is broken down. Second, the risk for a harmful race to the bottom cannot be verified or dismissed unless the specific nature of competition in the financial area is examined. I am convinced that the multi-faceted value of reputation in the business of banking diminishes considerably the hypothetical race towards 'less protective' jurisdictions. Firms want to exploit reputation by locating themselves in the country that offers the most sophisticated level of regulation and increased safety, soundness and stability. Regulators concerned with the stability and efficiency of their banking systems are unlikely to water down their standards and enter the race to laxity. Non-resident customers will dismiss offers from banks located in unsafe jurisdictions, whereas residents in the 'lax jurisdiction' will react with hostility against the lowering of standards of protection. In principle, the market is sensitive and capable of exercising disciplinary effects ensuring that states do not enter the path of laxity.

Key industry insiders, regulators and academics, most notably Braithwaite, Drahos, Jackson and Pan with their empirical studies, have confirmed this process.[76] Braithwaite and Drahos quote US Federal Reserve officials noting that 'it is a competitive advantage for our banks that they come from a solidly regulated home base' and in the Bank of England they were told that 'competition in market integrity is the main game'.[77] The authors themselves argue that bankers worry more about

---

[76] See John Braithwaite and Peter Drahos, *Global Business Regulation* (Cambridge: Cambridge University Press, 2000); Howell E. Jackson and Eric Pan, 'Regulatory Competition in International Securities Markets: Evidence from Europe in 1999' (Pt 1) (2001) 56 Bus Law 653, at 676–91.

[77] Braithwaite and Drahos, *Global Regulation*, pp. 130–1.

systemic risk and loss of reputation. Thus, the temptation to seek the low-cost location, while typical in relation to corporate taxation, is atypical in relation to financial regulation.

Take standard contract terms and conditions used in retail contracts as an example. Are firms and particularly banks not at the centre of powerful competitive forces? Are they not at the receiving end of dynamics and pressures that drive them towards constant revision and evaluation of their position? Do they not want to retain their customers? Insofar as this is the case, then the fairness of standard form contracts is bound to respond to competitive pressures and improve or deteriorate according to the improvement or deterioration of market competition and transparency. Instead of reflecting an institutional and incorrigible inclination towards corporate abuse and unfairness, standard form contracts imposed on consumers without individual negotiation can be mechanisms by which transaction costs are reduced and transaction risks are allocated to those most able to bear them but always in direct discourse with competitive pressures. The process relies on consumers understanding the implications of their choices and having information about better alternatives elsewhere. Users of Internet banking are well placed in both respects.

Statistics on user demographics show that the average user of online financial services is well placed to understand the legal implications of contractual terms. Moreover, there is no shortage of information about better alternatives. Financial portals, search engines and the convenience of gathering information on the Internet are all conducive to that end. Banking itself is a competitive market and the market for electronic banking services is potentially even more so insofar as the core Internet protocol enables pre-contractual contact and transactions with providers located anywhere in the world. There are risks and customers are naturally inclined to distrust network technology in the provision of financial services. Hence, banks must try harder to achieve customer acceptance and it seems that they actually do: it is often the case that financial institutions reserve their most competitive financial products and rates of interest exclusively for online customers.[78]

I have also examined how European banks allocate the risk of security failure. On the technical side, large sums have rightly been invested in

---

[78] For example, see http://www.halifax.co.uk/loans/home.shtml offering an exclusive online rate for personal loans not available to branch customers (last visited 10 September 2005).

order to sharpen up the security of IT systems.[79] The open network architecture, however, renders security events almost inevitable regardless of the level of investment, although adherence to good security practices is a significant mitigating factor. Unauthorized access to online accounts and misappropriation of funds are not unlikely to occur. If the proper access devices have been misused, the bank cannot distinguish between rightful mandate and unauthorized communication.

Based on the theory that standard form contracts imposed on consumers reflect an institutional abuse of bargaining power, one could predict that online banks, having satisfied a 'systemic' duty of care through reasonable investment in security procedures, would allocate the potential economic loss of security failures to consumers by means of appropriate standard form terms and conditions. Interestingly, I have found they almost invariably agree to undertake the risk unless the customer is negligent in keeping the security devices secret. My empirical research has shown that in most cases, particularly in the United Kingdom and Germany, transactions unauthorized by the account holder will not be treated as the customer's mandate and the account will not be debited unless the customer has failed to adhere to standards of good practice relating to the use of the Internet service in general and the security devices in particular. It seems that the high level of investment in better systems and products and the fair allocation of contractual liability in the case of unauthorized transactions indicate that the caricature of the race towards a poorly regulated or 'unsafe' location does not fairly reflect the true dynamics operating in the market for financial innovation and new technology, where reputation and trust is of paramount importance. It is simple: online banks want to attract customers off the high street and undertake to cover the economic loss in case of security failures as a customer incentive.

With regard to the level of convergence between the laws of the 'home' and 'host' countries, some degree of diversity in the quality of supervision will always exist however strong the incentives of the 'home country' might be. Having conceded that, I see no reason why this diversity and, why not, the higher level of transparency and effectiveness in handling complaints, enforcing consumer rights, providing effective mechanisms of out-of-court redress, and simple human values such as professionalism, accuracy, responsiveness, customer care and simplicity cannot be

---

[79] See Joris Claessens and others, 'On the Security of Today's Online Electronic Banking Systems' (2002) *Computers and Security* 253.

part of the package that efficient financial centres will export and firms will use as a competitive asset. In principle, this is one of the key benefits of the single market. In practice, it is unrealistic and probably undesirable to expect full convergence of qualitative elements before attempting full market integration.

There is no doubt that without consumer interest and confidence the project of the single financial market will fail. For that degree of confidence to be attained, a high level of transparency, substantial protection on the basis of high consumer standards and efficient and affordable mechanisms of consumer redress are essential, but local protection through the mandatory application of local rules is not. The financial market is better served through choice and unimpeded circulation of financial products, while consumer confidence may be adequately addressed through a measured and targeted programme of legal harmonization. While the principles of country of origin and free choice of law can put consumer confidence to the test, and even drive policy makers and firms towards better rules and contracts, the untested presumption of distrust, which 'imperfect' mutual recognition implies, is a substantial obstacle to further financial integration.

It is also unclear why the consumer, particularly from a less financially developed Member State, would not have confidence in services originating in Member States with efficient financial services regulation, consumer protection, law enforcement and procedures of redress. Responsible consumers surely can decide whether financial services originating overseas make financial sense for their own circumstances and whether, despite the benefits, the reputation of the firm, the applicable law or the Member State in question ensure an adequate level of protection. The governing law can also be a competitive asset. Banks may attract profitable customers through increased levels of protection or perhaps consider whether, in the light of the appealing size of the foreign market, choice of the consumer's law and full regulatory adaptation to the demands of the country of destination is in their interests. But this should be a free choice and not an institutional mandate. In parallel, the informed consumer will protect the uniformed. To the extent that banks strive to implant consumer confidence and compete on reputation, the existence of enough well-informed consumers, who understand the terms of the deal, the quality of supervision and the protection afforded by law and who are prepared to migrate to better deals, may effectively discipline the entire market driving up the general quality of services, supervision, applicable law and contractual terms.

Those arguments are reinforced by the transparency and quality of information available on the Internet. Even voices that are less enthusiastic about the forces of globalization and free trade concede that global information networks entail too positive an impact on consumers' power to access information not to trigger thought for regulatory reform.[80] In addition to high quality research, formerly unavailable to anyone without sound financial resources, the Internet is a goldmine of information in plain language about available firms and services, consumer rights and mechanisms of redress, made available by reputable commercial intermediaries and governmental or not-for-profit agencies. Further, the unique ability to search and, most importantly, to read online or store information without the pressure of time or aggressive sales techniques adds important value to the availability of information. Furthermore, some supervisory authorities are leaders in educating and informing consumers electronically. Consumers consult the register and check the status of regulated firms. They submit information and complaints and seek redress. Authorities are keen to transform their Internet sites into sources of investor and consumer education and advice. The FSA has established what essentially constitutes a fully functional directory containing searchable comparative tables of similar services and products supplied by different firms[81] and consumers are increasingly seizing this opportunity to strengthen their position by the thousands every day.[82] It is now emerging in empirical studies that the average Internet user is in a far better position than the average non-Internet user seeking financial services on the high street.[83]

Translating the foregoing ideas into normative legal principles, it seems that the Court has taken some notice. In the recent case *Deutscher Apothekerverband*[84] the Court accepted that the characteristics of network technology and the facilities offered by advanced software, in particular the convenient availability of information and the direct interaction between the supplier and the customer, will necessarily influence the decision as to whether restrictive national measures are strictly necessary for, and proportionate to, the promotion of worthy regulatory

---

[80] See John Goldring, 'Consumer Protection, Globalization and Democracy' (1998) 6 *Cardozo Journal of International and Comparative Law* 1.
[81] See http://www.fsa.gov.uk/consumer/tools/tools.html (last visited 10 September 2005).
[82] See Financial Services Authority, *Annual Report 2001–2002* (London, 2002), p. 41.
[83] See IOSCO, *Second Internet Report*.
[84] Case C-322/01, *Deutscher Apothekerverband eV v. 0800 DocMorris NV and Jacques Waterval* [2003] ECR I-14887.

objectives. In particular, the Court examined whether the prohibition to sell medicines outside pharmacies, whether via the Internet or otherwise, was necessary to ensure the safety of medicines and further ensure that the customer receives individual information and advice from the pharmacist when the product is purchased. The intervening national governments argued that even if the mail-order buyer is able to obtain advice on the Internet or by telephone, that is no substitute for advice given in a pharmacy in a direct face-to-face conversation with the customer because the customer's physical and psychological state, his bearing, his life-style and his current medication are factors which must be taken into account during the consultation.[85] The Court replied that as regards the need to provide the customer with advice and information, adequate advice and information may be provided via the Internet and it pertinently pointed out that electronic commerce may have certain advantages, such as the ability to place the order from home or the office, without the need to go out, and to have time to think about the questions to ask the pharmacists, advantages which must be taken into account.[86] The Court further observed that as regards incorrect use of the medicine, the risk thereof could be reduced through an increase in the number of online interactive features, which the customer must use before being able to complete a purchase.[87]

## Minimum harmonization of national laws and enforcement practices as prerequisites of mutual recognition of national laws and 'home country' control

The relationship between mutual recognition and legal harmonization has been a turbulent one. It was the futility of full harmonization and uniformity that strengthened the argument for mutual recognition and 'home country' control. And it is the perceived absence of sufficient equivalence of national standards and mutual trust among national authorities that may potentially undermine the policy of 'perfect' mutual recognition.

In the single European market, legal harmonization will never iron out all differences in national laws and therefore cannot alone remove all legal impediments. A certain degree of harmonization is, however, determinative of the success of mutual recognition, which is conceptually

---

[85] See para. 82.   [86] See para. 113.   [87] See para. 114.

linked to an adequate level of convergence of national standards. Mutual recognition and targeted legal harmonization work together to remove legal obstacles to financial integration. Has a sufficient level of harmonization been attained to underpin mutual recognition? Then a perfect model of mutual recognition will ensure free economic movement and render the remaining legal differences harmless and irrelevant to European economic integration. Otherwise, even the most trivial differences in national laws will disturb cross-border financial activities. Mutual recognition and harmonization join forces to achieve the end objective and complement one another, the former acting as the spearhead and the latter guaranteeing that the venture has strong legal foundations. The EU version of legal harmonization is the principal but not the only source of equivalence or similarities in national laws. Other forces, such as common historical roots, regulatory competition or even pure chance may be producing similar national rules. After all, the boundaries of human knowledge pose obvious restrictions in the scope for national choices that are radical, innovative and like no other.

### *The optimal level and content of minimum harmonization measures*

The optimal level of legal convergence has been achieved when free economic movement has been attained without compromising significant regulatory interests. With less harmonization than needed, full mobility of financial services will fail for lack of legal convergence. With more harmonization than absolutely required, the outer limits of valid centralization of legislative functions are overstepped.[88]

Excessive harmonization does not necessarily disturb free economic movement, but it entails 'transaction' and 'policy' losses that are not tolerated by the EC Treaty. It is also uneconomical in the light of the scarcity of harmonization resources. Having said that, the trick is to identify which laws need harmonization and which laws can be left to national authorities without undermining the single market. The 'trick' is rarely performed in accordance with textbook solutions. It requires astute political steering through the perilous waters of conflicting group interests, national legacies and subjective personal tastes. There is of course no single wisdom as to what the content of the common rules should be. The dividing line between what should be harmonized

---

[88] See EC Treaty, art. 5.

and what should be left to the discretion of national authorities is fine and subject to revision because what is considered to be 'essential' may change over time. It would therefore be extremely unwise to disguise one's subjective views as an objective benchmark of the optimal level of harmonization. There is however guidance to be found in the EC Treaty and the case law of the Court.

In checking the compatibility of specific instruments of legal harmonization with the Treaty, the Court has been mindful of a delicate problem:[89] an overly restrained policy of judicial review could permit the law-making institutions of the European Union to encroach impermissibly on the powers of Member States; but an overzealous exercise of control might tie the hands of the Community in strengthening economic integration.

Harmonization may be pursued as a means of reconciling different national laws which in the absence of coordination may justify trade restrictions in the interest of 'general good'.[90] Even when no express EU competence exists, harmonization may be pursued in order to improve the legal framework of the single market.[91] Nevertheless, the fact that different Member States maintain different laws and the abstract risk of trade obstacles or of distortions of competition are insufficient to justify EU harmonization.[92] The emergence of such obstacles must be likely and the measure in question must be designed to prevent them.[93]

Even when the constitutional conditions are met, the European Union cannot go beyond what is necessary to achieve the objective. Harmonization instruments must respect the free movement provisions and not prejudice the progress already attained in the internal market.[94] Common rules must be as simple as possible; framework Directives are to be preferred over detailed instruments; and as much scope as possible should be left for national decision-making.[95]

Despite all that, the EU legislature enjoys a generous margin of discretion. The Court has felt that assessing the validity of harmonization

---

[89] See AG Fennelly in Case C-376/98 *Germany* v. *Parliament and Council* [2000] ECR I-8419, para. 4.
[90] See *Germany* v. *Parliament and Council* [1997] ECR I-2405, para. 17.
[91] *Ibid.* para. 83; EC Treaty, art. 95.
[92] See Case C-233/94 *Germany* v. *Parliament and Council*, [1997] ECR I-2405, para. 84.
[93] *Ibid.*, para. 86.
[94] See Case C-15/83 *Denkavit Nederland BV* v. *Hoofdproduktschap Voor Akkerbouwprodukten* [1984] ECR 2171.
[95] See EC Treaty Protocol on the Application of the Principles of Subsidiarity and Proportionality OJ No. C340/140 10 November 1997.

instruments involves the kind of political considerations about the best level and method of government that courts have in general no business making. On two separate occasions, the Court expressly conceded that specific EU rules were contrary to the basic economic freedoms but it took a carefully concealed political position and declined to intervene because 'in view of the complexity of the matter and the differences between the legislation of the Member States, the Parliament and the Council were empowered to achieve the necessary harmonization progressively'.[96] In the event of unanimous adoption of Community legislation in the Council, the constitutional issues are likely to be kept at the margin of the discussion insofar as the legal act receives a strong dosage of political immunity to technical judicial review.[97]

The established Community order envisages the process of harmonization as being subordinate to the primary objective of achieving free economic movement. And in building the internal market, as much scope as possible should be left for national decision-making. Taken together and combined with the express provision of Article 100b inserted in the original Treaty of Rome by the Single European Act,[98] those principles indicate that mutual recognition must be the motor of integration whereas harmonization must be employed as an auxiliary contributor of essential legal convergence. This state of affairs, although lamented by those who would like to see regulatory interests such as consumer protection being emancipated from the 'internal market' project and autonomously pursued, has clear implications for the depth and breadth of harmonization instruments and the content of common rules: harmonization must be pursued only in cases where had it not been for a 'level playing field', perfect mutual recognition would entail disturbances and risks of market failure which the internal market does not tolerate.

Different people, whose views may range from the Marxist to the neo-liberal tradition, of course understand the concept of market failure differently. The process of harmonization however must be treated as regulation proper and, as such, it must be carried out in accordance with the established economic order of a market economy with free

---

[96] See Case C-193/94 *Skanavi and Chryssanthakopoulos* (Criminal Proceedings) [1996] ECR I-929, para. 27.

[97] See Stephen Weatherill, 'The Commission's Options for Developing EC Consumer Protection and Contract Law: Assessing the Constitutional Basis' (2002) EBLR 497.

[98] See pp. 000–00 above.

competition in which restrictions on enterprise should be exceptional and properly justified.

Ideally, when that level of convergence has been attained, the risk of 'competition in laxity' has been addressed and a more interventionist approach towards deeper centralization is not necessary. In particular, the adoption of overly protective and essentially redistributive measures of consumer, investor and depositor protection, which reflect a socio-legal understanding of what a market failure is, must be left to the national political process. The notion of redistributive social protection in the field of financial services, however worthy and socially desirable, is a matter to be dealt with at the national level, in accordance with local resources, choices and political tastes, perhaps in a framework of healthy competition, without national choices being used as a pretext for inhibiting free and open financial markets.

There is also scope for some complementary initiatives to be taken at the European level. I have already referred to the list of non-legal barriers preventing open electronic finance in Europe. Any action which may increase the contestability of the market and consumer confidence, through initiatives for consumer education and awareness, the flow of information on local market conditions and the creditworthiness of customers, technical standardization of clearing and settlement systems or security of information and network technology, is welcome and within the principle of financial liberalization. But first and foremost, to the extent that harmonization is a form of regulation proper, the discussion must focus on the quality of the harmonization process and the form and content of the common rules.

The process must be transparent. An open and meaningful stage of consultation must involve the main interest groups. Consequently, the rules must be designed, discussed and implemented in full accordance with the state of the art. The best rules are those that effectively address market failures while being sufficiently flexible to address new and formerly unknown circumstances without having to go through protracted and time-consuming procedures of revision. Further, there is no reason to waste efforts in reinventing the wheel. The convergence of regulatory principles and standards at the EC level can and should benefit from the abundant sources of international standards that constitute the global version of a sound regulatory framework. Whether banking regulation or electronic commerce, there is no shortage of international institutions and 'institutionalized' groups of experts producing standards of high quality (e.g. Basel Committee, Organization for Economic Cooperation and Development (OECD), IOSCO, International Monetary Fund (IMF), Financial Stability Forum, ICC, United Nations Commission on International Trade Law (UNCITRAL etc.). EU Member States, particularly the largest, are of course central players in all these standard-setting institutions.

Once the required convergence has been secured in substance, the pursuit of exhaustive uniformity in trivial aspects of regulation entails 'high transaction' costs and poor policy benefits. The case for uniformity of the procedural aspects of standard setting and supervision is equally unpromising. The internal structure and procedural mechanics of national agencies reflect national administrative traditions, available resources and political preferences, the convergence of which is both impossible and undesirable. Finally, it should be noted that legal harmonization must not contradict the values of the single financial market. To the extent that consumer choice is one of them, the harmonization of 'product rules' and 'financial techniques' should be resisted.

### Establishing mutual trust among national regulatory agencies

The Court has observed that the model of mutual recognition and 'home country' control 'is a particular application of a more general principle of mutual trust between the authorities of the Member States'.[99] Indeed, participating countries must have confidence that Member States in their capacity as 'home states' have the motivation and the ability to enforce the applicable rules. Confidence is easier to build in a climate of supervisory cooperation and coordination, particularly in the case of electronic banking activities where the bank providing services is far removed from the territory of the 'host authorities'. Sharing important information with regard to cross-border legal enforcement and supervisory concerns is an essential ingredient of mutual trust. Fundamental differences in the law relating to bank secrecy rules and the authorities' duty of confidentiality may undermine the quality of cooperation and mutual trust. 'Host' authorities may reasonably suspect that online banking activities originating in countries with strict secrecy rules and non-cooperative supervisory authorities entail risks of criminal activity and can be reluctant to commit to perfect forms of mutual recognition without residual 'host country' supervisory and enforcement powers.

---

[99] See Case 25/88 *Ministère Public* v. *Buchara* [1989] ECR-1105, para. 18.

The required level of mutual trust presupposes that the exchange of information among competent authorities is honest, efficient and ongoing. The list of essential institutional preconditions further includes the ongoing monitoring and assessment of compliance, mutual assistance in times of supervisory and enforcement urgency and avoidance of arbitrary behaviour which violates the terms of the mutual recognition arrangement.

Going back to the earlier discussion about the structural weakness of mutual recognition through the jurisprudence of national or supranational courts, the required level of trust among participating countries is more difficult to build where the responsibility for 'home country' control is vested in 'home country' courts rather than on supervisory agencies with a clear mandate and resources to ensure compliance and provide a single point of reference for market participants and fellow regulators. It is advisable that the mandate and scope *rationae materiae* of competence of financial regulatory agencies is broadly similar in all participating countries to ensure that no issue worthy of attention escapes supervisory scrutiny. This is not always the case in Europe given the differences in the structure of financial markets and the legacy of national regulatory regimes.

This question relates to the recent trend of consolidation of national supervisory agencies and the creation of mega-regulators with responsibility for many different types of financial activities. This is not the place to discuss the advantages and disadvantages of integrated supervision in respect of operational cost, efficiency and accountability of the competent authority. It is arguable however that, whether as intended or unintended collateral effect of supervisory consolidation, the operation of a single supervisory authority per national market reduces the regulatory burden for internationally active financial institutions and may potentially improve the consistency in the treatment of these international players, which would deal with a single rather than two or three regulatory agencies in every 'host country'. A consolidated supervisory authority constitutes a single point of reference for regulated entities and consumers, ensures better communication and cooperation with regulatory agencies overseas and may potentially increase the transparency and simplicity of domestic regulatory standards and supervisory practices, thus reducing the regulatory burden of internationally active banks promoting the cause of financial integration.

A second essential condition of perfect mutual regulation is consumer confidence in the quality of supervision and law enforcement by 'home country' authorities. In addition to consumer awareness of applicable rules and enforcement practices, it is important to establish efficient institutions for cross-border protection of consumer rights, dispute resolution and out-of-court redress.

Thirdly, one of the most important safeguards of mutual recognition is the institutional privilege of the 'host country' to resume supervisory and enforcement activities when domestic regulatory interests are at risk but confidence in capacity or motivation of the 'home' country has been lost. The emergency 'host country' powers are radically different from the current 'imperfect' form of mutual recognition. They would not allow for the *a priori* application of 'host country' rules but will solely permit *ad hoc* supervisory intervention against specific risks and identified financial institutions in cases where the fellow 'home' authorities have failed to adequately perform effective 'home country' supervision. The risk of 'host' authorities acting arbitrarily against overseas financial institutions, outside the spirit and the letter of such emergency powers, could be addressed with reasonable institutional precautions. For example, the exercise of such powers could be made conditional on the prior consultation with the competent 'home country' authorities in view of preventing emergency interventions and, if necessary as a last resort, it could be accompanied by the legal obligation to act only to the extent necessary to address the risk and not beyond that (principles of necessity and proportionality).

The Internet can make a substantial contribution towards the fulfilment of the foregoing conditions. At an early stage, Perritt identified the significance of the Internet in strengthening supervisory cooperation and facilitating the flow of information among national authorities, enhancing awareness of applicable practices elsewhere and reducing dramatically delays and supervisory gaps.[100] Its full implications received worldwide attention in 1997, when the Nobel Peace Laureate Jody Williams told the world how she managed to overcome her poor financial resources and coordinate via e-mail over one thousand governmental and non-governmental agencies leading to the signing of the Mine Ban Treaty in 1997.[101] The efficient use of electronic government in financial

---

[100] See Henry Perritt, 'The Internet as a Threat to Sovereignty? Thoughts on the Internet's Role in Strengthening National and Global Governance' (1998) 5 *Indiana Journal of Global Legal Studies* 423.

[101] See Jody Williams, *The International Campaign to Ban Land Mines – A Model for Disarmament Initiatives* (1997) at http://www.nobel.se/peace/articles/williams/index.html (6 December 2003).

regulation and supervision and the exploitation of the Internet as a means of sharing information on laws, regulatory and enforcement practices have increased international regulatory transparency. They have also facilitated the communication among national regulatory agencies, thus laying the foundations of meaningful cooperation between 'home' and 'host' authorities in financial areas governed on the basis of perfect mutual recognition and 'home country' control. It should be noted that electronic filing of supervisory returns and online communication between regulators and regulated entities have already been established as ordinary supervisory practices.[102]

On the institutional front, good spirited cooperation and coordination between the 'home' and 'host' authorities are mandated by the overarching duty of loyalty to the cause of European integration and the specific aspects thereof.[103] Member States shall take all appropriate measures to ensure the fulfilment of obligations arising out of Community law and shall abstain from taking any sort of prejudicial action. The duty involves, *inter alia*, an obligation addressed to all kinds of national judicial and administrative authorities,[104] to ensure that Community law is implemented in a timely manner[105] and effectively in a spirit of good faith;[106] to cooperate with one another and with Community institutions and provide information in a climate of transparency about national regulatory actions which affect the internal market;[107] to avoid international commitments which may undermine the Community *acquis*;[108] and to ensure that national authorities enjoy the de facto capacity to fulfil their obligations arising out of Community law.[109]

Although the scope for further improvement is wide, the current institutional framework is close to meeting the foregoing key conditions. At the international level, the work of the Basel Committee on Banking Supervision has been instrumental in increasing the mutual understanding and trust among key banking supervisors. Indeed, the original mandate of the Committee was to close gaps in the international supervisory

---

[102] See http://www.fsa.gov.uk/pages/Doing/Regulated/Firms/index.shtml (9 September 2005).
[103] See EC Treaty, art. 10.
[104] See Case C-344/98 *Masterfoods Ltd v. HB Ice Cream Ltd* [2000] ECR I-11369, para. 49.
[105] See Case C-315/95 *Commission v. Italy* [1996] ECR 5743, para. 7.
[106] See Case C-320/99 *Commission v. France* [2000] ECR I-10453, para. 9.
[107] See Case C-478/01 *Commission v. Luxemburg*, Transcript 6 March 2003, para. 22.
[108] See Opinion of the ECJ 2/91 [1993] ECR I-1061, para. 11.
[109] See Case 130/78 *Salumificio di Cornuda Sp A v. Amministrazione delle Finanze dello Stato* [1979] ECR 867, para. 27.

coverage of cross-border banking activities. In 1983, the Committee emphasized the importance of effective cooperation between home and host country authorities in the supervision of banks' international operations[110] and in 1990 it strongly recommended the key national authorities shall engage in ongoing exchange of information regarding the activities of international banks.[111]

The Committee observed that mutual trust can only be achieved if supervisory information can flow with confidence in both directions. 'Home country' authorities were made responsible for overseeing the internal structure and operations of internationally active banks, while 'host authorities' were encouraged to facilitate the flow of information with regard to the local activities of banks established overseas by reforming, if needed, relevant bank and supervisory secrecy rules. With regard to cross-border banking in general, the 1996 Basel paper on the *Supervision of Cross-Border Banking* and the *1997 Core Principles for Effective Banking Supervision* regarded the exchange of information among national authorities as an essential condition of a sound international regulatory framework.[112] The position regarding cross-border electronic banking activities was refined in July 2003.[113]

The Committee does not feel that the practice of electronic banking affects the role of the 'home' supervisor in overseeing the risks associated with cross-border banking.[114] Coordination among bank supervisors is still a key element of the process: When the 'home' supervisor is contacted by a foreign supervisor regarding the online activities of a local bank under home country supervision, the former should cooperate as appropriate under its applicable laws and regulations.[115] The precise form of cooperation is bound to reflect the asymmetrical relationship of the 'home' and 'host' authorities with the regulated entity. The 'home' authority will be monitoring the operations, overall soundness and internal structure of the bank pursuant to its own supervisory and enforcement rules. The 'host' authority will most probably communicate its concerns relating to the 'local' activities of the overseas

---

[110] See Basel Committee, *Principles for the Supervision of Banks' Foreign Establishments* (Basel: BIS, 1983).
[111] Basel Committee, *Information Flows Between Banking Supervisory Authorities* (Basel: BIS, 1990).
[112] Basel Committee, *Core Principles for Effective Banking Supervision* (Basel: BIS, 1997).
[113] Basel Committee, *Supervision of Electronic Banking*.
[114] *Ibid.* at p. 9.   [115] See p. 10.

entity with the expectation that the competent 'home' authorities would effectively respond in a timely manner.

The legal framework in the single European market reflects the international consensus that obstacles to exchange of information should be eliminated, that the confidentiality of shared information should be secured and that supervisors should pursue proactively policies of full cooperation and mutual assistance.[116] In the national arena, the duty of bank confidentiality does not, in principle, preclude the flow of customer-related and transaction information from the bank to the competent authorities in the event of criminal investigation or similar procedures.[117]

International supervisory cooperation is practically implemented by bilateral or multilateral Memoranda of Understanding (MoUs) between supervisory agencies, which establish the reciprocal rights and obligations of cooperation. Having regard to the large number of MoUs currently outstanding, one may argue that the institutional foundations of efficient international cooperation have been laid.[118] On a more personal level, the frequent interaction of key national officials with each other in various European and international regulatory committees increases mutual awareness of supervisory practices and creates the basis for further collaboration. A characteristic example was the collaboration of key personnel from the FSA and its German counterparts in the case of the proposed merger of the London and Frankfurt Stock Exchanges (which failed eventually). From the outset, joint working groups were established to assess the market and regulatory implications of the proposed transaction, working as an integrated team, which appears to have left a satisfying sense of successful cooperation.[119]

---

[116] See Consolidated Banking Directive (Council and EP Directive 2000/12/ EC, OJ 2000 No. L126/1), arts. 28–33; §§ 8–9 KWG; FiSMA 2000, ss. 169, 348–54; C.monét.fin., art.(1).

[117] See §§ 27, 44 KWG; FiSMA 2000, ss. 165(1), 175(5) and 274(8); FSA Enforcement (ENF) 2.10.3G; C.monét.fin., arts. L 561 (1), L 511 (33).

[118] The FSA has entered into 150 MoUs. See Michael Foot, 'International Cooperation and Exchange of Information' (paper presented at the Guernsey Financial Service Commission Seminar, June 2003). The German *Bundesanstalt für Finanzdienstleistungsaufsicht* (BAFIN) has entered into 62; BAFIN *Annual Report 2002* (Bonn: BAFIN, 2003), Annex 8.

[119] See Susanne Bergsträsser, 'Regulatory Implications of an Exchange Merger' in Guido Ferrarini, Klaus J. Hopt and Eddy Wymeersch (eds.) *Capital Markets in the Age of the Euro: Cross-Border Transactions, Listed Companies and Regulation* (London: Kluwer, 2002), pp. 289–96.

The Regulation on Consumer Protection Cooperation will no doubt strengthen the quality of cross-border enforcement.[120] The main operative provisions obligate national supervisory authorities with consumer-related responsibilities, including financial regulatory agencies, to cooperate with each other and the Commission towards the full enforcement of consumer protection rules in cases of cross-border trade in goods and services, prompt notification of Community law violations, exchange of information and efficient handling of cross-border consumer complaints.[121]

Turning finally to consumers, the gradual departure from a litigation-based notion of redress towards cheaper, accessible and less confusing means of out-of-court procedures, with the establishment of national Ombudsman Schemes, may potentially contribute to a safer single financial area. Provided that consumers have access to 'out-of-court' redress procedures in the 'home country' and financial institutions enjoy access to similar schemes in the 'host country', Ombudsman services may offer what is currently missing in the field of cross-border consumer redress. Those schemes, whose services can be used by consumers in other Member States, such as the UK scheme that operates in several European languages,[122] can substantially strengthen the level of consumer redress in the single market. The EU-wide Consumer Complaints Network for Financial Services (FIN-NET) may also contribute to better consumer redress.[123] The project enables recipients of cross-border financial services to communicate their complaints in their own language to the local ombudsman service, which in turn undertakes to forward the complaint to a special-purpose multilingual unit of the fellow 'home country' scheme.[124]

---

[120] See Council and EP Regulation 2006/2004/EC of 27 October 2004 on cooperation between national authorities responsible for the enforcement of consumer protection, OJ 2004, No. L364 1, 9 December 2004.
[121] See *ibid.*, arts. 6, 7 and 8.
[122] See Financial Ombudsman Service, *Annual Report 2002–2003* (London, 2003).
[123] See generally http://finnet.jrc.it/en/ (10 September 2005).
[124] See Memorandum of Understanding on a Cross-Border Out-of-Court Complaints Network for Financial Services in the European Economic Area, at http://europa.eu.int/comm/internal_market/finservices-retail/docs/finnet/memo-understanding_en.pdf (10 September 2005).

# PART III

EU harmonization and convergence of national laws relating to electronic banking activities

# 5

# Risks and regulatory concerns relating to electronic banking activities and the convergence of national prudential regulatory standards

In the previous chapter I argued that online banks providing services across borders should be subject to the mandatory law of the country in which they are established and be free to select the law governing their contracts provided that a minimum level of convergence in national prudential standards, consumer and investor protection rules has been attained. This chapter is descriptive rather than normative and aims to discuss the legal harmonization of prudential regulatory standards in the European Union with particular regard to the special risks and regulatory interests relating to electronic banking activities.

The discussion begins with the jurisprudence of the European Court of Justice ('the Court') concerning the regulatory interests that the 'host country' may invoke to justify restrictions on the free movement of services. It is perhaps useful to understand which national regulatory objectives, and under which conditions, justify derogations from the principle of mutual recognition because this information could be determinative of what needs to be harmonized prior to accepting mutual recognition of national laws and regulatory practices.

## Convergence of national laws and the notion of 'general good' in the single European market

The judicial concept of the 'general good' is the key to unlock the normative elements of mutual recognition and, perhaps, to understand the required scope of legal harmonization prior to establishing a pure form of mutual recognition.

### The 'general good' in the market for financial services

The 'general good' derogation from the economic freedoms guaranteed by the EC Treaty[1] is the principle that free economic movement based on

---
[1] Treaty Establishing the European Community (Rome, 25 March 1957); consolidated text at OJ 2002 No. C325, 24 December 2002.

mutual recognition of laws and regulatory standards can be restricted by measures taken by the 'host country' only insofar as these measures are justified by imperative reasons relating to the public interest,[2] unless that 'public interest' is adequately protected by the laws of the country of origin of the goods or services in question.[3] A bank operating in the single market under the freedom to provide services could be forced to bring their services in compliance with the legislation of the host country only if the pertinent measures were in the interest of the general good and met five strict conditions subject to judicial review by the Court: they must be applied in a non-discriminatory manner to domestic and overseas financial institutions; they must be justified by imperative requirements in the general interest; they must be suitable for securing the attainment of the objective which they pursue; they must not go beyond what is necessary in order to attain those objectives and if less restrictive measures are adequate to protect the public interest, those measures shall be preferred; and finally the pertinent public interest must not be adequately protected by the rules to which the financial institution providing the services is subject in the country in which this person is established.[4]

This notion of proportionality in restricting cross-border services on worthy public policy grounds reveals the conceptual link between the 'general good' and the normative scope of mutual recognition. Insofar as the legal standards of the country of origin are sufficient to satisfy the imperative public interest of the country of destination, the effects of mutual recognition can eliminate legal barriers without compromising the regulatory interests of the 'host country'. If, however, the attained legal and institutional convergence of the laws of participating countries is insufficient to satisfy the country of destination that its regulatory concerns have been addressed, the latter may regulate cross-border financial services but only in the necessary dosage to fill in the regulatory gap.

To the extent that the judicial review of 'host country' measures by the Court reveals the Court's binding opinion as to whether the regulatory interests and measures of the 'host country' justify restrictions on

---

[2] See Case C-76/90 *Säger v. Dennemeyer & Co. Ltd* [1991] ECR I-4221, para.15.

[3] See Case C-165/98 *Mazzoleni and ISA*, [2001] ECR I-2189 (Criminal Proceedings) para. 22.

[4] See Case C-55/94 *Gebhard* v. *Consiglio dell'Ordine degli Arrocati e Procuratori di Milano* [1995] ECR I-4165.

the free movement of services, the 'general good' jurisprudence may offer guidance on the appropriate level of legal convergence to be achieved before national measures restricting the free movement of financial services can no longer be justified on 'general good' grounds. In other words, one may argue that in the current governance model of mutual recognition based on minimum legal convergence, the 'general good' jurisprudence reveals certain minimum legal and regulatory institutions that must be in place before the regulatory claims of 'host countries' can be set aside as unjustified restrictions on free economic movement. For the same reason, EU measures of legal harmonization have the effect of preventing Member States from invoking their national regulatory interest and lack of adequate legal convergence in the single market as grounds for restricting free economic movement. In the field of financial services, when Germany questioned the legal basis of the Deposit Guarantee Schemes Directive,[5] the Court indirectly recognized the conceptual link between the 'general good' exception and mutual recognition by asserting that the effect of the harmonization achieved by the Directive was 'to prevent the Member States from invoking depositor protection in order to impede the activities of credit institutions authorized in other Member States . . .'.[6]

Obviously the opinion of the Court reflects the law and the facts of the litigated case. Different circumstances may lead the Court to revisit the required level of legal convergence upwards or downwards. For example, the Court has ruled that less restrictive rules found in other Member States do not render other stricter rules necessarily disproportionate.[7] In exceptional circumstances the 'national public interest' may be so strong that there could be no common EU standards that would render national measures unjustified and disproportionate. Notwithstanding the shortcomings of judicial review as source of normative arguments, the value of the 'general good' jurisprudence as guidance of the requisite legal convergence remains strong.

The individual components of the notion of 'general good' correspond to different aspects of legal harmonization. The aims which the Court has recognized to be in the 'public interest' indicate the underlying objectives that legal harmonization may pursue. The test of suitability

---

[5] Council and EP Directive 94/19/EC of 30 May 1994 on deposit-guarantee schemes, OJ 1994, No. L135/5, 31 May 1994.
[6] See Case C-233/94 *Germany* v. *Parliament and Council* [1997] ECR I-2405, para. 19.
[7] Case C-3/95 *Reisebüro Broede* v. *Sand ker* [1996] ECR I-6511, para. 42.

may offer some guidance as to which techniques are not capable of meeting the set objective. Necessity may offer some insight as to the level beyond which harmonization is futile and excessive, at least as a mechanism of institutional and legal convergence, whereas proportionality may be used to assess whether the depth or scope of harmonization goes beyond what is needed to secure acceptable levels of convergence and eventually a pure model of mutual recognition.

The list of regulatory interests that may justify restrictions on free economic movement is open-ended. From the numerous motives successfully invoked to date, the protection of the recipients of the service,[8] the protection of consumers,[9] the protection of creditors and the efficient administration of justice,[10] the cohesion of the tax system,[11] the compliance with professional ethics,[12] the maintenance of the good reputation of the financial sector,[13] the fairness of commercial transactions,[14] the prevention of fraud[15] and the protection of investors and depositors[16] are the most relevant for the conduct of electronic banking activities.

### The 'general good' concept and the online provision of banking services

The conduct of electronic banking activities raises several different types of risks and regulatory concerns. Policy makers are primarily concerned with the systemic stability and soundness of banks and the adequate protection of ordinary consumers, depositors and investors. Furthermore, the conduct of cross-border activities raises the question of international cooperation in the supervision of increasingly integrated

---

[8] See Joined Cases 110/78 and 111/78 *Ministère public* v. *Van Wesemael* [1979] ECR 35, para. 28.
[9] See Case 220/83 *Commission* v. *France* [1986] ECR 3663.
[10] See Case C-3/95 *Reisebüro Broede*, above note 7, para. 36.
[11] See Case C-264/96 *ICI* v. *Colmer* [1998] ECR I-4695, para. 29.
[12] See Case C-288/89 *Stichting Collectieve Antennevoorziening Gouda* v. *Commissariaat voor de Media* (the '*Mediawet* I' case) [1991] ECR I-4007, para. 14.
[13] See Case C-384/93 *Alpine Investments* BV v. *Minister van Financien* [1995] ECR I-1141, para. 44.
[14] See Case 120/78 *Rewe-Zentral AG* v. *Bundesmonopolverwaltung für Branntwein* (the *Cassisde Dijon* case) [1979] ECR 679.
[15] See Case C-275/92 *HM Customs and Excise* v. *Schindler* [1994] ECR I-1039.
[16] See Case C-101/94 *Commission* v. *Italy* [1996] ECR I-2691.

financial markets. Moreover, the reliance of financial institutions on advanced information technology and computer networks entails risks that may affect the safety, soundness and security of individual banks and broader repercussions for the financial system as a whole. These are all areas of law where legal convergence among EU Member States would probably facilitate the acceptance of the pure form of mutual recognition. And the lack of sufficient harmonization would probably justify restrictions on the free movement of services.

### Prudential standards of safety and soundness

The solvency and soundness of financial institutions was first recognized by the Court to be in the interest of consumers and a valid ground for restricting the free movement of services in the *German Insurance* case.[17] The specific question of bank safety and soundness was addressed in *Parodi*,[18] where the Court accepted that in the absence of sufficient legal convergence of prudential banking regulation, national measures restricting the freedom to provide banking services were justified because the banking sector was regarded as a particularly sensitive area from the point of view of consumer protection.[19] Prudential and consumer protection standards such as deposit guarantee schemes were legitimate grounds for national measures because they increased 'the stability of the banking system and the protection of savers.'[20]

What makes *Parodi* particularly interesting is the Court's zeal to emphasize that the overarching objectives of systemic stability and protection of consumers do not offer unfettered discretion in taking measures that restrict cross-border services. The Court emphasized the nature of the banking activity in question (mortgages) and the actual risks that it posed to retail consumers and concluded that, had it been a different banking service, risk or type of customer, the regulatory measures of the 'host country' might have been unnecessary and disproportionate.[21] The Court demonstrated the confidence to look carefully and weigh a broad range of factors in determining whether restrictive financial regulation is worth pursuing in light of the burdens posed on the single market in financial services. The principle of proportionality is the

---

[17] Case C-205/84 *Commission v. Germany* [1986] ECR 3755, para. 39.
[18] Case C-222/95 *Societé Parodi v. Banque H. Albert de Bary et Cie* [1997] ECR I-3899.
[19] Ibid., para. 22.
[20] See Case 233/94 *Germany v. Parliament and Council* [1997] ECR I-2405, para. 13.
[21] See Case 222/95 *Parodi*, above note 18, para. 19.

instrument that the Court uses in *Parodi* to apply a risk-based approach to good financial regulation in the single European market: the permissible regulatory response of the 'host country' must vary depending on the nature and scale of risks generated by the cross-border financial activity in question. Restrictive regulatory measures against the free movement of banking services, while justified on grounds of protection of mortgage borrowers, may be totally unnecessary and unjustified if imposed on financial institutions engaging in a different type of financial activity.

## Protection of consumers of financial services: depositors, borrowers and investors

The protection of consumers of financial services is the second main rationale of financial regulatory measures. The fear that consumers lack information and expertise to understand financial services and markets, the standardization of financial products and the limited scope for individual negotiations between consumers and financial institutions and the complexity and long-term economic implications of certain financial commitments are common justifications of regulatory measures that aim to protect consumers of financial services.

The question of consumer protection is crucial for the settlement of the political antagonism between the concepts of cross-border electronic finance, protectionism and promotion of legitimate regulatory values. Whatever the difficulties in reconciling competing claims of financial liberalization and social protection, the Court has firmly asserted that the protection of consumers is an overriding requirement of public interest which may block the free movement of services provided that the 'general good' requirements have been met.[22]

## Transparency and disclosure

In their most basic form, transparency and disclosure denote the negative obligation not to provide misleading or inaccurate information as a means of inducing the conclusion of a contract. In their positive form, they refer to positive information that financial institutions must disclose to the market. Informed consumers are better placed to make rational and efficient choices about what they want to bargain for. They

---

[22] See Case C-6/98 *ARD* v. *Pro Sieban* [1999] ECR I-7599, para. 50.

are better placed to negotiate a fair treatment and subsequently check that the contract is in accordance with their rational bargain.

Transparency and mandatory disclosure of information in transactions between consumers and financial institutions improve the position of consumers with the additional benefit that they do not restrict voluntary exchanges and the freedom of contract. For that reason, the Court has ruled that restrictions on commercial freedom are disproportionate and must be abolished if the disclosure of information would suffice to protect the general interest in question.[23] For online financial services where the lack of physical proximity between the customer and the financial institution renders mutual trust and confidence more difficult to establish, the case in favour of regulatory standards that enhance transparency and disclosure of information is even stronger.

More specifically, the protection of consumers from unfair marketing and misleading advertising practices may justify measures restricting the free movement of services.[24] Moreover, measures that rely on transparency and disclosure of information must be preferred to measures that substantially interfere with free economic movement. When Germany argued in *Cassis de Dijon*[25] that the prohibition to sell certain alcoholic beverages with low alcoholic content was intended to protect consumers from confusion and misleading trading practices by producers and distributors, the Court dismissed the measure as disproportionate to the set objective on grounds that it was sufficient to ensure that 'suitable information is conveyed to the purchaser by requiring the display of an indication of origin and of the alcohol content on the packaging of products.'[26] The Court subsequently confirmed in *GB-INNO-BM*[27] that the consumer's right to information and education was a central tenet of EU consumer protection policy because it empowered the consumer to make her choice in full knowledge of the facts.[28]

Article 153 EC has elevated the consumers' right to information into a binding principle that should inform the content of EU policies. Consumer information features prominently in EU consumer policies in

---

[23] See Case 120/78 *Cassis de Dijon*, above note 14, para. 13.
[24] See Case C-288/89 *Mediawet I* [1991] ECR I-4007, para. 27.
[25] See Case 120/78 *Cassis de Dijon*, above note 14.
[26] *Ibid.*, para. 13.
[27] See Case C-362/88 *GB-INNO-BM* v. *CCL* [1990] I-667.
[28] *Ibid.*, paras. 14–18.

general[29] and financial services in particular. At the international level, the values of fairness, accuracy and full disclosure of information to bank customers as part of a sound electronic banking service are promoted by the policy recommendations of the Basel Committee on Banking Supervision[30] and other international initiatives, such as the *Guidelines for Consumer Protection in the Context of Electronic Commerce*.[31]

## Honesty and integrity

Investors in securities markets assume a dual role: investors of capital and users of investment services provided by financial intermediaries such as online brokers. With regard to the relationship between investment services and investor protection, the Court confirmed in *Alpine Investments*[32] that investor confidence is an essential condition for creating and maintaining liquid, vibrant and competitive financial markets.[33] It is therefore a matter of public interest not only to ensure the free movement of investment services but also to implant and enhance investor confidence by means of professional regulatory measures serving to ensure the competence and trustworthiness of the financial intermediaries on whom investors are particularly reliant.[34] Professional ethics and rules of professional behaviour in the provision of investment services are also in the interest of the 'general good' and may justify restrictions on free economic movement.[35]

The Court's jurisprudence reveals the dual contribution of investor protection rules in the single European market. From a regulatory perspective, they impose on financial intermediaries appropriate standards of professional conduct in executing client instructions and handling client money. From a liberalization perspective, they enhance investor confidence in domestic and pan-European capital markets, thus encouraging cross-border investments of capital and consumption of investment services.

---

[29] See European Commission, Consumer Strategy 2002–2006, pp. 2–9.
[30] See Basel Committee on Banking Supervision, *Risk Management Principles for Electronic Banking* (Basel: BIS, 2003), Principle 11.
[31] See Organization for Economic Cooperation and Development, *Guidelines for Consumer Protection in the Context of Electronic Commerce* (Paris, 2000).
[32] See Case C-384/93 *Alpine Investments*, above note 12.
[33] *Ibid.*, para. 42.
[34] *Ibid.*
[35] See Case C-294/89 *Commission* v. *France* [1991] ECR I-3591, para. 31.

## The beneficiaries of consumer protection measures

The persons benefiting from consumer protection measures in the single market are invariably limited to those persons 'who are acting for purposes which are outside their trade, business or profession'.[36] The protection is therefore typically afforded to natural persons,[37] who are not engaged in trade or professional activities at the time of the conclusion of the contract, in other words the transaction is entirely concluded for the purpose of satisfying the customer's own needs in terms of private consumption.[38]

The purpose of the service as the sole determinant of potential vulnerability of the customer does not seem to be in line with a risk-based approach to regulation. It does not help us understand the consumer's ability to assess risks and make responsible choices. It is a crude measure of vulnerability that, although dominant in EC harmonization instruments, on close inspection it poses an anomaly to the constitutional balance between regulation and free trade.

What sort of consumer attitudes should restrictive regulation be measured against? At what moment would the level of protection be sufficient to protect individual consumers and enable free economic movement to operate without mandatory restrictions? At what point are common rules sufficiently protective to facilitate a genuine model of mutual recognition? The answer depends on the notional model of consumer which the Community legal order purports to protect and may range from persons of the highest skills and abilities to the most naïve and vulnerable members of our communities. The higher the level of the consumer's intellectual rigour, resources and analytical skills, the narrower the asymmetry of information between the firm and the consumer, and therefore, the lower the required level of protection and interference with free choice and contract.

To the extent that the least intellectually and emotionally capable persons can only be protected by measures which are too restrictive to

---

[36] See e.g. Council Directive 87/102/EEC of 22 December 1986 for the approximation of the laws, regulations and administrative provisions of the Member States concerning consumer credit, OJ 1987, No. L42/48, 12 February 1987, art. 1(2)(a); Council and EP Directive 2002/65/EC of 23 September 2002 concerning the distance marketing of consumer financial services, OJ 2002, No. L271/1b, 9 October 2002, art. 2(d).

[37] See Case C-541/99 *Cape SNC* v. *Ideal Service Srl* [2001] ECR I-9049.

[38] See Case C-96/00 *Rudolf Gabriel* v. *Schlank & Schick GmbH* [2002] ECR I-6367, paras. 17, 39.

sustain a functional financial market, the optimal model of regulation amounts essentially to a painful choice of whom the common EC rules must leave unprotected. This will rarely be expressed out loud. The selection of means of protection, however, is an unmistakable indicator of the underlying political choice. Information requirements, for example, cannot protect individuals who lack the intellectual or emotional foundations to make informed decisions based on sufficient information. Thus, there is a controversial political choice to be made regarding the objectives of protective legislation and the means to achieve them.

For the Court the objective is to protect the active and responsible consumer who can and shall decide on her own affairs at her own risk when presented with all necessary information.[39] She is an active information seeker who will make the right choice and further her welfare provided that quality information is available. The Court describes her as the average consumer who is reasonably well-informed and reasonably observant and circumspect.[40] With the exception of two cases regarding aggressive marketing techniques,[41] the Court has declined to justify restrictive national measures taken for the protection of consumers whose intelligence and business understanding was less than average.

This state of affairs appears to be hardly surprising. The EC Treaty, with the strong and binding provisions on free trade and the milder, declaratory and almost apologetic references to the so-called 'social agenda' regards free trade as a form of consumer policy in itself insofar as it enhances consumer choice and brings about broader macroeconomic benefits. In parallel, the principle of strict conferment of powers points to the nation state for non-expressly defined policies of social cohesion.

For those promoting the free trade agenda, consumer protection is at best a necessary prerequisite of systemic confidence and legal convergence as a means to sustain free trade policies or, at worst, a justified or prohibited disturbance of free economic movement but, either way, an auxiliary concept. Free competitive markets work better when they are

---

[39] See Case 407/85 *Drei Glocken* v. *Kritzinger* [1988] ECR 4233, paras. 15–22.
[40] See Case C-210/96 *Gut Springenheide GmbH and Tusky* v. *Oberkreisdirektor des Kreises steinfurt* [1998] ECR I-4657, paras. 30–2.
[41] See Case C-286/81 *Osthoek's Uitgeversmaatschappij* [1982] ECR 4575; Case C-382/87 *Buet and EBS* [1989] ECR 1235.

based on rational decisions of informed and responsible individuals and therefore the success of the single market project can only rely on the uncoordinated acts of those who can responsibly decide for themselves what they want to bargain for.

As a result, I do not believe that common EC rules must go beyond what its necessary to protect a responsible 'reasonably circumspect and rational information-seeker' to the extent that the confidence in the level of consumer protection of only those persons is strictly required to set the single financial market in motion. A 'social' agenda of consumer protection would probably emphasize the need for substantive limitations of party autonomy and compulsory redistribution of the costs and benefits of financial contracts. This approach would underestimate the ability of competitive markets to deliver value to consumers. Moreover, regulation entails costs and overly costly or restrictive regulation is reflected in the price of services and products.[42] Firms are likely to seek a way out of costly regulation, perhaps by taking themselves outside the scope of application of these standards. One way of doing so is to turn to the less regulated 'cream' of the market and abandon the high volume/low value services which are most relevant to social groups that the legislation intended to protect; or price out those groups indirectly, by raising fees and prices for overly regulated retail services. A stringent regulatory framework is also likely to halt financial innovation.

The merit of essential but not full harmonization lies in the scope for discretion afforded to national polities to set their own priorities. And there is no reason why competition cannot be encouraged. Centralization is necessary only to the extent required for stimulating the confidence of rational well-informed depositors and investors. Beyond this point, consumer protection should be left to the Member States without compromising the effects of mutual recognition. On the other hand, a revised Treaty mandate to pursue consumer protection policies autonomously and without regard to the single market project would no doubt send a strong signal towards a more expansionist EC consumer policy. This is however another story.

In short, the jurisprudence of the Court reveals its commitment to examine the justifications offered by Member States for restricting free trade against the specific risks posed by the relevant activity. Prudential and consumer protection concerns offer a sound rationale for common

---

[42] See Charles Goodhart and others, *Financial Regulation, Why, How and Where Now?* (London: Routledge, 1998), pp. 61–72.

rules but priority is to be given to disclosure of information and transparency rather than outright restrictions on commercial freedom. In setting the threshold of adequate legal convergence the Court has chosen to disallow measures that purport to protect social groups whose diligence and sense of personal responsibility is less than average. It is a clear signal that the single market agenda must not be allowed to atrophy under claims for establishing more regulation than required.

## Risks and prudential regulatory concerns caused by electronic banking activities

Notwithstanding the significant benefits of technological innovation and the growth of electronic finance, the rapid development of electronic banking applications carries risks as well as benefits and it is important that these risks are identified and managed by financial institutions in a prudent manner under the supervisory oversight of regulatory agencies.

The regulatory approach towards electronic finance internationally can be summarized by the concept of technological neutrality: in enforcing applicable laws regulatory agencies shall make no distinction between different channels for delivering financial services except in cases where the medium generates special risks that justify special regulatory treatment. The general framework of financial regulation and supervision applies to online financial services but specific rules relating to e-finance are introduced to address special risks where appropriate.

Starting with financial risks, the impact of the Internet on the essential elements and structure of banking services and products has largely been manageable and less dramatic than its impact on operational and non-financial risks. The risk of the borrower's default in the business of lending, the risk of liquidity shortages and the risk of losses due to movements in asset prices and interest rates in the inter-bank, foreign exchange and securities markets are not affected by electronic banking applications as much as the operational and legal risks associated with the use of advanced technologies in the financial sector. Financial institutions are however advised to review their lending policies in the light of the impersonal nature of electronic finance and consider the liquidity implications of providing their customers with direct access to deposit accounts.[43]

---

[43] See Basel Committee, 'Electronic Banking Risk Management Issues for Bank Supervisors', in *Electronic Banking Group Initiatives and White Papers* (Basel: BIS, 2000).

With regard to non-financial risks, financial institutions and supervisory authorities have identified a wide range of risks associated with e-finance applications, such as the virtually total reliance on automated operations and information technology, the remote interaction with customers and other market participants over publicly accessible computer networks, the constant innovation in internal systems and procedures and the vast concentration of sensitive data in inter-connected and electronically administered databases.[44]

As early as in 1977, the US National Commission on Electronic Fund Transfers attributed the link between electronic banking and IT security issues to the fact that electronic banking entails the flow of information by electronic means, the proliferation of electronic records and easier access to protected information.[45] One of the main concerns in that respect is the security of systems and procedures. The 'open network' structure of the Internet as a means of delivery of banking services creates new security issues for banks with respect to confidentiality, protection and integrity of information, non-repudiation of properly authorized transactions, authentication of users, control and prevention of unauthorized access to the bank's electronic systems and banking applications.

In addition to ensuring a secure internal network for conducting electronic banking activities, financial institutions recognize the importance of ensuring the uninterrupted availability of services. The failure of information technology systems and networks and the resulting denial and unavailability of service are commonly attributable to limited capacity to handle large volumes of transactions or, less frequently, to intentional action by malicious third parties. In any case, poor capacity planning and ineffective systems of network security may potentially undermine consumer confidence and the reputation of online banking operators.

From a legal perspective, the special prudential regulatory interest in the safety and security of electronic banking operations complements a wide range of legal and regulatory institutions that share the same objective, such as the criminal law of computer misuse, the duty of bank secrecy

---

[44] See generally European Central Bank, *The Effects of Technology on the EU Banking Systems* (Frankfurt, 1999); Basel Committee, *Risk Management Principles*; Deutsche Bundesbank, 'Electronic Banking from a Prudential Supervisory Perspective', *Monthly Report*, December 2000, 43–58; Banque de France and Commission Bancaire, *Internet: The Prudential Consequences* (Paris, 2000); Financial Services Authority, *The FSA's Approach to the Regulation of E-Commerce* (London, 2001).
[45] See Arora 'Electronic Banking', pp. 139–40.

and the statutory protection of privacy and personal data. The ongoing development and perfection of technical standards and regulatory scrutiny are justified by the economic and systemic consequences of technical failures for consumer confidence and the operation of financial markets.

## Non-EU international initiatives of legal harmonization concerning electronic banking activities

In the domain of international finance, the lack of a formal process of international legal harmonization exists side by side with the relentless production of legally informal standards, rules, codes and principles by an assortment of international standard-setting bodies such as the Basel Committee, IOSCO, the Financial Action Task Force of the OECD (FATF) and many others.[46] These rules and standards aim to distil and set out the recommended mode of conduct of national authorities and market participants in almost every conceivable aspect of financial regulation, including but not limited to prudential banking regulation, investor protection and market integrity, corporate governance and money laundering. The principal driving force of international cooperation in the production of international financial standards is the observation that globally integrated markets require international institutions to solve collective problems that permeate national boundaries and can only be addressed through coordinated corrective action at the international level. It was also felt at the aftermath of the regional financial crises of the late 1990s that in most developing and emerging market countries the pertinent crises were caused or at least exacerbated, among other things, by the inadequacies of domestic legal and regulatory institutions in the field of financial regulation and supervision.[47] As most of these countries lacked the required technical capacity and resources to propose and implement those essential standards that would strengthen national financial systems, the task was promptly assigned to established international groups of experts.[48]

---

[46] See Mario Giovanoli, 'A New Architecture for the Global Financial Market: Legal Aspects of International Financial Standard Setting' in Mario Giovanoli (ed.), *International Monetary Law: Issues for the New Millennium* (Oxford: Oxford University Press, 2000).
[47] See Group of Ten, 'Report of the Working Party on Financial Stability in Emerging Market Economies' (1997), pp. 15–19.
[48] See World Bank and International Monetary Fund, *International Standards: Strengthening Surveillance, Domestic Institutions and International Markets* (Washington DC, 2003), p. 4.

Moving from the policy rationale to its components, the process of setting international financial law standards is decentralized and based on informal arrangements.[49] From an institutional perspective, a great number and variety of institutions, entities and bodies are involved in developing the standards, while other organizations such as the IMF play a coordinating and 'supervisory' role as a result of their institutional function and broad membership. On the basis of their legal form and membership, the list of standard-setting institutions includes fully-fledged international organizations (IMF, OECD), de facto political groupings (G-7, G-10, G-20), sector-specific international groups of national officials and experts (Basel Committee, IOSCO, International Accounting Standards Board, FATF), cross-sector bodies with a coordinating role such as the Financial Stability Forum, associations of market professionals and institutions concerned with the harmonization of aspects of private law relating to international finance (the United Nations Commission on International Trade Law (UNCITRAL), the International Institute for the Unification of Private Law (UNIDROIT), the Hague Conference).[50]

The coverage *rationae materiae* of the standards is broad. The core list would probably include principles for bank capital adequacy[51] and effective banking regulation and supervision,[52] objectives and principles for securities regulation,[53] payment and settlement systems,[54] actions against money laundering[55] and corporate governance.[56] Equally

---

[49] See Giovanoli, *A New Architecture*, p. 10.
[50] The Hague Conference on private international law is a global inter-government organization, comprising more than fifty Member States. The activities of the Conference are administered by a small operating unit – the Permanent Bureau – located in The Hague. Between 1951 and 2005, the Conference drafted thirty-six international Conventions that have had a profound influence upon national legal systems, in both Member and non-Member States. Among the Conventions adopted by the Conference, the Convention on the Law Applicable to Certain Rights in respect of Securities held with an Intermediary has been instrumental in the harmonization of the law relating to international securities and capital markets transactions (http://www.hcch.net/index-en.php).
[51] See Basel Committee, *International Convergence of Capital Measurement and Capital Standards: A Revised Framework* (Basel: BIS, 2004).
[52] Basel Committee, 'Core Principles'.
[53] See IOSCO, *Objectives and Principles for Securities Regulation* (Madrid, 2002).
[54] See Committee on Payment and Settlement Systems (CPSS), *Core Principles for Systemically Important Payments Systems* (Basel, 2001); CPSS, *Recommendations for Securities Settlement Systems* (Basel, 2001).
[55] See Financial Action Task force, *The Forty Recommendations* (Paris, 2003).
[56] See Organization for Economic Cooperation and Development, *Principles of Corporate Governance* (Paris, 2004).

relevant for online financial services are a number of 'soft' harmonization initiatives in the field of 'private' financial law,[57] consumer protection in the delivery of financial services,[58] electronic commerce,[59] security of information systems and networks[60] and data protection.[61]

With specific regard to electronic banking activities, the design and implementation of sound regulatory and supervisory practices has been assigned to the Electronic Banking Group of the Basel Committee on Banking Supervision. From its establishment in 1975 as an informal forum of representatives of the Governors of central banks (and supervisory authorities) of key developed nations, the Basel Committee has played a dominant role in the formulation of broad supervisory principles and guidelines of best practice with the aim to strengthen the stability of the international financial system. Despite the Committee's lack of formal status under international law, its non-binding recommendations have found their way into national law and enforcement practices and shaped regulatory standards at the national and EU levels.

The involvement of the Basel Committee in the formulation of regulatory standards and principles for Internet banking activities is an integral part of the Committee's broader agenda to strengthen regulatory and supervisory control in the light of the unique nature and risks associated with different financial activities.

The Committee's first contribution came in 1989 with a short paper on the *Risks in Computers and Telecommunications Systems* which stressed the importance of senior management responsibility, rigorous systems of internal control and regular audit operations for efficient and secure computer and telecommunications systems.[62] In 1998, the Committee reviewed the changes in the risk profile of electronic banking

---

[57] See United Nations Commission on International Trade Law (UNCITRAL), *Model Law on International Credit Transfers* (1992); UNCITRAL, *Legal Guide on Electronic Funds Transfers* (1987).

[58] See UN Guidelines for Consumer Protection (Resolution 39) (New York, 1985); OECD, *Guidelines for Protecting Consumers from Fraudulent and Deceptive Practices Across Borders* (Paris, 2003).

[59] See UNCITRAL *Model Law on Electronic Signatures* (2001); UNCITRAL *Model Law on Electronic Commerce* (1996); International Chamber of Commerce, *Guidelines on Advertising and Marketing on the Internet* (Paris, 1998).

[60] See OECD, *Guidelines for the Security of Information Systems and Networks* (Paris, 2002).

[61] See OECD, *Guidelines on the Protection of Privacy and Transborder Flows of Personal Data* (Paris, 1980); Council of Europe Convention of 28 January 1981 for the Protection of Individuals with Regard to Automatic Processing of Personal Data (1981).

[62] See Basel Committee, *Risks in Computers and Telecommunications Systems* (Basel: BIS, 1989).

activities[63] and considered it appropriate to establish an *ad hoc* working group with the mandate to look into the regulatory aspects of electronic banking activities.

The first report of the Electronic Banking Group of the Basel Committee on risk management and supervisory issues arising from e-banking developments was released in October 2000.[64] The report carried out a survey of risks associated with the impact of technology in electronic banking operations and set out broad principles of an effective and proportionate supervisory response based on the following principles: the development of regulatory standards which do not inhibit innovation and competition; the importance of senior management involvement and responsibility; adaptation to continuing market developments; and international supervisory cooperation and exchange of information on risks, market developments and national responses.

The final version of the Electronic Banking Group's guidelines for risk management for electronic banking activities was released in July 2003.[65] The Committee reaffirmed the high level principles summarized in its earlier work and proposed fourteen principles for strengthening the safety and soundness of banks providing electronic banking services:

(a) establish effective senior management responsibility and oversight of e-banking activities; a rigorous process of security control; and due diligence in sourcing out e-banking functions;
(b) operate security controls for authenticating customers; ensure non-repudiation and accountability of transactions; separate the corporate functions concerning the administration of duties relating to e-banking systems, databases and applications; protect the integrity of data in transactions and electronic records; ensure that clear audit trails exist for all electronic transactions; preserve the confidentiality of information;
(c) disclose information on the bank's corporate and regulatory status; ensure full compliance with customer privacy legal requirements; ensure that the availability of service is guaranteed by effective business capacity, continuity and contingency planning; implement contingency plans to deal with unexpected external events, including malicious action.

---

[63] Basel Committee, *Risk Management For Electronic Banking and Electronic Money Activities* (Basel: BIS, 1998).
[64] See Basel Committee, *Electronic banking*.
[65] Basel Committee, *Risk Management Principles*.

## EU harmonization measures in the field of prudential banking regulation

The European harmonization of prudential regulatory standards is now quite advanced dating back to the First and Second Banking Directives.[66] The Banking Directive currently in force is the cornerstone of this legislative programme.[67] It consolidates seven core and twelve amending directives relating to credit institutions in one single text.[68] As a measure adopted pursuant to Article 47(2) EC, the Directive harmonizes the law relating to the 'taking-up' and 'pursuit' of banking activities, essentially the law of prudential banking regulation and supervision. From a regulatory perspective, the Directive strengthened the 'safety and soundness' of credit institutions operating in the single market. From a 'liberalization' perspective, it created the essential level of legal convergence as basis for the operation of the single 'passport' for banking services by neutralizing the risk that mutual recognition may generate regulatory competition in supervisory laxity.[69]

The Directive harmonizes the national law relating to bank licensing,[70] initial capitalization,[71] place of administration and incorporation,[72] composition, integrity and quality of management,[73] control of shareholders,[74] business names,[75] financial reports,[76] adequacy of regulatory capital,[77] restrictions on large exposures to credit risk[78] and participation of credit institutions in non-financial companies.[79] Moreover, the Directive requires the close cooperation of national regulatory agencies,[80] introduces the agencies' duty of professional secrecy,[81] which cannot however prevent the exchange of information between national authorities or other law enforcement agencies,[82] and establishes the right of judicial redress of credit institutions against unlawful supervisory

---

[66] Council Directive 77/780/EEC of 12 December 1977 on the coordination of laws, regulations and administrative provisions relating to the taking up and pursuit of the business of credit institutions, OJ 1977 No. L322/30, 17 December 1977; Council Directive 89/646/EEC of 15 December 1989 on the coordination of laws, regulations and administrative provisions relating to the taking up and pursuit of the business of credit institutions, OJ 1989 No. L386/1, 30 December 1989.

[67] See Council and EP Directive 2000/12/EC of 20 March 2000 relating to the taking up and pursuit of the business of credit institutions, OJ 2000, No. L126/1, 26 May 2000.

[68] See recital 1. [69] See recitals 3 and 7. [70] See arts. 4, 9, 10, 13, 14.
[71] See art. 5. [72] See art. 6(2). [73] See arts. 6(1) and 17.
[74] See arts. 7 and 16. [75] See art. 15. [76] See art. 31.
[77] See arts. 34–47. [78] See arts. 48–50. [79] See art. 51.
[80] See art. 28. [81] See art. 30. [82] See art. 30(2).

actions. The Directive does not preclude Member States from establishing their own national standards of prudential supervision. Provided that the minimum rules are transposed into national law, Member States retain full discretion to regulate national markets by selecting the scope,[83] intensity,[84] method and instruments of regulatory intervention and enforcement.

Other EU measures that complement the Banking Consolidation Directive in regulating the 'internal organisation' and 'soundness' of credit institutions are the Directive on Financial Conglomerates,[85] the Directive on the Reorganisation and Winding-Up of Credit Institutions,[86] the Bank Accounts Directive,[87] the Deposit-Guarantee[88] and Investor Compensation[89] Directives and the Money Laundering Directive.[90]

The Money Laundering Directive is, alongside the Council of Europe Convention on Laundering, Search, Seizure and Confiscation of the Proceeds from Crime,[91] the European response to the international legal apparatus against the legitimization of the proceeds of crime. It requires banks to identify their customers in all initial transactions,[92] particularly when the customer is not physically present for identification

---

[83] See recitals 17, 22, 34, 35; arts. 5(1), 17, and 31.
[84] See recital 12; arts. 31, 47, and 49(4).
[85] See Council and EP Directive 2002/87/EC of 16 December 2002 on the supplementary supervision of credit institutions, insurance undertakings and investment firms in a financial conglomerate, OJ 2003, No. L35/1, 11 February 2003.
[86] See Council and EP Directive 2001/24/EC of 4 April 2001 on the reorganisation and winding up of credit institutions, OJ 2001, No. L125/15, 5 May 2001.
[87] See Council Directive 86/635/EEC of 8 December 1986 on the annual accounts and consolidated accounts of banks and other financial institutions, OJ 1986, No. L372/1, 31 December 1986.
[88] Directive 94/19/EC. See above note 5.
[89] See Council and EP Directive 97/9/EC of 3 March 1997 on investor-compensation schemes, OJ 1997, No. L84/22, 26 March 1997.
[90] See Council Directive 91/308/EEC of 10 June 1991 on prevention of the use of the financial system for the purpose of money laundering, OJ 1991, No. L166/77, 28 June 1991.
[91] Council of Europe Convention on Laundering, Searches, Seizure and Confiscation, Strasburg, 8 November 1990, 30 ILM 148, 150 (entered into force 1 September 1993). This Convention was recently updated, to include provisions against the financing of international terrorism, by the Council of Europe Convention on Laundering, Search, Seizure and Confiscation of the Proceeds from Crime and on the Financing of Terrorism, Warsaw, 16 May 2005, Council of Europe Treaty Series – No. 198 (not yet effective), available at http://conventions.coe.int/Treaty/EN/Treaties/Word/198.doc (last visited 27 February 2006).
[92] See art. 3(1).

purposes,[93] in all transactions above a specified value[94] and in all suspicious transactions.[95] It also requires financial institutions to keep records of their dealings with their clients,[96] to cooperate with enforcement authorities,[97] to train staff and maintain rigorous internal control mechanisms.[98] Member States are free to adopt stricter provisions.[99]

## The prudential regulation of electronic banking activities in key European countries

### Prudential regulation in the United Kingdom

The treatment of electronic banking activities by the FSA is a core aspect of the FSA's risk-based and qualitative approach to regulation and supervision, which requires regulatory agencies to promote the safety and stability of the financial system without inhibiting technological innovation and enterprise.

The FiSMA 2000 is the statutory framework of that supervisory approach. In discharging its functions, the FSA must have regard to the principle that the burdens of regulation should be proportionate to the expected benefits and the desirability to facilitating innovation, thus minimizing the adverse effects of regulation on competition and using scarce supervisory resources economically.[100] In considering what degree of consumer protection is appropriate, the Authority must have regard to the differing degrees of risk associated with different transactions; the differing degrees of experience and expertise that different kinds of consumer may have; the needs that consumers may have for advice and accurate information and the general principle that consumers should take responsibility for their decisions.[101] The FSA has also promised to create incentives for voluntary compliance, to focus its supervisory resources on areas of greater risk to statutory objectives, to identify risks before they occur, to select the most appropriate and proportionate regulatory tool available and to take full advantage of technology in improving efficiency, understanding markets and delivering information to consumers.[102]

---

[93] See art. 3(11).
[94] See art. 3(2).
[95] See art. 3(8).
[96] See art. 3(11).
[97] See arts. 6, 8 and 9.
[98] See art. 11.
[99] See art. 15.
[100] See FiSMA 2000, s. 2(3).
[101] See ibid., s. 5(2).
[102] See FSA Supervision (SUP) 1.3G and ENF 1.3G.

With regard to electronic finance, the FSA summarized its position in June 2001.[103] In general, the FSA endorses technological innovation in the financial services industry and pledges not to impose special regulatory restrictions on regulated electronic financial activities unless the specific activity in question poses a risk to the four statutory objectives of maintaining systemic confidence, protecting consumers, eliminating financial crime and promoting public understanding of the financial system.[104] It further confirms that it does not discriminate in its supervisory approach on the basis of delivery channel alone, unless the risks to the statutory objectives justify it.[105] The overarching principle is that electronic commerce in financial services is subject to the full regulatory framework of the FiSMA 2000, the statutory instruments enacted under the authority of the Act and the FSA Handbook. Internet-related regulatory risks are adequately addressed through careful adaptation of the existing rules in appropriate circumstances.[106]

A number of regulatory requirements in the FSA Handbook are particularly relevant for the management and containment of operational risks relating to electronic banking activities. As a general principle of sound financial operations, regulated financial institutions must conduct their business with due skill, care and diligence and take reasonable care to organize and control their affairs responsibly and effectively, with adequate risk management systems.[107] With particular regard to the management of operational risks, regulated financial institutions must take care to establish and maintain appropriate systems and controls that can arise in response to inadequacies or failures in their processes and systems (and, as appropriate, the systems and processes of third-party suppliers, agents and others).[108] In doing so, financial institutions should have regard to the nature, scale, diversity and complexity of their operations.[109] These regulatory principles are further specified with particular regard to IT systems and networks.

For the purposes of the FSA Handbook, IT systems include the computer systems and infrastructure required for the automation of

---

[103] See FSA, Regulation of E-Commerce.
[104] See *ibid.*, pp. 11–15.
[105] *Ibid.*
[106] See pp. 31–43.
[107] See FSA Handbook, PRIN 2.1 R.
[108] See *ibid.*, SYSC 3.1.1 R and SYSC 3A.7.1 G.
[109] *Ibid.*

processes, such as application and operating system software; network infrastructure; and desktop, server, and mainframe hardware.[110] The FSA requires financial institutions to establish and maintain systems and controls for the management of their IT system risks, having regard to their organizational structure, the extent to which technology requirements are addressed in their business strategy, the appropriateness of their systems acquisition, development and maintenance activities and their activities supporting IT systems and networks.[111]

The FSA is also concerned with failures in processing information and the security of the systems and networks which can lead to significant operational losses. Hence, regulated financial institutions are required to establish and maintain appropriate systems and controls to address their information security risks,[112] with particular regard to confidentiality,[113] integrity,[114] availability and authentication,[115] non-repudiation and accountability.[116]

In addition to the generally applicable regulatory standards, a separate set of prudential standards, reserved exclusively for banks, are set out in the *Interim Prudential Sourcebook for Banks* which continues to apply until the phased implementation of the *Integrated Prudential Sourcebook* (PRU(FSA)).[117] The purpose of the prudential standards applying to *banks* is to ensure that banks maintain capital and other financial resources commensurate with their risks and appropriate systems and controls to enable them to manage those risks. With particular regard to the management of operational risks relating to Internet banking

---

[110] See FSA Handbook, SYSC 3A.7.5 G.
[111] See *ibid.*, SYSC 3A.7.6 G.
[112] See *ibid.*, SYSC 3A.7.7 G.
[113] 'Information should be accessible only to persons or systems with appropriate authority, which may require firewalls within a system, as well as entry restrictions' (FSA Handbook, SYSC 3A. 7.7G(1)).
[114] 'Safeguarding the accuracy and completeness of information and its processing' (FSA Handbook, SYSC 3A. 7.7. G(2)).
[115] 'Ensuring that appropriately authorised persons or systems have access to the information when required and that their identity is verified' (FSA Handbook, SYSC 3A. 7.7 G(3)).
[116] 'Ensuring that the person or system that processed the information cannot deny their actions' (FSA Handbook, SYSC 3A. 7.7 G(4)).
[117] From 31 December 2004 the FSA began the phased implementation for banks of its Integrated Prudential Sourcebook. This will eventually replace the set of sectoral prudential sourcebooks applied on an interim basis, including the Interim Prudential Sourcebook applying to banks.

activities, the standards and principles set out in the 'AR' section of the Sourcebook (Accounting and Other Records and Internal Control Systems) are worth mentioning.

In particular, the FSA puts banks on notice that the information held in electronic form within a bank's information systems is a valuable asset that needs to be protected against unauthorized access and disclosure.[118] It is the responsibility of management to understand the extent to which a bank relies upon electronic information, to assess the value of that information and to establish an appropriate system of controls. According to the FSA, the types of risk most often associated with the use of information technology in financial systems may be classified as follows:[119]

(1) Fraud and theft: access to information and systems can create opportunities for the manipulation of data in order to create or conceal significant financial loss. Additionally, information can be stolen, even without its physical removal or awareness of the fact, which may lead to loss of competitive advantage. Such unauthorized activity can be committed by persons with or without legitimate access rights.
(2) Errors: although they most frequently occur during the manual inputting of data and the development or amendment of software, errors can be introduced at every stage in the life cycle of an information system.
(3) Interruption: the components of electronic systems are vulnerable to interruption and failure; without adequate contingency arrangements this can lead to serious operational difficulty and/or financial loss.
(4) Misinformation: problems may emerge in systems that have been poorly specified or inaccurately developed. These might become immediately evident, but can also pass undetected for a period during which they could undermine the veracity of supposedly sound information. This is a particular risk in systems where audit trails are poor and the processing of individual transactions difficult to follow.

As to the appropriate response to these challenges, the FSA requires that management be aware of its responsibility to promote and maintain

---

[118] See FSA Handbook, AR 3.3.6 (19).
[119] See *ibid.*, AR 3.3.6 (20).

a climate of security awareness and vigilance throughout the organization. In particular, senior managers should give consideration to (a) IT security education and training, designed to make all relevant staff aware of the need for, and their role in supporting, good IT security practice and the importance of protecting company assets; and (b) IT security policy, standards, procedures and responsibilities, designed to ensure that arrangements are adequate and appropriate.[120]

### Prudential regulation in France

The supervision of banks in France is carried out in accordance with the provisions of the *Code Monétaire et Financier* (Monetary and Financial Code), secondary legislation and regulatory standards issued by the competent authorities. The Code was enacted in December 2000 consolidating in one single text the entire body of banking and financial services law.[121] In August 2003, the Financial Security Act[122] established a single supervisory agency with responsibility in the domain of investment services and capital markets, the *Autorité des Marchés Financiers* (Financial Markets Authority),[123] consolidating three regulatory agencies.[124] The reform was limited to the institutional structure of supervision without affecting the applicable regulatory standards. Similarly, except for the transfer of primary rule-making powers from the *Comité de la Réglementation Bancaire et Financière* (CRBF) to the Ministry of Economic Affairs,[125] the institutional structure of banking regulation and supervision remained unaffected. The licensing procedure of newly established banks is still administered by the *Comité des Etablissements de Crédit et des Entreprises d'Investissement*,[126] who is also the 'competent authority' for purposes of administration of the single European 'passport' for banking and investment services.[127] The *Banque de France*, the country's influential central bank, and the *Commission Bancaire* retained

---

[120] See *ibid.*, AR 3.3.6 (21).
[121] See Ordonnance No. 2000–1223, 14 December 2000.
[122] See Loi No. 2003–706, 1 August 2003.
[123] See C.Monét.fin., art. L 621(1).
[124] The Commission des Opérations de Bourse (COB), the *Conseil des Marchés Financiers* and the Conseil de Discipline de la Gestion Financière (CDGF).
[125] See C.monét.fin., art. L 611(1).
[126] See art. L 612(1).
[127] See art. L 612(2).

their overall responsibility for carrying out the prudential supervision of banks and administering the deposit insurance scheme.[128]

The primary source of prudential regulation is the fifth book of the French Monetary and Financial Code and the technical details are found in secondary regulatory instruments. Overall, the legal and institutional framework accords with international standards of good regulatory practice and implements the relevant EU measures relating to banking regulation and supervision.[129] The supervisory approach is based on risk and varies from case to case depending on the specific risk profile of the regulated entity.[130]

There are specific regulatory standards addressing the risks associated with electronic finance. Financial institutions are required to establish and maintain robust and efficient systems of internal control,[131] so as to ensure compliance will applicable law, the swift flow of information to senior management, the integrity of accounting and reporting systems and the functionality and security of IT applications, networks and telecommunications.[132] It is also required that applicable systems of internal control are adaptable to the development of new services and delivery channels and the emergence of new types of risk.[133] The security of computer networks and electronic data should be periodically tested and contingency plans must be in place to ensure the continuity of operations in case of disruptive events.[134]

The treatment of electronic banking activities by the *Banque de France* and the *Commission Bancaire* was the subject of public consultation, with the final position contained in the White Paper on the Prudential Consequences of the Internet published in December 2000.[135] The French authorities emphasized the largely 'unexceptional' characteristics of electronic banking activities, which should be subject to the entire

---

[128] See art. L 613(3).
[129] See Gavalda and Stoufflet, Droit Bancaire, pp. 35–75; International Monetary Fund, *Assessment of the Compliance by France with the 1997 Basel Committee's Core Principles for Effective Banking Supervision* (Washington DC, 2001).
[130] See Jean-Louis Fort, *Banking Supervision and the Evolution of Banking Risks* (General Secretary, *Commission Bancaire* (Speech Delivered on the Occasion of the Bicentennial of the Bank of France, Paris, 25 May 2000).
[131] See C.monét.fin., art. L 511(41); Règlement No. 97-02, 21 February 1997.
[132] See Règlement No. 97-02, art. 5.
[133] See art. 11.
[134] See art. 14.
[135] See Banque de France, *Internet and Prudential Consequences*.

body of banking law and regulation.[136] Attention was drawn to the applicable regulatory requirements to establish rigorous mechanisms of internal control so as to ensure the safe conduct of electronic banking operations.[137] The security of computer networks, electronic data and IT systems is the subject of prudential supervision from the very moment that an application for authorization to engage in electronic banking activities is filed.[138] Of particular supervisory interest are cases where certain internal functions relating to information technology applications and networks are outsourced to external providers, in which case the agencies require that the allocation of primary responsibility and risks between the financial institution and the service provider be clear and transparent.[139] During the authorization stage the agency collects information concerning the structure of IT networks and systems and contingency plans so as to form a view on the safety and soundness of the proposed venture. Once the licence to engage in electronic banking activities has been granted, the bank is required to vest responsibility for designing and implementing the security of computer networks and systems with senior managers,[140] to update and test it regularly[141] and to provide adequate safeguards against unauthorized access,[142] abuse of customer data[143] and unavailability of service due to technical failures.[144]

## Prudential regulation in Germany

Prudential regulation and supervision in Germany are carried out in accordance with the Banking Act and other secondary statutory and regulatory instruments.[145] In 2002, the Integrated Financial Services Supervision Act[146] established the Federal Financial Supervisory Authority (*Bundesanstalt für Finanzdienstleistungsaufsicht – BaFin*) as a single financial services authority which assumed the functions of three separate agencies, each one formerly responsible for banking, securities or insurance regulation. The complementary role of the *Bundesbank* in various stages of the supervisory process remained unchanged.[147]

---

[136] See pp. 31–2.   [137] See pp. 96–7.   [138] See p. 103.
[139] See pp. 103–4.   [140] See p. 109.   [141] *Ibid.*
[142] *Ibid.*   [143] See p. 111.   [144] See p. 110.
[145] See generally H.-P. Burghof and B. Rudolph, *Bankenaufsicht: Theorie und Praxis der Regulierung* (Wiesbaden: Wiesbaden Gabler Verlag, 1996).
[146] See Finanzdienstleistungsaufsichtsgesetz (FinDAG).
[147] See KWG, § 7.

German authorities have fully endorsed the principle of risk-based qualitative and measured supervision, alongside the operation of quantitative constraints, and this principle informs their approach to supervising electronic banking activities.[148] In the 2000 Annual Report, the Banking Supervisory Office (BAKRED) highlighted the role of computer networks and IT applications in generating new risks in the business of banking.[149] Safeguarding the security and continuity of networks and systems was regarded as the main regulatory concern and the agency stressed its determination to address these issues nationally and through cooperation at the international level, primarily within the Electronic Banking Group of the Basel Committee.[150] The Authority released a statement in January 2001[151] where it manifested its belief that the best response to security and continuity risks is what may be termed regulation through 'code' (or technology) rather than legal formalism. The most appropriate response was the establishment of sound security measures through investment in secure systems and IT applications. In that regard, the Office committed to working closely with the experts, in particular the Bundesamt für Sicherheit in der Informationstechnik (BSI) (Federal Agency for Security in Information Technology), so as to identify the most appropriate technologies and security measures for online banks. Moreover, the Supervisory Office endorsed the recommendations of the BSI for building a security strategy in three levels, namely the protection of communication, the verification of identity of the communication partners and the security of system components,[152] in accordance with international standards of good practice such as internal and external access controls with security devices, firewalls, contingency plan and similar practices.[153]

The *Bundesbank* issued a statement on *Electronic Banking from a Prudential Supervisory Perspective* in December 2000.[154] It too confirmed the principle of 'neutrality' of law towards different delivery channels.[155] Care, however, must be taken to adapt traditional principles to the

---

[148] See Federal Banking Supervisory Office, *Annual Report 2000* (Bonn, 2001), pp. 11–12.
[149] See *ibid.*, pp. 8–11.
[150] *Ibid.*
[151] See Federal Banking Supervisory Office, *German Banking Supervisors to Perform Security Analyses of E-Banking Platforms* (Press Release) (Bonn, 18 January 2001).
[152] See Federal Banking, Annual Report 2000, p. 21.
[153] See *ibid.*, pp. 23–4.
[154] See Deutsche Bundesbank, *Electronic Banking*.
[155] See *ibid.*, p. 56.

new risks associated with Internet technology.[156] To that end, it proposed 'minimum requirements for the conduct of e-banking activities' with emphasis on the security of computer networks and systems and emphasized that any special prudential standards for electronic banking activities should develop strict rules regarding the security and robustness of IT resources and networks.[157] That would entail, for instance, the bank explaining to the agency its e-banking strategy and how it fits into the bank's overall business strategy.

On the micro-level of security policy, banks are expected to invest in secure network and IT systems, to adopt appropriate systems of internal control and to review regularly the performance of those systems. The *Bundesbank* endorses the idea of international cooperation for the purpose of responding efficiently to the challenges of the new business model.[158]

---

[156] *Ibid.*
[157] See *ibid.*, p. 57.
[158] See *ibid.*, p. 58.

# 6

# EU measures of legal harmonization concerning electronic commerce and distance marketing of financial services, data protection, banking contracts and investor protection

Following the discussion on the level of convergence of prudential regulatory standards, this chapter turns on the legal convergence of non-prudential national laws and regulations relating to electronic banking activities. The discussion begins with laws of general application to online financial services such as the E-Commerce[1] and Distance Marketing[2] Directives and subsequently turns to rules governing specific types of electronic banking activities such as rules relating to consumer credit, electronic funds transfers and online securities activities.

## E-commerce and distance marketing of financial services

The provision of banking and financial services via the Internet is subject to national laws implementing the E-Commerce and Distance Marketing Directives. By establishing consumer protection requirements and facilitating the formation of financial contracts electronically, the two Directives are the basic components of the institutional framework for online financial services in the single European market.

### The E-Commerce Directive

The aim of the Directive is to approximate the laws of the Member States to the extent necessary for ensuring the free movement of 'information society services' in the European internal market.[3] It applies only to

---

[1] EP and Council Directive 2000/31/EC of 8 June 2000 on certain legal aspects of information society services, in particular electronic commerce, in the internal market, OJ 2000 No. L1781, 17 July 2000.

[2] EP and Council Directive 2002/65/EC of 23 September 2002 concerning the distance marketing of consumer financial services, OJ 2002 No. 27115, 9 October 2002.

[3] See E-Commerce Directive, art. 1.

'information society services' which are defined as any service normally provided for remuneration, at a distance, by means of electronic equipment for the processing and storage of data, and at the individual request of a recipient of service.[4] It suffices to note here that the Directive applies to a wide range of services provided via the Internet, including services which are not remunerated by those who receive them, such as the availability of online information, commercial communications, access to and retrieval of data.[5]

## The subject-matter of harmonization

The Directive harmonizes national provisions relating to the establishment of firms engaging in electronic commerce activities, the right to provide online services in the single European market, commercial communications, electronic contracts and the liability of intermediaries. It does not override but merely complements the level of legal convergence already achieved by the remainder of EU measures relating to financial services.[6] The Directive prohibits Member States from rendering the establishment and operation of websites and the provision of online services subject to initial authorization requirements or equivalent administrative formalities, provided that the conditions for taking up and pursuing the underlying economic activity have been met.

The most radical institutional reform is perhaps the introduction of the principle of 'country of origin' which will be fully discussed in chapter 8. The Directive aims to eliminate the uncertainty as to which national laws apply to cross-border electronic commerce activities by requiring the country of origin of the service provider to enforce local laws and regulations regardless of the location of the recipient of the services and, simultaneously, the country of destination of services to refrain from restricting online services originating in another Member State.[7] Given the limited scope of legal harmonization achieved by the Directive, it is paradoxical that the scope of mutual recognition of national laws under the principle of 'country of origin' applies to virtually all aspects of national law with the exception of consumer contract requirements as we shall see in chapter 8. This oddity seems to inaugurate unprecedented tactics towards the completion of the internal market. In contrast with earlier EU Directives, which carefully established the

---

[4] *Ibid.*, art. 2(a).   [5] See recital 18.
[6] See recital 11; arts. 1(3), 6, 7.   [7] See art. 3(1), (2).

model of 'home country control' after having approximated the rules being subject thereto, the E-Commerce Directive moved towards the principle of 'country of origin' based upon a seemingly weak basis of prior legal harmonization. It should be noted, however, that the Directive was intended to operate cumulatively to the substantial corpus of EU measures relating to consumer protection and financial services, which had already achieved a high level of legal convergence of national laws relating to electronic commerce activities.

## National implementation

The deadline for Member States to transpose the Directive into national law was 17 January 2002.[8] Despite some delays in certain countries, national laws and regulations have generally been in accordance with its provisions.[9]

In the United Kingdom, the Directive was transposed by the Electronic Commerce (EC Directive) Regulations 2002[10] ('General Regulations') and the Electronic Commerce Directive (Financial Services and Markets) Regulations 2002[11] (the 'Treasury Regulations'). The 'General Regulations' are of general application to online activities and transpose the Directive in its entirety. The 'Treasury Regulations' are of special application to financial activities governed by the FiSMA 2000 and the FSA Handbook and implement the principle of 'country of origin' in cross-border financial services. The Treasury Regulations and the E-Commerce Directive module of the FSA Handbook (ECO) complement but do not override the 'General Regulations' in the field of financial services.[12]

In Germany, the Directive was implemented in most respects by the EGG (E-Commerce Act).[13] A separate regulatory instrument (*Verordnung*) transposed the information and disclosure duties relating to the formation of electronic contracts.[14] Rather than enacting a new statute, the E-Commerce Act implements the Directive by amending the earlier

---

[8] See art. 22(1).
[9] See European Commission, *First Report on the Application of Directive 2000/31/EC on Electronic Commerce*, COM(2003) 702 final.
[10] SI 2002/2013.
[11] SI 2002/1775.
[12] See SI 2002/2013, Explanatory Note.
[13] See *Gesetz über Rechtliche Rahmenbedingungen für den Elektronischer Geschäftsverkehr* (EGG).
[14] See BGB-InfoV.

TDG (Teleservices Act).[15] The purpose of the Teleservices Act is to regulate the entire corpus of electronic information and communication services,[16] which are designed for the individual use of combinable data such as characters, images, or sounds and are based on transmission by means of telecommunication (teleservices).[17]

Teleservices are services offered in the field of individual communication such as online banking[18] as well as goods and services offered and listed in electronically accessible databases with interactive access and direct-order facilities.[19] Teleservices are services which may be provided simultaneously to a potentially unlimited number of users through the transmission of data at no individual request (distribution services)[20] or at the individual request of a single user (on demand services).[21] Online banking services are on-demand teleservices because the relevant data are transmitted electronically at the individual request of a single user.

In France, the E-Commerce Directive was belatedly implemented in June 2004 by Articles 14–28 of Loi 2004-575 (the Act 2004-575 for confidence in the digital economy).[22] The Act defines electronic commerce as the activity by which a person, acting in a professional capacity, offers or performs the provision of goods or services at a distance and by electronic means.[23]

## Distance Marketing Directive

The Distance Marketing Directive is a consumer protection measure which applies to consumer contracts concerning services of a banking, credit, payment, insurance, pension or investment nature,[24] supplied by firms making exclusive use of any means of communication which may be used for the marketing of banking and financial services without the simultaneous physical presence of the supplier and the consumer such

---

[15] See *Gesetz über die Nutzung von Telediensten* (TDG).
[16] See §1 TDG.
[17] *Ibid.*, §2 Abs. 1.
[18] See §2 Abs. 2(1).
[19] See §2 Abs. 2(5).
[20] See §3 Abs. 3.
[21] See §3 Abs. 4.
[22] See Loi No. 2004-575 du 21 Juin 2004 pour la confiance dans l'économie numérique (Electronic Commerce Act).
[23] *Ibid.*, art. 14.
[24] See Distance Marketing Directive, art. 2(b).

as the Internet, mail or telephone.[25] In the case of services consisting of an initial contractual agreement which is followed by successive operations or a series of separate operations of the same nature performed over the time, the Directive applies only to the initial agreement.[26] For example, the consumer protection requirements of the Directive attach in the case of a consumer opening a bank account electronically but do not apply in subsequent services provided in the context of the bank account. If the customer applies for a service of a different nature, the duties imposed by the Directive re-attach.[27]

### The subject-matter of legal harmonization

The Directive establishes harmonized information requirements, which must be met prior to the conclusion of the contract, and the consumers' right of withdrawal. Moreover, the Directive prohibits the unsolicited provision of financial services if the firm makes a request for immediate or deferred payment. Based on the principle that conflicting or inconsistent national rules of consumer protection could impede the functioning of the internal market, the Directive requires Member States to avoid differences in the implementing national provisions,[28] with the exception of the information requirements of Article 3, for which Member States may adopt more stringent standards of consumer protection.[29] Member States are also permitted to extend the scope of application of the Directive to financial services which are not covered by the definitions of Articles 1 and 2.[30] National provisions implementing the Directive should be read and apply cumulatively with the consumer protection requirements imposed by the Consumer Credit,[31] Cross-Border Credit Transfers[32] and Investment Services Directives,[33] which all established similar information requirements.[34] Finally, it should be noted that the

---

[25] *Ibid.*, art. 2(e).
[26] *Ibid.*, 1(2) and recitals 16–17.
[27] See *ibid.*, recital 17.
[28] See *ibid.*, recital 12 and art. 13.
[29] See *ibid.*, art. 4(3).
[30] See *ibid.*, recital 29.
[31] See Council Directive 87/102/EEC of 22 December 1986 on consumer credit, OJ 1987 No. L42/48, 12 February 1987.
[32] See EP and Council Directive 97/5/EC of 27 January 1997 on cross-border credit transfers, OJ 1997 No. L43/25, 14 February 1997.
[33] See Council Directive 93/22/EEC of 10 May 1993 on investment services in the securities field, OJ 1993, No. L141/27, 11 June 1993.
[34] See Distance Marketing Directive, art. 4(1) and recitals 14 and 22.

scope of application of the E-Commerce and Distance Marketing Directives coincides in the case of financial services, which are provided to consumers at a distance by means of electronic equipment for the processing and storage of data. Both Directives apply cumulatively to the provision of banking services electronically.[35] Non-financial services provided at a distance by means of electronic equipment are only subject to the E-Commerce Directive. Financial services provided at a distance by non-electronic means are only subject to the Distance Marketing Directive, unless the recipient of service is not a consumer in which case none of the Directives applies. Financial services provided at a distance by means of electronic equipment to non-consumer recipients are also only subject to the E-Commerce Directive.

## National implementation

The Distance Marketing Directive entered into force in October 2002 and Member States were required to implement the Directive not later than 9 October 2004.[36] In the United Kingdom, the Directive was transposed into national law by the provisions of the Financial Services (Distance Marketing) Regulations 2004 that came into force on 31 October 2004.[37] Furthermore, the Financial Services Authority carried out the necessary amendments of several modules of the FSA Handbook by adopting the Distance Marketing Directive Instrument 2004.[38] The implementation of the Directive by the FSA resulted in changes being made in certain consumer protection requirements imposed by the Handbook, primarily by the Conduct of Business Sourcebook (COB (FSA)). In Germany, the authorities implemented the Directive in December 2004 by enacting the Distance Marketing Act,[39] which updated certain provisions of the Civil Code[40] and the information requirements imposed by the BGB-InfoV.[41] While the general information requirement is prescribed in the Civil Code, the actual information to be provided is listed in the BGB-InfoV. Finally, the French authorities transposed the Directive through the adoption of implementing legislation

---

[35] See recital 6.
[36] See art. 21.
[37] SI 2004/2095.
[38] FSA 2004/39.
[39] See *Gesetz zur Änderung der Vorschriften über Fernabsatzverträge bei Finanzdienstleistungen*.
[40] See §§ 312b–312d BGB.
[41] See § 1 BGB-InfoV.

which amended a range of consumer protection requirements in the Consumer Code.[42]

### The convergence of national laws relating to advertising and distance marketing of online financial services

Following the overview of the basic provisions and methodology of the E-Commerce and Distance Marketing Directives, it is now expedient to examine the attained legal convergence of national laws relating to advertising and marketing of online financial services. Although the normative effect of the two Directives in that field is substantial, information made available electronically via the Internet, which presents or describes the bank's services or simply renders the availability or quality of the services known to potential customers is also subject to the law of advertising, fair trading practices and commercial communications, whether it is of general application or specifically related to the business of banking. There are also several EU measures contributing to legal convergence of national laws in this area, which all apply cumulatively to the provision of banking services via the Internet.

#### Advertising and marketing laws and regulations

The main EU harmonization measure of general application is the Misleading and Comparative Advertising Directive[43] which aims to protect the public from the effects of misleading commercial advertisements and to lay down the conditions for lawfully engaging in comparative advertising.[44] Moreover, most EU Member States are bound by the 1883 Paris Convention for the Protection of Industrial Property,[45] which commits Member States to assure effective protection against acts of unfair competition, such as dishonest practices in industrial or commercial matters, acts creating confusion with the establishment or commercial activities of a competitor, false allegations in the course of trade, and indications or allegations misleading the public as to the

---

[42] See Ordonnance No. 2005-648 du 6 juin 2005 relative à la commercialisation à distance de services financiers auprès des consommateurs (Ordinance 648/2005 of 6 June 2005 relating to the distance marketing of consumer financial services); C.consom., arts. L 121 (20)(8)–121(20)(16).
[43] See Council Directive 84/450/EEC of 10 September 1984 on misleading and comparative advertising, OJ 1984, No. L250/17, 19 September 1984.
[44] See *ibid.*, art. 1.
[45] Paris, 20 March 1883, 11851 UNTS 828.

nature, the characteristics and the suitability for their purpose of goods and services.[46]

The Distance Marketing Directive promotes fairness and transparency in marketing practices by prohibiting the unsolicited provision of financial services to consumers without their prior individual request if there was request for immediate or deferred payment for those services.[47] The E-Commerce Directive established a number of additional regulatory requirements. More specifically, any form of communication designed to promote directly or indirectly the bank's services and any promotional offer by providers of online financial services and which constitutes or forms part of an electronic commerce activity shall

(a) be clearly identifiable as a commercial communication;
(b) clearly identify the person on whose behalf the commercial communication is made;
(c) clearly identify as such any promotional offer (including any discount, premium or gift) and ensure that any conditions which must be met to qualify for it are easily accessible, and presented clearly and unambiguously; and
(d) clearly identify as such any promotional competition or game and ensure that any conditions for participation are easily accessible and presented clearly and unambiguously.[48]

The notion of 'commercial communication' means a communication, in any form, designed to promote, directly or indirectly, the goods, services or image of any person pursuing a commercial, industrial or craft activity or exercising a regulated profession.[49]

The E-Commerce Directive deferred to the Member States to decide whether unsolicited commercial communications by electronic mail (spamming) would be prohibited without the recipient's prior consent (opt-in method) or permitted without the client's prior objection (opt-out method). The Directive merely required Member States to impose a duty on a service provider to ensure that any unsolicited commercial communication sent by him was clearly and unambiguously identifiable as such as soon as it was received.[50] Unsolicited emails promoting

---

[46] Ibid., art. 10bis.
[47] See Distance Marketing Directive, art. 9(1).
[48] See E-Commerce Directive, art. 6.
[49] Ibid., art. 2(f).     [50] Ibid., art. 7(1).

services and products are now subject to national provisions implementing the Directive on Privacy and Electronic Communications.[51] The Directive requires Member States to ensure that a person shall neither transmit nor instigate the transmission of unsolicited communications for the purposes of direct marketing by means of electronic mail unless the recipient of the electronic mail has previously notified the sender that he consents for the time being to such communications being sent by, or at the instigation of, the sender.[52]

Additional protection against unfair marketing practices will be provided by national provisions implementing the 2005 Directive on Unfair Commercial Practices,[53] which aims to clarify consumers' rights and boost cross-border trading by harmonizing EU rules on business-to-consumer commercial practices. The new legislation outlines 'sharp practices' which will be prohibited throughout the EU, such as pressure selling, misleading marketing and unfair advertising. The Directive will complement but not replace the remainder of national provisions regulating marketing and advertising practices. Given the rather general and abstract character of the Directive and the extensive regulatory framework already in place with regard to marketing and promotion of financial services, this Directive is not expected to change significantly the existing legal framework relating to online banking activities.

At the national level and against the context provided by this rich corpus of EU measures, the fairness of advertising and marketing practices is regulated by a hybrid framework consisting of private, administrative and criminal law.[54]

Turning to key European countries and starting with France, the general law of unfair marketing practices is based on civil liability in tort.[55] Unfair acts of competition are actionable in civil courts in accordance with Articles 1382–3 of the French civil code. A rich body of case

---

[51] See EP and Council Directive 2002/58/EC of 12 July 2002 concerning the processing of personal data and the protection of privacy in the electronic communications sector, OJ 2002 No. L201/37, 31 July 2002.
[52] *Ibid.*, art. 13(1).
[53] See EP and Council Directive 2005/29/EC concerning unfair business-to-consumer commercial practices in the internal market, OJ 2005 No. L149/22, 11 June 2005.
[54] See Reiner Schulze and Hans Schulte-Nölke (eds.), *Analysis of National Fairness Laws Aimed at Protecting Consumers in Relation to Precontractual Commercial Practices and the Handling of Consumer Complaints by Business* (Brussels: European Commission, 2003).
[55] See Cédric Montfort, 'France', in Schulze and Schulte-Nölke (eds.), *Analysis of National Fairness Laws*.

law specifies what constitutes 'unfair' conduct such as discrediting or denigrating competitors or their services, creating confusion as to the trader's own identity, business organization and services or profiting at the expense of the work and reputation of others.[56] Misleading advertising carries a criminal penalty,[57] whereas the practice of comparative advertising is permissible on certain conditions in accordance with the provisions implementing the Misleading and Comparative Advertising Directive.[58] Following the implementation of the E-Commerce Directive, unsolicited e-mails are now prohibited unless the client's prior consent has been obtained.[59] Online banks providing information via the Internet are subject to special rules regulating bank advertising. For example, misleading advertising for the purposes of soliciting deposits or promoting banking services is prohibited.[60] The unsolicited offer of banking and investment services to persons other than sophisticated investors is subject to special provisions.[61] The thrust of the French rules is that financial institutions may not address unsolicited offers without the customer's prior consent, without enquiring about the customer's experience and financial circumstances and without informing the customer of the right to walk away from the contract within a period of fourteen days.[62]

In English law, there is no special economic tort of unfair marketing practices, although it is possible that misleading or inaccurate advertising may occasionally satisfy the requirements of special economic torts such as misrepresentation, passing-off or deceit.[63] Basic duties of commercial fairness and transparency are imposed by statutory provisions which prohibit false and misleading representations in the course of providing services,[64] misleading advertisements[65] and the provision of misleading

---

[56] Ibid.
[57] See C.consom., arts. L 121(1), L 121(6) and L 213(1).
[58] Ibid., arts. L 121(8) et seq.
[59] See Loi No. 2004-575, art. 22.
[60] See CA Rennes, 31.03.2000 JCP E 2000, no. 48, p. 1092.
[61] See C.monét.fin., arts. L 341–L 343.
[62] Ibid.
[63] See Hazel Carty, An Analysis of the Economic Torts (Oxford: Oxford University Press, 2000).
[64] See Trade Descriptions Act 1968, s. 4.
[65] See Control of Misleading Advertisements Regulations 1988, SI 1988/915; Consumer Credit Act 1974, s. 46.

price information.[66] Business associations are encouraged to self-regulate their advertising practices.[67]

In the financial context, the provisions of the FiSMA 2000 and the FSA Handbook relating to marketing of financial services and products apply without exception to commercial communications transmitted via the Internet. Any form of communication, including promotional information on a website and e-mails,[68] which is being addressed whether verbally or in legible form to a particular person or group of persons[69] or to the public in general[70] and contains an invitation or inducement to enter or offer to enter into a contract for the conduct of 'regulated activities'[71] must comply with the financial promotion rules of the FSA Handbook, primarily that the promotion must be clear, fair and not misleading.[72] More specifically, firms promoting their online financial activities must take steps to ensure that:

(a) any promotional information is not in any way disguised or misrepresented and that any statement of fact, promise or prediction is clear, fair and not misleading;
(b) any statement of opinion is honestly held and does not contain any false indications, particularly as to the firm's independence, resources and scale of activities, or the scarcity of any investment or service;
(c) its design, content or format does not obscure or disguise any requirement for mandatory disclosure of information; and
(d) any promotional information does not create the impression that the offering was approved by the FSA.[73]

Furthermore, recipients of promotional communications via the Internet must be given the opportunity to view the full text of the relevant key features, contract terms and any other relevant information required by the Handbook.[74] This can be achieved through the use of a hypertext

---

[66] See Consumer Protection Act 1987, s. 20.
[67] See Stephen Weatherill, 'United Kingdom' in Schulze and Schulte-Nölke (eds.), *Analysis of National Fairness Laws*.
[68] See Financial Services and Markets Act 2000 (Financial Promotion) Order 2001, SI 2001/1335, arts. 7(3) and 2(1).
[69] *Ibid.*, art. 6(b).
[70] *Ibid.*, art. 6(c).
[71] See FiSMA 2000, s. 21(8)(a).
[72] See FSA Handbook, PRIN 2.1.1R and COB (FSA) 3.8.4 R.
[73] *Ibid.*, COB (FSA) 3.8.4R and 3.8.5R.
[74] *Ibid.*, COB (FSA) 3.14.5G.

link, as long as it is not hidden away in the body of the text where a recipient could miss it when browsing through the pages.[75] Although the client shall not be prevented from applying for products and services electronically before actually reading the required information, financial institutions must draw the potential client's attention to that information and emphasize the importance of reading it.[76]

With regard to the activity of accepting deposits, the FSA highly recommends that banks comply with the British Bankers' Association Code of Conduct.[77] The terms of this Code apply to the advertising of all interest-bearing accounts with banks and building societies in the United Kingdom. Advertisements circulating via the Internet are subject to the Code. In general, advertisements of interest-bearing current accounts should observe the spirit and letter of this Code, the British Code of Advertising, Sales Promotion and Direct Marketing, the standards imposed by the FSA Handbook and the remainder of applicable legislation. Banks advertising the offering of interest-bearing accounts are required to ensure that potential customers are informed of the nature of any commitment, including the type of deposit (e.g. whether it is a notice account or an instant access account) into which they may enter as a result of responding to an advertisement. They must also ensure that all advertising and promotional material is clear, fair, reasonable and not misleading.

Finally in Germany, the main legal source is the Unfair Competition Act (UWG).[78] Competitive acts which are contrary to honest competitive practices[79] and deceptive advertising statements in the course of business violate the statute.[80] German courts have produced a substantial volume of case law which is reputed to be far more stringent than international standards concerning restrictions on trading practices, although it is currently being updated towards a more liberal approach.[81] Online banks are unexceptionally subject to the general and bank-related law.[82] The federal financial supervisory authority has yet to issue specific rules in

---

[75] Ibid.  [76] Ibid.
[77] See COB (FSA) 3.8.6G; see also British Bankers' Association, *Code of Conduct for the Advertising of Interest Bearing Accounts* (London, 2003).
[78] *Gesetz gegen den Unlauteren Wettbewerb.*
[79] See §1 UWG.
[80] Ibid., §3.
[81] See Hans Schulte-Nölke and others, 'Germany', in Schulze and Schulte-Nölhe (eds.), *Analysis of National Fairness Laws*.
[82] See OLG Coblence, WRP 1997, 874.

exercise of the power granted by the Banking Act to regulate misleading advertising by credit institutions.[83]

## Pre-contractual information requirements

In the interests of transparency and consumer protection, providers of online financial services are required to provide consumers with comprehensive information prior to the contract being formed. Disclosure requirements may be regarded as necessary because of the type of financial product, the nature of the risk or the method of communication between the financial institution and the customer. The application of information requirements by several legal provisions according to the type of financial transactions or methods of delivering financial services is cumulative.[84] Online banking services are subject to national information requirements implementing the E-Commerce Directive, the Distance Marketing Directive and, depending on the specific type of activity, the Consumer Credit or Credit Transfers Directives. Furthermore, these mandatory statutory protections do not override but complement the general law of pre-contractual information such as the common law of misrepresentation and deceit and the civilian doctrine of pre-contractual good faith (*culpa in contrahendo*).[85] Pending further harmonization at the European level, Member States may maintain or adopt more stringent rules than the requirements imposed by the E-Commerce and Distance Marketing Directives.[86]

According to the national statutes implementing the E-Commerce Directive,[87] providers of electronic commerce services are required to make available to the recipient of the service and any relevant enforcement authority, in a form and manner which is easily, directly and permanently accessible, the following information:[88]

(a) the name of the service provider;
(b) the geographic address at which the service provider is established;

---

[83] See §23 KWG.
[84] See Electronic Commerce (EC Directive) Regulations 2002, SI 2002/2013, reg. 10; E-Commerce Directive, recital 11, arts. 1(3) and 5(1); Distance Marketing Directive, art. 4(1).
[85] See Distance Marketing Directive, art. 3(4).
[86] See E-Commerce Directive, art. 5(1); Distance Marketing Directive, art. 4.
[87] See SI 2002/2013, reg. 6; FSA ECO 3 Annex 1R; § 6 TDG; Loi no. 2004-575, arts. 19–21.
[88] See E-Commerce Directive, art. 6.

(c) the details of the service provider, including his electronic mail address, which make it possible to communicate with him in a direct and effective manner;
(d) where the service provider is registered in a trade or similar register available to the public, details of the register in which the service provider is entered and his registration number, or equivalent means of identification in that register;
(e) where the provision of the service is subject to an authorization scheme, the particulars of the relevant supervisory authority; and
(f) where the service provider exercises a regulated profession
   (i) the details of any professional body or similar institution with which the service provider is registered;
   (ii) his professional title and the member State where that title has been granted; and
   (iii) a reference to the professional rules applicable to the service provider in the Member State of establishment and the means to access them; and price information indicating whether prices are inclusive of tax and delivery charges.

To the extent that the provision of online banking services to customers acting for purposes outside their trade or profession falls within the scope of application of national laws implementing the Distance Marketing Directive,[89] a number of additional information requirements attach. The information must be provided in good time before the consumer is bound by any distance contract or offer,[90] in a clear and comprehensible manner with due regard, in particular, to the principles of good faith in commercial transactions, and the principles governing the protection of those who are unable to give their consent such as minors.[91] Furthermore, the supplier of financial services is required to communicate to the consumer on paper or in another durable medium, which is available and accessible to the consumer, all the contractual terms and conditions and the information specified in the Directive either in good time before or immediately after the conclusion of the contract.[92] The definition of 'durable medium' covers any instrument which enables a consumer to store information addressed personally to him in a way accessible for future reference for a period of time adequate for the

---

[89] See pp. 168–70.
[90] See Distance Marketing Directive, art. 3(1).
[91] Ibid., art. 3(2).   [92] Ibid., art. 5(2).

purposes of the information and which allows the unchanged reproduction of the information stored,[93] such as floppy disks, CD-ROMs, DVDs and the hard drive of the consumer's computer on which the electronic mail is stored.[94] The supplier must also communicate the contractual terms and conditions to the consumer on paper, if the consumer so requests during their contractual relationship, unless the supplier had already communicated the contractual terms and conditions to the consumer on paper during that contractual relationship, and those terms and conditions had not changed since they were so communicated.[95] Table 6.1 summarizes the information requirements imposed on providers of online banking services by the combined provisions of the rules implementing the E-Commerce Directive and the rules implementing the Distance Marketing Directive.

## Privacy and data protection

Electronic banking is a data-intensive activity based on the constant processing of financial and personal data internally and their circulation externally among the bank, the customer, supervisory authorities, credit reference agencies, clearing and settlement systems and securities markets. The legal framework aims to reconcile the tension between the protection of personal data, which is a significant aspect of the fundamental human right to show respect for one's private and family life,[96] and the swift circulation and processing of large volumes of data, which is essential in the business of banking. The basic legal instrument is the Data Protection Directive.[97]

The Directive is an 'internal market' measure justified by the importance of the processing of data for a wide range of economic activities in the single market and the real risk that differences in national laws may restrict cross-border transactions.[98] It establishes the principle that the lawful processing of personal data requires the prior consent of the data subject.[99] Exceptionally, no consent is required when the processing

---

[93] Ibid., art. 2(f).    [94] Ibid., recital 20.    [95] Ibid., art. 5.
[96] See Convention for the Protection of Human Rights and Fundamental Freedoms, Rome, 4 November 1950, ETS No. 8, art. 8.
[97] See EP and Council Directive 95/46/EC of 24 October 1995 on the protection of individuals with regard to the processing of personal data and on the free movement of such data, OJ 1995 No. L281/31, 23 November 1995.
[98] Ibid., recital 7.    [99] Ibid., art. 7.

Table 6.1. *Information requirements under ECD and DMD*

*Information concerning the bank*
- the identity and the main business of the supplier, the geographical address at which the supplier is established and any other geographical address relevant for the customer's relations with the supplier (ECD, DMD)
- the details of the service provider, including his electronic mail address, which allow him to be contacted rapidly and communicated with in a direct and effective manner (ECD)
- the identity of the representative of the supplier established in the consumer's Member State of residence and the geographical address relevant for the customer's relations with the representative, if such a representative exists (ECD, DMD)
- where the supplier is registered in a trade or similar public register, the trade register in which the supplier is entered and his registration number or an equivalent means of identification in that register (ECD, DMD)
- the particulars of the relevant supervisory authority (ECD, DMD)

*concerning the service (DMD)*
- a description of the main characteristics of the financial service
- all the contractual terms and conditions which must be in conformity with the contractual obligations which would result from the law presumed to be applicable to the distance contract if the latter were concluded
- the total price to be paid by the consumer to the supplier for the financial service, including all related fees, charges and expenses, and all taxes paid via the supplier or, when an exact price cannot be indicated, the basis for the calculation of the price enabling the consumer to verify it
- where relevant notice indicating that the financial service is related to instruments involving special risks related to their specific features or the operations to be executed or whose price depends on fluctuations in the financial markets outside the supplier's control and that historical performances are no indicators for future performances
- notice of the possibility that other taxes and/or costs may exist that are not paid via the supplier or imposed by him
- any limitations of the period for which the information provided is valid
- the arrangements for payment and for performance
- any specific additional cost for the consumer of using the means of distance communication, if such additional cost is charged

*concerning the distance contract (DMD)*
- the existence or absence of a right of withdrawal in accordance with Article 6 and, where the right of withdrawal exists, its duration and the conditions for

Table 6.1. (cont.)

- exercising it, including information on the amount which the consumer may be required to pay on the basis of Article 7(1), as well as the consequences of non-exercise of that right
- the minimum duration of the distance contract in the case of financial services to be performed permanently or recurrently
- information on any rights the parties may have to terminate the contract early or unilaterally by virtue of the terms of the distance contract, including any penalties imposed by the contract in such cases
- practical instructions for exercising the right of withdrawal indicating, *inter alia*, the address to which the notification of a withdrawal should be sent
- the Member State or States whose laws are taken by the supplier as a basis for the establishment of relations with the consumer prior to the conclusion of the distance contract
- any contractual clause on law applicable to the distance contract and/or on competent court
- in which language, or languages, the contractual terms and conditions, and the prior information referred to in this Article are supplied, and furthermore in which language, or languages, the supplier, with the agreement of the consumer, undertakes to communicate during the duration of this distance contract

*concerning redress (DMD)*
- whether or not there is an out-of-court complaint and redress mechanism for the consumer that is party to the distance contract and, if so, the methods for having access to it
- the existence of guarantee funds or other compensation arrangements not covered by the relevant EC Directives

is necessary for the performance of a contract or in taking steps at the request of the data subject in view of entering into a contract.[100] Moreover, no consent is required if the processing is necessary for compliance with a legal obligation which the controller of data is subject to or for the purposes of the legitimate interests pursued by the controller or by the third party or parties to whom the data are disclosed, except where such interests are overridden by the fundamental rights and freedoms of the customer. In any case, the processing must be fair, accurate and proportionate to its legal purpose.[101] The controller of data is also

---

[100] *Ibid.*     [101] *Ibid.*, art. 6.

subject to information requirements and the data subject is entitled to have access to the data[102] and object to them being processed.[103]

The Directive aims to strengthen the security of information systems and networks of firms controlling substantial volumes of data. Firms are required to implement appropriate technical and organizational measures to protect personal data against accidental or unlawful destruction or accidental loss, alteration, unauthorized disclosure or access, especially where the processing involves the transmission of data over a network, and against all other unlawful forms of processing.[104]

The Commission examined the state of implementation of the Directive in May 2003.[105] Most countries, including the United Kingdom,[106] France[107] and Germany,[108] have transposed the Directive into national law. It seems that, despite the generally successful national implementation of the Directive, certain remaining minor differences in national laws prevent internationally active firms and organizations from adopting a single data protection policy for all their branches and other establishments situated in different Member States.[109] These remaining differences do not, however, obstruct the cross-border provision of banking services from within a single location to clients in different Member States because the Directive adopted a conflict of laws solution based on strict territoriality. Each Member State should apply its data protection rules only to the processing of data that is carried out by firms established on the territory of the Member State.[110] The concept of establishment implies the effective and real exercise of activity through stable arrangements, such as branches and subsidiaries.[111] Neither the domicile of the customer to whom the data relate nor the use of local technical facilities for the collection, storage or processing of data triggers the application of national data protection rules.[112]

---

[102] *Ibid.*, arts. 10–11.  [103] *Ibid.*, arts. 12, 14–15.  [104] *Ibid.*, art. 17.
[105] See European Commission, *First Report on the Implementation of the Data Protection Directive*, COM(2003) 265 final.
[106] See Data Protection Act 1998.
[107] See Loi No. 2004-801 du 6 août 2004 relative à la protection des personnes physiques à l'égard des traitements de données à caractère personnel (Law 801/2004 of 6 August 2004 relating to the protection of individuals against the processing of personal data).
[108] *Bundesdatenschutzgesetz*.
[109] See European Commission, Report on the Data Protection Directive, pp. 10–14.
[110] See Data Protection Directive, art. 4(1)(b).
[111] *Ibid.*, recital 19.
[112] See § 1 Abs. 5 *Bundesdatenschutzgesetz*; Loi No. 2004-801, art. 5; Data Protection Act 1998, s. 5(1).

## The harmonization of national laws of banking contracts

Legal restrictions on the free movement of financial services belong predominantly to the domain of 'public law' and therefore European policies towards financial integration have taken the form of mutual recognition and legal harmonization of economic regulatory law. The establishment, however, of the single banking licence on the basis of 'home country' control and the progressive reduction of legal barriers generated by national regulatory measures has exposed the (formerly concealed) adverse economic effects on financial integration of national contract laws.

### Financial integration and the law of contracts

The idea that contract law may restrict the cross-border provision of financial services may sound surprising. After all, having in place legal rules regulating contractual relationships is the minimum essential condition for creating functional domestic and international markets. On the other hand, national differences in domestic laws regulating contractual relationships can increase the cost of cross-border transactions and the operating costs of internationally active financial institutions. Against this context, it should be noted that the EU measures adopted so far in the domain of contract law have achieved partial harmonization of selected legal topics, which do not constitute a coherent system of European contract law. In my view, the limited scope of legal harmonization of the law of contracts is justified.

Contract law relies on the autonomy and freedom of contracting parties. In cross-border contracts within an integrated economic area, the parties can easily achieve legal certainty and insulate the contract from undesirable national laws by freely selecting the law governing the contract. National authorities in Member States may have an interest in the free choice of law but only to the extent that the chosen law conflicts with or overrides national rules adopted in the general interest, which commonly take the form of mandatory requirements of consumer protection and other social policies applicable regardless of the otherwise governing law. Insofar as the free choice of governing law by the parties is only limited by certain mandatory requirements, a selective process of legal harmonization of the relevant mandatory standards suffices to reconcile different national approaches towards mandatory contract rules, thus facilitating the acceptance of free choice of applicable law as the overriding principle in the single European market. The selective harmonization of mandatory contract requirements and the convergence of national conflicts of laws around the principle of free choice of law in contractual matters are effective integration policies which entail far lower institutional and economic costs than the alternative path of replacing the continental civil codes and the Anglo-Saxon common law with a uniform European Civil Code.

### *The convergence of national contract laws of general application*

National laws relating to contracts for the online provision of banking services have been the subject matter of a broad range of EU measures of legal harmonization. One may distinguish between harmonization measures of general application to contractual relationships and measures that specifically regulate certain types of banking contracts. This section examines rules of general application, such as information requirements, the law governing the validity and formation of contracts concluded by electronic means, the consumer's right of withdrawal from the contract and the law regulating unfair terms in consumer contracts. The following section will discuss the legal convergence of national laws specifically relating to certain banking activities.

#### Information requirements

In addition to information requirements imposed by the remainder of Community law, the E-Commerce Directive requires that, except where otherwise agreed by parties who are not consumers, at least the following information be provided by the online bank clearly, comprehensibly and unambiguously and prior to the request for services being placed by the customer:[113]

(a) the different technical steps to follow to conclude the contract;
(b) whether or not the contract will be filed with the bank and whether it will be accessible;
(c) the technical means for identifying and correcting input errors prior to the request for services being placed;
(d) the languages offered for the conclusion of the contract;

---

[113] See E-Commerce Directive, art. 10; SI 2002/2013, reg. 9; FSA ECO 3 Annex 1; C.civ., art. 1369(1); Loi 2004-575, art. 25; § 312e BGB and § 3 BGB-InfoV.

(e) any relevant codes of conduct to which the bank subscribes and information on how those codes can be consulted electronically;
(f) contract terms and general conditions in standard form in a way that allows the customer to store and reproduce them.

### Validity and formation of electronic contracts

The European Union has not elaborated a complete and systematic legal framework relating to electronic contracts but merely sought to prevent Member States from maintaining or adopting rules which were likely to obstruct the formation of contracts by electronic means.[114] Mindful of the need to ensure consistency with international standards, the Commission relied to a great extent on the 1996 UNCITRAL Model Law on Electronic Commerce in drafting the relevant provisions of the E-Commerce Directive.[115]

With regard to the validity of contracts concluded by electronic means, the Electronic Commerce Directive specifically aimed to prevent EU Member States from maintaining or adopting rules relating to the form of contracts, which were likely to 'curb the use of contracts by electronic means',[116] thus disturbing the development of the new electronic market. To that end, the Directive requires Member States to ensure that their legal system allows contracts to be concluded by electronic means. In particular, Member States must ensure that the legal requirements applicable to the contractual process neither create obstacles for the use of electronic contracts nor result in such contracts being deprived of legal effectiveness and validity on account of their having been made by electronic means.[117] Article 9 of the Directive allows Member States to provide for exceptions to this principle, notably in 'contracts that create or transfer rights in real estate, except for rental rights' and 'contracts for suretyship granted and on collateral securities furnished by persons acting outside their trade, business or profession'.[118]

The drafters of the Directive were also keen to emphasize that the Directive would not affect Member States' possibility of maintaining or establishing general or specific legal requirements for contracts which can be fulfilled by electronic means, in particular requirements

---

[114] See E-Commerce Directive, recital 34.
[115] *Ibid.*, recital 60.  [116] *Ibid.*, recital 34.
[117] *Ibid.*, art. 9(1).  [118] *Ibid.*, art. 9(2).

concerning secure electronic signatures.[119] It is also clear that a legal requirement that a financial contract must be 'in writing' cannot deprive contracts concluded electronically of their validity, legal effect or *ad probationem* value, *unless* the pertinent provision requiring the written form is prescribed by rules which implement other instruments of European Community law.[120] For example, notwithstanding the provisions of the E-Commerce Directive, consumer credit agreements must still be concluded in writing because the pertinent formality reflects the provisions of the Consumer Credit Directive.[121]

As to the required conditions for upholding the validity of contracts concluded electronically, the E-Commerce Directive defers to the Member States. The provisions of the Directive introduce essentially a *negative obligation*, in the sense that the conclusion of contracts electronically is not a sufficient ground for failing to meet applicable requirements of form. Whether a mere exchange of electronic communications, via email or through the bank's website, is sufficient to satisfy legal requirements that a contract be made 'in writing' or be signed by the parties is not resolved by the Directive which defers to the Member States.

At first sight, the implementation of the E-Commerce Directive would require the United Kingdom to revise a substantial portion of its law on contractual formalities, at least to the extent that this law requires a contract to be contained or evidenced in writing and/or signed. It turned out, however, that no substantial reform was required. In the view of the Law Commission, requirements of 'writing' and of 'signature' can generally be met via some electronic means of communication without any change of the law.[122] In English law, information stored in an electronic form (whatever that form) is a 'document' and would (except where the context otherwise dictates) satisfy a statutory requirement for a document.[123] The Law Commission concluded that the definition of 'writing' by the Interpretation Act of 1978 as 'typing, printing, lithography, photography and other modes of representing or reproducing words in a visible form'[124] includes its natural meaning as well as the specific forms referred thereto. The natural meaning will include any

---

[119] *Ibid.*, recital 35.   [120] *Ibid.*, recital 38.
[121] See Council Directive 87/102/EEC, art. 4(1).
[122] See Law Commission, *Electronic Commerce: Formal Requirements in Commercial Transactions* (London: Law Commission of England and Wales, 2001).
[123] See *Victor Chandler International* v. *Customs and Excise Commissioners* [2000] 1 WLR 1296.
[124] See Interpretation Act 1978, sch. 1.

updating of its construction, for example, to reflect technological developments.[125] Writing requirements appear very rarely in practice and there is broad consensus that contracts concluded on the world wide web or via e-mail will satisfy writing requirements as interpreted by the Interpretation Act 1978.[126] Moreover, the Law Commission's view is that requirements of signature can generally be interpreted in a functional way, by asking whether or not the conduct of a would-be signatory indicates an authenticating intention to a reasonable person without it being required that the signature is in a specified form.[127] As a result, and depending on the authenticating intention of the signatory, digital signatures, scanned manuscript signatures, typing one's name (or initials) and clicking on a website button will satisfy a statutory signature requirement.

Although the electronic form may be used in cases where a statutory writing requirement is imposed under both German[128] and French[129] laws, the parties' electronic communications must be verified by means of 'advanced electronic signatures' as defined by national statutes implementing the Electronic Signatures Directive.[130] In effect, German and French law do not recognize the equivalence of contracts concluded electronically with contracts concluded 'in writing' unless a public key encryption system, which involves a trustworthy certification authority and a digital signature, is used.[131] The condition is not met in the usual case of a customer placing electronically a request for the provision of banking services via the Internet. Moreover, digital signature technology as a means of verifying identities is unlikely to be available to ordinary consumers. In fact, the notion that banking contracts will be formed over the Internet among parties with no prior contacts, through reliance on digital signature certificates issued by trusted third parties as a means of verifying identities, appears to be somehow premature. European banks have developed mechanisms to verify and vet the customer's identity,

---

[125] See Law Commission, Electronic Commerce, para. 3.7.
[126] Ibid., pp. 8–12.
[127] Ibid., paras. 3.28–29.
[128] See § 126 Abs.3 BGB.
[129] See C.civ., art. 1108(1).
[130] EP and Council Directive 1999/93/EC of 13 December 1999 on a Community framework for electronic signatures, OJ 2000 No. L13/12, 19 January 2000. See also § 126a BGB; C.civ., art. 1316(4).
[131] See J. Bizer, 'Elektronische Signaturen im Rechtsverkehr' in D. Kröger and M. Gimmy, Handbuch zum Internetrecht (2nd edn, Berlin: Springer-Verlag, 2002).

some of which actually rely on information received by 'trusted third parties' such as credit reference agencies, other banks and public utilities. The use, however, of digital signatures in this context is not ordinary banking practice.

Turning to other consumer protection requirements, in cases where the customer has transmitted an order or request for services via the Internet, for example by electronically submitting an application form, the bank should acknowledge the receipt of the order without undue delay and by similar means of communication.[132] Moreover, the customer should be allowed to identify and correct input errors before submitting the online request by an appropriate and accessible technical means.

In the wider context of Internet banking, a distinction should be made between the initial establishment of the banker–customer relationship and the contract for the provision of Internet services. It should be noted that both contracts may be concluded either electronically, through the postal delivery of documents or by other means of contract formation. With regard to the establishment of the banker–customer relationship, opening a bank account is not subject to legal formalities under English and German law. Informal offer and informal acceptance (duly complemented by valid intention to be bound and consideration under English law), which may be communicated either orally, in writing, by conduct or electronically, suffice to create a legally binding contract establishing the banker–customer relationship, the commission agency agreement for executing securities transactions and the 'Internet service' agreement for the provision of online services.[133]

The position is different in France, where the bank may agree to accept the customer's deposits only by means of a written contract, which must prescribe key terms of the banker–customer relationship.[134] Although the violation of the rule constitutes a criminal offence,[135] the validity of the contract is probably not affected because to suggest otherwise would penalize the customer whom the rule intends to protect. A 'written agreement' regulating the provision of online investment services on

---

[132] See E-Commerce Directive, art. 11; SI 2002/2013 reg. 11; FSA ECO 3 Annex 1R; C.civ., art. 1369(2); § 312e BGB.
[133] See *Morgans* v. *Launchbury* [1973] AC 127; Law Commission, Electronic Commerce, paras. 3.9 and 3.23; OLG Hamm NJW 2001, 1142.
[134] See C.monét.fin., art. L312(1)(1).
[135] *Ibid.*, art. L 351(1).

commission and the operation and administration of the client's securities and cash account is also required for each customer for whom the bank executes trading orders in securities.[136]

There is also a general legal requirement that financial institutions should not provide banking and investment services before verifying the customer's name, identity and place of residence on the basis of suitable documentation and other reliable sources.[137] The rule is one of the OECD Forty Recommendations on money laundering.[138] It is also a national legal requirement following the implementation by Member States of the EU Money Laundering Directive.[139]

It is standard practice in online banking to identify customers through the postal delivery of documents to the bank. Online banks may also use the services of a trusted third party such as a credit reference agency to verify the customer's identity. In Germany, online banks frequently use the so-called '*Post-Ident Verfahren*' (identification process through the postal service) to verify the identity of potential customers. Customers appear in person at the local branch of the Deutsche Post AG, the national postal service. The clerk verifies the identity of the person signing the application form, for example by inspecting his or her passport, and signs a confirmation slip, which is sent to the bank. The German bank regulator has approved this practice.[140] A third method of customer identification requires the assistance of another financial institution, which had verified the customer's identity in the past. The financial institution that verified the client's identity in the past may send a confirmatom letter to the bank or simply the first deposit in the online

---

[136] See Règlement Général AMF, art. 321–68.
[137] See Basel Committee, *General Guide to Account Opening and Customer Identification* (Basel, 2003); Loi No. 90-614 du 12 juillet 1990 relative à la participation des organismes financiers à la lutte contre le blanchiment des capitaux provenant du trafic des stupéfiants (Law 614/1990 of 12 July 1990 relating to the participation of financial institutions in the fight against the laundering of the proceeds of the trade in narcotics), art. 12; Règlement Général AMF, art. 321-56; BAKRED, *Guidelines Concerning Measures to be Taken by Credit Institutions to Combat and Prevent Money Laundering* (Bonn, 1998); Money Laundering Steering Group, *Guidance Notes for the Financial Sector* (London: British Bankers' Association, 2001) paras. 4.1–4.100.
[138] See OECD Financial Action Task Force on Money Laundering (FATF), *The Forty Recommendations* (Paris, 2003), recommendation 5.
[139] See § 154 *Abgabenordnung* (AO); §§ 1 and 8 GwG; Money Laundering Regulations 2003, SI 2003/3075; FSA Handbook Money Laundering (ML) 3.1.3R; C.monét.fin., art. L 563 (1); Règlement Général AMF arts. 321(43) and 332(32).
[140] See BAKRED, Guidelines, Guideline 10.

bank account may be paid in with funds transferred from the customer's account with the other financial institution.

With regard to cross-border electronic banking, there are currently no established special procedures for verifying bank customers who reside in another Member State.[141] In that respect, the engagement of trusted third parties could be a smart way of identifying non-resident account holders.[142] For example, the verification of the customer's identity and the authentication of identification documents by the online bank in country A could take place in the bank's branch, subsidiary or correspondent bank located in the customer's country B or other trusted organization such as the home country's diplomatic mission in that country.[143]

## Right of withdrawal

The Distance Marketing Directive requires Member States to provide recipients of financial services which are marketed at a distance with a statutory right to withdraw from the contract without penalty and without giving any reason within a statutory cancellation period of fourteen calendar days.[144] In particular, if notice of cancellation is properly given by the consumer to the supplier within the cancellation period, the notice of cancellation shall operate to cancel and terminate the distance contract at the time at which the notice of cancellation is given. The cancellation period begins on the day on which the distance contract is concluded ('conclusion day') and ends on the expiry of fourteen calendar days beginning with the day after conclusion day, *provided that* the supplier communicated all the contractual terms and conditions and the information specified in the Distance Marketing Directive on or before conclusion day.[145] Where the supplier did not communicate that information on or before conclusion day, but subsequently communicates to the consumer on paper or in another durable medium, which is available and accessible to the consumer, all the contractual terms and conditions and the information required under

---

[141] See European Commission, *A Possible Legal Framework for the Single Payment Area in the Internal Market: Non-Resident Accounts* (MARKT/4006/2003, 14 April 2003).
[142] See OECD FATF, The Forty Recommendations, Recommendation 9.
[143] See Money Laundering Steering Group, Guidance Notes; BAKRED, Guidelines.
[144] See Distance Marketing Directive, art. 6(1); SI 2004/2095, reg. 9(1), 2); §§ 312s and 355 BGB; C.consom., art. L 121(20)(12).
[145] *Ibid.*

the Directive, the cancellation period ends on the expiry of fourteen calendar days beginning with the day after the day on which the consumer receives the last of those terms and conditions and that information. Effectively, the cancellation period does not expire before the consumer duly receives the required information.[146]

A notice of cancellation is a notification which, however expressed, indicates the intention of the consumer to cancel the contract by that notification. The right to cancel is not available, *inter alia*, in cases of contracts for a financial service where the price of that service depends on fluctuations in the financial market outside the supplier's control, which may occur during the cancellation period, such as services related to foreign exchange, money market instruments, transferable securities, units in collective investment undertakings and various financial derivative instruments.[147] The right to cancel is also not available in contracts whose performance has been fully completed by both parties at the consumer's express request before the consumer gives notice of cancellation.[148]

The cancellation of the contract generates the immediate obligation of the firm to refund any sum paid by or on behalf of the consumer under or in relation to the contract to the person by whom it was paid, less any charge for any service actually provided by the supplier in accordance with the contract as soon as possible and in any event within a period not exceeding thirty calendar days beginning from the day on which the cancellation event occurred.[149] The charge cannot be disproportionate to the service already provided in comparison with the full coverage of the contract and, in any case, it cannot be such that it could be construed as a penalty for withdrawal.[150]

## Regulation of contracts in standard form

Standard form contracts or contracts of adhesion play a major role in the provision of electronic banking services. Their significance reflects the increasing standardization of modern consumer contracts. It is also encouraged by the suitability of the online environment for this type of contractual arrangement.

---

[146] See Case C-481/99 *Heininger v. Bayerische Hypo- und Vereinsbank AG* [2001] ECR I-9945.
[147] See Distance Marketing Directive, art. 6(2)(a).
[148] See art. 6(2)(b).  [149] See art. 7.  [150] *Ibid.*

**A brief survey of banking practices in key Member States**  The Federal Banking Association in Germany introduced model terms and conditions, which are almost invariably adopted by individual firms in a uniform manner in regulating the banker–customer relationship.[151] They are structured into *General Terms* and *Special Terms* of Contract. The former provide the general framework of the banker–customer relationship (*Allgemeine Geschäftsbedingungen*).[152] The latter regulate specific types of contracts, including securities transactions (*Sonderbedingungen für Wertpapiergeschäfte*), credit transfers (*Bedingungen für den Überweisungsverkehr*), and even the 'Internet service' agreement (*Bedingungen für den Zugang über elektronische Medien*).

Banks in the United Kingdom use standard form contracts for the banker–customer relationship, specific banking services and the contract for online Internet services. Although there is no universally adopted list of uniform terms and conditions, the existing similarities in the terms used by different banks reflect the influence of the Banking Code whose contractual standards are expressly incorporated by most UK banks.

Implementing statutory requirements,[153] French banks should present their customers with a copy of the deposit account agreement (*convention de compte de dépôt*), which must set out the terms of the contract (*conditions générales des contrats*). They also drafted a self-regulatory Charter of Deposit Account Contracts, which indicates the terms governing that service.[154] The uniform terms established by the Charter cover deposit accounts for persons acting outside their trade or profession and therefore leave scope for competition among banks in setting the terms and conditions of the online services. The written agreement regulating the provision of online investment services is also required to contain certain mandatory terms of contract, including the identity, residence, and legal status of the bank and the customer; the documents required for the identification of the account holder; the services covered by the agreement; the scale of fees and charges; the duration of the contract; the duty of confidentiality; what sort of trading orders may be placed; the medium by which the orders are to be transmitted; the information to be provided to the customer upon

---

[151] See Jürgen Sonnenhof, 'Änderungen der AGB-Banken zum 1. April 2002' (2002) WM 1269.
[152] *Ibid.*
[153] See C.monét.fin., art. L312-1-1.
[154] See Fédération Bancaire Française, *Charte Relative aux Conventions de Compte de Dépôt* (Paris: Fédération Bancaire Française, 2003).

execution, including the nature of the financial instrument, the market, the date and price, and the amount of the transaction; the period within which the customer may challenge the terms of the execution; and if applicable, the names of other intermediaries holding the customer's securities and cash accounts.[155]

To incorporate standard form contracts in the banker–customer relationship, it suffices that the customer is given notice prior to the conclusion of the contract. The principle is adhered to with variations in England, France and Germany.[156] In English and French law, actual notice is not required unless the bank failed to take reasonable steps to ensure that the terms had been brought to the attention of the customer.[157] In accordance with French consumer protection law, notice of standard terms must be given in a clear, legible and comprehensible manner.[158] It is also a statutory requirement that the terms of the deposit account be communicated to the customer prior to the conclusion of the contract[159] and the same applies for the terms of the 'online trading' contract.[160]

The German Civil Code establishes special consumer protection rules. The bank should draw the customer's attention to the terms either expressly or by means of a clearly visible sign at the place where the contract is concluded.[161] The consumer must be offered the opportunity to become aware of their content in a reasonable manner.[162] It is good practice to set out the terms in full on the website or make them individually available via e-mail and ensure that the application form technically cannot be submitted by the customer until it has been demonstrated that the customer has taken notice of and approved the terms, perhaps by ticking a box or clicking 'I agree'. It is now required by the E-Commerce and Distance Marketing Directives to disclose standard contract terms in advance.[163]

---

[155] See Règlement Générale AMF, arts. 321(70)–(75) and 321(54)–(67).
[156] See *Thornton v. Shoe Lane Parking* [1971] 2 QB 163, 170; BGH, NJW 1992, 1232; B. Starck, H. Roland and L. Boyer, *Droit Civil des Obligations: Contrat* (6th edn, Paris: Litec, 1998), pp. 52–6.
[157] See *Olley v. Marlborough Court Ltd* [1949] 1 KB 532; Cass.Civ. 09.02.1999, 44 RTD civ. 836.
[158] See C.consom., art. L 133(2).
[159] See Décret No. 84-708, art. 7.
[160] See Règlement Générale AMF, arts. 321(57) and (71).
[161] See § 305 Abs. 2 BGB.
[162] *Ibid.*
[163] See E-Commerce Directive, art. 10(3); Distance Marketing Directive, art. 5.

**The Unfair Terms Directive**  The Unfair Contract Terms Directive[164] aimed to harmonize national laws concerning unfair terms in contracts for the sale of goods and the provision of services to consumers.[165] To the extent that one in five litigated cases of unfair contract terms are generated by consumer contracts for the provision of financial services,[166] the Directive is rightly regarded as a key measure towards the completion of the single financial market.

The Directive applies to consumer contracts.[167] Contract terms which reflect mandatory statutory and regulatory provisions are not covered by the Directive.[168] The main operative provision of the Directive requires Member States to ensure that unfair terms used in consumer contracts are not binding on the consumer and that the contract shall continue to bind the parties upon those terms if it is capable of continuing in existence without the unfair terms. Whether a contract term is unfair or not is a matter to be decided by national courts case by case.[169] The Directive defines unfair terms as contractual terms, which have not been individually negotiated and, contrary to the requirement of good faith, cause a significant imbalance in the parties' rights and obligations arising under the contract, to the detriment of the consumer.[170] A term shall always be regarded as not individually negotiated where it has been drafted in advance and the consumer has therefore not been able to influence the substance of the term, particularly in the context of a pre-formulated standard contract.[171] There is also an Annex containing an indicative, non-binding and non-exhaustive list of terms which are usually regarded as unfair but Member States are free to adopt their own lists.[172] It should be noted that the assessment of the unfair nature of the terms should relate neither to the definition of the main subject matter of the contract nor to the adequacy of the price and remuneration

---

[164] See Council Directive 93/13/EEC of 5 April 1993 on unfair terms in consumer contracts, 1993 OJ No. L95/29, 21 April 1994.
[165] *Ibid.*, recitals 3–5.
[166] See the European Database on Case Law Concerning Unfair Contractual Terms at http://europa.eu.int/clab/ (last visited 9 October 2005); the database contains 12,566 litigated cases, of which 2,433 cases concern contracts for the provision of financial services.
[167] See Unfair Terms Directive, art. 1(1).
[168] See art. 1(2).
[169] See Case C-473/00 *Cofidis SA v. Fredout* [2002] ECR I-10875.
[170] See Unfair Terms Directive, art. 3(1).
[171] See art. 3(2).   [172] See art. 3(3) and recital 16.

for the services provided in exchange, in so far as these terms are in plain intelligible language.[173]

From a policy perspective, the Directive was not based on the rather simplistic view that unfair terms in consumer contracts of adhesion reflected the inherently unequal bargaining position of the parties.[174] Instead, the fairness of contract terms should be assessed in the light of several factors that influence the content of the contractual agreement. The explicit instruction to the national judge is revealing. The unfairness of a contractual term shall be assessed, taking into account the nature of the goods or services for which the contract was concluded and by referring, at the time of conclusion of the contract, to all the circumstances attending the conclusion of the contract and to all the other terms of the contract or of another contract on which it is dependent.[175] Particular weighting must be afforded to the nature and the ratio of price to quality of the services,[176] the strength of the bargaining positions of the parties, whether the consumer agreed to the term in exchange for a benefit and whether the services were supplied to the special order of the consumer.[177] This is a circumstantial evaluation of fairness case by case. For example, a prejudicial term is likely to be unfair if the cost of the service or good is relatively high but the same term in another contract may simply demonstrate a fair exchange of disadvantageous terms in return for a lower price. Finally, the drafters of the Directive were keen to emphasize the value of transparency in agreeing contract terms as a means of stimulating better terms for consumers. Member States are required to ensure that consumer contracts are drafted in plain and intelligible language and where there is doubt about the meaning of a term, the interpretation most favourable to the consumer shall prevail.[178]

The Directive does not stop Member States from regulating contract terms which are outside the scope of application of the Directive, for example terms in non-consumer contracts or terms which have been individually negotiated.[179] Within the scope of application of the Directive, Member States may adopt or retain more stringent provisions

---

[173] See art. 4(2).
[174] See Leone Niglia, *The Transformation of Contract in Europe* (The Hague: Kluwer, 2003), p. 3.
[175] Unfair Terms Directive, art. 4(1).
[176] See *ibid.*, recitals 17–18.    [177] See *ibid.*, recital 15.
[178] See *ibid.*, art. 5.    [179] See *ibid.*, recital 12.

to ensure a higher level of consumer protection than the common EU rules.[180]

In April 2000 the Commission published the report on the implementation of the Directive.[181] While the minimum provisions of the Directive have been transposed into national law, Member States appear to have extended the scope of protection beyond the areas regulated by the Directive.[182] Table 6.2 presents the state of national implementation in France, Germany and the United Kingdom.

The statutory regulation of unfair terms in France applies to contract terms, whether individually negotiated or not, regardless of whether they reflect mandatory statutory and regulatory provisions.[183] In Germany, the protection applies without distinction to consumer and non-consumer contracts.[184] Moreover, unlike the non-binding list of the Directive, Germany introduced a binding list of 'black terms', which are always regarded as unfair. In the United Kingdom, the scope of application of national requirements was not extended beyond the subject matter of the Directive,[185] while the Unfair Contract Terms Act 1977 provides additional protection which is not limited to consumer contracts.

The definition of 'unfairness' was implemented rather inconsistently. In the national arena, the perception of 'unfairness' of contract terms relates to various economic and political views of consumer protection, fairness, efficiency, social conditions and the role of the state in regulating the operation of consumer markets. In that respect, legislative and judicial choices as to the scope and scale of consumer protection in the law of contracts are in direct discourse with local cultural identities and political choices.[186] Niglia demonstrates that from the early development of standard form contracts, national laws developed marked differences as to how to reconcile the underlying tension between party autonomy and mandatory consumer protection.[187] When he carefully

---

[180] See *ibid.*, art. 8.
[181] See European Commission, *Report on the Implementation of Council Directive 93/13/EEC of 5 April 1993 on Unfair Terms in Consumer Contracts* COM(2000) 248 final.
[182] *Ibid.*, pp. 13–20.
[183] See C.consom., art. L 132(1).
[184] See § 305 Abs. 1 BGB.
[185] See Unfair Terms in Consumer Contracts Regulations 1999, SI 1999/2083.
[186] See Hugh Collins, 'European Private Law and the Cultural Identity of States' (1995) 3 *European Review of Private Law* 353.
[187] See Niglia, *The Transformation of Contract*, pt 1.

Table 6.2. *Coverage of Unfair Contract Terms Regulation in key EU countries*

|  | Directive | France | Germany | UK |
|---|---|---|---|---|
| Terms not individually negotiated | ● | ● | ● | ● |
| Terms individually negotiated |  | ● |  |  |
| Consumer contracts | ● | ● | ● | ● |
| Non-consumer contracts |  |  | ● |  |
| Terms which reflect mandatory rules of law |  | ● |  |  |
| Terms which reflect the subject-matter, price and remuneration |  |  |  |  |
| Binding list of terms which are necessarily unfair |  |  | ● |  |
| Non-binding list of terms which may be regarded as unfair | ● | ● | ● | ● |

examined the extent to which national views of unfairness of contract terms were adapted to the circumstantial and risk-based assessment of 'unfairness' established by the Directive, he concluded that national practices of regulation of unfair contract terms did not fully conform to the provisions of the Directive.[188]

English courts duly apply the circumstantial test of 'unfairness'. This is partly due to the fact that, unlike other European countries, English law received the Directive without carrying the historical burden of a different approach. In fact, the test of 'reasonableness' introduced by the Unfair Contract Terms Act 1977 for assessing contract terms excluding liability is very similar to the rationale underpinning the Directive: the court must have regard to the circumstances which were, or ought reasonably to have been, known to or in the contemplation of the parties when the contract was made,[189] whereas the bargaining position of the parties is only one among several elements informing this assessment.[190] In the landmark case *Director General of Fair Trading* v. *First National Bank*,[191] the House of Lords used the provisions and recitals of the

---

[188] *Ibid.*, pt 2.
[189] See Unfair Contract Terms Act 1977, s. 11(1).
[190] See Jack Beatson, *Anson's Law of Contract* (28th edn, Oxford: Oxford University Press, 2002), pp. 194–7.
[191] [2002] 1 AC 481 (HL).

Directive to construct the right approach. The court held that the criterion of the significant imbalance in the parties' rights and obligations to the detriment of the consumer must be assessed in the light of the contract as a whole.[192] The requirement of good faith in this context is one of fair and open dealing. Openness requires that the terms should be expressed fully, clearly and legibly. Appropriate prominence should be given to the terms which might operate disadvantageously to the customer, whereas a high level of transparency may in the circumstances lead to the conclusion that a prima facie disadvantageous term is in fact a fair one.

France and Germany appear to have disregarded the concept of unfairness as defined by the Directive.[193] In Germany there is no case law that actually applies a circumstantial test and the courts continue to use the concept of 'unreasonable prejudice'.[194] This concept was developed by the courts at the beginning of the twentieth century and codified in 1977, almost twenty years before the implementation of the Directive, by the Act on the Regulation of the Law of General Business Conditions (AGBG).[195] Against the spirit of circumstantial evaluation, German courts apply a list of 'black' terms which must always be considered as unfair.[196] In further contrast, German courts have distanced themselves from the requirement of plain and intelligible language. The Federal Court (BGH) has held that in cases where the drafter is inhibited by various kinds of legal and factual difficulties, the use of legal jargon is acceptable even when the other party may have to spend a considerable amount of time to understand the relevant terms.[197] There is no shortage of terms in banking contracts, including contracts for the provision of electronic banking services, which were found to be 'unreasonably prejudicial' by German courts: exclusion of liability for the breakdown of the online banking system for technical reasons;[198] right to interrupt the online banking service at any time for maintenance;[199] limitation of liability in selecting an intermediate agent bank;[200] and a

---

[192] Ibid. per Lord Bingham 496.
[193] See Niglia, *The Transformation of Contract*, pt 3.
[194] Niglia, *The Transformation of Contract*, p. 192.
[195] *Gesetz zur Regelung des Rechts der Allgemeinen Geschäftsbedingungen.*
[196] See § 309 BGB.
[197] See BGH NJW 1998, 3114.
[198] See BGH (12 December 2000) AZ: XI ZR 138/00.
[199] See OLG Köln (14 April 2000) AZ: 6 U 135/199.
[200] See LG Köln (1 December 1999) 26 O 79-1998.

right to charge fees for non-performance of a giro transaction for lack of sufficient cover.[201]

The circumstantial test prescribed by the Directive is now part of the French Consumer Code.[202] It is however subject to the general rules of contractual interpretation of Articles 1156 to 1161, 1163 and 1164 of the French Civil Code. Further, the *Conseil d'Etat* is empowered to establish binding lists of unfair terms that the courts have to apply regardless of the circumstances of the particular case.[203]

It should be noted that whether national courts may lawfully distance themselves from the interpretation adopted by the Directive is controversial.[204] The Directive aims to harmonize national laws. Member States have no common concept of fairness and on that basis it seems that the test proposed by the Directive must be universally applied. If the meaning of the test is doubtful or vulnerable to the possibility of differing interpretations in different Member States, the European Court of Justice ('the Court') could be asked to rule on the proper interpretation. The House of Lords shares this view.[205] In terms of Community law, national courts must interpret implementing legislation in the light of the provisions and the recitals of the Directive and, necessarily, respect the interpretation given by the Court. The Court invariably interprets Directives by giving its legal terms a genuine European 'autonomous' meaning.[206] Harmonized EU rules entail obligations for Member States. In the context of the Unfair Terms Directive, it cannot be argued that the circumstantial test of 'unfairness' is equally compatible with the Directive with a fixed notion of unfairness applied by some national courts. In *Commission v. Sweden*[207] the Court confirmed that the assessment of specific terms should take into account the circumstances attending the conclusion of the contract and – in so prescribing – the Directive defines the result which must be achieved.[208]

---

[201] See BGH (13 February 2001) XI ZR 197/00.
[202] See C.consom., art. L 132(1).
[203] See Niglia, *The Transformation of Contract*, pp. 181–2.
[204] See Irene Klauer, 'General Clauses in European Private Law and "Stricter" National Standards: The Unfair Terms Directive' (2000) 8 *European Review of Private Law* 187.
[205] See *Director General of Fair Trading v. First National Bank* [2002] IAC 481 (HL) at 496.
[206] See Case 53/81 *Levin v. Staatssecretaris van Justitie* [1981] ECR 1035, paras. 9–11.
[207] See Case C-478/99 *Commission v. Sweden* [2002] ECR I-4147.
[208] *Ibid.*, para. 18.

### The harmonization of national laws of electronic banking contracts

In addition to national laws of general application to commercial and consumer contracts, the legal and institutional framework for the conduct of electronic banking activities comprises statutory and regulatory provisions of special application to certain types of online financial services, such as bank deposits and electronic transfers of funds, consumer loans and online investment services. These are all areas of national law where EU measures of legal harmonization have had substantial impact.

### Bank deposits, accounts and electronic fund transfers

Leaving aside the impact of EU measures of general application such as the Unfair Terms Directive, national laws relating to bank deposits, accounts and electronic transfers of funds have largely remained unaffected by EU measures of legal harmonization. The law of the banker–customer relationship is largely unconstrained by mandatory requirements of EU law with the notable exception of EU measures aiming to create a single European payment area, namely the Cross-Border Credit Transfers Directive and the Regulation on Cross-Border Euro Payments (in this section 'the Regulation').[209]

**The Cross-Border Credit Transfers Directive** The execution of the customer's mandate in accordance with the 'Internet service' agreement may fall within the scope of application of national provisions implementing the Cross-Border Credit Transfers Directive. The Directive establishes standards of good performance and transparency in 'cross-border credit transfers' in the currencies of the Member States up to the equivalent of €50,000 executed by financial institutions.[210] The Directive regulates transactions carried out on the initiative of an originator via a financial institution or its branch in one Member State, with a view to making available an amount of money to a beneficiary at a financial institution or its branch in another Member State.[211] The originator and the beneficiary may be one and the same person. The conditions are met when the customer in Member State A instructs via the Internet her

---

[209] See EP and Council Regulation 2560/2001/EC of 19 December 2001 on cross-border payments in euro, OJ 2001 No. L344/13, 28 December 2001.
[210] See Cross-Border Credit Transfers Directive, art. 1.
[211] See art. 2f.

bank in Member State B to transfer funds in a bank account held in State A or a third State C. The transmission of the originator's mandate via the Internet constitutes a 'cross-border credit transfer order' which is expressly defined as an unconditional instruction *in any form*, given directly by an originator to an institution to execute a cross-border credit transfer.[212]

The Directive establishes certain information requirements. The customer must be informed in a readily comprehensible form, in writing or by electronic means, of the terms of the service, such as the time needed for the funds to be credited to the account of the beneficiary's bank and the beneficiary; the manner of calculation of fees and charges; details of complaints and redress procedures; and indication of the reference exchange rates used.[213] Unless otherwise agreed, minimum information should also be supplied after the transfer has been executed, namely a reference number, the amount of the transfer and the amount of charges and commission fees.[214]

Unless the originator's bank does not wish to perform the transfer, it must give an undertaking as to the estimated completion time and total cost.[215] If the transfer is not executed within the indicated period of time or, in the absence of any such time limit, if the funds have not been transmitted to the beneficiary's bank within five business days, the originator's bank must compensate the originator,[216] unless the bank can establish that the delay was caused by the customer.[217] The amount of compensation is calculated by applying a national reference rate of interest to the amount of the transfer for the period of delay.

If the relevant amounts have not been credited to the account of the beneficiary's bank, the originator must be refunded within fourteen business days with the amount of the transfer up to the equivalent of €12,500 plus interest for the period between the order and the date of the credit,[218] unless the non-execution was caused by error or omission in the instructions given by the originator.[219] The originator's bank is released from the obligation in the event of abnormal and unforeseeable circumstances beyond its control, the consequences of which would have been unavoidable despite all efforts to the contrary.[220] National laws may adopt more stringent rules of consumer protection.[221]

---

[212] See art. 3(g).
[213] See art. 3.
[214] See art. 4.
[215] See art. 5.
[216] See art. 6(1).
[217] See art. 6(3).
[218] See art. 8(1).
[219] See art. 8(3).
[220] See art 9.
[221] See recital 8.

The Directive has been implemented in all Member States.[222] In September 2001, the European Commission released a pan-European study of national laws implementing the Directive,[223] which concluded that notwithstanding a few minor differences the implementing national measures reflect the spirit and the letter of the Directive. Certain legal impediments to cross-border banking activities may be caused by national differences in the scope of application of implementing rules. For example, Germany has extended the scope of application of national provisions to purely domestic credit transfers and to credit transfers to bank accounts in non-European Economic Area (EEA) countries. It also extended its scope of application to credit transfers up above €50,000.[224] To the extent that the scope of application of the relevant legislation in Germany is wider than in other Member States, certain cross-border transactions which are unregulated in the bank's 'home country' could be subject to statutory regulation in Germany.

**The Regulation on Cross-Border Euro Payments** The Directive sought to improve the efficiency of cross-border credit transfers but its implementation did not produce the intended benefits. Empirical evidence published in 2001 showed that while the cost of domestic credit transfers was negligible, the average cost of low-value cross-border transfers equaled almost a quarter of the value of the transfer.[225] It was also realized that the high economic cost of cross-border bank payments was largely caused by the fragmentation and non-standardization of national payment systems rather than the lack of legal harmonization in the standards of transparency and consumer protection. Furthermore, the mobilization of market forces was thought to be insufficient to trigger the requisite structural reforms towards the integration of national payment systems.

The creation of common technical standards and integrated clearing and settlement systems for bank payments are subject to network effects. Individual banks are reluctant to invest in integrated payment systems

---

[222] See Cross-Border Transfers Regulations 1999, SI 1999/1876; C.monét.fin., art. L 133(1); §§ 676a–676c BGB and § 12 Info-V.
[223] See Oppenheimer, Wolff & Donnelly LLP, *Study on the Verification of a Common and Coherent Application of the Cross-Border Credit Transfers Directive* (Brussels: Oppenheimer, Wolff & Donnelly LLP, 2001).
[224] See §§ 12–13 Info-V; §§ 676a–676c BGB.
[225] See European Central Bank, *Towards a Single Euro Payments Area: Progress Report* (Frankfurt, 2003), p. 9.

without being certain that others would join in, whereas individual investments in new technology and payment systems are meaningless unless other institutions follow suit and economies of scale are achieved. Simultaneously, the high economic cost of cross-border bank payments drives down consumer demand at the retail level, thus discouraging institutional investment in better cross-border payment facilities. The whole situation has been described in terms of a classical *chicken-and-egg* problem.[226] The European Commission and the European Central Bank regarded the fragmentation of national bank payment systems unacceptable within a single currency area and came up with a simple and radical idea. Charges levied on cross-border credit transfers and electronic payments could not be higher than corresponding transactions carried out domestically. In reality, banks would continue to incur the high costs caused by the fragmentation of national payment clearing and settlement systems but they would be legally prevented from shifting the cost to consumers. It was hoped that the prohibition would provide incentives for investment in the integration of national bank payment systems and technical standards for cross-border bank payments.

The Regulation was adopted in December 2001. With effect from 1 July 2003, charges levied by a bank in respect of cross-border electronic funds transfers up to €12,500[227] should be the same as the charges levied by the same bank in respect of corresponding transactions carried out within the Member State in which the bank is established.[228] Euro-denominated credit transfers in EU countries outside the European Monetary Union are also covered. Moreover, customers are entitled to receive prior information on the applicable fees, charges and exchange rates.[229] To facilitate the transfer of funds, uniform standards have been introduced. Each bank account must be identified with an International Bank Account Number (IBAN) and each bank with a Bank Identifier Code (BIC). The statutory protection only attaches if the originator communicates to the bank the IBAN of the beneficiary and the BIC of the beneficiary's bank.[230] Member States are required to guarantee the application of the Regulation by establishing effective and proportionate sanctions.

---

[226] See Kari Kemppainen, *Competition and Regulation in European Retail Payment Systems* (Bank of Finland, Discussion Paper 16) (Helsinki, 2003), p. 12.
[227] €50,000 from January 2006.
[228] See Council and EP Regulation 2560/2001/EC, art. 3(2).
[229] Ibid., art. 4.    [230] Ibid., art. 5.

### The banker–customer relationship and mandatory rules adopted in the general interest

In view of the limited scope of EU harmonization, Member States are left with substantial discretion to regulate the banker–customer relationship and certain banking services at national level. Policy makers in the United Kingdom have largely declined to regulate bank deposits, accounts and core banking services by way of mandatory statutory and regulatory standards. A certain degree of self-regulation was introduced by the British Bankers' Association in the form of the UK Banking Code. Moreover, bank deposits are outside the scope of application of the Conduct of Business module of the FSA Handbook with the exception of regulatory requirements relating to financial promotion.[231]

The French tradition is quite different, with statutory regulation being a major source of the French law of the banker–customer relationship. For example, if the bank wishes to reject the customer's application to open an account, it must do so in writing and communicate its decision to the applicant.[232] Alternatively, the bank may agree to accept the customer's deposits only by means of a written contract which must prescribe specified terms.[233] It must also inform its clients and the public of the general terms and conditions, including the terms of use of the account, applicable fees and parties' obligations.[234] The payment of interest on deposit accounts is severely restricted by statute. With the exception of certain types of savings accounts, deposits which can be withdrawn at any time without notice (on-sight deposits) do not generate interest.[235] Accounts held by non-residents are also caught by the restriction.[236] Furthermore, the provision of combined banking services is prohibited, unless the services are capable of being requested and purchased separately or they are inseparable in nature.[237] The bank is free to set the amount of fees and charges for the performance of the service but any alteration must be communicated to the customer in writing at least three months prior to the changes taking effect.[238]

---

[231] See Conduct of Business Rules (COB (FSA)) 1.3.2 R and 3.8.
[232] See C.monét.fin., art. R 312(3).
[233] See C.monét.fin., art. L 312-1-1.
[234] See C.monét.fin., art. R 312(1).
[235] See C.monét.fin., art. L312(3); Règlement. CRBF No. 86/13 as amended.
[236] See Décision No. 72-05 du Conseil National du Crédit.
[237] See C.monét.fin., art. L 312(1)(2).
[238] See art. L 312(1).

The German law of the banker–customer relationship is largely subject to the autonomy of the parties to regulate their contractual relationship with the exception of the law relating to unfair contract terms and other provisions implementing EU measures. For example, the parties are free to set the rate of interest payable on deposit accounts and the level of the bank's remuneration.[239]

## Online bank loans and the Consumer Credit Directive

The Consumer Credit Directive established the legal framework for consumer credit in the European Union with a view to creating a single market in consumer credit and protecting consumers who benefit from such credit.[240] The underlying idea was that the convergence of national laws would elevate the level of consumer protection and level the field of competition in the single European market for goods and services. Insofar as it harmonizes certain aspects of the law relating to 'loans and other similar financial accommodation',[241] the Directive reduces legal barriers in the provision of credit as a financial service, facilitating this particular type of online banking activity.

Personal consumer loans granted via e-finance applications are within the scope of the Directive unless (a) their amount is less than €200 or more than €20,000[242] or (b) the credit is repayable either within a period of less than three months or by a maximum number of four payments within a period less than twelve months.[243] Credit in the form of advances on a current account granted by the bank is only subject to the information requirements of Article 6.[244] The Directive enhances the level of transparency at the advertising, pre-contractual and contractual stage but it does not otherwise intervene in the substantive rights and obligations of the lender and the borrower.

First, any advertisement in which a person offers credit or offers to arrange a credit agreement and in which a rate of interest or any figures relating to the cost of credit are indicated must also include a statement of the 'annual percentage rate of charge' which reflects all costs, including interest and other charges which the consumer has to pay for the

---

[239] See H. Schimansky, H. J. Bunte and H. J. Lwowski, *Bankrechts-Handbuch* (2nd edn, Munich: C. H. Beck 2001), ch. 70.
[240] See Consumer Credit Directive, recitals 3, 5–7 and 9.
[241] See art. 1(2)(c). [242] See art. 2(1)(f).
[243] See art. 2(1)(g). [244] See art. 2(1)(e).

credit, expressed as an annual percentage of the amount of the credit and calculated in accordance with a mathematical formula set out in the Directive.[245]

Second, the agreement must be made in writing and a copy be given to the consumer.[246] It will be recalled that the provisions of the E-Commerce Directive concerning electronic contracts do not override 'writing' requirements imposed by other EC Directives.[247] The written agreement must include[248] a statement of the annual percentage rate (APR); the conditions under which the APR may be amended; the amount, number and frequency or dates of credit instalments as well as of the payments for interest and other charges; the charges levied for non-compliance with the undertaken commitments, for insurance and guarantees, for the transfer of funds and for keeping an account intended to receive payments in reimbursement of the debt.[249] The written agreement must also include the other essential elements of the contract[250] including the credit limit, an indication of the security required, the terms of repayment, any right of withdrawal and an indication that the consumer will be entitled, as provided in Article 8, to a reduction if he repays early. Finally, the consumer is entitled to discharge his obligations before the time fixed by the agreement in which case he is entitled to an equitable reduction of the total cost of credit.[251]

With regard to overdraft credit facilities, the account holder must be informed in writing at the time or before the agreement is concluded of the credit limit; the annual rate of interest, applicable charges and the conditions under which these may be amended; the procedure for terminating the agreement[252] and the terms of use and repayment of the facility and the cooling-off period, if any.[253] During the period of the agreement, the consumer must be informed, in a statement of account or in any other acceptable manner, of any change in the annual rate of interest or in the relevant charges at the time it occurs.[254] In Member States where overdrafts may be agreed tacitly, the consumer

---

[245] See art. 3.  [246] See art. 4(1).
[247] See E-Commerce Directive, recital 11.
[248] See Consumer Credit Directive, art. 4(2).
[249] See arts. 4(2) and 1(a)(2).
[250] See art. 4(3); Annex I, para. 4.
[251] See art. 8.  [252] See art. 6(1).
[253] See art. 4(3) and Annex I, para. 2.  [254] See art. 6(2).

must be informed of the annual rate of interest and applicable charges where the overdraft extends beyond a period of three months.[255]

The Directive does not preclude Member States from retaining or adopting more stringent provisions to protect consumers consistent with their obligations under the Treaty.[256] Member States may, for example, regulate non-consumer credit agreements or bring within the scope of national measures of consumer protection credit agreements of value higher than the monetary limits established by the Directive.[257]

Unsurprisingly, the scope of application of national consumer credit requirements varies considerably from country to country.[258] Unregulated contracts in one country are potentially regulated in another and vice versa. Personal loans of less than €20,000 are invariably subject to national consumer credit requirements in all Member States but the remaining national differences in the scope of application of national standards largely prevent suppliers of credit in one country from serving consumers in another country under a single set of advertising regulations, contract formalities and documentation. For example, loans granted to natural persons for professional purposes are outside the scope of the Directive and outside the scope of French consumer credit law[259] but, below a certain value, within the scope of the UK Consumer Credit Act 1974[260] and the German equivalent.[261] Table 6.3 compares the scope of application of consumer credit rules in the three EU countries.

The convergence of substantive national laws is also incomplete, with national laws imposing additional requirements concerning the content and form of disclosure of information to consumers.[262] The Directive requires consumer credit agreements to be made in writing and consumers to receive a copy of the written agreement with the financial and other essential terms of the contract. The UK Consumer Credit Act 1974 establishes extensive requirements of form, content and execution of

---

[255] See art. 6(3).   [256] See art. 15.
[257] See Case C 208/98 *Berliner Kindl Brauerei AG* v. *Siepert* [2000] ECR I-1741.
[258] See §§ 491 and 507 BGB; C.consom., arts. L 311(2), L 311(3) D 311(1), D 311(2); CCA 1974, ss. 8 and 189.
[259] See C.consom., art. 311(3).
[260] See CCA 1974, ss. 8–20 and 189.
[261] See § 507 BGB.
[262] See CCA 1974, s. 44; Consumer Credit (Advertisements) Regulations 2004, SI 2004/1484, regs. 2–9; §§ 1 and 6 *Preisangabenverordnung* (Regulation on the Disclosure of Price Information); C.consom., art. L 311(4).

Table 6.3. *Coverage of Consumer Credit Regulation in key EU countries*

|  | Directive | France | Germany | UK |
|---|---|---|---|---|
| Consumer loans more than €200 but less than €20,000 | • |  |  |  |
| Any consumer loan more than €200 |  |  |  | • |
| Any consumer loan less than €21,500 |  | • |  | • |
| Loans by any natural person regardless of professional purpose of less than €50,000 |  | • |  |  |
| Loans by any natural person regardless of professional purpose of less than £25,000 |  |  |  | • |
| Loans with a repayment period of more than 3 months | • | • |  |  |

regulated agreements.[263] Non-compliance with the prescribed formalities means that the agreement may only be enforced with the permission of the court for lack of proper execution.[264] Furthermore, the agreement is not properly executed unless a document in the prescribed form, containing all financial and essential contract terms, is signed in the prescribed manner both by the debtor and by or on behalf of the creditor and the document embodies all the terms of the agreement.[265] The prescribed terms are clarified by regulations.[266] A copy of the executed agreement and of any document referred to in the agreement must be delivered to the debtor when the unexecuted agreement is presented to her for signature.[267] The form and content of the copies are also prescribed by regulations.[268]

It should be noted that the Consumer Credit Act 1974 (Electronic Communications) Order 2004 ('the Order')[269] was made under sections 8 and 9 of the Electronic Communications Act 2000 to modify certain provisions of the CCA 1974 for the purpose of enabling and facilitating

---

[263] See Consumer Credit (Agreements) Regulations 1983 SI 1983/1553 as amended.
[264] See CCA 1974, s. 65.
[265] See CCA 1974, s. 61.
[266] See Consumer Credit (Agreements) Regulations 1983, reg. 6(1) and sch. 6.
[267] See CCA 1974, s. 63.
[268] See Consumer Credit (Cancellation Notices and Copies of Documents) Regulations 1983, SI 1983/1557.
[269] SI 2004/3236.

the use of electronic communications for concluding regulated agreements and when sending notices and other documents. Electronic communication is defined as a communication transmitted by means of an electronic communications network or by other means but while in an electronic form.[270] The Order amends the CCA 1974 and Regulations made under it so that references to 'post' and 'postal address' are expanded to enable electronic communications between the provider and the recipient of credit.

In Germany, the credit agreement must be in writing, at the exclusion of any other form (including the electronic form).[271] It must include the prescribed financial particulars and other terms and a copy must be delivered to the customer.[272] Both the letter and spirit of the Directive regarding the transparency of terms, particularly financial terms and the cost of credit, are given due prominence. A survey of litigated cases before the BGH has shown that the court requires a high level of transparency in the way that the interest is fixed and has been prepared to set aside terms introducing complex, unusual or poorly understood methods of interest computation.[273]

In France the agreement must be concluded under the terms of a prior offer which the bank must deliver to the borrower in duplicate.[274] The offer must reproduce certain statutory provisions and include prescribed terms relating to the financial elements of the agreement and the essential terms of the contract.[275] The offer must be in the form and content of one of the model agreements annexed to the code.[276] The offer must remain open for at least fifteen days[277] and the agreement becomes complete as soon as the borrower accepts the offer.[278] The bank may reserve the right to approve the borrower after the borrower's acceptance in which case the contract is concluded when the borrower is informed of the bank's decision to grant the loan.[279]

The Directive establishes the right of early repayment. According to the UK CCA 1974, the debtor is entitled at any time, by notice to the creditor and the payment to the creditor of all amounts payable by the

---

[270] See Electronic Communications Act 2000, s. 15(1).
[271] See §§ 492–3 BGB; BGH NJW 2000, 3496.
[272] See § 492 Abs. 1 BGB.
[273] See BGH XI ZR 223/90; BGH XI ZR 119/91; BGH XI ZR 275/89.
[274] See C.consom., arts. L 311(8), (9), (10) and R 311(6).
[275] *Ibid.*, art. L 311(10).   [276] See art. R 311(6).
[277] See art. L 311(8).   [278] See art. L 311(15).
[279] See art. 311(16).

debtor to discharge the debtor's indebtedness under the agreement.[280] The debtor is entitled to receive by the creditor a rebate of charges for credit which is proven to be unused because of the early repayment.[281] Under German law the consumer may terminate the agreement six months after the loan was granted at the earliest by giving three months' notice,[282] while in France this right can be exercised at any time.[283]

Overdraft facilities are outside the scope of the Directive, with the exception of Article 6 which prescribes disclosure and transparency requirements. The German law has followed the choices of the Directive.[284] Similarly in the United Kingdom, the provisions relating to the form, content and cancellation of credit agreements do not apply to overdrafts.[285] It suffices that the advertisements disclose the rate of interest,[286] that the bank notifies the customer of the terms of the agreement and that the customer is given information on the state of her account and periodic statements.[287] In France the general law of consumer credit, with all its formalism, applies to overdraft facilities.[288]

The Directive has not harmonized the law governing the parties' contractual rights and obligations and, therefore, the differences of national laws as to whether and how to restrict party autonomy in the interest of consumer protection have remained considerable. Table 6.4 demonstrates a few notable examples.

In reality, the Directive intended to achieve only minimum harmonization of certain information and transparency requirements in the provision of credit, whereas the convergence of national consumer credit laws relating to parties' substantive rights and obligations was never one of the objectives. My own survey into the laws of three EU countries has shown that the Directive has been properly implemented 'as to the result to be achieved', to recall the threshold of proper implementation. The remaining differences of national consumer credit laws are mostly differences in detail concerning the form of contracts and of pre-contractual

---

[280] See CCA 1974, s. 94.
[281] See s. 95; Consumer Credit (Rebate on Early Settlement Regulations) 2004, SI 2004/1483.
[282] See § 489 BGB.
[283] See C.consom., art. L 311(29).
[284] See § 493 BGB.
[285] See CCA 1974, s. 74.
[286] See Consumer Credit (Advertisements) Regulations 2004, reg. 4, 8, sch. 2
[287] See CCA 1974, s. 78.
[288] See Cass. Avis 09.10.1992: *La Semaine Juridique* 1993, II, 22024.

Table 6.4. *National laws limiting party autonomy in consumer credit contracts*

|  | UK | Germany | France |
|---|---|---|---|
| **Right of withdrawal** | Not available in consumer credit agreements entered into at a distance or without oral representations (CCA 1974, ss. 67–73) | Yes – must be exercised within two weeks (355 BGB) | Yes – must be exercised within seven days (C.consom., art. L 311–15) |
| **Restriction of remedies in the event of default** | Seven days default notice in the prescribed form to the borrower before commencement of enforcement (CCA 1974, ss. 87–9) | No right of enforcement unless the borrower defaulted in two successive instalments which amount to at least 10% of the loan<br>In any case, two weeks, default notice<br>Opportunity to pay and discuss the possibility of consensus must be offered (498 BGB) | Discretionary court powers to evaluate the financial conditions of the parties and on that basis suspend enforcement, freeze interest, demand restructuring and rescheduling of instalments (C.civ., 1244–1 and C.consom., L 313(1)) |

Table 6.4. (*cont.*)

| | UK | Germany | France |
|---|---|---|---|
| **Interest rate regulation** | Freedom to determine the rate of interest but discretionary court powers to reopen grossly exorbitant or unfair credit bargains. Case-law suggests very rarely used. (CCA 1974, ss. 137–139) Right to compound interest upon interest (*NBG v. Pinios Shipping Co.* [1990] 1 AC 637) | Freedom to determine the rate of interest but courts have disallowed, on grounds of unfairness, contractual rates more than twice the market rate or in absolute numbers 12% above market rate. Prohibition to compound interest upon interest (289 BGB) | Freedom to determine the rate of interest unless the total applicable rate of charge is in excess of the statutory threshold of usurious rate of interest, currently 1/3 above the average market rate. The restriction applies to consumer loans and any type of overdraft facility (C. consom., L 313(3)). The contractual rate of interest is void unless fixed in writing (C.civ. 1907) No right to compound interest upon interest for periods less than one year (C.civ. 1154) |

disclosures. There are of course sharp differences in the regulation of substantive rights and obligations as shown in Table 6.4 but it should be noted that the Directive never aimed to achieve legal convergence in that respect.

Recognizing the need for modernizing the legal framework relating to consumer credit, the Commission published a proposal for a revised Directive in September 2002, which was later withdrawn and replaced by a new proposal in October 2005.[289]

## Convergence of national laws regulating the provision of online investment services

From an early stage in the development of electronic finance applications, national regulatory and supervisory agencies, working under the aegis of the IOSCO, have sought to develop international standards of good regulatory practice to address the regulatory and supervisory challenges posed by the provision of investment services via the Internet, especially the electronic reception and transmission of trading orders for unsophisticated retail investors.[290] The underlying principle of comparative regulatory practice is that regulation of securities activities should not inhibit innovation in financial products and services nor the use of advanced information technology, telecommunications and computer networks in primary and secondary capital markets. Insofar as the fundamental principles of securities regulation do not vary according to technological developments, the totality of regulatory provisions should attach to online securities activities unless special risks associated with electronic finance justify targeted regulatory reforms where appropriate.[291] With regard to online reception and transmission of trading orders, the IOSCO identified three main risks that may justify special regulatory and supervisory interest: first, the risk that unauthorized third parties may obtain access to client assets and accounts; second, the operational risk that the available capacity of IT systems, computer networks and telecommunications may be insufficient to serve large volumes of trading activity; and, finally, the risk that online services

---

[289] See European Commission, *Amended Proposal for a Directive of the European Parliament and of the Council on consumer credit*, COM(2005) 483 final.

[290] See International Association of Securities Commissions, *Report on Securities Activities on the Internet III* (Madrid, 2003); IOSCO, Second Internet Report; IOSCO, First Internet Report.

[291] See IOSCO, Second Internet Report, pp. 16–20.

may be unavailable because of technical failure, thus disrupting client access to securities markets. Regulatory authorities are encouraged to examine whether technical standards currently in place are capable of addressing those risks or whether some additional action would be necessary, for example additional investment in technology concerning network and IT security, ongoing assessment of potential vulnerabilities and review of existing contingency plans in case of failure.

## The Directive on Markets in Financial Instruments

To ensure that the regulatory objectives of investment services regulation are pursued on the basis of function rather than form and to create equal conditions of competition between providers of similar services, European banks providing investment services are subject to national securities laws implementing the 1993 Investment Services Directive.[292] The 1993 Investment Services Directive sought to establish the minimum legal conditions under which authorized investment firms and banks could provide specified services or establish branches in other Member States on the basis of home country authorization and supervision. To this end, that Directive aimed to harmonize the initial authorization and operating requirements for investment firms including conduct of business rules. It also provided for the harmonization of some conditions governing the operation of regulated markets.

In 2004, the Directive on Markets in Financial Instruments (MiFiD),[293] a central component of the Financial Services Action Plan, was adopted in view of repealing and replacing the 1993 Directive not earlier than October 2006.[294] The MiFiD will apply to investment firms and banks offering investment services and will establish an effective 'single passport', allowing them to operate throughout the European Union on the basis of authorization in their home Member State. The MiFiD establishes a high level of investor protection and, for the first time, a comprehensive regulatory framework governing the organized execution of securities transactions by organized securities markets,

---

[292] See Investment Services Directive, art. 2(1).
[293] See EP and Council Directive 2004/39/EC of 21 April 2004 on markets in financial instruments, OJ 2004 No. L145/1, 30 April 2004.
[294] *Ibid.*, arts. 70 and 71; see also Proposal for a Directive of the European Parliament and of the Council amending Directive 2004/39/EC on markets in financial instruments, as regards certain deadlines, COM(2005) 253 final.

alternative trading systems and financial institutions. In addition to allowing financial institutions to provide their services across borders on the basis of their home country authorization and supervision, it will substantially harmonize national regulations on the provision of investment services.

The Directive is a framework measure in line with the 2002 Resolution of the European Parliament,[295] which endorsed the Lamfalussy recommendations for speeding up financial services legislation in the single European market. It therefore confines itself to establishing the general high-level principles of the national legal framework, whereas more detailed implementing measures will be set out by the Commission in consultation with market participants and national authorities.

The Directive is of limited application to online banks providing investment services. The normative impact of the Directive is clearly focused on the regulation of the bank–client relationship and market conduct. Member States shall ensure that credit institutions comply only with those national provisions that implement the Directive rules on investor compensation schemes, regulatory requirements of internal organizational structure, conflicts of interest and investor protection, including conduct of business rules, market transparency and integrity and the right to provide investment services across borders.[296]

Regulatory requirements of organizational structure are set out in Article 13. As a general principle, financial institutions should maintain and operate effective organizational and administrative arrangements designed to prevent conflicts of interest arising in the course of business between themselves and their clients or between one client and another and establish adequate policies and procedures sufficient to ensure compliance with all applicable laws and regulations.[297] If those arrangements are not sufficient to ensure with confidence that risks of damage to client interests with be prevented, the investment firm shall clearly disclose the general nature and/or sources of conflicts of interest to the client before undertaking business on its behalf.[298] Another obligation is to ensure continuity and regularity in the performance of investment services and, crucially for online services, to employ appropriate systems, resources and procedures.[299] It should also maintain sound

---

[295] See European Parliament resolution on the implementation of financial services legislation, OJ 2002 No. C284 E/115, 21 November 2002.
[296] See Directive on Markets in Financial Instruments, art. 1(2).
[297] See art. 13(2), (3).   [298] See art. 18(2).   [299] See art. 13(4).

administrative and accounting procedures, internal control mechanisms, effective methods of risk assessment and security arrangements for information technology and processing systems.[300] Records must be kept of all services and transactions[301] and, when holding client funds or securities, adequate arrangements must be made so as to safeguard the client's ownership rights over his or her assets and prevent the use of a client's assets without the client's express consent.[302] To take account of technical developments, including developments in electronic finance applications, the Commission is expected to adopt measures which will specify concrete organizational requirements for financial institutions performing different services and activities.[303]

Unlike the 1993 Investment Services Directive, which achieved very limited harmonization of national investor protection rules,[304] the MiFiD established extensive regulatory requirements of conduct of business and market transparency.[305] Following international standards of good regulatory practice, the Directive establishes information requirements. All information and marketing communications addressed to clients or potential clients shall be fair, clear and not misleading and marketing communications shall be clearly identifiable as such.[306] It becomes compulsory to provide appropriate information about the firm and its services, financial instruments and proposed investment strategies, the risks associated with particular investments, execution venues and markets, costs and associated charges.[307]

The Directive requires financial institutions to know and appreciate their clients' financial situation, investment objectives and knowledge and experience of investment products or services by obtaining all relevant information.[308] There is also a duty to warn the client if the financial institution considers that the product or service is not appropriate to the client or potential client.[309] Member States shall, however, allow financial institutions providing online services that only consist of execution and/or reception and transmission of client orders (without investment advice) to provide those services without the need to obtain information on their clients' financial situation, investment objectives,

---

[300] See art. 13(5).
[301] See art. 13(6).
[302] See art. 13(7), (8).
[303] See art. 13(10).
[304] See Investment Services Directive, art. 11.
[305] See Directive on Markets in Financial Instruments, arts. 19–30.
[306] See art. 19(2).
[307] See art. 19(3).
[308] See art. 19(4), (5).
[309] See art. 19(5).

knowledge and experience, provided that (a) the services relate to securities admitted to trading on regulated markets, (b) the service is provided at the initiative of the client, (c) the client is informed that the firm is not required to assess the suitability of the investment, (d) the firm complies with its obligations concerning conflicts of interest.[310]

The firm shall also establish a record that includes the document agreed between the firm and the client that sets out the rights and obligations of the parties and the terms of the service.[311] The client is further entitled to receive adequate reports relating to the costs of transactions and the services undertaken on behalf of the client.[312] In adopting detailed measures implementing the Directive, the Commission shall take into account the nature of the service and of the financial instrument and the retail or professional nature of the client.[313] This reflects a proportionate and risk-based approach to regulation which establishes divergent standards of protection for different types of risks, securities activities and types of investors.

In addition to conduct of business rules that must be respected by all financial institutions providing investment services, online banks and firms providing execution or reception/transmission services are subject to special regulatory standards. When executing trading orders, they shall be required to take all reasonable steps to obtain the best possible result for the client, taking into account price, costs, speed, likelihood of execution and settlement, size, nature or any other consideration relevant to the execution of the order, unless there is a specific instruction from the client, in which case the firm shall execute the order following the specific instruction.[314] They will also be obliged to ensure the prompt, fair and expeditious execution of client orders, relative to other client orders or to the proprietary trading interests of the firm, executing comparable client orders in strict accordance with the time of their reception by the firm.[315]

In the interest of transparency and market integrity, investment firms will be required to keep at the disposal of regulatory agencies, for at least five years, the relevant data relating to all their transactions in securities,[316] whereas those firms executing transactions in securities admitted to trading on regulated markets will be additionally required

---

[310] See art. 19(6).
[311] See art. 19(7).
[312] See art. 19(8).
[313] See art. 19(10).
[314] See art. 21(1).
[315] See art. 22(1).
[316] See art. 25(2).

to report details of such transactions to the authorities as quickly as possible and no later than the close of the following business day.[317] The latter firms will also be required to make public the volume and price of those transactions and the time at which they were concluded as close to real time as possible, on a reasonable commercial basis and in a manner which is easily accessible to other market participants.[318]

Based on the extensive harmonization of national rules of investor protection by the Directive's high-level provisions and, crucially, the Commission's broad mandate to introduce detailed EU rules implementing those high-level principles and standards, the MiFiD paves the way for the full mutual recognition of national investor protection laws on the basis of home country control. In their capacity as 'host countries', Member States shall ensure that any financial institution authorized and supervised by the authorities of another Member State may freely perform investment services within their territories provided that such services and activities are covered by the firm's authorization.[319] The legal framework relating to investor protection would be the law of the 'home country', because 'host' Member States 'shall not impose any additional requirements on such an investment firm or credit institution in respect of the matters covered by this Directive'.[320]

### Online investment services and national laws of investor protection

National provisions regulating the conduct of firms providing online investment services still reflect the 1993 Investment Services Directive. It should be noted that although Member States have all adopted rules regulating the marketing of investment services, the internal organizational structure of financial institutions, the required disclosure of information to investors, the handling of client funds and assets and the conduct of business, the remaining differences in the detail and form of national provisions and the methods of supervision and enforcement are substantial. In the early stages of the Financial Services Acton Plan the Commission conducted a thorough review of national conduct of business rules and concluded that, although the general principles and requirements of Article 11 of the Investment Services Directive had been successfully implemented, the content and form of national provisions

---

[317] See art. 25(3).   [318] See art. 28(1).
[319] See art. 31(1).   [320] Ibid.

still differed substantially in detail from country to country.[321] It was also observed that the applicable national criteria for distinguishing between professional and retail investors remained so inconsistent in their detail that financial institutions serving clients of similar sophistication in different Member States were likely to fall into different regulatory frameworks from country to country for serving the same type of clients. The Commission eventually concluded that the level of harmonization of national laws of investor protection was inadequate to support the mutual recognition of national laws, paving the way for the ensuing reform of the legal framework by the MiFiD.

## United Kingdom

In the United Kingdom the legal framework regulating the internal organizational structure of firms providing investment services comprises the 'threshold conditions' for carrying out regulated activities,[322] several modules of the FSA Handbook such as the *Principles for Business* (PRIN), *Senior Management Arrangements, Systems and Controls* (SYSC), *Threshold Conditions* (COND), *Fit and Proper Test for Approved Persons* (FIT) and substantial parts of the *Conduct of Business* (COB (FSA)) module regulating Chinese walls,[323] conflicts of interest,[324] the protection of client assets,[325] transactions by employees for their own interest,[326] recording and reporting requirements.[327]

Although 'private customers' (who are not classified as 'expert private customers') enjoy the full protection of the regulatory framework,[328] firms providing execution and/or reception and transmission services are subject to a 'lighter' regulatory regime provided that no investment advice is offered.[329]

---

[321] See European Commission, *The Application of Conduct of Business Rules Under Article 11 of the Investment Services Directive* COM(2000) 722 final; European Commission., *Upgrading the Investment Services Directive* COM(2000)729 final.
[322] See FiSMA 2000, sch. 6.
[323] See Conduct of Business (COB (FSA)) 2.4R.
[324] See COB (FSA) 7.1R.
[325] See COB (FSA) 9.
[326] See COB (FSA) 7.13.
[327] See COB (FSA), sch. 1 and sch. 2.
[328] See COB (FSA) 4.1.
[329] The following do not apply: COB (FSA) 4.2 (Terms of Business and Client Agreements); COB (FSA) 5.2 (know your customer); COB (FSA) 5.1 (Polarization and Status Disclosure).

Online banks inviting or inducing the public to engage in investment activities are subject to the financial promotion requirements of COB (FSA) 3. Furthermore, they shall ensure that non-real time communications include a fair and adequate description of the nature of the service, the risks involved and the commitment required.[330] They shall also disclose all necessary information relating to the legal status of the firm,[331] remuneration and fees.[332] Excessive fees are prohibited[333] and the firm's own transactions must be executed fairly and in due turn.[334] Further, to provide best execution, a firm must take reasonable care to ascertain the price which is the best available for the customer order in the relevant market and execute the order at a price which is no less advantageous to the customer unless the firm has taken reasonable steps to ensure that it would be in the customer's best interests not to do so.[335] The execution must be timely.[336] There are also rules which regulate the orderly aggregation and allocation of the firm's own and client transactions,[337] the realization of customers' assets,[338] confirmation of transactions[339] and periodic statements.[340] Investors enjoy a private right of action for breach of statutory duty against financial institutions violating the conduct of business rules unless the loss is suffered by persons acting in a professional capacity in the course of business.[341]

## France

With regard to requirements of organizational structure and investor protection under French law, the Monetary and Financial Code reflects the provisions of the 1993 Investment Services Directive. With regard to prudential requirements, online banks providing investment services are required to maintain financial soundness, liquidity and adequate resources,[342] to adopt internal policies on the execution of employees' orders for their own account,[343] to protect their clients' proprietary interests in their assets and funds and refrain from trading in their own account with client assets or using client funds without the client's

---

[330] See COB (FSA) 3.8.8R.
[331] See COB (FSA) 5.5.
[332] See COB (FSA) 5.7.
[333] See COB (FSA) 5.6.
[334] See COB (FSA) 7.4.
[335] See COB (FSA) 7.5.5R.
[336] See COB (FSA) 7.6.4R.
[337] See COB (FSA) 7.7.
[338] See COB (FSA) 7.8.
[339] See COB (FSA) 8.1.
[340] See COB (FSA) 8.2.
[341] See FiSMA 2000, s. 150; Financial Services and Markets Act 2000 (Rights of Action) Regulations, SI 2001/2256, reg. 3.
[342] See C.monét.fin., art. L 533(1).
[343] Ibid., art. L 533(6).

prior consent.[344] The conduct of business rules of Article 11 of the 1993 Directive were adopted *verbatim* by Article L 533(4) of the French Monetary and Financial Code. More detailed conduct of business regulations in content and form are set out in the 3rd Book of the General Regulation of the Autorité des Marchés Financiers (*Règlement Général AMF*).[345]

Starting from the requirements of organizational structure, investment firms are required to appoint a compliance officer with wide powers to oversee the implementation of rigorous systems of internal control.[346] Orders submitted by staff for their own account cannot have priority, in terms of transmission or execution, over orders placed by customers and must be routed and executed using procedures comparable to those used for such customers.[347] Under no circumstances may staff transmit orders directly to the market or to a trading desk.[348] Employees exposed to risks of conflicting interests or having access to confidential information shall not trade for their own account.[349]

The conduct of firms providing online investment services is regulated from the moment that a potential client is likely to enter into a contract for the provision of services.[350] The law requires the parties to reduce their agreement into a written contract that contains a number of mandatory terms prescribed by law.[351]

As general principle, the firm is a *del credere* agent of the client. It guarantees the delivery of and payment for securities bought or sold on the customer's behalf.[352] The bank must act with care and diligence and give absolute priority to the interests of its customers as regards reception, transmission and execution of trading orders and the placement of securities.[353] Moreover, the bank is under a legal duty to provide its customers with the best possible execution, taking into account the instructions it receives, the conditions in the relevant market(s) and

---

[344] See art. L 533(7), (8).
[345] See H. de Vauplane and J.-P. Bornet, *Droit des Marchés Financiers* (3rd edn, Paris: Litec, 2001), pp. 882–98.
[346] See *Règlement Général AMF*, art. 321-24.
[347] *Ibid.*, art. 321-34.
[348] *Ibid.*
[349] See arts. 321-37 and 321-39.
[350] See de Vauplane and Bornet, *Droit des Marchés Financiers*, pp. 884–6.
[351] See *Règlement Général AMF*, arts. 321-44 and 321-68.
[352] See *Règlement Général AMF*, art. 321-20.
[353] See C.monét.fin., art. L 533(4); C.civ., art. 1991.

the securities involved.[354] The bank is prohibited from trading for its own account with client money[355] and must provide regular information as to the state of the customer's account and the execution of his transactions.[356] Before executing a transaction in a financial instrument for a new customer, the intermediary must verify the identity of the customer.[357] The use of the authentication devices provided for in the 'Internet service' agreement is a rebuttable presumption that the customer's authority has been obtained.[358]

The bank must assess the professional competency of the customer to master the envisaged transactions and the attendant risks.[359] The assessment must take into account the customer's financial condition, investment experience and objectives. The customer must be informed of the characteristics of the securities, the transaction and the relevant risks taking into account his investment experience.[360] In that respect, the General Regulation establishes transparency and disclosure requirements from which, unlike the UK and German framework, execution-only services are not exempted.[361] When a customer envisages carrying out a transaction that differs from those he generally does, either by nature or in terms of the securities or amounts involved, the firm has a duty to ask him to explain the objectives of the transaction[362] and, on that information, the firm must reassess the customer's expertise and provide new information before the execution of the transaction. The rule would render online trading disproportionately onerous and for that reason firms must ensure that the contract prescribes the customer's trading limitations in markets, instruments and amount so as to preclude the transmission of instructions which 'differ from those that the customer generally performs'.

Financial institutions providing online investment services across borders are required to provide additional information on the legal status of the overseas market and its recognition by the French authorities,[363]

---

[354] See *Règlement Général AMF*, art. 321-42.
[355] See C.monét.fin., art. L 533(7).
[356] See *Règlement Général AMF*, arts. 321-47 and 321-49.
[357] See art. 321-43.
[358] See L. Ruet, 'La Passation des Ordres de Bourse via Internet' (2000) *Revue de Droit Bancaire et Financier* (May/June) 194, at 199–200.
[359] See *Règlement Général AMF*, art. 321-46.
[360] See Cass.Com. 05.09.1991, RTD com. 1992, 436.
[361] See *Règlement Général AMF*, art. 321-57.
[362] See art. 321-48.   [363] See art. 251-3.

the legal nature of the service under the applicable law,[364] the competent supervisory authority and procedures for the resolution of disputes between the firm and the customer.[365] The information must be drafted in the French language and made available to the customers prior to the commencement of trading on the regulated market.[366] A copy of this information must be sent to the French competent authority.[367]

The General Regulation (*Règlement Général AMF*) contains specific provisions adapting the general law to services provided via the Internet.[368] More specifically, commercial communications must clearly identify the status of the firm and the persons who perform auxiliary services such as clearing, settlement and safe custody.[369] The verification of the customer's identity is carried out by means of the standard identification documents.[370] The bank must ensure that the client systematically receives the information relating to nature and risks of performed operations in screen-readable or downloadable form, before the client is able to place his first Internet order.[371] Whoever maintains the client's cash and securities accounts must have an automated account-verification system.[372] In the event of insufficient funds and margin or if the trading limits have been overstepped, the system must block order entry. The client is informed on-screen of the reasons for such blocking and is requested to remedy the situation. The firm must acknowledge on-screen that the client's order has been registered and the customer must be invited to confirm the order.[373] The 'Internet service' agreement must prescribe that the firm assumes responsibility for proper execution once acknowledgment has been sent and the order has been confirmed. In light of industry-wide IT security standards, firms must ensure the security of order-reception systems.[374] In the event of malfunction every effort should be taken to inform users of the nature and foreseeable duration of the failure.[375] The firm must strive to achieve sufficient capacity of order-reception systems, including back-up systems, alternative means of communication in the event of IT malfunction and human resources in IT and network technology.[376] It is suggested that the violation of conduct of business rules triggers civil liability in tort if

---

[364] Ibid.   [365] See art. 251-5.   [366] Ibid.
[367] See art. 251-6.   [368] See arts. 321-54 to 321-69.
[369] See art. 321-54.   [370] See art. 321-56.
[371] See arts. 321-59 to 321-61.   [372] See arts. 321-62 to 321-63.
[373] See art. 321-64.   [374] See art. 321-67.
[375] See art. 321-65.   [376] See art. 321-66.

economic loss can be established[377] but the issue remains controversial in legal doctrine.[378]

## Germany

The German framework of investor protection comprises the Securities Trading Act[379] (WpHG), the Guidelines issued by the competent authority and the duties implied by the general law of contract.[380]

Articles 33 and 34 of the WpHG impose requirements of internal organizational structure with regard to resources and procedures, avoidance of conflicts of interest, procedures of compliance and internal control and requirements to keep and retain records. The statute is complemented by interpretative regulatory Guidelines.[381] The German regulator requires that the measures taken for the implementation of the organizational duties be proportionate and commensurate to the size, types of business activity and structure of the firm.[382] Among such necessary means and procedures are measures to ensure the confidentiality of insider information and the avoidance of conflicts of interest such as confidential areas (Chinese walls) and restrictions on the flow of information;[383] the development of an internal culture of compliance; and arrangements designed to minimize delays in the execution or transmission of orders in case of failure or faults of the system.[384] This implies that care must be taken to strengthen the capacity of networks and IT systems and maintain contingency plans in the event of technical failure.[385]

Although the regulatory requirement to maintain robust IT systems is not in itself a legal basis of contractual or tortious liability in the event of technical failure, German courts under certain circumstances are

---

[377] See A. Leborgne, 'Responsabilité Civile et Opérations sur le Marché Boursier' (1998) 48 RTD com 261, at 274–6.
[378] See T. Bonneau, 'De l'Inulité du Droit Contractuel pour Assurer le Respect des Règles de Marché' (1999) 52 RTD com 257.
[379] *Wertpapier-Handelsgesetz.*
[380] See Kümpel, *Bank- und Kapitalmarktrecht*, pp. 1894–929.
[381] See Bundesaufsichtsamt für den Wertpapierhandel (BAWe), *Richtlinie zur Konkretisierung der Organizationspflichten von Wertpapierdienstleistungsunternehmen gemäss § 33 Abs. 1 WpHG* (Frankfurt, 1999).
[382] *Ibid.*, art. 2.1.
[383] See arts. 3.2, 3.3.
[384] See art. 2.2.
[385] See OLG Schleswig ZIP 2000, 1721; LG Nürnberg-Fürth NJW-RR 2000, 1650.

prepared to infer an enforceable duty to ensure 'unimpeded availability' of service from the language used in advertising and pre-contractual material and other surrounding circumstances.[386] Liability for breach of contract was found, for example, in cases where a promise to provide 'reliable and 24/7' services was made in corporate literature and the interruption of the service resulted in economic loss due to adverse price movements in the market.[387]

Conduct of business rules are established by Articles 31 and 32 of the WpHG and further elaborated by regulatory Guidelines.[388] In consonance with the provisions of the 1993 Investment Services Directive, the German provisions require firms to perform their obligations with the requisite degree of expertise, care and conscientiousness in the interests of their customers.[389] They must endeavour to avoid conflicts of interest and to ensure that customers' orders are executed with due regard to customers' interests.[390] Firms are required to obtain information on their clients' experience or knowledge of securities transactions, their investment objectives and their financial situation.[391] Firms should not treat their own or their employees' trading orders better than their clients' orders.[392] Customer orders must be promptly executed or transmitted, unless later execution or transmission is in the interest of the customer.[393] In principle, all orders and instructions must be executed or transmitted in the order they were received.[394] If orders are to be executed on a stock exchange, the firm should take care to transmit them without delay.[395]

There is no duty to provide investment advice to experienced customers in contracts for the provision of execution-only services.[396] The bank can expressly disclaim the offer of investment advice by appropriate

---

[386] See § 276 BGB; G. Mai, 'Wertpapierhandel', at pp. 206–7; Peter Balzer, 'Legal Aspects in Direct Banks Securities Business. A German Perspective' in Norbert Horn (ed.), *Legal Issues in Electronic Banking* (The Hague: Kluwer, 2002), pp. 247–50.
[387] See LG Itzehoe (10 July 2001) AZ: 1 S 92/01; AG Pinneberg (16 February 2001) AZ: 64 C 376/00; Landgericht Nürnberg-Fürth (19 May 1999) AZ: 14 O 9971/98.
[388] See BAWe, *Richtlinie zur Konkretisierung der §§ 31 und 32 WpHG für das Kommissionsgeschäft, den Eigenhandel für andere und das Vermittlungsgeschäft der Wertpapierdienstleistungsunternehmen* (Frankfurt, 2001).
[389] See § 31 Abs. 1(i) WpHG.
[390] See § 31 Abs. 1(ii) WpHG.
[391] See § 31 Abs. 2 WpHG.
[392] See BAWe, Richtlinie zur Konkretisierung der § 31 und 32, art. 3(1).
[393] Ibid., art. 3(2); BGH (24 July 2001) XI ZR 164/2000.
[394] Ibid.    [395] Ibid.    [396] See BGH WM 1996, 906.

terms in the 'Internet service' agreement.[397] Standard corporate literature in electronic form explaining the basic risks and opportunities of various investment markets, instruments or strategies is sufficient. The position regarding inexperienced investors is more controversial[398] although the Court of Appeal has accepted that there is no duty of information and advice beyond general explanatory literature.[399]

Execution-only services are subject to reduced regulatory requirements. According to section 2(6) of the Guideline, providers of execution-only services must inform the customer about the scope of their services prior to accepting any orders. The information must be brought in line with the customer's knowledge of and experience in the envisaged forms of investment. If additional information is provided, including market reports and analysis, it must be made clear that this information does not amount to investment advice. The usual disclosure requirements on corporate status, applicable fees, commissions and costs, terms and conditions and type, elements and risks of intended transactions apply.[400] The violation of those provisions in the Act which promote the protection of investors establishes a private right of action for damages for breach of statutory duty under Article 823(2) of the German Civil Code.[401] The Federal Court appears to have endorsed the view,[402] although it is also argued that a personal right of action is not available to investors.[403]

### Assessing the level of convergence of national laws regulating Internet banking

The process of legal harmonization in the single European market is complex. The threshold of its success is significantly lower if the overarching aim is to underpin mutual recognition of national laws through the attainment of minimum convergence acceptable to all participating nations. The threshold becomes however substantially higher if

---

[397] See Balzer, 'Legal Aspects', pp. 232–3.
[398] See P. Balzer, 'Aktuelle Rechtsprechung zum Discount Broking' (2001) 1 *Die Bank* 51.
[399] See OLG München ZIP 1998, 1954.
[400] See BAWe, Richtlinie zur Konkretisierung der § 31 and 32, arts. 1(1), 1(2), 2(2), 2(6); see also § 31 Abs. 2(ii) WpHG.
[401] See Balzer, 'Legal Aspects', p. 245.
[402] See BGH (24 July 2001) XI ZR 329/00.
[403] See U. Florian, *Internet Wertpapierhandels*, pp. 74–5.

legal harmonization is the sole mechanism of financial integration with exclusive objective to eliminate legal diversity across Member States.

The second route is not attractive nor is it what EU law is all about. It is impossible to expect legal uniformity through the centralization of legislative functions at the EU level while the implementation and enforcement of common rules remains the responsibility of national authorities. Even if EU rules are transposed into national law, there are occasions where national courts continue to interpret national provisions in the light of domestic legal and cultural experiences and according to national rules of interpretation, particularly in cases of general clauses or common standards of an abstract or imprecise nature. The test of unfairness in the Unfair Terms Directive is a typical example.

By relying on Directives which are binding only as to the result to be achieved, EU harmonization generates diverse national methods and practices of implementation and fails to create a complete system of European law. It normally addresses specific issues, while in most cases Member States are allowed to maintain or adopt more stringent standards of consumer or investor protection.

Measured against an overarching aim of uniformity, the end result is difficult to portray otherwise than as an unsystematic and piecemeal approximation of national laws, far short of the level required to eliminate diversity. The remaining noticeable differences in the scope of application of implementing legislation, the intensity of harmonization, the substance and form of national rules, even the most trivial diversity in systemically unimportant commercial conduct, will disturb free economic movement unless claims of more than one country to regulate are dismissed.

From the perspective of mutual recognition, harmonization assumes an auxiliary function which reduces considerably the requirements of success. Common EU rules become the 'floor' of economic regulation and protection and the lower acceptable threshold of legal convergence. By default, the adequacy of depositor, investor or borrower protection is measured against the needs of rational and responsible information seekers. Although the protection of more vulnerable individuals is by all means a noble task, it should neither serve as a pretext for inhibiting free markets nor should it be carried out at the EC level.

Common rules amount to regulation proper. Regulation must not constrain individual freedom beyond what is necessary to address identifiable risks in the light of the circumstances of each case. Disclosure of information must take precedence over outright limitations of commercial freedom unless more stringent rules are justified. What matters is the qualitative response to risks and the enjoyment of equivalent protection in the Member States. More stringent national rules are welcome but should not restrict the cross-border provision of services. Sufficient legal convergence does not require uniformity in legal methodology and national legal instruments. Differences in trivial matters pose no risks for the internal market but the substantive quality of enforcement and supervision is as important as the enactment of common rules.

Turning our attention to national approaches, national authorities are consistent in treating electronic banking in accordance with the general risk-based supervisory framework. The emerging regulatory standards and supervisory practices epitomize successfully the recommendations of the Basel Committee. The key risks are fully identified and supervisory authorities seem to have agreed on the basic framework of supervision. They have all emphasized the importance of constant review and international cooperation.

The position of investors and depositors has become stronger. With the full implementation of the Distance Marketing and E-Commerce Directives, the disclosure of information will be unprecedented, while the statutory right of withdrawal from the contract will offer an 'after-the-event' exit from unsatisfactory agreements, thus enhancing consumer confidence. Whether in implementation of EU or national policies, the basic framework of investor, depositor and borrower protection is in place. Remaining differences in conduct of business regulation, consumer credit law and the law of bank transactions do not always correspond to different regulatory perspectives. They largely represent differences in methods and style of presentation which are fatal in the event of conflicting national laws but harmless in a single market of mutual recognition and 'home country' control. The most recent reforms in the framework of the Financial Services Action Plan will increase the level of European harmonization even further. More extensive harmonization and unrestricted mutual recognition are already the institutional choices of key measures such as the Directive on Markets in Financial Instruments and the Unfair Commercial Practices Directive. The implementation of the Lamfallussy recommendations will contribute to the speedier adoption of legal instruments, better common rules and a better institutional framework for reconciling political controversies as to the content of common rules. The ultimate responsibility for the end result depends on the political rigour with which those opportunities are explored.

# PART IV

Applicable law and allocation of regulatory responsibility in cross-border electronic banking activities

# 7

# Cross-border Internet banking and the principle of 'home country' control in the EU Financial Services Directives

## Introduction

From the early development of the single market programme, the principle of 'home country' control was intended to operate as one of the three pillars of the single European market in financial services. More specifically, the harmonization of substantive rules on such matters as initial authorization, prudential supervision and internal organization of banks and other credit institutions was thought to offer a strong basis of mutual recognition of national laws and the attribution of the primary task of supervising the internationally active financial institution to the competent authorities of the Member State of its origin ('home country' control).[1] It was also implicit that the authorities of the country of destination of financial services, while not deprived of all power, would assume a complementary role.[2]

The fourth and last part of the book will examine the extent to which cross-border electronic banking activities in the single European market are subject to the legal and supervisory control of the 'home country' of the bank and whether Member States in their capacity as recipient countries may impose their own legal requirements to online services originating in another EU state. This chapter will outline the normative content of the principle of 'home country' control of the Banking Consolidation Directive[3] and how this institutional arrangement influences the allocation of legislative and supervisory jurisdiction for prudential matters between the 'home' and 'host' state in the case of cross-border banking services. Subsequently, chapter 8 will discuss the extent to which the principle of 'country of origin' of the E-Commerce

---

[1] See European Commission, *Completing the Internal Market*, p. 28.
[2] Ibid.
[3] EP and Council Directive 2000/12/EC of 20 March 2000 relating to the taking up and pursuit of the business of credit institutions, OJ 2000 No. L126/1, 26 May 2000.

Directive[4] has expanded the scope of application of 'home country' control with regard to online banking services. Finally, chapter 9 will examine the question of governing law for cross-border consumer banking contracts which have remained unaffected by the 'home country' rules of the Banking and E-Commerce Directives. Taken together, these three chapters present the conflicts of national laws and economic regulations relating to cross-border electronic banking and the extent to which the institutional reforms carried out by EU Directives have contributed to legal clarity and certainty in the single market for e-commerce in financial services.

## Cross-border Internet banking without the benefit of 'home country' regulation and supervision

The liberalizing effects of the principle of mutual recognition and 'home country' control in the single European market are substantial. It suffices to examine the regulatory treatment afforded by EU (or EEA) Member States to cross-border services provided by non-EU (or non-EEA) banks to indicate just how much the single market programme has improved the legal framework by permitting financial institutions to provide services to non-residents without being subject to the legal and supervisory framework of the 'host country'. The applicable legal framework to financial institutions providing cross-border services outside the framework of EU financial services Directives demonstrates that in cases where the principle of 'home country control' does not apply, the institutional choice of EU countries has been to always regulate online services directed at domestic residents regardless of the location of the financial institution domestically or overseas.

### The regulatory laws of the United Kingdom without the benefit of 'home country' control

Section 19 of the FiSMA 2000 provides that the requirement to be authorized under the Act only applies in relation to regulated activities that are carried on 'in the United Kingdom'. Section 418(5) clarifies the position of overseas firms which maintain an establishment in the

---

[4] EP and Council Directive 2000/31/EC of 8 June 2000 on certain legal aspects of information society services, in particular electronic commerce, in the internal market, OJ 2000 No. L178/1, 17 July 2000.

United Kingdom but makes no reference to services provided to UK residents at a distance from outside the United Kingdom, via the Internet or otherwise. In the view of the FSA, a firm based outside the United Kingdom may potentially be regarded as carrying on activities in the United Kingdom even if the firm does not have a place of business maintained in the United Kingdom (for example, by means of the Internet or other telecommunications system or by occasional visits).[5] The FSA has been reluctant to establish and apply a single determinative criterion for identifying the location where certain electronic activities are carried on. It suggested however that in most cases it will be relevant to consider whether what the firm is doing satisfies the so-called 'business test' established by the FiSMA 2000. In addition, it will also be relevant whether the firm may be able to rely on the exemptions enjoyed by certain 'overseas persons'.[6] In other words, the FSA suggests that financial institutions based outside the United Kingdom will be regarded as carrying on activities in the United Kingdom for regulatory purposes *provided that* the pertinent regulated activities satisfy the 'business test' and, simultaneously, lie outside the scope of application of certain exclusions enjoyed under the Act by 'overseas persons'.

Under section 22 of the FiSMA 2000, for an activity to be a regulated activity it must be carried on 'by way of business', which expressly depends on the type of activity.[7] With regard to online banking activities, the determinative activity is the acceptance of deposits. The activity of accepting deposits will not be regarded as carried on by way of business by a person if he does not hold himself out as accepting deposits on a day-to-day basis and if the deposits he accepts are accepted only on particular occasions.[8] In determining whether deposits are accepted only on particular occasions, the frequency of the occasions and any distinguishing characteristics must be taken into account. It therefore appears that online banks based outside the United Kingdom will be regarded as carrying on activities in the United Kingdom if they hold themselves out as accepting deposits from persons in the United Kingdom on a day-to-day regular basis.

A non-EEA bank engaging in online banking activities would still be outside the scope of application of the 'general prohibition', if the activities were among those activities for which 'overseas persons' are

---

[5] See FSA Handbook AUTH 2.4.6 G.
[6] *Ibid.* [7] See AUTH 2.3.2 G. [8] *Ibid.*

excluded.[9] It turns out that the relevant provisions regarding 'overseas persons' do not apply to firms engaging in core banking activities,[10] and therefore financial institutions based on non-EEA countries are required to obtain a Part IV permission to engage in electronic banking operations if they hold themselves out as accepting deposits from persons in the United Kingdom on a day-to-day regular basis via the Internet or otherwise.

The application of the 'general prohibition' to non-EEA financial institutions based outside the United Kingdom, which triggers the obligation to obtain a Part IV permission to carry on regulated activities, does not automatically require those firms to comply with the regulatory provisions of the FSA Handbook, including conduct of business rules. There are special provisions which determine the territorial scope of application of the various parts of the Handbook to cross-border activities. Subject to expressly defined exceptions, the general principle is that the conduct of business module (COB) applies in relation to activities carried on from an establishment maintained by the firm in the United Kingdom only. Thus, an overseas bank advertising or engaging in electronic banking activities with persons in the United Kingdom via the Internet would remain outside the scope of application of COB unless an exception to the rule provided otherwise.[11] There is only one exception relevant for banks based in non-EEA countries but it is a very wide one which effectively brings most online banking activities between foreign banks and UK customers within the scope of application of COB. Pursuant to Rule COB 1.4.3 the COB Sourcebook applies in relation to activities *not* carried on from an establishment maintained by the firm in the United Kingdom, *if* the activity is carried on with or for a client in the United Kingdom. None of the exceptions to this rule applies to online banking activities.[12] Finally, rule COB 3.3.1 defines the scope of territorial application of the rules on financial promotion. According to the rule, the financial promotion regime applies only in relation to the communication of a financial promotion to a person inside the United Kingdom. Thus, in principle and without prejudice to the liberalizing effects of EU Directives, the UK financial regulatory laws apply to online banking services, which are marketed or provided to UK residents, even when the provider of services is established outside the United Kingdom.

---

[9] See AUTH 2.4.6 G.
[10] See AUTH 2.9.15 G.
[11] See COB 1.4.2 R.
[12] See COB 1.4.3 R

Another interesting question is whether the FSA rules apply to banks based in the United Kingdom that provide or market online services to clients based outside the United Kingdom. In light of section 19 of the FiSMA 2000, which limits the application of the UK rules to activities carried on 'in the United Kingdom', section 418 of the Act clarifies that for regulatory purposes an activity is regarded as being carried on in the United Kingdom, if it is carried on by a UK-based person and the day-to-day management of the activity is the responsibility of an establishment in the United Kingdom. The location of the customer in the United Kingdom or elsewhere is not determinative.

### The regulatory laws of Germany without the benefit of 'home country' control

According to section 32 of the German Banking Act, the requirement to be authorized under the Act applies to anyone wishing to conduct banking business or to provide financial services in Germany commercially or on a scale which requires a commercially organized business undertaking. Regulated business is conducted in Germany not only when the bank has its head office or an established place of business within the country but also when it is established outside the country and purposefully addresses the German market in order to offer, regularly and by way of business, banking or financial services to businesses and/or individuals established within Germany.[13]

Financial institutions based on a non-EU (and non-EEA) country may only provide services to German residents after obtaining the requisite regulatory approval and only on the condition that the services are provided to German residents from within a local branch or subsidiary.[14] In other words, financial institutions that do not enjoy the institutional benefits of the single financial market are prohibited from offering online banking services from a commercial establishment outside Germany. It should be noted that this prohibition applies without prejudice to the constitutionally guaranteed right of German residents to request services from banks established outside the country.[15] German law therefore

---

[13] See Bundesanstalt für Finanzdienstleistungsaufsicht (BAFIN), *Hinweise zur Erlaubnispflicht nach § 32 Abs. 1 KWG in Verbindung mit § 1 Abs. 1 und Abs. 1a KWG von Grenzüberschreitend Betriebenen Bankgeschäften und/oder Grenzüberschreitend erbrachten Finanzdienstleistungen* (Bonn, 2003).
[14] *Ibid.* [15] *Ibid.*

makes a distinction between services 'purposefully directed at German residents' – in which case cross-border services from an establishment outside Germany are prohibited – and cross-border services that German residents can enjoy under their fundamental constitutional rights. The Federal Supervisory Authority applies a range of criteria to determine whether cross-border services by non-EU (and non-EEA) banks are permissible or not.[16] In principle, it is not determinative to identify the location where the electronic data were loaded from or where the equipment hosting the website is located. What matters is the content of the communication. Internet sites in German will be considered an offer in Germany unless expressly and clearly directed at other German-speaking nations. Conversely, Internet sites in a foreign language will not be considered an offer in Germany provided that additional elements of the offer point to the same direction, for example a prominent disclaimer that the offer is not addressed to German residents or the absence of contact persons in Germany. Other factors such as the domain name, the legal and financial particulars of the available services, the standard terms of contract or the currency, are taken into account. The strongest criterion of all is the actual provision of services to persons in Germany, which in the words of the Federal Authority 'speaks for' services purposefully directed to German residents. Effectively, the criteria used by the German authority imply that German residents enjoy the constitutional right to sign up to unsolicited services provided by foreign banks, but if services were actually provided to German residents, that would be a strong criterion of active solicitation in Germany, which would be prohibited to non-EU and non-EEA firms.

### The regulatory laws of France without the benefit of 'home country' control

In France, the requirement of regulatory authorization applies to legal persons which carry out by way of regular business banking operations[17] or provide investment services.[18] The French authorities have accepted that the conduct of cross-border electronic banking activities takes place

---

[16] Ibid.; Bundesaufsichtsamt für das Kreditwesen (BAKRED), *Marketing of Foreign Collective Investment Schemes on the Internet* (Berlin, 1998); BAWe, Bekanntmachung zum Wertpapier-Verkaufsprospektgesetz.
[17] See C.monét.fin., arts. L 311-1, L 511-1, L 511-9.
[18] See arts. L 321-1, L 531-1 and L 532-1.

within the territory where the bank's central operational and administration system is located, thus requiring online banks to obtain regulatory approvals in their 'home country'.[19] To determine, however, whether additional regulatory authorization would be required in France, they use the criterion of the 'manifest intention' of the bank to market or provide services to French residents as this intention is expressly stated on the website or, in the absence of an express statement, as it is indirectly inferred from an open-ended list of criteria such as the use of the French language, a French domain name, whether the design, structure and content imply an offer addressed to French residents, the use of links to other French websites, standard form contracts which imply a local connection and the accessibility of the site through French financial portals and search engines.[20]

## Mutual recognition of national laws on the basis of 'home country' control in the Banking and Investment Services Directives

In the banking sector, the principle of 'home country control' in prudential regulatory matters was first established by the Second Banking Directive,[21] now repealed and replaced by the Banking Consolidation Directive.[22] The Directive provides that a 'credit institution', defined as any undertaking whose business is to receive deposits or other repayable funds from the public and to grant credits for its own account,[23] should be authorized in the Member State in which it has its registered office (home state).[24] The head office must always be situated in the home Member State and actually operate there.[25] Once incorporated and authorized in the 'home country', the bank may carry on within the territories of other Member States, either by the establishment of a branch or by way of the provision of services, the activities listed in Annex I to the Directive.[26] Within the scope of the so-called 'passport' are core banking services, for example accepting deposits, lending,

---

[19] See Banque de France, Internet: and Prudential Consequences, pp. 37–9.
[20] See pp. 40–4; see also *Règlement Général AMF*, art. 321-55.
[21] Council Directive 89/646/EEC of 15 December 1989 on the coordination of laws, regulations and administrative provisions relating to the taking up and pursuit of the business of credit institutions, OJ 1989 No. L386/1, 30 December 1989.
[22] See Directive 2000/12/EC.
[23] See art. 1(a).   [24] See recital 9 and art. 1(6).
[25] See art. 6(2).   [26] See art. 18.

transmitting funds and issuing and administering means of payment, and investment services, for example trading for the account of customers in transferable securities.

The 'passport' is available on three substantive conditions:[27] first, the activities which the bank intends to carry on are listed in the Annex I to the Directive; second, the bank has obtained authorization to carry on those activities in accordance with the law and the procedure of the 'home country'; third, the activities should be carried on within the territory of the 'host' country either by way of a permanent establishment or by way of free movement of services. On those conditions, the passport is available even when the law of the country of destination precludes local firms from providing similar services.

Regarding the typology of cross-border market entry, the scope of the 'passport' appears to be narrower than the scope of the freedom to provide services under the EC Treaty.[28] Unless activities are carried on 'within the territory' of the host country, cross-border services are solely within the scope of the basic economic freedoms of establishment and services.[29] The basic Treaty freedoms are therefore wider than the 'passport'. They cover four models of cross-border services, namely: services provided by means of a local establishment; by temporary movement of the bank in the host country; at a distance without the provider being physically present in the 'host country'; and, finally, by the customer's temporary movement towards the bank's home country.[30] The 'passport', however, explicitly covers services by local establishment and temporary movement within the territory of the host country but it does not cover the movement of the customer towards the 'home state'. And of course there is the open question of whether services provided at a distance, via the Internet or otherwise, constitute 'activities carried on within the territory' of the host state.

This uncertainty, however, does not upset the mandatory attribution of supervisory responsibility to the home state authorities. Primary 'home state' control is not conditional upon the criteria for the operation of the single banking licence being met. The question of allocating

---

[27] See FiSMA 2000, sch. III; §§ 1 and 53b Abs.1 KWG; C.monét.fin., arts. L 511-22 and L 532-18.
[28] Treaty Establishing the European Community (Rome, 25 March 1957); consolidated text at OJ 2000 No. C325, 24 December 2002.
[29] See Banking Consolidation Directive, art. 18.
[30] See Joined Cases C-286/82 and 26/83 *Luisi and Carbone v. Ministero del Tesoro* [1984] ECR 377, para 10.

powers between home and host authorities arises from the moment that a regulated service crosses the borders of the 'home country' for consumption *within the territory* of another Member State. Member States may have different views as to the place where regulated activities are carried on but they invariably – and rightly so – accept that the 'home state' authorities retain exclusive regulatory and supervisory powers when a regulated activity conducted by a local firm is not considered to have crossed the borders.[31]

The scope *rationae materiae* of 'home country' control comprises the national law adopted in implementation of the harmonized prudential standards relating to the initial taking-up and subsequent pursuit of the listed activities.[32] It encompasses the prudential rules consolidated by the Banking Directive,[33] the law of deposit-guarantee[34] and investor compensation,[35] and the remainder of rules pertaining to the internal organizational structure of the bank.[36] Finally, it extends to identification, reporting and due diligence requirements adopted in implementation of EU and international provisions relating to money laundering.[37]

The way that the Banking Consolidation Directive portrays the scope of 'home country' supervision is potentially misleading. Article 26 provides that the model of home country control applies without prejudice to those provisions of the Directive which give responsibility to the authorities of the host Member State. The 17th Recital further provides that there should be no obstacles to carrying on in the 'host country' activities enjoying mutual recognition in the same manner as in the home Member State, as long as the latter do not conflict with legal provisions protecting the general good in the host country. These two provisions somehow seem to imply that cross-border services are in principle

---

[31] See FSA AUTH 5 Annex 3; § 53b Abs. 2a and 3 KWG; Règlement CRBF No. 86/13, art. 5.
[32] See Banking Consolidation Directive, art. 26.
[33] See arts. 4–17 and 34–56.
[34] See EP and Council Directive 94/19/EC of 30 May 1994 on deposit-guarantee schemes, OJ 1994 No. L135/5, 31 May 1994, arts. 3–5.
[35] See EP and Council Directive 97/9/EC of 3 March 1997 on investor-compensation schemes, OJ 1997 No. L84/22, 26 March 1997, art. 7.
[36] See EP and Council Directive 2001/24/EC of 4 April 2001 on the reorganization and winding up of credit institutions, OJ 2001 No. L125/15, 5 May 2001; Council Directive 86/635/EEC of 8 December 1986 on the annual accounts and consolidated accounts of banks and other financial institutions, OJ 1986 No. L372/1, 23 November 1988.
[37] See FSA ML 1.1.2R; § 1 Abs. 3 GwG; C.monét.fin., art. L 562 (1)1.

subject to the law and supervision of the country of origin unless otherwise stated in the Directives. On close inspection, this is not true.

Member States have residual powers to legislate and supervise cross-border services at will. Unless special commitments are undertaken by way of secondary Community law, those powers are limited only by the Treaty provisions, which do not systematically establish the principle of 'home country' control as overriding principle of EU economic law. The Treaty freedom to provide services establishes criteria for judicial review of legal barriers caused by national legal requirements without, however, systematically favouring the application of the law of the 'home country'. This view is consistent with case law suggesting that the law of the firm's 'home country' is also a potential source of prohibited restrictive measures.[38] The principle of 'home country control' is based on secondary, not primary, Community law,[39] and its precise scope of application should be specifically defined by secondary EU measures, as it is actually the case with the Banking, Investment Services[40] and Deposit Guarantee[41] Directives. More specifically in the Banking Consolidation Directive, home country regulation and supervision is expressly reserved for the 'prudential' rules harmonized therein.[42] This choice reflects the guiding principle that mutual recognition is unworkable without mutual trust and some common rules. The remainder of the law governing banking services has not been harmonized and therefore no other inroad to the legislative and supervisory competence of Member States is implied. Arguably, the wording of the 17th Recital of the Banking Consolidation Directive is confusing. But recourse to the recital is not permitted in cases where the provisions of the Directive are clear and precise.[43] Where there is a conflict between the wording of a provision in a Directive and the recital, the former prevails[44] and,

---

[38] See Case C-384/93 *Alpine Investments BV* v. *Minister van Financiën* [1995] ECR I-1141.
[39] See Case C-233/94 *Germany* v. *Parliament and Council* [1997] ECR I-2405, para. 12.
[40] Council Directive 93/22/EEC of 10 May on investment services in the securities field, OJ 1993 No. L141/27, 11 June 1993.
[41] EP and Council Directive 94/19/EC of 30 May 1994 on deposit-guarantee schemes, OJ 1994 No. L135/5, 31 May 1994.
[42] See Banking Consolidation Directive, recital 7 and art. 26(1).
[43] See Case C-238/94 *García* v. *Mutuelle de prevoyance Sociale d'Aquitaine* [1996] ECR I-1673, para. 10.
[44] See Case C-412/93 *Société d'Importation Edouard Leclerc-Siplec* v. *TFI Publicite SA* [1995] ECR 179, paras. 45–7.

likewise, a recital cannot be relied upon to derogate from the provision in question.[45]

The principle of 'home country' control applies to national rules falling within the scope of prudential regulation and supervision. Regarding that content alone, host authorities are given the right to consult and exchange information with the home authorities;[46] the duty to collaborate closely in order to address systemic and micro-level risks;[47] and the right to exercise emergency supervisory powers, after prior consultation with the home authorities, particularly when the bank is persistent in violating the conditions of the 'passport' and the response of the home authorities is not satisfactory.[48] Additional powers in the field of monetary policy are reserved against incoming services by way of local establishment.[49] The wider host powers in the event of establishment are justified by common sense and reflect a broader principle of Community law that regulation must always be in proportion to the actual connection of the activity with the territory of the regulating jurisdiction and therefore less intrusive in relation to services provided on a cross-border basis than those pursued by way of local establishment.[50]

An important procedural right of the 'host' authorities is the right to be notified prior to the exercise of 'passport' rights. A bank which intends to provide services for the first time within the territory of another Member State must notify the competent authorities of the 'home' Member State of the activities which it intends to carry on.[51] Subsequently, the host authorities have the right to receive the notification from the home authorities within one month of its receipt by the latter.[52] The failure to notify the required information on time or in the prescribed manner does not affect the validity of contracts entered into in the course of the relevant services but it may trigger administrative measures.[53]

---

[45] See Case C-162/97 *Gunnar Nilsson* (Criminal proceedings) [1998] ECR I-7477, para. 54.
[46] See Banking Consolidation Directive, art. 22(9).
[47] See art. 28.
[48] See arts. 22(2)–(5).
[49] See art. 27.
[50] See Case C-279/80 *Webb* (Criminal proceedings) [1981] ECR 3305, para. 16.
[51] See Banking Consolidation Directive, art. 21(1); FiSMA 2000, sch. 3, paras. 14 and 20; Règlement CRBF, No. 93/13 and 93/12 (for banking services), Décret No. 96-880, arts. 7 and 15 (for investment services); §§ 24a and 53b KWG.
[52] See Banking Consolidation Directive, art. 21(2).
[53] See Case C-193/94 *Skanavi and Chrissantha Ropoulos* (Criminal Proceedings) [1996] ECR I-943.

With regard to other fields of economic regulatory law, notably investment services regulation relevant for online securities trading, the MiFiD established the principle of mutual recognition of national regulatory laws within the scope of the Directive and exclusive 'home country control' by prohibiting EU countries 'receiving' cross-border investment services from imposing any additional requirements on firms providing those services in respect of the matters covered by this Directive.[54]

## The notion of 'general good' in the Banking Consolidation Directive

Notwithstanding the application of the principle of 'home country control', the host Member State may require compliance with specific provisions of its own national laws or regulation provided that the conditions of the 'general good' are satisfied.[55] It may also take all appropriate measures to prevent or punish irregularities committed within its territory contrary to those provisions.[56] Those rules may govern, *inter alia*, the form and the content of advertising.[57] The concept of the 'general good' refers to the well-known notion developed by the European Court of Justice.

It should be clarified from the outset that the notion of the 'general good' in the Banking Consolidation Directive does not refer to the residual 'host country' powers in the prudential matters harmonized by the Directive within the scope of primary 'home country' supervision. This is dealt with by the provisions of Article 22(2)–(5) which establishes the emergency powers of the 'host authorities' to impose their own prudential rules when confidence in 'home country' control is broken down.

The 'general good' concept is a different animal which relates to the remainder of national law, outside the subject-matter of home country supervision. It purports to coordinate the application of the single banking licence against applicable national rules in the country of destination that reflect eligible notions of public policy, for example in the domain of advertising or financial promotion. Insofar as applicable 'host country' rules are capable of restricting the exercise of the freedom

---

[54] See EP and Council Directive 2004/39/EC of 21 April 2004 on markets in financial instruments, 2004 OJ No. L145/1, 30 April 2004, art. 31(1).
[55] See Banking Consolidation Directive, recitals 16–17.
[56] *Ibid.*, art. 22(5).    [57] *Ibid.*, art. 22(11).

to provide banking services under the passport, the Directive requires that any restrictions should satisfy the 'general good' requirements. In other words, instead of expanding the legislative and enforcement competence of host Member States in derogation from the supposedly automatic application of prudential and non-prudential 'home country' rules, which the Directive never established, the 'general good' notion purports to achieve precisely the opposite: to limit 'host country' powers.

Had it not been for the 'general good' requirements, 'host country' rules outside the scope of prudential supervision would continue to restrict cross-border services. If they were found applicable to cross-border services under the operation of conflict of laws, they would have been limited solely by the Treaty provisions on free economic movement. The Directive brings into play the concept of the 'general good' to impose limits in that process by requiring Member States in their capacity as host countries to apply non-prudential rules subject to the stringent requirements set out in the 'general good' jurisprudence. Furthermore, the Banking Consolidation Directive concept of the 'general good' does not provide the legal basis for enforcing 'host state' rules unless those rules are prima facie applicable in accordance with the conflict of laws and the territorial application of economic regulatory law: the prima facie application of substantive 'host country' rules is determined by the conflict of laws and, subsequently, applicable substantive rules are assessed against the free movement jurisprudence in which case they must pass the 'general good' test if they pose restrictions to cross-border trade. With regard to sources of applicable 'host country' laws, the most commonly invoked 'general good' motives, such as consumer protection or systemic financial stability, are typically promoted by an assortment of national rules that may be of either 'public' or 'private' law nature.

## 'Host country' powers to apply domestic laws in non-prudential matters

Outside the subject-matter of 'home country' control, the various financial services Directives do not dictate specific rules concerning the allocation of regulatory responsibility and the territorial application of national laws. In the following sections, I will examine the extent to which national authorities enforce non-prudential legal and regulatory requirements against financial institutions directing services to local residents via the Internet. The ensuing discussion covers the regulatory law relating to online securities trading (insofar as the recently adopted 'home country' control provisions of the MiFiD have yet to be transposed into national law) and national rules concerning marketing and advertising activities. These are all areas of law where the recently implemented 'country of origin' principle of the E-Commerce Directive removed the primary regulatory responsibility of the recipient country but this set of reforms will be discussed in chapter 8. Finally, the question of applicable law in cross-border contracts for banking services will be examined separately in its own right in chapter 9.

## *The localization of online banking services and the question of applicable law*

The Banking Consolidation Directive requires financial institutions providing cross-border services to 'notify' the competent authorities of their own 'home country' before carrying on regulated activities 'within the territory' of another EU country. Although the territorial location where online banking activities are carried on is strictly determinative of the notification requirement, the EU and national views on this matter may well influence the extent to which national authorities may enforce non-prudential requirements against cross-border electronic banking activities.

### The notification requirement

The circumstances which trigger the notification requirement are not technically connected with the scope of territorial application of host country law. The obligation is addressed to the bank and notification must be given to the home country authorities, which should clarify the territorial circumstances that trigger the notification requirement.[58] In practice, national authorities in their capacity as 'home country' authorities will always respect the request of their fellow regulators to receive notification whenever a given service is regarded as being provided 'within the territory' of other EU countries. The 'home country' of the financial institution will always encourage notification of cross-border services to the authorities of other EU countries in cases where these authorities believe that the pertinent activities are carried on within

---

[58] See *ibid.*, art. 21 (1).

their territories, even if the 'home authorities' actually believe otherwise.[59] Moreover, the national criteria of localization used for determining the requirement of notification almost certainly influence the criteria used for determining the scope of application of national laws to cross-border services. National authorities are unlikely to require notification of cross-border services because the relevant activities 'are carried on within the territory' but refrain from requiring compliance with local laws because the requisite territorial connection is lacking. Nevertheless, the opposite cannot be true: it seems that the territorial criteria for the application of local laws could be wider than the criteria used in the notification procedure, resulting in circumstances in which certain 'host country' laws apply to cross-border services that do not trigger a notification requirement.

### The European Commission's views on the localization of online banking activities

The position of the European Commission was published in 1997.[60] Having examined various criteria for identifying the location of cross-border services, such as the customer's place of residence, the supplier's place of establishment or the place where the contracts are signed, the Commission conceded that they were not suitable for all banking services covered by the Banking Consolidation Directive.[61] Instead, it opted for a literal interpretation of the Directive, according to which only activities carried on within the territory of another Member State should be the subject of prior notification. It then endorsed the criterion of the place of provision of the 'characteristic performance of the service', i.e. the essential supply for which payment is due.[62]

The final criterion of the place of provision of the characteristic performance of the service operates in two stages. The starting point is to identify the performance, which is characteristic of the particular service and, on that basis, to determine the place where the performance is to be provided. The Commission came to the conclusion that the distance provision of banking services, for example through the Internet, should not require prior notification because the supplier cannot be deemed

---

[59] See FSA Handbook Supervision (SUP) 13.12.1 G; BAKRED, *Anzeige gemäss § 24a Abs. 1 Satz 1 KWG Errichtung einer Zweigniederlassung* (Bonn, 2001).
[60] See European Commission, *Freedom to Provide Services and the Interest of the General Good in the Second Banking Directive* SEC(97) 1193 final.
[61] Ibid., at p. 6.     [62] Ibid.

to be pursuing its activities in the customer's country. The conclusion is based on the valid assumption that it is always the supplier of the service which has to provide the characteristic performance of the service but the Commission wisely qualified its statement through the observation that 'this solution will require a case-by-case analysis, which could prove difficult'.[63] It is now clear that the conduct of a case-by-case analysis has not been the only difficult point. The criterion itself was not happily received by all Member States, which were perfectly entitled to disregard the non-binding views of the Commission.[64]

## The position of the French authorities

With regard to cross-border investment services, the *Comité des établissements de crédit et des entreprises d'investissement* (CECEI) disagreed with the views of the Commission in November 1998,[65] and the Banque de France followed suit in December 2000 in respect of cross-border electronic banking activities.[66] The French authorities clarified the national position for both the notification requirement and the territorial circumstances that trigger the application of French laws to 'incoming' cross-border services.

The French authorities were unhappy with the criterion recommended by the Commission because the place 'where the characteristic performance of the service takes place' would typically be the 'home country' of the bank, thus negating the 'host authorities' right to receive notification and therefore defeating the aim of the notification procedure to provide information to residents of those countries to which cross-border services were directed.[67] They also pointed to the functional difficulties in determining with precision which particular aspect of the service is the most 'characteristic'. They questioned, for example, whether in the provision of online investment services the 'characteristic performance' would take place in the location where the securities were traded or in the place where the customer's securities or cash account was held and administered.

---

[63] *Ibid.*, at p. 7.
[64] See Case C-57/95 *France* v. *Commission* [1997] ECR I-1627.
[65] See Comité des Etablissements de Crédit et des Entreprises d' Investissement, *La Libre Prestation de Services en Matière de Services d'Investissement* (Paris, 1998).
[66] See Banque de France, *Internet and Prudential Consequences*, pp. 42–3.
[67] See CECEI, *Libre Prestation de Services*, p. 112.

The approach adopted by the French authorities goes beyond the question of whether the service is strictly provided within the territory of the recipient country. Instead, it focuses on the bank's intention to offer services to residents of a Member State other than its 'home country'. In the French view, the notification procedure is triggered as soon as the service provider has demonstrated his intention to enter into a contract with residents of another Member State. The French authorities have taken the view that the suggested criterion is met as soon as the bank expressly states that it intends to provide via the Internet services to customers in other Member States. In the event that an explicit statement of that kind is lacking, the bank will be deemed to be providing services within the territory of the 'host country' if there is an actual connection between the service and the recipient country, for example actual provision of services to residents in that country, or presentation of the website in the language of that country or advertisement of the site in Internet portals and search engines located in the recipient jurisdiction.

Consistent with their views, the French authorities require compliance with domestic legal and regulatory requirements adopted in the interest of 'general good' from the moment that services are directed at local residents. More specifically, there is an official list of French laws and regulations which automatically apply to branches of EU and EEA banks.[68] The French authorities have also confirmed that services provided on a cross-border basis (and not by way of local establishment) are also subject to the listed laws and regulations but only insofar as these cross-border activities would be prima facie subject to French law, which is a matter for the conflict of laws and the scope of application of economic regulatory law.[69] There is no further guidance as to which rules apply to cross-border services but it can safely be argued that most legal instruments appearing in this statutory list would not apply to non-established foreign firms because they regulate matters of internal organizational structure which could reasonably be enforced against local branches but not against non-established foreign banks. Leaving aside those requirements of organizational structure, a sizeable amount of French laws relating to consumer protection and specified financial products and services impose mandatory requirements regardless of the

---

[68] See Règlement CRBF No. 93/13, art. 5(1).
[69] *Ibid.*, art. 5(2).

otherwise applicable law and should be respected by EU and EEA banks providing distance services via the Internet.

## The position of the UK authorities

Unlike its French counterparts, the FSA believes that UK banks and investment firms should apply the 'characteristic performance' test as explained by the European Commission but they should nevertheless note that other EU and EEA countries may apply the 'solicitation test' examining whether it is the consumer or the provider of the service that initiated the business relationship.[70] The FSA considers, for example, that accepting deposits and, arguably, receiving and executing trading orders are typical examples of services taking place within the territory of the bank, whereas providing secured loans and offering investment advice are seen as taking place in the country where the recipient of the service is based.[71]

## The position of the German authorities

The official German position on the notification requirement was released in 2001.[72] The German regulator appeared to have accepted the criterion of the 'characteristic performance' insofar as it encouraged German banks to consult the Commission's Interpretative Communication to decide whether their activities amounted to services carried on within the territory of another Member State. The regulator noted, however, that the Commission's views were not binding and tacitly expressed its approval of the Commission's position by emphasizing that 'other foreign authorities' did not necessarily share the view of the Commission on the concept of the 'characteristic performance'. From a regulatory perspective, cross-border activities of EU and EEA banks in Germany are subject to certain regulatory requirements of non-prudential nature imposed by the Banking Act,[73] but these are not normally enforced against European banks providing online services at a distance.[74]

---

[70] See FSA Handbook SUP App 3.6.8 G.
[71] See Financial Services Authority, *Implementing the E-Commerce Directive* (Consultation Paper 129) (London, 2002), pp. 11–16.
[72] See BAKRED, *Errichtung einer Zweigniederlassung*.
[73] See §§ 53b Abs. 3, 3, 23a, 37, 44c, 49 & 50 KWG.
[74] See K.-H. Boos, R. Fischer and H. Schulte-Mattler, *Kreditwesengesetz* (Munich:, C. H. Beck 2000), pp. 1066–8.

## Discussing the EU and national views on localization

The 'place of the characteristic performance of the service' is a *sui generis* criterion developed for the purposes of the Banking and Investment Services Directives. It resembles the criterion of the 'performance which is characteristic of the contract', a concept appearing in the Rome Convention,[75] and the 'place of performance of the obligation in question', which is used in the Brussels Convention,[76] without being identical to either concept. For the purposes of the Banking Consolidation Directive, the Commission believes that services are provided in the place where the essential aspect of the service is performed. In the Rome Convention what matters is the place where the *performer* of the characteristic obligation of the contract is established[77] and in the Brussels Convention the place where under the applicable law the litigated claim is to be performed.[78] The Commission's criterion has however direct similarities with '. . . the place in a Member State where, under the contract, the services were provided or should have been provided . . .' which offers an alternative basis for jurisdiction under Article 5(1)(b) of the Brussels Regulation.[79]

In my view, the choice of the Commission is sound. If the wording of the Directive is to be respected, the sole criterion must be the place where the activities are carried on. The criterion of the 'characteristic performance' rightly assumes that different aspects of the service may be carried on within the territories of different Member States, for example, preliminary enquiries as to status of the customer or advertising. On the other hand, the Directive requires a single location to be determined. It is therefore appropriate to invoke the concept of the 'essential element' of the service for the purpose of avoiding multiple locations. In essence, the recommended criterion poses the following question: when the bank carries on one of the activities listed in the Annex, what is the essential,

---

[75] See Convention on the Law Applicable to Contractual Obligations (Rome, 19 June 1980); Consolidated Version at OJ 1998, No. C27/34, 26 January 1998.
[76] See Convention on Jurisdiction and the Enforcement of Judgments in Civil and Commercial Matters (Brussels, 27 September 1968); Consolidated Version OJ 1998, No. C27/1, 26 January 1998.
[77] See Rome Convention, art. 4(1).
[78] See Brussels Convention, art. 5(1).
[79] See Council Regulation (EC) No 44/2001 of 22 December 2000 on jurisdiction and the recognition and enforcement of judgments in civil and commercial matters, OJ 2001 No. L121, 16 January 2001.

characteristic element of this activity for which the customer is prepared to part with her money? The 'characteristic performance' of the service is neither the preliminary steps nor the administrative settlement of the transaction. It is the economically most important obligation of the bank, the 'centre of gravity' and the defining element of the services listed in the Annex to the Directive.

'Performance' is an act by which the obligation due by the bank to the customer is fulfilled. Performance extinguishes the claim and relieves the bank from the obligation to perform. The term 'performance' also means that one of the contractual objectives defined by the contractual agreement has been fully achieved. Thus, the place of performance is the place where the creditor's claim is extinguished by the debtor's having performed the obligation required of him and the place where the aim of the contract is wholly or partly achieved.[80]

The 'essential obligation required of the bank' shall be construed with reference to the activities listed in the Annex to the Directive and not in accordance with national definitions of regulated activities which may vary. Care must be taken not to confuse the 'characteristic performance' of the service with what in economic terms might be the most important operation from the customer's point of view. For example, to open and operate a bank account in accordance with the customer's instructions is not *per se* listed in the Annex to the Directive as a regulated activity even though it is economically a core banking activity. For the purposes of the Banking Consolidation Directive it is therefore irrelevant whether this particular service might be considered as taking place in part within the country of the customer, where the Internet service is enjoyed. With regard to bank accounts, the relationship between the bank and the customer consists of a number of activities listed in the Annex, namely acceptance of deposits, issuance and administering means of payment and money transmission services. And each one of them must be looked at individually in order to determine what the characteristic element is and where it is to be performed.

The place of performance is a matter of fact. It does not refer to the place where under the applicable law the service must be performed. It must be determined where the regulated service is actually provided with no particular reference to national legal definitions of the place of

---

[80] See AG Lenz in Case 288/92 *Custom Made Commercial Ltd* v. *Stawa Metallbau GmbH* [1994] ECR I-2913, para. 25.

performance. It is also not affected by the agreement of the parties as to where a service ought to be performed although it is normally expected that the service is actually performed in accordance with the parties' understanding as to the place of performance.

The contrary view of the French authorities is not convincing. First, it is doubtful whether it respects the wording of Articles 18 and 21 of the Directive. The *intention* of the service provider, however demonstrated, cannot be assimilated to activity actually *carried on within* a territory. The exercise of the notification rights on that basis extends the restrictive effects of the Directive to circumstances where the activities are manifestly not carried on within the territory of the 'host country'. By doing so it fails to construe narrowly an exemption from the scheme established by the Directive as compelled by a fundamental principle of interpretation.[81]

Second, it is settled law that when the wording of secondary Community law is open to more than one interpretation, preference should be given to the interpretation which renders the provision consistent with the Treaty.[82] Hence, an interpretation which imposes obstacles to free trade must concede priority to an interpretation which facilitates free economic movement. The notification is of course an administrative burden on free trade which the Banking Consolidation Directive superimposed on the general law as concession to those countries opposing the operation of exclusive home state supervision. Third, against a wide interpretation of the notification requirement one may also invoke the notion that restrictions against the provision of services at a distance are less tolerable than restrictions against services physically supplied within the host country. This must no doubt inform the interpretation of the Directive in the event of ambiguity. The French authorities justify their *contra legem* interpretation on grounds of investor and consumer protection. This is not convincing. The notification pursues a simple objective of exchange of information between supervisory authorities. After the implementation of the Distance Marketing[83] and E-Commerce Directives, full information regarding the location and status of the bank will be routinely available on the bank's website for purposes of investor and consumer protection, thus rendering this justification redundant.

---

[81] See Case C-54/84 *Paul v. Emmerich* [1985] ECR 915, para. 17.
[82] See Case 220/83 *Commission v. France* [1986] ECR 2663, para. 17.
[83] EP and Council Directive 2002/65/EC of 23 September 2002 concerning distance marketing of consumer financial services, OJ 2002 No. L271/16, 9 October 2002.

In my view, cross-border services via the Internet are outside the scope of the 'passport' and the notification procedure, unless they are performed within the territory of the 'host Member State'. The 'passport' intended to remove an additional layer of control over cross-border services which would otherwise have been subject to duplicate supervision. It is not surprising that those countries which were ready to claim competence on the basis of a wide notion of 'local effects' adopted a similar approach towards notification. The scope of 'host state' supervision and the interpretation of the notification requirement were bound to be symmetrical. After all, this was a measure which was offered in exchange for agreement towards a model of full country control.

The real root of the controversy lies, in my view, in the difficulty to predict back in the late 1980s, when the Directive was negotiated, that a fourth model of cross-border services would develop. The Directive drew a demarcation line between services by local establishment and temporary movement in the host country on the one hand and the right of the consumer to visit the home state on the other, which remained within the sole scope of the Treaty rules. The overzealous readiness of national authorities to extend the long arm of local mechanisms of control over Internet services as soon as local consumers take advantage of technological developments to enjoy cross-border services is part of the broader discomfort of established principles of law, including Community law, with this new form of free economic movement.

What is really required is a new consensus around a perfect model of one-stop home country supervision. The Commission's attempt, however, to find a practical solution by going back to the letter of the provision was in the right direction. On the other hand, a strong line of communication and exchange of information between the home and host authorities over cross-border ventures is arguably a precondition for creating mutual trust and confidence between national authorities.[84] The right of host authorities to protect local consumers when trust in the ability of the home authorities is broken down pre-supposes that the former have information about cross-border Internet offers. Information may be obtained by a simple consumer complaint or by the

---

[84] As Peter Parker, a senior official from the UK Financial Services Authority put it to me, 'there is a reasonable feeling among banking regulators across Europe that actually notification is a good thing to do and therefore it is something to encourage on the basis of regulatory cooperation'.

regulator's own research and notification of one form or another may help in that direction.

Turning to specified types of online services, the service of accepting deposits and other repayable funds from the public is performed in the location where the bank accepts the deposit and opens an account in the name of the depositor. The service performed by the bank is the reception of the customer's instruction via the Internet and the subsequent execution by debiting the customer's account and either crediting the beneficiary's account held with the bank or instructing the beneficiary's bank to do so. It is not within the scope of the service to discharge the underlying payment obligation, although in many cases that will be the result. The 'characteristic performance' of the service occurs in the place where the bank receives the instruction and initiates the payment and not in the place where the beneficiary's account is credited, unless both the originator's account and the payee's account are held in the same Member State. The essential element of lending services is that the bank makes available to the customer the specified amount of funds. It is the performance for which the customer is prepared to part with his money. In the case of overdraft credit where the proceeds of the loan are made available through the customer's account with the lending bank or another account in the same country, the service is provided in the bank's 'home country' and it is outside the scope of the 'passport'. It cannot be ruled out, however, that the funds are made available through a bank account in the customer's Member State. In that case, it is my view that the bank is providing services within that territory and the notification procedure must be activated. Finally, the essential element of online investment services is the sale or purchase of securities on behalf and for account of the customer. The service is generally covered by the 'passport'.[85] Neither the establishment of the necessary infrastructure for the distant communication between the bank and the customer nor the post-market settlement of the customer's accounts constitutes 'trading in financial instruments'. The service is performed within the territory of the Member State where the market is located. For securities traded in the bank's home country, no notification is required. For securities traded in the customer's Member State or a third Member State without the bank having a place of business in that jurisdiction, it has been suggested that the remote access of the market via electronic

---

[85] See Banking Consolidation Directive, Annex I, pt 7.

terminals is insufficient to denote services provided in the recipient jurisdiction.[86] I am more inclined to suggest that trading in the form of selling and purchasing instruments occurs in the country where the market is located. Remote access denotes precisely market access at a distance and not the creation of some 'virtual' market in the bank's home country. This is also the reason why I generally oppose the claims of the consumer's country of residence to enforce local laws. The Internet facilitates access to banks and markets regardless of location. It does not create a 'virtual' presence in the client's home country, which would justify the enforcement of local laws.

## The application of 'host country' rules regulating online investment services

Until the future implementation of the MiFiD, the allocation of regulatory responsibility between the 'home' and 'host' countries in the field of cross-border investment services will be subject to national laws implementing the 1993 Investment Services Directive. The 1993 Directive did not extend the scope of 'home country' control to conduct of business regulation, which remained the responsibility of the country in which investment services 'were provided'.[87] There was no explicit attribution of special powers to 'home authorities' and no limitation of Member States' powers in their capacity as 'host countries' to regulate the behaviour of financial intermediaries dealing with local residents. It should be noted that the 1993 Directive did not preclude 'home countries' from regulating local firms providing cross-border services. It simply refrained from requiring 'host countries' to concede priority to the regulatory powers of 'home countries'. In effect, the 1993 Directive was reluctant to coordinate the application of national investor protection laws, thus allowing a potential situation to arise in which a firm established in country A providing investment services to a client established in country B in respect of securities traded in the markets of country C is required to comply with conduct of business rules of all three jurisdictions.

---

[86] See Guido Ferrarini, 'Pan-European Securities Markets: Policy Issues and Regulatory Responses' (2002) 3 EBOL Rev 249, at p. 265.
[87] See Council Directive 93/22/EEC of 10 May 1993 on investment services in the securities field, OJ 1993, No. L141/27, 11 June 1993, art. 11.

### UK investor protection rules and cross-border services

The rules defining the territorial scope of application of investor protection rules of the FSA Handbook are set out in COB 1.4. According to the main operative provision, the UK requirements would not apply in relation to activities carried on with or for a client in the United Kingdom but not from an establishment maintained in the United Kingdom, if the firm did not solicit or otherwise communicate offers to UK clients in any way.[88] They would however apply if the activity was regarded as carried on 'in the United Kingdom', in other words if the services were provided to UK clients by way of regular business and no 'overseas persons' exclusions were available. In effect, financial institutions actively soliciting clients in the United Kingdom via the Internet would have to comply with UK investor protection requirements regardless of the actual location where the services were performed.[89]

### German investor protection rules and cross-border services

German rules of conduct do not apply to firms providing distant services to local investors unless so required *both* by the nature of the rule and the degree of proximity of the service with the territory of the jurisdiction. The required degree of proximity is expressly set out in the provisions of Articles 31(3) and 32(3) of the Securities Trading Act. Services provided by firms established in another jurisdiction to customers having their habitual place of residence or registered office in Germany are subject to German rules of conduct, provided that the investment services or non-core investment services and related ancillary services are not provided *exclusively* abroad.

It is evident that a lesser degree of proximity with national territory is required than would have been the case under the criterion of the 'characteristic performance'. Provided that the client is established in Germany, the performance of a partial aspect of the service therein or, in the case of supply of more than one type of services, a partial aspect of any one service, for example the delivery of securities or the transfer of the proceeds of sale in Germany or the provision of investment advice via the Internet to the investor, is sufficient.[90] Only services provided 'exclusively abroad' escape local requirements. In relation to German

---

[88] See FSA COB 1.4.3 R.
[89] See FSA COB 2.4.6G.
[90] See U. Florian, *Internet Wertpapierhandels*, pp. 30–1.

investors, the performance of the obligations under the 'Internet service' agreement may be considered as partly located in Germany where the Internet service is enjoyed. The customer's residence in Germany would also suffice to establish the civil jurisdiction of German courts in the event of litigation for breach of statutory duty relating to conduct of business regulation.[91] The location of the market, however, as the place of the performance of the characteristic aspect of the service is not determinative. Finally, legal requirements of internal organization do not apply unless the firm maintains a physical establishment in Germany.[92]

### French investor protection rules and cross-border services

Firms providing investment services by way of cross-border services to investors with residence in France should comply with local investor protection requirements with the exception of the following provisions of the General Regulation AMF:[93] Articles 321-25 to 321-32 relating to the internal organization of the firm and the functions of the compliance officer and Articles 321-33 to 321-40 relating to the conduct of personnel.

### The need for reform

The reluctance of the drafters of the 1993 Directive to establish a clear model of 'home country' control and mutual recognition of investor protection requirements preserved the economic costs of cumulative national regulation and legal uncertainty in the single financial market. Based on the extensive harmonization of investor protection rules, the recently adopted MiFiD corrected the imbalance in prudential and non-prudential regulations by the establishment of 'home country control' in non-prudential investor protection standards.

### *The application of 'host country' rules regulating the marketing and advertising of online banking services*

The Banking Consolidation Directive provided that credit institutions were not precluded from advertising their services by all available means

---

[91] *Ibid.*, at p. 19.
[92] See Bundesanstalt für Finanzdienstleistungsaufsicht, *Bekanntmachung zur Auslegung einzelner Begriffe in § 34b Wertpapierhandelsgesetz* (Bonn, 2003).
[93] See C.monét.fin., arts. L 533 (4) and L 532 (18); Conseil des Marchés Financiers, *Note sur l'Applicabilité du Titre III aux Prestataires de Services d'Investissement Intervenant en Libre Etablissement ou en Libre Prestation de Services en France* (Paris, December 2003).

of communication in other Member States subject to any rules governing the form and the content of such advertising adopted in the interest of the general good.[94] Whether the law of the host state applies to commercial communications and advertising at a distance by electronic means is a matter for the territorial scope of application of national statutes or the private international law of unfair competition.

## UK requirements and cross-border services

The part of the FSA Handbook relating to financial promotion applies to an invitation or inducement to engage in regulated activities made to a person who receives it inside the United Kingdom or which is directed generally at persons inside the United Kingdom.[95] To determine whether the conditions are met, the usual indicators relating to the content and the information available on the bank's website will be taken into account.[96]

Regarding the statutory provisions which regulate the advertising of services in general or special types of financial services in particular,[97] it is settled law that if a person located outside England initiates an offence, part of the essential elements of which take effect in England, that person is amenable to English jurisdiction in the absence of express indications in the statute.[98] It has yet to be decided by courts whether promotional material which is stored outside the jurisdiction and made available to UK clients via the Internet amounts to an act committed wholly or partly in England. It may be argued, however, that any solution in accordance with the 'local effects' or 'targeted at' criteria would be hardly surprising. First, it accords with the approach taken by English courts in relatively comparable trade mark cases according to which the application of English law to Internet content located outside but intentionally directed at the jurisdiction cannot be avoided.[99] Second, it also accords with the private international law of economic torts other than defamation as it is established by Private International Law

---

[94] See Banking Consolidation Directive, art. 22(11).
[95] See FSA Handbook COB 3.3.1 and 3.3.5R.
[96] See COB 3.3.6R.
[97] See Trade Descriptions Act 1968, s. 4; Control of Misleading Advertisements Regulations 1988 SI 1988/915 (as amended); Consumer Credit Act 1974, s. 46; Consumer Protection Act 1987.
[98] See *R v. Munton* (1793) 1 Esp 62; *R v. Oliphant* [1905] 2 KB 67.
[99] See *Euromarket Designs Inc. v. Peters* [2000] ETMR 1025, 1031 (Ch D); *1–800 Flowers Inc. v. Phonenames Ltd* [2000] ETMR 369.

(Miscellaneous Provisions) Act 1995. Under section 11(2)(c), in the event that the elements constituting the economic tort occur in different countries, the applicable law is to be taken as being the law of the country in which the most significant element or elements of those events occurred. If the act and the effects of the wrongful conduct occur in different jurisdictions, as is the case with publication over the Internet, it is accepted that the law of the place where the harmful effects are produced applies.[100] In the case of inaccurate or misleading representations by telephone or facsimile it is submitted that the applicable law is the law of the country where the statements are relied and acted upon.[101] I see no reason why Internet content would be treated differently.

Further, it is consistent with the EC law relating to international jurisdiction for civil wrongs. In accordance with Article 5(3) of the Brussels Regulation, matters relating to tort, delict or quasi-delict, which include acts of unfair competition and civil liability for inaccurate, misleading and defamatory statements,[102] may also be litigated in the place where the harmful event occurred or may occur. The concept covers both the causative event giving rise to and being at the origin of the damage and the place where the damage occurred or the adverse effects of the harmful act were felt, at the plaintiff's option.[103] This position has been endorsed by national courts in the United Kingdom,[104] France[105] and Germany.[106]

In *Shevill*[107] the European Court of Justice accepted that in the event of a libel by a newspaper article distributed in several Member States, the place of the event giving rise to the damage can only be the place where the publisher of the newspaper is established, because that is the place where the harmful event originated and from which the libel was issued and put into circulation.[108] Regarding the place where the damage occurred, the court held that this is the place where the event giving rise to the damage 'produced its harmful effects upon the victim', even

---

[100] See Lawrence Collins (ed.), *Dicey and Morris on the Conflict of Laws* (13th edn, London: Sweet and Maxwell, 2000), p. 1547.
[101] *Ibid.*
[102] See Case C-68/93 *Shevill* v. *Presse Alliance* [1995] ECR-I 415.
[103] See Case C-364/93 *Antonio Marinari* v. *Lloyds Bank* [1995] ECR I-2719.
[104] See *Cronos* v. *Palatin* [2002] EWHC 2819 (Comm), para. 14.
[105] See *Schimmel Pianoforte D* v. *M. Bion* (1991) IR 37 Cour de Cassation, 1st civ.ch., 08.01.1991.
[106] See OLG München NJW-RR 1994, 190.
[107] See above note 102.    [108] *Ibid.*, para. 24.

though the wrongdoer may be regarded as having entirely acted in a different Member State.[109] The European Court of Justice emphasized that in the case of an international libel through the press, the injury caused by a defamatory publication to the honour, reputation and good name of a natural or legal person occurs in the places where the publication is distributed and comprehended by readers, provided that the victim is known in those places.[110]

Applying those principles to civil wrongs committed via the Internet, one may conclude that jurisdiction may be assumed in Member States where the 'harmful effects' of unfair or misleading statements and Internet content are produced, even if the wrongdoer's unlawful conduct technically occurs in the territory of another jurisdiction where the Internet site is hosted, maintained and administered.[111] It is also dictated by common sense to the extent that information or communication in any form cannot be said to have produced any effects unless received or perceived by the intended audience. This principle was recently reaffirmed in the High Court of Australia case *Dow Jones Inc. v. Joseph Gutnick*,[112] where it was held that in the event of material made available on the world wide web harmful effects can only be produced in the place where the reader 'downloads' the information and at no point before the information can be comprehended by the reader.

### Cross-border services and legal requirements in France and Germany

In civil law jurisdictions, the law governing civil liability for torts, including misleading or inaccurate advertising and unfair competition, is the law of the place where the wrong has been committed.[113] It is a settled principle that the forum will apply the law of the place where the unfair or misleading communication has harmed private interests, that of consumers and competitors, and public policy.[114] The position under both German[115] and French[116] law is that unfair or misleading promotional

---

[109] See para. 28.   [110] See para. 29.
[111] See OLG München CR 2000, 464.   [112] [2002] HCA 56.
[113] See CGJ Morse, 'Choice of Law in Tort: A Comparative Study' (1984) 32 AmJCompL 51.
[114] See BGH NJW 1962, 37 (38); Cour de Cassation 14.01.1997, 86 RCDIP 504–505; CA Paris D. 2002, p. 1389.
[115] See OLG Frankfurt MMR 1999, 427; LG Hamburg, MMR 1999, 612 (criteria the language, means of payment); LG Braunschweig, MMR 1998, 272; LG Berlin, MDR 2001, 391; LG Paderborn MMR 2001, 710.
[116] See J. Huet, 'Le Droit Applicable dans les Réseaux Numériques' (2002) 129 JDI 737, at 747.

material made available on the world wide web or communicated to individual customers is subject to the law of the place to which offers or services are directed.

French statutes relating to misleading and comparative advertising,[117] the use of the French language in commercial communications[118] and other statutory provisions associated with the form or content of consumer credit, core banking and investment services advertisements, establish criminal liability and will apply to acts where at least one of their constitutive elements has taken place in France.[119] The application of French criminal law triggers automatically the international jurisdiction of French criminal courts.[120] French courts have taken the position that material directed at customers with residence in France in view of establishing commercial relationships is caught by the scope of domestic statutory offences.[121] The Consumer Code has clearly encouraged this approach by stating that the law of consumer credit advertisements applies to advertisements implemented, received or perceived in France whatever the medium of communication.[122]

For similar statutory offences, German law applies to acts committed within the territory of Germany.[123] For the purposes of criminal law, an act is committed at every place the perpetrator acted or, in case of an omission, should have acted, or at every place where the result-element of the crime occurs or the perpetrator intended it to occur.[124] The result of the crime occurs in the territory within which the protected legal interest is violated.[125] In German case law and doctrine, there is no consensus as to whether information made available via the Internet is subject to German criminal law under an *objective* or a *subjective* test.[126] The German government has taken the view that German criminal law

---

[117] See C.consom., arts. L 121(1)1, L 121(6) and L 213(1).
[118] See Loi No. 94-665, art. 2.
[119] See C.pen., art. L 113(2).
[120] See C.proc.pen., art. 689.
[121] See TGI Paris (26 February 2002) in [2002] 4 Electronic Business Law 14; TGI Paris, 12.02.1999, aff. Chaumet, *La Semaine Juridique*.E 1999, p. 695.
[122] See C.consom., art. L 3(4).
[123] See § 3 StGB.
[124] *Ibid.*, art. 9.
[125] See A. Schönke and others (eds.) *Strafgesetzbuch* (26th edn, Munich: C. H. Beck, 2001), art. 9.
[126] See M. Schreibauer 'Strafrechtliche Verantwortlichkeit für Delikte im Internet' in D. Kröger and M. Gimmy, *Handbuch zum Internetrecht* (2nd edn, Berlin: Springer Verlag, 2002), pp. 596–8.

applies to criminal acts, which *objectively* produce effects in German territory or were intended by the perpetrator to have effects in the territory, regardless of whether the act constitutes a criminal offence under the law of the place where the perpetrator physically acted.[127] The Federal Court (BGH) shares the view.[128]

---

[127] *Ibid.*
[128] See BGH [2001] 2 *Electronic Business Law* 15.

# 8

# Mutual recognition of national laws under the principle of 'country of origin' of the Electronic Commerce Directive

For financial services provided by electronic means, the principle of country of origin of the E-Commerce Directive, also known as the 'internal market' clause, was advertised as a decisive contribution to legal certainty and one-stop home country control. The Directive established the mutual recognition of the law relating to electronic commerce in the hope to eliminate legal obstacles arising from divergences in legislation and from the legal uncertainty as to which national rules apply to online services.[1]

Article 3 of the E-Commerce Directive introduces the 'country of origin' rule in the following terms:

> Each Member State shall ensure that the information society services provided by a service provider established on its territory comply with the national provisions applicable in the Member State in question which fall within the coordinated field.[2] Member States may not, for reasons falling within the coordinated field, restrict the freedom to provide information society services from another Member State.[3]

## Scope of application of the 'country of origin' rule

The 'country of origin' rule has been drafted in carefully chosen terms of art. It applies to information society services (ISS) and only within the scope of the 'coordinated field' as defined by the Directive. Its outer limits are also dictated by the general scope of application of the Directive, the applicable exceptions and the general derogations from the 'country of origin' rule as set out in the Annex to the Directive.

---

[1] See EP and Council Directive 2000/31/EC of 8 June 2000 on certain legal aspects of information society services, in particular electronic commerce, in the internal Market, OJ 2000 No. L178/1, 17 July 2000, recital 5.
[2] *Ibid.*, art. 3(1).   [3] See art. 3(2).

*Limitations posed by the general scope of application of the Directive*

The Directive does not change in any way the law relating to data protection, taxation, agreements and practices governed by cartel law, activities of notaries or equivalent professions, the judicial representation of a client and gambling activities.[4] Moreover, it does not affect measures taken at Community or national level in order to promote cultural and linguistic diversity and to ensure the defence of pluralism.[5]

The concept of 'information society services'

The Directive applies to 'information society services'. In the legal glossary of the European Union the term 'information society' appeared for the first time in the 1994 Bangemann Recommendations for the development of European information networks.[6] In that paper, the 'information society' was defined as the social and commercial revolution based on technological progress which enables the processing, storage, retrieval and communication of information and human intelligence in whatever form it may take – oral, written or visual – unconstrained by distance, time and volume.[7] Insofar as the E-Commerce Directive covers only ISS, the definition of ISS necessarily defines the scope of application of the 'country of origin' rule. According to Article 2(a) of the Directive, ISS are 'services within the meaning of Art. 1(2) of Directive 98/34/EC as amended by Directive 98/48/EC': they are services as defined by the EC Treaty,[8] normally provided for remuneration, at a distance, by electronic means and at the individual request of a recipient of services.[9] We shall briefly discuss the components of this definition.

**'Services normally for remuneration'** ISS are services within the meaning of Article 50 EC: activities of a commercial character, which are normally provided for remuneration, insofar as they are not

---

[4] Art. 1(5).   [5] Art. 1(6) and recital 63.
[6] See High-Level Group on the Information Society, *Europe and the Global Information Society, Recommendations to the European Council* (the 'Bangemann Recommendations') (Brussels, 1994).
[7] *Ibid.*, p. 3.
[8] Treaty Establishing the European Community (Rome, 25 March 1957); consolidated text at OJ 2002 No. C325, 24 December 2002.
[9] See EP and Council Directive 98/48/EC of 20 July 1998 amending Directive 98/34/EC laying down a procedure for the provision of information in the field of technical standards and regulations, OJ 1998 No. L217/18, 19th recital; E-Commerce Directive, 6th and 18th recitals.

governed by the provisions relating to freedom of movement for goods, capital and persons.[10] Remuneration is the consideration for the service in question and it is the product of agreement between the provider and the recipient of the service.[11] The consideration is not necessarily in the form of a pecuniary obligation and it is not required that it be provided by those for which the service is performed,[12] as long as the provider receives consideration in one form or another. In electronic banking services, remuneration exists even if no fee or commission is payable to the bank. The deposit of funds finances the bank's lending business and this is sufficient consideration for the service that the customer receives.

Financial services are 'services' within the meaning of the EC Treaty regardless of the application of the rules on the free movement of capital where appropriate. In cases such as *Svensson and Gustavsson*[13] and *Parodi*[14] cross-border bank loans were recognized as falling simultaneously within the scope of freedom of services and free movement of capital. In any case, the characterization of online activities as 'provision of services', 'trade in goods' or 'movements of capital' for purposes of the Treaty economic freedoms do not determine the scope of application of the E-Commerce Directive. For example, selling and delivering goods online is an expressly enumerated 'information society service',[15] even though it is regulated by the Treaty chapter on the free movement of goods for purposes of the Treaty economic freedoms. In the same way, online financial services are 'information society services' if they meet the criteria of the relevant definition regardless of whether they are 'services' or 'movements of capital' for purposes of the Treaty economic freedoms. The E-Commerce Directive, together with the Distance Marketing of Consumer Financial Services Directive,[16] aims to contribute to creating a legal framework for providing online financial services.[17] The definition of 'information society services' is an autonomous concept and whether online financial activities are ISS is an

---

[10] *Ibid.*, recitals 6 and 18.
[11] See Case 263/86 *Belgium* v. *Humbel* [1988] ECR 5365, para. 17.
[12] See Case C-352/85 *Bond van Adverteerders* v. *The Netherlands* [1988] ECR 2085, para. 16.
[13] See Case C-484/93 *Svensson and Gustavsson* v. *Ministre du Logement et de l'Urbanisme* [1995] ECR I-3955.
[14] See Case C-222/95 *Société Parodi* v. *Banque H. Albert de Bary et Cie* [1997] ECR I-3899.
[15] See E-Commerce Directive, Recital 18.
[16] EP and Council Directive 2002/65/EC of 23 September 2002 concerning distance marketing of consumer financial services, OJ 2002 No. L271/16, 9 October 2002.
[17] Recital 27.

independent question from their legal nature as movements of capital or services under the EC Treaty.

**'At a distance'**   ISS are provided without the parties being simultaneously present. The pertinent factor is space, not time. The provider and the recipient must not be physically present in the same area but it is not required that the service is provided in real time.[18]

**'By electronic means'**   ISS are provided by electronic means if the service is initially sent and subsequently received at its destination by means of electronic equipment for the processing (including digital compression) and storage of data and entirely transmitted, conveyed and received by wire, by radio, by optical means or by other electromagnetic means.[19]

The first requirement is that the service is *sent* and *received* by means of electronic equipment for the processing and storage of data. The service essentially consists of data, which are capable of being processed and stored in the provider's equipment and subsequently sent to the recipient, where they are received by means of similar equipment. Second, the transmission and exchange of the data from the provider's to the recipient's 'equipment' must be effected via wire, radio, optical means or other electromagnetic means. Services, which are not provided *entirely* by means of transmission of data between the provider's and the recipient's 'electronic equipment' are not ISS. In particular, it does not suffice that the service is sent in the form of information by means of electronic equipment but it is received otherwise than in the same way, for example cash withdrawal in ATMs, or that it is transmitted by cable or other eligible means but not from or to electronic equipment for the processing and storage of data, for example telephone banking.[20]

In respect of banking services provided entirely via the Internet, the condition is fulfilled. Advertising, disclosure of information, contractual offer and acceptance, transmission of the customer's mandate, performance, administration and settlement of the parties' claims may take the form of data which are stored, transmitted and received over the network. What matters is the reception and transmission of data between the bank's and the customer's computing equipment.

---

[18] See Directive 98/48/EC, above note 9, Annex V para.1.
[19] *Ibid.*, art. 1(2)(t).
[20] *Ibid.*, Annex V, para. 2.

The deposit of funds does not appear to satisfy the conditions. The deposit of coins and notes is certainly not an information society service. Moreover, the deposit of funds by way of cashless fund transfers is not a reception and transmission of data between the bank and the customer but between the bank and a third bank communicating a payment instruction at the request of the depositor or a third party such as an employer or a commercial debtor. With the exception of deposits of funds, the 'Internet service' contract entails the performance of services that satisfy the definition, such as electronic fund transfers at the customer's instructions transmitted via the Internet, online access to account information or electronic transmission of orders for the purchase or sale of securities.

**'Individual request'** ISS must be provided through the transmission of data on individual request, which aims to exclude television and radio broadcasting.[21] The pertinent criterion is whether data have been transmitted on the recipient's individual request. The condition is met even if the information is *intended* to reach an unlimited number of individual receivers, as in most commercial websites, or the information has been communicated to individual recipients via electronic mail without their prior demand.[22]

## The 'coordinated field'

The 'coordinated field' designates the subject-matter of mutual recognition of national laws that the principle of country of origin entails. The coordinated field consists of the requirements laid down in Member States' legal systems applicable to ISS providers or to ISS, regardless of whether they are of a general nature or specifically designed for them.[23]

First, the 'coordinated field' covers requirements with which the service provider has to comply *before* the commencement of the activity in order to meet legal conditions of market entry,[24] including general requirements concerning qualifications, authorization or notification. Second, it encompasses requirements relating to the actual pursuit of the activity of providing ISS, such as rules applicable to advertising,

---

[21] See E-Commerce Directive, recital 18.
[22] *Ibid.*
[23] See E-Commerce Directive, art. 2(h).
[24] Art. 2(h)(i).

including the format, content, fairness and control of advertising and promotional information,[25] which (a) may relate either to the underlying services, for example rules on consumer credit advertisements, (b) may be of a general nature, for example the law of unfair advertising and competition, or (c) apply specifically to online communications. It also covers rules regulating the conduct of the service provider in providing financial services, such as conduct of investment business rules, including rules of pre-contractual disclosure of information to investors, depositors or consumers.[26] Furthermore, it covers requirements regarding the quality or content of the service[27] and the law relating to contractual obligations regardless of whether it is of a general nature or specifically applicable to online electronic contracts.[28] Here one may list the law relating to the conduct of the parties immediately prior to forming a contract such as the rules on pre-contractual disclosure of information, misrepresentation and liability during negotiations (*culpa in contrahendo*), the law relating to the formation of contracts, for example offer, acceptance and formalities, especially the requirement of a written contract, the use of electronic signatures and the validity of contracts concluded online and the law relating to the performance of contractual obligations, whether it is of a general nature or specifically applicable to consumer contracts. Finally, the 'coordinated field' covers requirements concerning the liability of the service provider, which may be either contractual or in tort for civil wrongs occurred during the advertising, pre-contractual or contractual stage of the service.

The 'coordinated field' does not cover requirements that apply to services 'not provided by electronic means'.[29] The derogation refers to national rules which cannot reasonably apply to services provided at a distance by electronic means (objective criterion) as well as rules which *in concreto* refer to a non-electronic aspect of the service, notwithstanding the application of the Directive in some other respect (subjective criterion). The pertinent criterion is whether the rule applies to activities that are *actually* carried on by electronic means. For example, legal requirements relating to the validity of contracts are outside the scope of the coordinated field, insofar as a particular type of contract cannot be validly concluded electronically under the applicable law in question. Here it is *objectively* impossible to conclude a valid contract by electronic means. If no such restriction exists, the valid formation of an

---

[25] Art. 2(h)(i) and recital 21.
[26] Ibid.    [27] Ibid.    [28] Ibid.    [29] See art. 2(h)(ii).

electronic contract is *objectively* possible. Yet, the rules relating to the validity of contracts would still be outside the 'coordinated field' in the specific case of electronic services performed under a contract formed otherwise than by electronic means despite the permissive legal framework.

For the systematic understanding of the Directive, the definition of the 'coordinated field' is crucial. The definition concept itself follows the vague chronological order of the key events in the economic cycle of financial services, in particular initial market entry of financial institutions, advertising activities, pre-contractual behaviour, formation of contracts, content and performance of contractual obligations. By bringing under the generic concept of the 'coordinated field' legal requirements, which are not related in any respect other than by being applicable to online services, the Directive effectively dictates the normative effects of the 'country of origin' rule with total disrespect to the traditional distinction between public and private law. This is an unprecedented development in the field of EU law relating to financial services where the principle of 'home country' control has been until now strictly confined within the boundaries of prudential financial regulation – essentially regulatory law falling within the domain of 'public law'. Because the E-Commerce Directive has extended the normative impact of the principle of country of origin to a broad range of legal issues spanning from the law of contracts to key aspects of regulatory law, the reconciliation of the principle of country of origin with established rules of private international law or conflict of laws has not been an easy task. It is clear, however, that the characterization of a given domain of national law as 'private' or 'public' is not determinative of the potential position of the pertinent national rules 'in' or 'out' of the field coordinated by the E-Commerce Directive.

*Mutual recognition under the principle of 'country of origin'*

The broad coverage of the 'coordinated field', which defies the distinction between private and public law, and a number of conflicting and apparently ambiguous provisions of the Directive have triggered a lively academic debate, especially in Germany, on the likely normative effects of the 'internal market' clause.

### The theories

In broad terms, three different approaches have emerged. First, it has been argued that the 'country of origin' rule constitutes a conflicts rule proper, which requires that ISS and ISS providers be subject to a single system of law, namely the law of the country of origin of the provider.[30] Another version of this theory suggested that the 'most favourable' law to the provider be applicable, which in the circumstances could be either the law of the country of origin or even that of the country of destination.[31]

The second major proposition regarded the model of country of origin as a rule of negative integration akin to the Treaty economic freedoms.[32] It was argued that the Directive established no special arrangement as to the allocation of exclusive supervisory responsibility to the 'home state', let alone a conflict of laws proper. It was merely intended as a rule of negative integration dictating the elimination of national rules obstructing the provision of online services. The third view stands in the middle and regards the 'country of origin' rule as a mandatory requirement of secondary Community law, which entails specific obligations for national authorities but without determining *in abstracto* the law governing online activities.[33]

## The critique

The second view that the principle of country of origin simply reiterates the prohibition of restrictions on the free movement of online services has obvious strengths. The Directive emphatically provides that it does not aim to establish additional rules on private international law relating to conflicts of laws[34] and does not affect the process of designating the applicable law insofar as the applicable substantive rules do not restrict the freedom of suppliers to provide ISS.[35] Furthermore, the actual wording of the principle of country of origin is remarkably similar to the jurisprudence of the Court concerning the freedom to provide services: Article 3(2) provides that Member States may not restrict the freedom of service providers to provide ISS from another Member State,

---

[30] See Peter Mankowski, 'Das Herkunfslandprinzip als Internationales Privatrecht des E-Commerce Richtlinie' (2001) 100 ZvglRWiss 137.
[31] See e.g. Reich and Helfmeier, 'Consumer Protection in the Global Village'.
[32] See Herbert Kronke, 'Applicable Law and Jurisdiction in Electronic Banking Transactions' in Norbert Horn (ed.), *Legal Issues in Electronic Banking* (The Hague: Kluwer, 2002), p. 77.
[33] See Gerard Spindler, 'Herkunftslandprinzip und Kollisionsrecht-Binnenmarktintegration ohne Harmonisierung?' (2002) 66 RabelsZ 633.
[34] See E-Commerce Directive, art. 1(4) and recital 23.
[35] See recital 23.

while Article 3(4) concedes that restrictions may nonetheless be imposed in order to safeguard eligible public policy objectives of the country of destination.

On that basis, it appears that the 'country of origin' rule operates in three consecutive stages. First, the law applicable to ISS and ISS providers is determined in accordance with common conflict of laws and the territorial application of regulatory and public law of Member States. Second, insofar as the applicable law restricts the freedom to provide ISS and falls within the 'coordinated field', the Member State of destination shall refrain from requiring compliance. Third, provided that the procedural and policy conditions of Article 3(4) are satisfied, the *status quo ante* shall be reinstated and the service provider would still have to comply with the applicable rules in the 'host country'.

Despite the apparent force of that theory, substantial doubts remain. First despite the unusual drafting of Article 3, which does not explicitly state that ISS shall be governed by the law of the country of origin, the Directive makes clear '. . .that information society services should in principle be subject to the law of the Member State in which the service provider is established.'[36] Second, the Annex to the Directive exempts from the normative effects of the principle of country of origin the freedom of parties to choose the applicable law and contractual obligations concerning consumer contracts. The drafters' care to exclude key aspects of private international law demonstrates *a contrario* that other areas of conflict of laws are within the scope of and replaced by the 'country of origin' rule. Third, if the provision was reduced to a mere negative covenant akin to the Treaty economic freedoms, the value added by the Directive would be virtually negligible and the shortcomings of regulatory reform through litigation, namely the piecemeal and *ad hoc* elimination of barriers, the uncertainty as to whether national measures constitute restrictions and whether those restrictions could be justified would still burden the internal market in online services. The only normative difference between the Directive and the Treaty would have been the 'general good' derogation of Article 3(4), which replaces the open-ended list of justifications under Article 49 EC with a *numerus clausus* of four public policy objectives and a more stringent consultation procedure. But in disregarding the crucial question of which national law applies to ubiquitous online services and concentrating on the

---

[36] See recital 22.

restrictive effects of applicable law, the theory has misunderstood the objective and rationale of the Directive and must be dismissed.

The Directive never intended to put the country of origin at par with the country of destination. It recognizes that cross-border electronic commerce is restricted not only by divergence in national law but also by legal uncertainty as to which national rules apply to such services.[37] Although negative integration in the form of a 'restriction test' analogous to the Treaty freedoms suffices to remove the most disturbing elements associated with legal plurality and diversity, the uncertainty as to which law applies requires a more aggressive strategy. It is precisely this point where the parity between the country of origin and the country of destination, as the EC Treaty recognizes it, is replaced by legal clarity and certainty in accordance with a strong form of mutual recognition. In the words of the Directive, ISS should in principle be subject to the law of the Member State in which the service provider is established 'in order to effectively guarantee freedom to provide services and legal certainty for suppliers and recipients of services. . .' and therefore '. . . ISS should be supervised at the source of the activity. . .'[38] In principle, 'the competent authority provides such protection not only for the citizens of its own country but for all Community citizens. . .' and it is therefore 'essential to state clearly this responsibility on the part of the Member State where the services originate.'[39]

On those grounds, the 'most favourable law' theory must also be dismissed. The country of origin must ensure that the firm complies with domestic law, regardless of whether it is more or less favourable to the provider than the rules of the country of destination. An initial attempt by Austria and Germany to implement the Directive in the form of a flexible rule, according to which the most favourable law should apply, raised considerable criticism, it almost set in motion infringement proceedings on the part of the European Commission and was eventually abandoned by its sponsors.[40] There is more to the Directive than a restatement of Article 49 EC on the basis of a more stringent 'general good' derogation. But can we infer a proper conflicts rule?

The arguments of the pure 'conflicts theory' are equally unconvincing. The unequivocal provision of Article 1(4) cannot be simply bypassed as

---

[37] See recital 5.   [38] See recital 22.   [39] *Ibid.*
[40] See Peter Mankowski, 'Herkunftslandprinzip und Günstigkeitsvergleich in Art.4 TDG-E' 2001 CR 630.

*falsa demonstratio*. The Directive expressly provides that it does not add to the rules of private international law and, as such, it must be respected. Furthermore, conflicts rules share common characteristics that are lacking in Article 3 of the Directive. For example, the conflict of laws is based on objective connecting factors, which designate the applicable law *in abstracto*. International treaties harmonizing national conflicts of laws such as the Rome Convention on the Law Applicable to Contractual Obligations[41] establish objective connecting factors to be applied by all countries where a contract might be litigated. In contrast, the E-Commerce Directive imposes different obligations on Member States depending on their respective capacity as country of origin or country of destination of ISS. Furthermore, the construction of an abstract conflicts rule encompassing the entire corpus of public and private law is impractical and rather impossible. Unsurprisingly, no such rule can be detected in Article 3 and it is unwise to extract one.

## A mandatory rule of community law

In my view, the principle of 'country of origin' as defined in Article 3 of the E-Commerce Directive incorporates the typical characteristics of EU Directives as framework rules addressed to Member States, binding only as to the result to be achieved but leaving to the national authorities the choice of form and methods. It should be noted that, unlike other internal market Directives, which set out sufficiently precise rules, the principle of country of origin can only be understood as a mandatory requirement imposing obligations on Member States, the precise effects of which cannot be appreciated in isolation from implementing legislation and out of the national legal context.

On careful inspection, Article 3 is revealing. It does not designate the applicable law in an abstract form, operating as *lex specialis* vis-à-vis existing conflict of laws. It imposes specific obligations on Member States in their respective capacities as country of origin or country of destination, which have to be implemented by whatever methods Member States consider appropriate. It is nothing more than a mandatory rule of Community law, which must be implemented by national authorities. Crucially, if national law, whether substantive or conflict of laws, is incompatible with the changes required by the Directive, the Directive prevails and the national rule must be set aside.

---

[41] See Convention on the Law Applicable to Contractual Obligations (Rome, 19 June 1980); consolidated version at OJ 1998, No. C27/34, 26 January 1998.

The first obligation imposed on Member States is to ensure that services provided by service providers established on their territories comply with the national provisions applicable in the Member State in question which fall within the coordinated field.[42] The concept of 'national provisions applicable in the Member State in question' refers to substantive rules and does not include domestic conflicts of laws, which could designate the law of another Member State in a potentially endless process of *renvoi*.[43] The Directive purports to eradicate restrictions relating to legal uncertainty as to the application of national law. That objective is served by requiring Member States in their capacity as 'countries of origin' to ensure that firms established therein comply with their own law. The obligation is addressed indistinctly to Member States and must be invariably implemented by national legislative, executive and judicial authorities.[44]

In the hypothetical case that conflicts rules in the country of origin designate a different applicable law, there is no option but to give priority to the Directive and disregard the conflict of laws in question. The forum judge is required by the Directive to apply the substantive law of the country of origin regardless of what the domestic conflict of laws would otherwise dictate. The scope of territorial application of economic regulatory law of the country of origin should also be amended so as to cover online services provided by local firms to clients in other EU countries.

The obligation imposed on Member States in their capacity as countries receiving online services is different. Article 3(2) of the Directive does not require the 'host country' to apply a specified national law, whether its own rules or the rules of the country of origin. The 'host country' is solely required not to restrict the freedom to provide ISS from another Member State. The term 'restrict' corresponds to the identical concept featuring in the jurisprudence of the Court concerning the free movement of services but improves the legal framework in one important respect: in the context of the E-Commerce Directive and within the boundaries of the coordinated field, private parties are no longer required to litigate whether a given measure imposed by the

---

[42] See E-Commerce Directive, art. 3(1).
[43] See also Ana P. Vallelersundi (Rapporteur), *Recommendation for Second Reading on the Council Common Position for Adopting the Directive on Electronic Commerce*, A5-0106/2000, 12 April 2000, at p. 11.
[44] See Case C-96/81 *Commission v. Netherlands* [1982] ECR 1791.

'host country' restricts the provision of online services. The obligation imposed on the country of destination to 'deregulate' *incoming* online activities must be examined in the light of the simultaneous obligation imposed on the 'country of origin' to 'exclusively regulate' *outgoing* online activities. Taken together, Article 3(1) and (2) of the E Commerce Directive introduces a *sui generis* model of 'home country' control.

The legal obligation of the country of origin to extend the territorial scope of application of domestic law to outgoing online services directed at recipients in other EU countries is an implicit instruction to the country of destination to reform its legal framework in view of deregulating the cross-border provision of online services by firms established in other EU countries. Because any regulatory requirement imposed on firms established in other Member States will add to the regulatory burden that the firm is subject to in the country of origin, extending the scope of application of domestic law to *outgoing* services in implementation of Article 3(1) without simultaneously deregulating *incoming* services pursuant to Article 3(2) violates Article 3 of the Directive. The proper implementation of Article 3 entails the correction of the spatial application of public law and regulation in appropriate circumstances, so as to achieve the full application of the 'coordinated field' to outgoing ISS and full deregulation of incoming ISS within the same limits, without prejudice to the exceptional powers set out in Article 3(4).

## The general derogations

The mandatory requirements imposed by Article 3 do not apply to insurance, units in collective investment schemes, the permissibility of unsolicited communications by electronic mail (which is regulated by the Directive on Privacy and Electronic Communications),[45] the freedom of parties to choose the law applicable to the contract and contractual obligations concerning consumer contracts.[46] The breadth of the 'coordinated field', which enhances dramatically the normative impact of mutual recognition regardless of whether minimum harmonization has been achieved or not, is the institutional context against which these 'general derogations' must be understood.

---

[45] See EP and Council Directive 2002/58/EC concerning the processing of personal data and the protection of privacy in the electronic communications sector, OJ 2002 No. L201/37 31 July 2002.
[46] See Annex to the E-Commerce Directive.

The negotiators of the Directive had to overcome a sharp contradiction: while the principle of country of origin works better if a minimum level of common rules has been attained, it was almost impossible to achieve a satisfactory level of convergence in such a broad range of legal topics falling within the coordinated field. Hence, the Directive itself emphasizes that it must be read in the context of the remainder of Community law relating to various types of online activities, such as financial services, movements of capital or sale of goods.[47]

Simultaneously, the 'coordinated field' was designed to extend beyond national requirements in force at the time of the adoption of the Directive, incorporating automatically any EU legislation adopted thereafter.[48] It therefore operates in the form of an institutional 'floating charge', the scope of which is intended to be evolving in accordance with developments in Community law, constantly reducing the non-harmonized standards which fall within the scope of the rule of 'country of origin'.

Turning to the existing derogations, the freedom of choice of the governing law of contracts has rightly been kept out of the model of country of origin. In matters where party autonomy is unrestricted, it makes no sense to impose the mandatory application of the law of the 'country of origin'.

With regard to consumer protection, particularly in relation to consumers' contractual commitments, the assurances given by the promoters of the Directive were not sufficient to secure political agreement in the Council. Member States were not prepared to revisit embedded principles of the conflict of laws for consumer contracts. The Directive leaves outside the model of country of origin contractual obligations concerning consumer contracts, which remain subject to traditional rules of private international law.

One could potentially question the wisdom of this choice, especially because consideration was taken at that time of the level of harmonization already attained in consumer contract law. As the rapporteur argued in the European Parliament,[49] consumer protection had been sufficiently harmonized at the EU level so as to sustain a workable model of home country control. Having indicated this, she acknowledged the existing national sensitivities on that issue and reluctantly proposed

---

[47] See recital 11.    [48] See recital 21.
[49] See Christine Oddy (European Parliament), *Report on the Proposal for the E-Commerce Directive*, PE 229.868/fin, 23 April 1999.

the adoption of the derogation but only for those elements that had not been dealt with at the EC level. The Council declined to revise its position and therefore consumer contracts remained outside the normative effects of the Directive regardless of the absence or not of sufficient convergence in the substantive laws of the Member States. Thus, the country of origin principle cannot have the result of depriving the consumer of the protection afforded to him by the mandatory rules relating to contractual obligations of the law of the Member State in which he has his habitual residence.[50] Those obligations should be interpreted as including information on the essential elements of the content of the contract, including consumer rights, which have a determining influence on the decision to contract.[51]

The derogation expressly covers the 'law applicable to contractual obligations' relating to consumer contracts and the protection afforded to the consumer by the mandatory rules of the law of the country of his or her habitual residence.[52] The reference to the Rome Convention is direct and unequivocal, bringing the private international law of consumer contracts outside the scope of the 'country of origin' principle. What this means in practice is that Member States in their capacity as the country of origin should still determine the law governing contractual obligations in consumer contracts in accordance with the provisions of the Rome Convention. In their capacity as the country of destination, they can disregard the obligation imposed by Article 3.

## The place of establishment

To determine the 'country of origin' for purposes of applicable law, one must identify the place of establishment of the provider of ISS. Establishment involves the actual pursuit of an economic activity through a fixed establishment for an indefinite period.[53] The presence and use of the technical means and technologies required to provide the service do not, in themselves, constitute an establishment of the provider[54] but it is not required that the 'fixed establishment' takes the form of a branch or agency. A mere office managed by the firm's own staff or even by a person who is independent but authorized to act on a

---

[50] See E-Commerce Directive, recital 55.
[51] See recital 56.   [52] See recital 55.
[53] See recital 19.   [54] Ibid.

permanent basis for the undertaking would suffice.[55] Unless the 'fixed establishment' has a permanent character and it is staffed by people, who can undertake legal commitments on behalf of the 'parent undertaking',[56] the likely location of the technology and equipment supporting the website as well as the place in which the website is accessible cannot trigger the application of the 'internal market' clause.[57] In cases where a provider has several places of establishment, it is important to determine from which place of establishment the particular service concerned is provided.[58] In the event of uncertainty, this is the place where the provider has the centre of his activities relating to this particular service.[59]

The 'place of establishment' of financial institutions for the purposes of the 'country of origin' rule is not necessarily the 'home Member State' as understood in the context of the Banking Consolidation Directive.[60] For example, if a branch located in country X of a credit institution authorized in country Z provides online services to clients in country Y, the country of origin for purposes of the E-Commerce Directive would be country X and not the 'home country' Z of the credit institution. If online services are provided from within the bank's 'home country', the country of origin for purposes of the E-Commerce Directive coincides with the home country for purposes of the Banking Directive. In that case, an interesting question would be whether the likely location in another country of electronic equipment storing the website or the electronic records of personal and account information, or even helpdesk staff and call centres dealing with enquiries regarding the 'Internet service' agreement, could be regarded as a permanent establishment.

In practice, it is unlikely that electronic equipment for the storage or processing of data would be located in a jurisdiction where the bank maintains no other form of establishment. Even in the unlikely case that a bank establishes several computers in another country, the 'place of technology' does not amount to a 'place of establishment'.[61] The real issue arises when the bank maintains a branch or subsidiary in another Member State, where aspects of the Internet service are performed, for

---

[55] See Case C-205/84 *Commission* v. *Germany* [1986] ECR 3755, para. 21.
[56] See Case C-33/78 *Somafer SA* v. *Saar-Ferngas AG* [1978] ECR 2183.
[57] E-Commerce Directive, recital 19.
[58] *Ibid.*
[59] *Ibid.*
[60] EP and Council Directive 2000/12/EC of 20 March 2000 relating to the taking up and pursuit of the business of credit institutions, OJ 2000 No. L126/1, 26 May 2000.
[61] *Ibid.*

example, the storage and administration of local customer information or even the website, but the performance and settlement of the transactions are actually carried on in the 'home country' headquarters. In that case, different forms of actual economic activity occur in different Member States but the characteristic aspect of the service is arguably carried on in the 'home' jurisdiction. In the event of uncertainty caused by the interaction of more than one place where various components of the economic activity in question are pursued, the Directive uses the concept of the 'centre of activities' to solve the problem. Arguably, services are provided from the place of establishment where characteristic aspects of the service and not merely ancillary operations are performed.

In the case of the French online bank Banque Cortal, which used to accept deposits and online trading instructions from UK residents directly in the books of its French headquarters, the FSA emphasized that the involvement of the London branch in the collection and transmission of applications from UK customers back to the 'home country' was purely facilitative and did not change the legal character of the 'passport' as one based on the freedom of cross-border services and not establishment.[62]

## The implementation of the 'country of origin' principle

### Implementation in the United Kingdom

The principle of country of origin was implemented in the United Kingdom by the Electronic Commerce (EC Directive) Regulations 2002 (the 'General Regulations')[63] and the Electronic Commerce Directive (Financial Services and Markets) Regulations 2002.[64] In accordance with the letter and the spirit of the E-Commerce Directive, online financial services provided to UK residents by financial institutions based in another EEA country have been taken outside the scope of application of UK laws, except for applicable 'consumer contract requirements' which must still be respected.[65] The exception refers to requirements in the FSA Handbook that a certain amount of information be provided to a consumer before he enters into a contract for the provision of one or more information society services or requirements as to the manner in which such information is to be provided.[66] The beneficiaries of this deregulation are

---

[62] See Interview with Leon Burt, Monitoring and Notification Department, Financial Services Authority, London, 4 July 2003, on file with author.
[63] SI 2002/2013.       [64] SI 2002/1775.
[65] SI 2002/1775, reg. 3(4).       [66] See SI 2002/1775, reg. 3(6).

'incoming electronic commerce activities', which are defined as ISS provided to persons in the United Kingdom by firms established in other Member States, which would be regulated activities under the FISMA 2000 but for the measures implementing the Directive.[67]

The ECO section of the FSA Handbook further specifies in rule ECO 1.1 that an EEA firm carrying on an electronic commerce activity from an establishment in an EEA country other than the United Kingdom with or for a recipient of electronic commerce services in the United Kingdom enjoys the freedom to carry on the electronic commerce activity in the United Kingdom. In doing that it is only required to comply with the applicable laws in the country of origin from which the service is provided and not the laws in the place where the customer is located, that is the laws of the United Kingdom, subject to derogations from that principle.[68] Rule ECO 1.1.6 succinctly confirms that the FSA Handbook does not apply to an incoming provider of electronic commerce services except for the provisions relating to prior information requirements set out in rule ECO 1.1.10, which implement the derogations from the principle of country of origin. Even this limited obligation to comply with applicable information requirements under the FSA Handbook is waived in the case of a provider of electronic commerce services from an establishment outside the United Kingdom, if the EEA country from which the activity is provided has implemented the Distance Marketing Directive with the result that the obligations provided for by the Directive are applied when the provider of electronic commerce services is carrying on the activity from an establishment in that EEA country with a UK person receiving electronic commerce services in the United Kingdom.[69] This provision is justified on grounds that the information requirements prescribed by the Distance Marketing Directive are more extensive than the information requirements set out in the Handbook and there is no reason to require compliance with the UK rules if the EEA firm already complies with the more extensive requirements in its country of origin.

The corollary of the rules implementing the principle of country of origin with regard to *incoming* providers of electronic commerce services from an EEA country to persons in the United Kingdom, are the rules which extend the scope of application of UK requirements to *outgoing*

---

[67] See FISMA 2000 (Regulated Activities) (Amendment) (No. 2) Order 2002, SI 2002/1776.
[68] See ECO 1.1.2 G.      [69] See ECO 1.2.5B R.

providers of electronic commerce services from an establishment in the United Kingdom to persons in another EEA country. Given that most parts of the FSA Handbook were in any case applicable to firms engaging in regulated activities from an establishment in the United Kingdom regardless of the location of the customer, the implementation of the E-Commerce Directive did not require a substantial restatement of the territorial scope of application of the Handbook in connection with electronic commerce services provided from an establishment in the United Kingdom. Rule ECO 2.2.3 renders electronic commerce communications made from an establishment in the United Kingdom to a person in an EEA State other than the United Kingdom subject to the Handbook rules on financial promotion. The effect of rule ECO 2.2.3 was to extend the scope of application of the financial promotion rules to UK firms providing electronic commerce services to recipients in another EEA country. These firms would have been outside the scope of application of the pertinent rules but for the rules implementing the E-Commerce Directive.[70]

## Implementation in Germany

Information society services or teleservices (*Telediensten*) in the terminology of the German E-Commerce Act, provided by financial institutions based in Germany, are subject to the 'requirements of German law' (*Anforderungen des deutschen Rechts*), regardless of whether they are commercially offered or rendered in another country.[71] Taking into account the applicable derogations relating to the private international law of contracts, the 'requirements of German law' encompass substantive rules and not the German conflict of laws.[72] In accordance with the Directive, the provision of teleservices in Germany by commercial providers established in another EEA country should not be restricted.[73] In the domain of public regulatory law, German authorities must refrain from requiring financial institutions based in another country to comply with German rules.[74]

---

[70] See COB 3.3 and MCOB 3.3.
[71] See *Gesetz über die Nutzung von Telediensten* (TDG), § 4 Abs.1.
[72] See Deutsche Bundestag, *Public Hearing on the Implementation of the E-Commerce Directive*, BT-Drucks. 14/6098 (2001).
[73] See TDG § 4 Abs. 2.
[74] See Deutsche Bundestag, *Report on the Electronic Commerce Bill*, BT-Drucks. 14/6098 (17 May 2001), at p. 18.

## Implementation in France

The E-Commerce Directive was implemented by Loi 2004–575 (the Act 2004–575 of 21 June 2004 for the Confidence in the Digital Economy).[75] Electronic commerce was defined as the economic activity in which a person proposes or achieves the provision of goods or services at a distance by electronic means.[76] The conduct of electronic commerce activities is unrestricted within the national territory to the extent provided for by the Act.[77] According to the main operative provisions, 'electronic commerce activities' are made subject to the law of the Member State on the territory of which the person pursuing the activities is established, unless the provider and the recipient of the services select by common agreement a different applicable law.[78] Despite its formulation as an abstract conflicts rule, the applicable law encompasses the entire corpus of the 'coordinated field' regardless of the public or private nature of the underlying rules.[79] The 'common agreement' of the parties to select a different governing law takes precedence over the 'country of origin' rule only in respect of contractual obligations subject to party autonomy. The application of the 'country of origin' rule must not have the effect of depriving those consumers who have their habitual residence in France of the protection afforded by the mandatory requirements of the French law relating to contractual obligations, in accordance with the international obligations undertaken by France.[80] The provisions relating to contractual obligations include the provisions applicable to the elements of the contract, including consumer rights, which have a determining influence on the decision to contract.[81]

### The case-by-case derogation of Article 3(4)–(6)

I argued in Chapter 4 that a working model of country of origin must provide for the emergency resumption of regulatory powers by the country of destination when trust and confidence in the political will

---

[75] See Loi No. 2004–575 du 21 Juin 2004 pour la confiance dans l'économie numérique, J.O. 22 June 2004.
[76] Ibid., art. 14.
[77] See art. 16 (I).
[78] See art. 17, para. 1.
[79] See Michèle Tabarot, Rapport sur le Projet de Loi pour la Confiance dans l'Economie Numérique, Assemblée Nationale 608 (11 February 2003), pp. 54–5.
[80] See Loi No. 2004–575, above note 75, Art. 17, para. 2(1).
[81] Ibid.

or ability of the 'home authorities' to enforce its laws adequately has broken down. By the provisions of Article 3(4)–(6) the Directive has established this mechanism that can be invoked by the 'host country' if certain 'substantive' and 'procedural' conditions are met.

## Substantive conditions

Based on Article 3(4) of the Directive, Member States may take measures to derogate from the country of origin rule in respect of a given service if those measures are necessary for reasons of public security and national defence, public policy and the protection of consumers and investors. This list is exhaustive and far narrower in scope and potential for raising obstacles than the concept of the 'general good' as defined by the Court. For example, the condition of 'public policy' is not met by whatever policy objective a rule of domestic law may pursue. In this specific context, 'public policy' is a technical concept which presupposes a 'genuine and sufficiently serious threat affecting one of the fundamental interests of society'[82] such as the prevention, investigation, detection and prosecution of criminal offences, including the protection of minors and the fight against any incitement to hatred on grounds of race, sex, religion or nationality, and violations of human dignity concerning individual persons.[83] It is also clear that policy objectives of a purely economic nature, for example the protection of local economic interests and revenue, are not permissible grounds for restricting online services. Reflecting this narrow scope, 'public policy' has seldom been invoked by Member States as legitimate ground for restrictions and even more rarely sustained by the Court.[84] In providing interpretative guidance on the notion of 'public policy' in the E-Commerce Directive, the Commission has rightly argued that

> It is difficult to see which financial services could meet this judicial condition of a serious threat affecting one of the fundamental interests of society with the exception of services provided illegally in the context of the financing of criminal activities (including terrorism) and money laundering.[85]

---

[82] See Joined Cases C-115 and 116/81 *Adoui* v. *Belgium* [1982] ECR 1665, para. 8.
[83] See E-Commerce Directive, art. 3(4)(a)(i).
[84] See Jukka Snell, *Goods and Services in EC Law* (Oxford: Oxford University Press, 2002), pp. 176–7.
[85] See European Commission, *Application to Financial Services of Article 3(4) to (6) of the Electronic Commerce Directive*, COM(2003) 259 final, at p. 6.

Turning to the remaining conditions, the measure must be taken against a *given* information society service which prejudices one of the eligible objectives or which presents a serious and grave risk of so doing. It is important to underline that Article 3(4) does not provide the legal basis upon which the country of destination may justify the adoption of measures against all incoming providers. It must be seen as a 'case-by-case' derogation, which enables exceptional and *ad hoc* measures to be taken against *individual* providers, the services of which prejudice or threaten to prejudice those objectives. A 'given' service is taken to mean here that the Member State of destination may not take general measures in respect of a category of financial services such as investment funds or loans. Nor is it justified to apply against a specific provider the entire corpus of national law applicable to a category of services, for example, the entire national legislation on consumer credit or collective investment schemes. The measures must be taken against a given service that prejudices one of the objectives spelt out or presents a serious and grave risk of so doing. This wording allows the Member State in which the service is provided to take not only punitive but also preventive measures where there is a serious and grave risk to those objectives. Furthermore, emergency measures must be proportionate to the policy objectives, which means that they must not go beyond what is necessary to achieve legitimate objectives.[86]

## Procedural conditions

Prior to taking the measures in question, the Member State must ask the country of origin to take measures that would satisfy the interests in need of protection. The Directive does not specify any precise deadline by which the Member State of origin must act following the notification received from the Member State of destination. However, Article 19(3) of the Directive stipulates that Member States must as quickly as possible provide the assistance and information requested by other Member States or by the Commission. The actual experience is primarily a matter of efficiency in the cooperation between the 'home' and 'host' authorities where individual circumstances and national approaches matter a great deal.

Banks and other intermediaries established in Member States in which the local authorities are not keen on performing those tasks will soon find

---

[86] See E-Commerce Directive, art. 3(4)(a)(iii).

out that their cross-border services are increasingly restricted by unilateral actions taken by the country of destination. Cooperation on the part of the country of origin is an excellent method to enhance the reputation of domestic firms and render restrictions imposed by the 'host' authorities less frequent. The responsiveness of the 'home' authorities to the concerns of their counterparts is a vital asset promoting the long-term interests of domestic firms with cross-border commercial aspirations.

On receiving the request for action, the country of origin must act without delay, in good faith and in a spirit of cooperation. Thereafter, the emergency procedure may only be initiated if no measures were taken or they were inadequate, after notifying the Commission and the Member State of origin of the intention to take such measures. It is also clear from Article 3(4)(b) of the Directive that the notification requirement in no way deprives the Member State in question of the right to institute court proceedings, including preliminary proceedings, and to carry out acts in the framework of a criminal investigation. Further, national courts, including civil courts, dealing with private law disputes may also take *ad hoc* measures to derogate from the principle of country of origin in conformity with the same policy and procedural conditions.[87]

In cases of urgency, Member States may derogate from the foregoing conditions and the measures shall be notified in the shortest possible time to the Commission and to the Member State of origin, indicating the reasons why the Member State considers that there is urgency. In any case, the Commission must examine the compatibility of the notified measures with Community law, especially the 'policy conditions' and, if found incompatible, it may ask the Member State in question to refrain from taking any of the proposed measures or urgently to put an end to the measures in question. It is important to note that this examination does not have suspensory effect. The Member State of destination may take the proposed measures without awaiting the result of the Commission's examination.

### *National implementation*

### Implementation in the United Kingdom

Pursuant to the residual powers of the 'host country', as defined by the E-Commerce Directive, the FSA may direct that an incoming EEA firm

---

[87] *Ibid.*, recital 26.

may no longer carry on a specified electronic commerce activity in the United Kingdom or may only carry it on subject to specified requirements which would normally not apply to incoming ISS providers.[88] The FSA has published its enforcement policy in relation to the application of the case-by-case derogation, particularly its understanding of the policy and procedural conditions that must be met before the FSA may preclude or restrict the freedom of EEA financial institutions to provide online services in the United Kingdom.[89] On obtaining information concerning possible financial crime facilitated through or involving an incoming ISS provider, or detriment to UK markets or recipients caused by the activities of an incoming provider, the FSA would contact the relevant EEA regulator of the incoming institution. The FSA would expect the relevant EEA regulator to consider the matter, investigate it where appropriate and keep the FSA informed about what action, if any, was being taken. The FSA may not need to be involved further if the action by the relevant EEA regulator addresses the concerns of the FSA. There may be however circumstances in which the FSA will need to use that power, for example when one of the policy conditions are met or the relevant EEA regulator has not taken or is unable to take action or it appears that action against the wrongdoing would be taken by the FSA more effectively.

The question of whether the FSA shall prevent or prohibit the incoming electronic commerce activity, or make it subject to certain requirements (for example, compliance with specified rules), will depend on the overall circumstances of the case. A non-exhaustive list of factors to be considered would include the extent of loss incurred by UK customers, the extent of risk that money laundering or other financial crime may be committed, the impact that a full prohibition would have on UK customers and the risk that the activity presents to the financial system and confidence in the financial system. Overall, the careful drafting of the Regulations and the high degree of transparency surrounding the enforcement policy of the FSA successfully implement the inherently discretionary Article 3(4)–(6) process and some of its most debated aspects.

In relation to the remainder of UK supervisory agencies with responsibility for certain financial services, for example, Office of Fair Trading

---

[88] See SI 2002/2013, reg. 6(1).
[89] See FSA Handbook Enforcement (ENF) 19.4.2G–19.4.6G.

for consumer credit, Article 3(4) is implemented by the 'General Regulations'. The UK rules restate Article 3(4)–(6) in its entirety.[90] In addition, it is confirmed that the notion of 'enforcement authorities', to which regulation 5 is addressed, may indeed encompass courts in exceptional circumstances: in the event that an enforcement authority with responsibility in relation to the requirement in question is not party to the proceedings, a court may, on the application of any person or of its own motion, apply any requirement which would otherwise not apply by virtue of application of the principle of country of origin in respect of a given ISS, provided that the policy conditions are met.[91] The procedural requirements of prior consultation with the 'home country' authorities do not apply to court proceedings.

### Implementation in France and Germany

The Act 2004-575 of 21 June 2004 for the Confidence in the Digital Economy restates *verbatim* the policy conditions of Article 3(4)(a)(i) and delegates the enactment of secondary legislation, which must fix the procedural conditions in consistency with the Directive.[92] The operative provision confirms the residual and exceptional character of the 'case-by-case' derogation and clarifies that the pertinent powers may only be exercised by administrative public authorities and not by national courts.

The German Act on Electronic Commerce restates the requirements of the Directive almost word for word.[93] The express reference to the procedure prescribed in the Directive clarifies that the derogation may only be invoked in exceptional circumstances against individual firms.

### The normative impact of the principle of 'country of origin'

Except for the law of contract, where the principle of 'country of origin' applies only in the unusual scenario of non-consumer contracts in which the parties have not chosen the applicable law, the Directive has been a significant contributor to the ideals of the single market in the domain of advertising, financial promotion and customer solicitation where no general derogation applies.

The correct implementation of Article 3 required the amendment of the scope of territorial application of domestic statutes relating to

---

[90] See SI 2002/2013, reg. 5.
[91] See reg. 5(2).
[92] See Loi, No. 2004-575 above note 75, art. 18.   [93] See TDG § 5.

advertising and promotion, either directly through the general revision of applicable laws to incoming electronic commerce activities, or indirectly by regulatory agencies and public authorities declining to enforce national standards against incoming firms while extending their enforcement and supervisory jurisdiction to services provided by domestic institutions to foreign residents across borders.

With regard to liability in tort for unlawful conduct of online marketing and advertising activities, legal suits litigated in the courts of the 'country of origin' must be litigated in accordance with the law of this country. This is the essence of the principle of country of origin in non-contractual matters, which takes precedence over contrary conflicts of laws of the forum judge. If the legal suit for non-contractual matters is litigated in the courts of the country of destination, the governing law will be determined in accordance with the conflicts of laws of the forum and, under the effects doctrine, it will most likely result in the law of the country of destination being applicable. In this case, there will be three possibilities.

First, there might be no cause of action under the applicable law of the country of destination. In that case, the action will be struck out and it will make no difference that a cause of action might have existed under the hypothetically more stringent law of the country of origin. This is the case where a bank established in a Member State with stringent rules of advertising and financial promotion or other forms of non-contractual liability provides services to customers in a Member State where the rules are more liberal, in which state an action is brought.

Second, there might be a cause of action against the provider under the applicable law but not under the law of the country of origin. To proceed in this case with the claim against the provider of services would effectively mean that the sole compliance with the law of the country of origin did not suffice to provide services in the Member State in question. This would be a violation of the principle of 'country of origin' unless the court invoked the 'case-by-case' derogation.

Finally, there might be a cause of action under the law of both countries. If a restriction is not found because in the circumstances of the case a valid cause of action arises in both legal systems, the case will proceed in accordance with the applicable law. Thereafter, the provider may not invoke the 'country of origin' rule as a means of defending against particular aspects of the applicable law which enhance the provider's obligations, restrict its rights or are unfavourable to its case in some other respect. In view of the negative obligation set out in Article

3(2), the courts of the country of destination may strike out the claim to ensure that cross-border trade is not restricted but they cannot selectively replace the applicable law with the law of the country of origin because such an action would effectively elevate the 'internal market' clause into a proper conflicts rule.

The institutional structure of financial regulation in the single European market, with the principles of mutual recognition and 'home country' control established by the Banking Directive, is not affected by the 'country of origin' rule. The regulatory responsibilities of the 'home' and 'host' authorities, including the single licence and the notification procedure, remain unaffected by the E-Commerce Directive.

With regard to investment services, especially online trading services, the 'country of origin' rule has significant implications for the territorial application of conduct of business rules in two respects. First, Member States in their capacity as country of origin of investment services must ensure that firms established within their territory comply with domestic conduct of business rules, regardless of the location of the investor. Second, the scope of territorial application of conduct rules vis-à-vis financial institutions established in other Member States must be amended to reflect the requirements imposed by Article 3 of the E-Commerce Directive.

The approach taken by the UK FSA in implementing the Directive is a good example of how the principle of 'country of origin' was supposed to work with regard to conduct of business rules: the scope of territorial application of the FSA Handbook was specifically revised so as to deregulate online investment services originating in another EEA country. In countries where the Directive was implemented by an Act of general application, as opposed to the specific legislative revision of financial regulatory standards, a certain degree of uncertainty concerning which local rules apply to online services originating overseas will always exist.

# 9

## Applicable law and jurisdiction in cross-border electronic banking contracts

The final chapter of this book will discuss the conflict of laws and questions of jurisdiction in contractual matters relating to cross-border electronic banking activities in the single European market. It will be recalled that the single market Directives in the field of financial services and electronic commerce do not regulate the question of which law governs international banking and financial contracts and which court decides international banking and financial contractual disputes in Europe.

The legal and institutional principles of mutual recognition and 'home country' control established in the field of financial services by measures such as the Banking Consolidation Directive,[1] the E-Commerce Directive[2] and the Directive on Markets in Financial Instruments (MiFiD)[3] harmonize important aspects of economic regulatory law without affecting the conflict of national laws in contractual matters. The scope of application of the Banking Directive and the MiFiD extends almost exclusively to matters of prudential and investor protection regulation and supervision, whereas the E-Commerce Directive expressly exempts the contractual choice of applicable law and contractual matters relating to consumer contracts from the normative impact of the principle of country of origin. Put simply, the contractual aspect of cross-border electronic banking activities, at least with regard to governing law and jurisdiction, remains unaffected by EU policies in the field of financial services and electronic commerce and subject to the general law relating to the conflict of laws and jurisdiction, primarily the Rome Convention

---

[1] EP and Council Directive 2000/12/EC of 20 March 2000 relating to the taking up and pursuit of the business of credit institutions, OJ 2000 No. L126/1, 26 May 2000.
[2] EP and Council Directive 2000/31/EC of 8 June 2000 on certain legal aspects of information society services, in particular electronic commerce, in the internal market, OJ 2000 No. L178/1, 17 July 2000.
[3] EP and Council Directive 2004/39/EC of 21 April 2004 on markets in financial instruments, OJ 2004 No. L145/1, 30 April 2004.

on the Law Applicable to Contractual Obligations[4] and the Brussels Regulation.[5] In determining the applicable law and jurisdiction, the distinction between consumer and non-consumer contracts will be crucial.

## International contracts, conflicts of laws and European financial integration

Contractual agreements between parties in different jurisdictions raise the question of which law applies to the contract and which court will be competent to hear potential disputes. The international harmonization of the national conflict of laws or private international law by way of a multilateral treaty or convention or, in the case of the single European market, by means of an EU Directive or Regulation, aims to ensure that cross-border contracts are governed by the same law regardless of the forum of litigation.

By having in place common international rules and criteria for designating the applicable law, the participating countries achieve a substantial degree of legal certainty and predictability by preventing a situation arising whereby the conflicts rules of country A designate a different system of law from the conflicts rules of country B. In other words, the law governing the contract would be different depending on the forum of litigation, thus generating uncertainty as to applicable substantive legal requirements. Uniform conflicts rules, which are identical in all countries participating in the international legal agreement or convention, ensure legal certainty and predictability of the governing law whatever the potential forum of litigation and enhance the protection of legal rights and legitimate contractual expectations against the perils of litigation in unpredictable jurisdictions. Transaction costs are reduced and the stability of contractual relationships is enhanced since the validity of contract needs to be checked solely against a single set of substantive legal requirements. Furthermore, the legitimate competition between the parties to select their own national law as the governing law of the contract requires certainty that the choice of law will not be frustrated by the forum judge

---

[4] Convention on the Law Applicable to Contractual Obligations (Rome, 19 June 1980); consolidated version at OJ 1998, No. C27/34, 26 January 1998.
[5] Council Regulation 44/2001 EC of 22 December 2000 on jurisdiction and the recognition and enforcement of judgments in civil and commercial matters, OJ 2000, No. L12/1, 16 January 2001.

applying his or her own conflicts criteria. Finally, for the objectives of the single European market, the harmonization of conflicts rules is a far simpler exercise and superior to the harmonization of substantive contract rules. There are only thirty-three articles in the Rome Convention against the potentially thousands of articles comprising a hypothetical European Civil Code.

The elimination of the economic cost of legal diversity in the single European market through the process of unification of national conflicts rules, as opposed to the harmonization of substantive contract laws, is not without certain disadvantages. The unification or harmonization of conflict of laws creates parity between foreign law and the domestic law of the forum of litigation because the forum judge is required to apply objective connecting factors designating the applicable law, which may or may not be the law of the forum. Thus, harmonization measures such as the Rome Convention are destined to result in the frequent application of foreign law by national courts, which do not have legal training in, sufficient information about, and practical access to legal sources of the applicable foreign law. The problem in practice is not as acute as it seems because the unification of the conflict of laws is invariably complemented, at least in Europe, by the unification or harmonization of the national laws determining the forum of litigation. To the extent that international legal instruments, such as the Rome Convention and the Brussels Regulation, establish the freedom of the parties to choose both the applicable law and the forum of litigation, it is most commonly the case that applicable law and forum of litigation are provided for by the same jurisdiction.

One could also argue that the harmonization of conflicts rules is not an adequate solution to legal uncertainty in cross-border activities because the mechanistic application of uniform connecting criteria such as 'the seat of the corporation' or 'the domicile of the consumer' enhances legal certainty in designating the applicable law at the expense of the 'fairness' or 'suitability' of the outcome. The underlying idea is that EU Member States should have an interest in the content of applicable substantive rules and distrust objective criteria that determine the applicable law *in abstracto*. They should be more willing to work towards the harmonization of substantive national laws instead of relying on the mechanistic coordination of conflicts of laws.

It is however questionable whether national governments should really have an interest in the content and application of substantive laws governing purely private contractual matters, where the parties are better informed of and freely select what is best for them. In those cases where the forum has a legitimate interest in imposing local substantive requirements, for example in the field of consumer protection, the problem is solved by harmonizing certain key aspects of substantive law as well as introducing mechanisms in the conflict of laws which enable the application of 'public policy' laws of the forum or of the country where the consumer domiciles whatever the otherwise applicable law.

## Choice of law and choice of jurisdiction in cross-border banking contracts

The unification of national conflict of laws in Europe in the form of the Rome Convention is justified by the benefits of having a contract governed by the same rules in any Convention country where it might be litigated.[6] The underlying principle of multilateralism in the conflict of laws is the equality of the conflicting legal orders, including the law of the forum, before the forum judge and the determination of the applicable law on the basis of objective and abstract connecting factors. The *lex fori* is not precluded from being the proper law of the contract but, in principle, it does not enjoy special treatment by the forum judge, who is instructed to apply the law of a foreign legal system and disregard the law of the forum if so compelled by the choice of the parties or the operation of the objective connecting factors introduced by the Convention.

The multilateral character of the Rome Convention is, however, diluted by the established privilege of the forum judge to disregard the prima facie applicable law for reasons of domestic public policy. Hence, despite the theoretical benefits of unification of the conflict of laws, it is not altogether irrelevant where a contract would be likely to be litigated. The largely discretionary right of the forum judge to override the applicable law and apply certain legal requirements of the *lex fori* at the stage of litigation may potentially restrict the firm's freedom to provide cross-border services by depriving the parties of the benefit to know in advance the full legal framework of their contractual agreement.

In banking practice, the use of standard contract terms on the applicable law and forum aims to reassure the bank providing cross-border

---

[6] See Giuliano and Lagarde, 'Official Report'.

services that their activities will benefit from legal certainty, low transaction costs and the advantage of being subject to a single governing law and forum of litigation. The chosen law and forum is invariably the law and forum of the country where the bank is established.

## Freedom of choice

The parties' right to choose the law applicable to their contractual relationship is the primary institutional principle of all sophisticated systems of conflicts of laws. The Rome Convention provides that a contract, either in whole or in part, shall be governed by the law chosen by the parties, and this choice must be expressed or demonstrated with reasonable certainty by the terms of the contract or the circumstances of the case.[7] Although no distinction is made between consumer and non-consumer contracts, the parties' freedom of choice of governing law in consumer transactions is severely diluted by the provisions of Article 5 of the Convention. In general, it is not essential to negotiate an agreement on the applicable law and, in practice, banks providing Internet services seldom do.

With regard to the forum of litigation in civil and commercial matters, including contractual disputes, the Brussels Regulation regulates the allocation of international jurisdiction among national courts. The Brussels Regulation replaces the 1968 Brussels Convention[8] in all Member States except Denmark.

According to the main operative provision of Article 2, persons domiciled in a Member State must be sued in the courts of that Member State unless the Regulation provides otherwise. In this respect, the express agreement of the parties to designate the courts of a Member State as having jurisdiction in potential disputes establishes an exclusive basis of jurisdiction, in derogation from Article 2, unless the parties provided otherwise.[9] The forum selection agreement between the parties should clearly and precisely demonstrate the consensus between the parties.[10] Furthermore, it is subject to formalities aiming to ensure

---

[7] See Rome Convention, art. 3(1).
[8] See Brussels Convention on Jurisdiction and the Enforcement of Judgments in Civil and Commercial Matters (Brussels, 27 September 1968); consolidated version OJ 1998 No. C27/1, 26 January 1998.
[9] See Brussels Regulation, art. 23.
[10] See Case C-24/76 *Estasis Salotti di colzani Aimo e Gianmario Colzani v. RUWA Polstereimaschinen GmbH* [1976] ECR 1831, para. 7.

that a genuine consensus was actually reached.[11] The agreement must be in writing or evidenced in writing or in a form which accords with mutually established practices or a usage of which the parties are or ought to have been aware in the relevant trade or commerce.[12]

In providing online services across borders, the bank will want to ensure that the courts of its 'home country' have exclusive jurisdiction. According to the Brussels Regulation, the exchange of electronic communications is equivalent to an agreement in writing if a durable record of the agreement can be supplied.[13] Standard contract terms made available on the bank's website or via electronic mail satisfy the 'writing requirement'. In general, the rules on the validity of jurisdiction clauses are strictly construed.[14] Mutual consent will not be established merely by making the terms available to the customer[15] unless the contract actually contains the forum selection clause or includes a direct reference to separately provided standard contract terms, of which the forum selection clause forms part.[16]

## Choice of law and forum in the absence of choice

In the absence of express choice of law, the contract is governed by the law of the country with which it is most closely connected.[17] With the exception of consumer contracts, it is presumed that contracts entered into in the course of trade are most closely connected to the country where the party who is to effect the performance which is characteristic of the contract maintains its principal place of business or, where under the terms of the contract the performance is to be effected through a place of business other than the principal place of business, the country in which that other place of business is situated.[18]

---

[11] See Case C-387/98 *Coreck Maritime GmbH* v. *Handelsveem BV* [2000] ECR I-9337, para. 13.
[12] See Brussels Regulation, art. 23(1).
[13] See art. 23(2).
[14] See Case 71/83 *Partenreedereims Tilly Russ* v. *NV Haven- & Verroerbedrij F Nova and NV Goeminne Hout* [1984] ECR 2417.
[15] See Case C-159/97 *Trasporti Castelletti Spedizioni Internazionali SpA* v. *Hugo Trumpy SpA* [1999] ECR I-1597.
[16] See Case C-24/76 *Estasis Salotti di Colunzi Aimo e Gianmario Colanzi* v. *RUWA Polstereimaschinen Gmb H* [1976] ECR 1831.
[17] See Rome Convention, art. 4(1).   [18] See art. 4(2).

To determine the applicable law one must first identify which party is to perform the obligation which is characteristic of the contract. The notion of the 'characteristic performance' must be understood as the legal obligation which constitutes the essence of the contract and the economically and sociologically most essential obligation to be performed.[19] In most bilateral or reciprocal contracts the principal obligation of one of the parties is the payment of a sum of money in exchange for the provision of services or the sale of goods and, therefore, the monetary obligation is not the distinguishing element of the contractual bond and the obligation 'characterizing' the contract.[20] The characteristic performance of the contract is the performance for which the payment is due, which usually constitutes the centre of gravity and the socio-economic function of the transaction, and therefore it is the provider and not the recipient of the service whose principal place of business will decide the governing law of the contractual relationship. In banking contracts, the party to perform the characteristic obligation is, in principle, the bank and, therefore, the contract is governed by the law of the country in which the bank's principal place of business is situated.[21]

The presumption must be disregarded on two occasions.[22] First, if the characteristic performance of the contract cannot be identified, the contract shall be governed by the law of the country with which it is most closely connected. The derogation refers to complex transactions where one cannot tell which party is to perform the characteristic obligation, for example a multilateral contract where a syndicate of banks enter into a loan agreement with one single borrower, where it is arbitrary to select any of the banks as the party which performs the characteristic obligation. It is therefore unlikely to be invoked in Internet banking where the 'characteristic performer' is easy to spot.

Second, the presumption will be disregarded if it appears from the circumstances as a whole that the contract is most closely connected with another country. Giuliano and Lagarde's Report on the Convention on the Law Applicable to Contractual Obligations (the 'Official Report')

---

[19] See Giuliano and Lagarde, 'Official Report', pp. 17–20.
[20] See *AIG Group (UK) Ltd* v. *The Ethniki* [1998] 4 All ER 301, at 310; BGH DtZ 1996, 51; Cass.Civ.1st, 15.05.2001, JDI 2001, 1121.
[21] See *Sierra Leone Telecommunications Co. Ltd* v. *Barclays Bank plc* [1998] 2 All ER 821; *Raiffeisen Zentralbank Osterreich AG* v. *National Bank of Greece SA* [1999] 1 Lloyd's Rep. 408, at 412; OLG Köln RIW 1993, 1025; OLG München RIW 1996, 330.
[22] See Rome Convention, art. 4(5).

emphasizes that there is no reason to rebut the presumption unless all the circumstances show the contract to be more closely connected with a country other than the place of business of the performer.[23] English courts accept that the presumption will be set aside only if the place of business of the party who is to carry out the characteristic performance has no real significance as a connecting factor.[24] Perhaps one cannot think of more striking circumstances where these conditions are not fulfilled than Internet services, where the place of business of the bank is the administrative centre and origin of marketing activities, operations and provision of services.

With regard to the question of international jurisdiction and in the absence of consensual choice of forum, claims must be brought in the courts of the domicile of the defendant unless an alternative special basis of jurisdiction can be established.[25] One alternative basis is Article 5 (1) of the Brussels Regulations which entitles the plaintiff to bring an action in the courts for the place of performance of the obligation in question.[26] If the contract involves the provision of services and in the absence of contrary agreement of the parties, the place of performance of the obligation in question shall be the place in a Member State where under the contract the services were provided or should have been provided.[27] Because this is a new provision that did not feature in the original Brussels Convention, there is currently no consensus as to how this alternative basis of jurisdiction must be interpreted, particularly in the case of financial services.[28]

### Choice of law and forum in consumer contracts

International consumer contracts are subject to special rules of private international law and international jurisdiction. These rules aim to restrict the parties' freedom of choice and designate the law of the consumer's jurisdiction as the applicable law because the imbalance in

---

[23] See Giuliano and Lagarde, 'Official Report', p. 22.
[24] See *Samcrete Egypt* v. *Land Rover Exports Ltd* [2001] EWCA Civ 2019, para. 41; *Iran Continental Shelf Oil Co.* v. *IRI International Corporation* [2002] EWCA Civ 1024, paras. 77–91.
[25] See Brussels Regulation, art. 2(1).
[26] See art. 5(1)(a).
[27] See art. 5(1)(b).
[28] See L. Bernardeau, 'Droit International Privé et Services Financiers de Détail' 2001–2 *Euredia* 313, at pp. 354–5.

the negotiating strength and economic resources available to the firm and the consumer is considered to be so significant that, from a policy perspective, the consumer should be entitled to sue in his own jurisdiction and undertake legal obligations governed by his own familiar consumer protection rules.[29]

## Choice of law in consumer contracts

The special consumer protection provisions of Article 5 of the Rome Convention do not eliminate but merely limit freedom of choice. The main operative provision provides that, on certain conditions, the choice of law made by the parties, valid though it may be, should not have the result of depriving the consumer of the protection afforded to him by the mandatory rules of the country in which he has his habitual residence.[30] The concept of 'mandatory rules' is controversial. It arguably encompasses rules which protect the consumer and cannot be derogated from by contrary agreement of the parties.[31] It suffices that the protection of consumers is one of the objectives pursued by the rules, even if it is not the only one or it is not expressly stated to be one.[32] It is, however, argued in Germany that the consumer may benefit from any rule which in the circumstances of the case is beneficial to the interests of the weaker party, regardless of whether it is of general application or specifically applicable to consumer contracts.[33] If the chosen law is more beneficial, the consumer has discretion to invoke either the chosen law or the law of the consumer's own country. In any case, the protection is not available to consumers unless the following requirements are met.

## Supply of services or provision of credit

First, the protection is available in consumer contracts, the object of which is the supply of goods or services, and in contracts for the

---

[29] See Brussels Regulation, recital 13.
[30] See Rome Convention, art. 5(2).
[31] See C. G. J. Morse 'Consumer Contracts, Employment Contracts and the Rome Convention' (1992) 41 ICLQ 1, at pp. 8–9; Cour de Cassation, 19.10.1999, Dalloz, Cahier Droit des Affaires [2000], pp. 8–9.
[32] See Trevor Hartley, 'Mandatory Rules in International Contracts: The Common Law Approach' (1997) 266 *Recueil des Cours de l'Académie de Droit International* 337, at pp. 371–2.
[33] See U. Magnus, J. von Staudingers *Kommentar zum BGB mit EGBGB und Nebengesetzen EGBGB/Internationales Privatrecht* (Berlin: Walter de Gruyter, 2002), at pp. 332–3.

provision of credit for that object.[34] Contracts for the provision of banking and investment services fulfil the condition.[35] It is, however, uncertain whether banking activities which are services for the purposes of EC law would necessarily fall within the definition of 'contract for the provision of services' for purposes of the Rome Convention.[36] In particular, it is questionable and doubtful whether consumer credit in the form of direct loans or overdraft facilities is covered. On one occasion the High Court of Justice held that direct loans were outside the scope of protection because a bank loan is not a contract for the provision of services.[37] Paradoxically, a consumer loan was the pertinent transaction in *Director General of Fair Trading* v. *First National Bank plc*[38] which is the leading English authority on the interpretation of the Unfair Terms Directive, an instrument applicable to 'contracts for the supply of services'.[39] In France, some lower courts held that loans are outside the scope of protection[40] but the view is resisted by others.[41] The German Federal Court has brought direct loans outside the scope of protection as well.[42]

In my view, the concept 'contracts for the provision of services' adequately covers direct bank loans and overdraft facilities, which should benefit from the consumer protection rules of the Rome Convention. First, it is contrary to Community law to construe narrowly – and thereby restrict – the scope of application of consumer protection measures.[43] Second, the Treaty freedom to provide services applies invariably to the provision of credit and the granting of loans across borders.[44] It would be inconsistent with the objectives of the single European market to define the scope of the same legal concept differently in the different

---

[34] See Rome Convention, art. 5(1).
[35] See Collins, *Dicey and Morris*, pp. 1286–7; BGHZ 123, 380.
[36] See Collins, *Dicey and Morris*, p. 1286; BGH, NJW 1997, 1697; Cour de Cassation, 19.10.1999, 89 RCDIP [2000] 29–34.
[37] See *N. M. Rothschild Limited* v. *Equitable Life Assurance Society* [2002] EWHC 1022.
[38] [2002] 1 AC 481 (HL).
[39] See Council Directive 93/13/EEC of 5 April 1993 on unfair terms in consumer contracts, 1993 No. OJ No. L95/29, 2 April 1994, art. 2.
[40] See TGI Strasburg, 02.04.2001, Recueil Dalloz Sirey, Cahier Droit des Affaires [2002] at p. 2935.
[41] See CA Colmar, 24.02.1999, 1999 ZIP 1210–11; J. Calais-Auloy and F. Steinmetz, *Droit de la Consommation* (6th edn, Paris: Dalloz, 2003), at p. 8.
[42] See BGH NJW 1997, 1697.
[43] See Case C-203/99 *Veedfald* v. *Aarhus Regional Authority* [2001] ECR I-3569, para. 15.
[44] See Case C-484/93 *Svensson and Gustavsson* v. *Ministre du Logement et de l'Urbanisme* [1995] ECR I-3955

contexts of the EC Treaty[45] and the Rome Convention. The most recently adopted Brussels Regulation does not repeat the conceptual ambiguity and expressly extends the application of the relevant consumer protection rules to consumer contracts concluded in 'the course of commercial and professional activities',[46] which no doubt encompass the totality of the financial services industry, including the provision of credit.

It should be noted that the special consumer rules apply to contracts for services and credit specifically provided for the purpose of the sale of goods or the provision of services, for example by way of deferred payment, instalment payment or direct financing either directly by the merchant or through an associated credit provider.[47] This separate reference to certain consumer credit agreements is not intended to exclude other credit agreements, particularly key banking services, from the protective rules. To the contrary, it purports to extend the protection not only to the principal transaction for the sale of goods or services but also to ancillary financing agreements as well.

### Specific invitation or advertising

The second requirement for protecting certain consumer contracts is that the contract must have been preceded by a specific invitation addressed to the consumer or advertising in the consumer's country of habitual residence and, in addition, the consumer must have taken in that country all the steps necessary on his part for the conclusion of the contract.[48] Those conditions purport to ensure that strong territorial connections exist between the contract and the country in which the consumer has residence.[49]

The first condition is that the formation of the contract was initiated by the bank. The provision describes situations where the bank has taken steps to market its services in the country where the consumer resides[50] and prescribes that these steps must either be a *specific invitation* addressed to the consumer or *advertising* in the country of the consumer's residence. An invitation by way of an *unsolicited* electronic mail is caught on the condition that the consumer is first approached by the bank

---

[45] Treaty Establishing the European Community (Rome, 25 March 1957); consolidated text at OJ 2002 No. C325, 24 December 2002.
[46] See Brussels Regulation, art. 15(1)(c).
[47] See Case C-150/77 *Bertrand* v. *Ott* [1978] ECR 1431, para. 20.
[48] See Rome Convention, art. 5(2).
[49] See Case C-96/00 *Rudolf Gabriel* v. *Schlank & Schlick GmbH* [2002] ECR I-6367, para. 41.
[50] See Giuliano and Lagarde, 'Official Report', p. 23.

and not vice versa.[51] Offers of services to the general public through a website are unlikely to be considered a specific invitation addressed to the consumer, so the question is whether the alternative condition is fulfilled.

The most controversial issue is whether the bank's website constitutes advertising in the consumer's country of habitual residence. The Report on the Rome Convention explains that the protection applies only if the bank has 'done certain acts such as advertising in the press, or on radio or television, or in the cinema or by catalogues aimed specifically at that country'.[52] The material must have been addressed to consumers in that country. The publication of an offer on the Internet to the whole world or in a publication with international readership is not sufficient. In the example used by the Report, the special rules do not apply when a German consumer responds to an advertisement in an American publication, even if that publication is made available in Germany, but they apply if the advertisement appears in editions of the same American publication which are aimed at European readers.[53]

The criterion covers situations where the bank took steps to market its services in the country where the consumer resides.[54] What the Convention is looking for is the solicitation of business. Protection will be afforded when the bank solicited the customer but it will be denied when the customer solicited the bank.[55] It is suggested that if the website makes explicit that services are addressed to certain jurisdictions and consumers in those jurisdictions are invited to take the necessary steps for the conclusion of the contract via the Internet, the website constitutes advertising in the consumer's country and the protection can be invoked.[56] It is also proposed that because the bank may employ various mechanisms to reject applicants from jurisdictions where services are not addressed, the actual provision of services implies an active solicitation of business there.[57]

---

[51] See *Andrew Rayner* v. *Richard Davies* [2002] EWCA Civ 1880 (CA), para. 26.
[52] See Giuliano and Lagarde, 'Official Report', p. 23.
[53] *Ibid.*, at pp. 23–4.
[54] See *Rayner* v. *Davies* [2002] EWCA Civ 1880 (CA), para. 43.
[55] *Ibid.*, para. 23.
[56] See Richard Plender and Michael Wilderspin, *The European Contracts Convention: The Rome Convention of the Choice of Contracts* (2nd edn, London: Sweet and Maxwell, 2001), at pp. 146–7.
[57] See P. Mankowski, 'Das Internet im Internationalen Vertrags- und Deliktsrecht' (1999) 63 *RabelsZ* 203, at pp. 242–52.

In my view, the distinction between the 'active' consumer and the 'solicited' or 'passive' consumer offers nothing but uncertainty in contracts concluded by consumers surfing the net and subsequently applying for banking services at a distance. Who is soliciting whom? Let us suppose that the bank wants to make full use of the Internet for marketing its services. It launches the website and aims to accept all applications. The services are addressed at all jurisdictions but at no one in particular. There is nothing in the website which constitutes an offer addressed to a specific jurisdiction, no disclaimer, nothing of that kind. The customer applies. Can we argue that the bank solicited the customer simply because it did not reject the application? I think not. Not taking steps to prevent services from being provided to certain countries is different from actively offering services to those countries, as the Convention expressly requires. But what is the impact of launching a website in the first place? This is surely a step to offer services and it is certainly addressed to the applicant among others. But if we accept that, we must conclude that the bank advertises in all countries of the world.

A different criterion would be the intention of the bank to offer its services in another country, which can be inferred from the languages used in the website, the currency in which transactions are denominated, the use of certain legal terms and conditions and other criteria. Is there an indication as to where the services are addressed? This is the place where customers are solicited. Is there a disclaimer that services are not available in that jurisdiction? No solicitation of local customers can be implied. It is obvious, however, that the distinction between 'active' and 'passive' consumers has something to do with their behaviour in response to the bank's activities, which are observed objectively rather than in the way in which the bank is subjectively treating its website. The bank could place a disclaimer and then accept all applications from that jurisdiction. Those people would be 'active' consumers and no protection would be justified but there is an obvious flaw in the bank's behaviour. To prevent that, one may superimpose the obligation to reject all those applications but it would again reverse the criterion of 'steps taken to solicit customers' with steps not taken to avoid being solicited by them.

It is just better to concede that the problem is caused by the properties and characteristics of the Internet which can achieve 'local connections' between certain content and certain geographic location without any 'special steps' being taken to that end. If the bank does not send advertising leaflets to German addresses, no advertising leaflet will reach that country unless a reader takes steps to bring it in. In that case, as the Official Report demonstrates, the protection is not available because no active solicitation has taken place. The Internet is different. The available technology empowers the customer to access the bank's computer systems and retrieve information at her convenience. On the customer's request, data will be delivered to the customer's equipment. It is the customer who requests information, while the bank either provides the online content or takes steps to repel incoming requests. In all meaningful ways it is the customer who is now able to take advantage of offers abroad. The uncertainty surrounding Article 5(2) of the Rome Convention reflects simply the legacy of the established principles of law that fail to adapt to the realities of online activities, exposing cross-border ventures to legal uncertainty and overregulation.

The second requirement is that the consumer must have taken all the steps necessary on his part for the conclusion of the contract in the country of his habitual residence. The concept of the 'necessary steps' avoids the classic problem of determining the place where the contract was concluded. Thus, the protection afforded by Article 5 can be relied upon even in the event that under the applicable law the contract is considered to have been concluded in the country where the bank is established. It suffices that the necessary factual steps on the part of the consumer, for example sending the application form via e-mail or post or responding to the online advertisement or indicating his acceptance to the contractual offer in the appropriate webpage, have been taken from within the country where the consumer has his habitual residence.[58]

### Services provided in another country

Even when the foregoing requirements were met, there would be no special consumer protection if the services were supplied exclusively outside the country of the consumer's residence.[59] The condition reflects the traditional view that the mandatory application of local protection is not justified when services are not provided within the territory of that country, even if the provider has performed therein certain commercial acts such as advertising or specific solicitation of clients.[60]

---

[58] See Case C-96/00 *Gabriel*, above note 49.
[59] See Rome Convention, art. 5(4)(b).
[60] See Giuliano and Lagarde, 'Official Report', pp. 24–5.

It is suggested that the determinative criterion for establishing whether services were provided entirely outside the consumer's country is the consumer's physical departure from the country of his residence.[61] The argument appears to have been implicitly endorsed by the Official Report, which offers as an example the case of consumers travelling abroad and enjoying accommodation services in hotels.[62] Because the service is entirely provided in another country, the consumer is rightly deprived of the protection of the laws of his country of origin.

The determinative criterion is not the departure of the consumer from his country but the territory within which services were provided, which will determine whether, at least in part, services were provided within the country of the consumer's residence and were therefore worthy of protection. The threshold is particularly low: it suffices that services were not provided exclusively outside the consumer's country of residence.

In the case of electronic banking activities, it appears that the service is not provided exclusively outside the consumer's country. The 'Internet service' is partly performed in that jurisdiction where the customer enjoys access to core banking services through the locally located equipment for the processing and storage of data. It does not matter that the characteristic obligation is performed in the bank's headquarters. Thus the second condition will always be met by the actual delivery of Internet services to consumers abroad.

### International jurisdiction in consumer contracts

The European Court of Justice held that terms in standard form contracts which confer jurisdiction in respect of all disputes arising under the contract on the courts of the place where the supplier has its principal place of business may on certain conditions be regarded as unfair and void, particularly when the transactions are of low value.[63] More protection is afforded, however, by special rules of international jurisdiction which empower the consumer to litigate in the courts of her domicile, whether as plaintiff or defendant.

On certain conditions which aim to establish a strong territorial connection between the contract and the jurisdiction of the courts, Articles 15–17 of the Brussels Regulation establish an exclusive basis of

---

[61] See BGHZ 123, 380 (389).   [62] See Giuliano and Lagarde, 'Official Report', p. 25.
[63] See Case C-240/98 *Oceano Grupo Editorial SA* v. *Roció Murcianio Quintero* [2000] ECR I-4941, paras. 22–4.

jurisdiction for consumer contracts.[64] Consumers as defendants can only be sued in the courts of their domicile,[65] but as plaintiffs they can sue either in the other party's domicile (unlikely in practice) or in their own domicile at their discretion.[66]

The protection is not available unless the bank pursues commercial or professional activities in the country of the consumer's domicile or 'by any means directs such activities to that Member State . . . and the contract falls within the scope of such activities'.[67] It is evident from the *travaux préparatoires* that the second alternative was inserted in light of the growth of electronic commerce in order to eliminate the uncertainties of having to establish the location of e-commerce activities.[68] It now suffices that the provider of services directs such activities to the jurisdiction of the consumer's domicile.[69] The protection is available when the bank actively solicits customers in other Member States, inviting them to conclude a contract with the bank and the contract is actually concluded in the scope of those activities without it being necessary that the contract is actually concluded online. I remain sceptical as to whether Internet services are convincingly portrayed as activities directed at a particular jurisdiction. Further, I am not keen on placing consumers acting in the same way, i.e. surfing the net in search of a better deal, in different groups of protection depending on whether the website indicates where services are provided, effectively depending on how the bank presents its activities. But I am in the minority. Legal concepts tend to apply to the online environment by way of analogy. Rephrasing the provision so as to extend protection to consumers in countries where the supplier has 'directed' its activities was expressly intended to cover cross-border e-commerce activities. The uncertainty is real but in practice the bank will most probably need to litigate in the consumer's country of domicile. To the best of my knowledge, the matter has yet to be clarified in courts but the overwhelming

---

[64] See Case C-96/00 *Gabriel*, above note 49, para 36.
[65] See Brussels Regulation, art. 16(2).
[66] See art. 16(1).
[67] See art. 15(1)(c).
[68] See European Commission, *Proposal for a Council Regulation on Jurisdiction and the Recognition and Enforcement of Judgments in Civil and Commercial Matters* COM(1999) 348 final, at p. 16.
[69] See European Council and Commission, *Statement on Article 15 of the Council Regulation 44/2001* (European Council, 2314th Meeting Justice, Home Affairs and Civil Protection, 1 December 2000).

experience regarding e-commerce litigation suggest that courts will assume jurisdiction if the local market is 'targeted' or 'solicited' in one form or another.

## Choice of law and the impact of mandatory rules

Although in practice the Brussels Regulation ensures that the contract will be litigated in the consumer's country of domicile, the protection afforded by Article 5 is available to the consumer whatever the forum of litigation. The special rules on consumer protection may restrict the parties' freedom of choice but do not undermine the principle that the Convention designates the applicable law regardless of where the contract is litigated.

This principle is eroded by Article 7(2) which has preserved the special position of the law of the forum in the conflicts process,[70] and provides that nothing in the Convention, whether the free choice of the parties or other connecting factors, may restrict the application of the rules of the law of the forum in a situation where they are mandatory irrespective of the law otherwise applicable to the contract.

This is a stark reminder that the Member State where litigation may arise will require compliance with local mandatory rules of a certain calibre and importance even if the governing law is that of another country. In the light of the Brussels Regulation, it is a reminder that the courts in the country of the consumer's domicile, where the bank directs its Internet services, may potentially override the law of the 'home state' and impose local standards of contractual behaviour at their unilateral discretion. Essentially Article 7(2) is an inroad on legal certainty. Whether local 'mandatory rules' apply in transnational contracts is no longer resolved in accordance with the uniform criteria of the Rome Convention. It depends on the unilateral views of Member States as to which rules are too important to concede priority to another system of law and what their scope of territorial application may be. The answer to both questions is likely to differ among jurisdictions.

The difference between *ius cogens*, which cannot be derogated from by contract, and internationally mandatory rules of the forum (*lois de police, Eingriffsnormen*) is one of quality and intensity. Internationally mandatory rules promote a public policy of the forum so fundamental

---

[70] See Giuliano and Lagarde, 'Official Report', pp. 28–9.

that the equality of value between the conflicting legal systems, which underpins the system of the Rome Convention, is replaced by the priority of the forum's claim to apply certain domestic rules in international contracts, whether these rules belong to the private or public law domain. The Convention does not enter the hazardous zone of making normative distinctions between private and public law, wisely conceding that Member States may pursue their overriding interests of public policy by whatever means they think appropriate.

National law regulating the economic organization of the state, such as the protection of undistorted competition, the protection of the national currency, or the stability of the financial system is the main supplier of international mandatory rules. Rules which are not strictly in the interest of the general public but purport to protect special social groups like consumers, investors or employees, are often intended to apply regardless of the otherwise applicable law.[71] Moreover, national measures implementing EU rules of consumer or social protection are adopted in the interest of the general good and must be applied by the courts of any Member State in cross-border contracts regardless of the otherwise applicable law, provided that there is close territorial connection between the Community and the facts of the case.[72]

There is no certainty in identifying national rules which are likely to override the applicable law. In the absence of a clear indication, the objective pursued by the rule will be the main criterion. Economic regulation which is likely to affect the banker–customer relationship appears to be a prime candidate. A key question for our purposes relates to national law of unfair terms, consumer credit, electronic fund transfers or the law of contracts which extends to matters not covered by EC Directives or goes beyond the minimum standards set out therein. Would the bank have to comply only if the conditions of Article 5 were satisfied or would Article 7(2) provide an alternative basis for imposing local standards of behaviour?

Despite an earlier German case, where the court failed to consider the option of Article 7(2) when the conditions of Article 5(2) were not fulfilled,[73] it is now accepted that local standards of consumer protection may be imposed in derogation from the Convention if they reflect a

---

[71] *Ibid.*, at pp. 28–9.
[72] See Case C-381/98 *Ingmar* v. *Eaton* [2000] ECR I-9305, paras. 20–5.
[73] See BGH NJW 1997, 1697.

fundamental policy of the forum.[74] Rules implementing EC Directives and more stringent national rules than the harmonized standards appear to satisfy the requirement unless specified otherwise in the implemented or implementing instrument.[75] More stringent national rules apply even if the bank has complied with the minimum standards as implemented in the 'home country' unless the harmonization instrument stipulates otherwise.[76] The freedom to provide services, however, provides a ceiling which national rules should not overstep.

Those rules which reflect purely national notions of consumer protection must be approached case by case. The test is satisfied in the event of mandatory rules which, while affecting the transactional aspect of the banking contract, belong to the wider public law domain. In all other cases, it is a matter of construction on the basis of the express or implied intention of the forum. In principle, banking regulation which affects the contractual aspect will apply in accordance with the unilateral intention of supervisory authorities,[77] whereas other rules adopted in the interest of the 'general good' such as the UK Consumer Credit Act 1974 are also likely to override the applicable law.[78] But exceptions are bound to exist.

A good example of mandatory banking regulation which, in implementation of domestic monetary and economic policy, imposed restrictions on cross-border banker-customer relationships (regardless of the otherwise applicable law) used to be the French rules against the payment of interest to bank depositors of deposits repayable on demand (sight deposits). More specifically, under the provisions of Article L 312 (3) of the *Code Monétaire et Financier* (Monetary and Financial Code), as they were implemented by Regulation No. 86–13 of the *Comité de la Réglementation Bancaire et Financière* (Committee for Banking and Financial Regulation), banks were prohibited from paying interest to current account depositors (unofficially, in return for offering free checking facilities). In the context of cross-border banking services and movements of capital, the prohibition applied to accounts held by French banks, regardless of the nationality or residence of the depositor. It also applied to accounts offered by overseas banks to French residents,

---

[74] See BGHZ 135,124; BGH WM 1994, 14, 1; Plender and Wilderspin, The Rome Convention, at pp. 195–6; Cass. Civ. 19.10.1999: D. 2000 jur p. 765.
[75] See *Ingmar* v. *Eaton* [2002] ECR I-9305.
[76] See Case C-382/87 *Buet and EBS* [1989] ECR 1235.
[77] See for example Banque de France and Commission Bancaire, Internet: The Prudential Consequences, p. 59.
[78] See *Huntpast Ltd* v. *Leadbeater* [1993] CCLR 15.

whenever an overseas bank proposed to provide services in France in pursuit of the freedom to provide services under the 'passport' established by the Second Banking Directive.[79] Even if the contract for the provision of banking services was subject to the law of the EEA country where the bank was established, the French prohibition reflected a fundamental domestic policy which overrode the otherwise applicable law. From a conflict of laws perspective, the enforcement of the aforementioned prohibiton by French courts would arguably rely on the provisions of Article 7(2). From a financial integration perspective, the normative impact of Article 7(2) on the free movement of banking services, electronic or otherwise, is amply illustrated by this example. As the European Court of Justice accepted in *Caixa*, where the French prohibition was litigated, a prohibition on the remuneration of sight accounts constitutes a serious obstacle to the pursuit of cross-border banking activities because it affects the access of overseas banks to the French market. In prohibiting overseas banks from paying interest on sight deposits, the rules deprived those banks of the possibility of competing more effectively with local banks, which have an extensive network of branches and therefore greater opportunities to raise capital from the French public than overseas institutions and especially overseas online banks which compete solely over the Internet.[80] By allowing national courts to override the governing law of the banking or financial contract so as to apply an open-ended list of national mandatory measures of monetary or economic policy, Article 7(2) of the Rome Convention could significantly undermine the objectives of financial integration to the extent that national mandatory laws affecting the banking contract could potentially restrict the freedom to provide banking services across borders.

In any case, those exceptional statutes do not apply to the entire world. The forum determines unilaterally the required degree of

---

[79] See Règlement No. 92–13 du 23 décembre 1992 relatif à la fourniture de services bancaires en France par des établissements ayant leur siège social dans les autres Etats membres des Communautés européennes.

[80] See Case C-442/02 *Caixa-Bank France* v. *Ministère de l'Economie, de Finances et de l'Industrie* [2004] ECR I-8961, paras. 13–16. Following the *Caixa-Bank* litigation, the prohibition of remuneration of sight deposits was repealed by the *Arrêté du 8 mars 2005 relatif à l'abrogation des textes réglementaires interdisant la rémunération des comptes de dépôts à vue*. See Règlement No. 86–13 du 14 mai 1986 relatif à la rémunération des fonds reçus par les établissements de crédit, as amended.

proximity between the contract and the territory of the jurisdiction.[81] The domicile or habitual residence of the consumer within the jurisdiction appears to be an essential condition[82] but an additional territorial factor is normally required, for example, advertising, forming or performing the contract within the country. Hence, while the conditions of Article 5 are not strictly determinative of the scope of application of Article 7(2), they provide a good indication of required proximity between the forum and the contract.[83]

In short, the precise effects of Article 7(2) on market integration are impossible to assess without having regard to the underlying rules of substance, the likely forum of litigation and, primarily, how the forum will exercise the discretion vested in it. These are matters which are unlikely to be known to the parties at the conclusion of the contract, particularly when services are provided from within a single location to recipients in many jurisdictions. In exercising that discretion, however, the forum must have regard to the economic freedoms protected by the Treaty and the general obligation imposed on Member States to promote the internal market objective. Unilateralism in the law of contracts may have disturbing effects on cross-border banking, and national courts must decline to apply restrictive rules unless properly justified in the interest of the general good. Insofar as this can only be checked through litigation, it does not fully correct the uncertainty and overregulation caused by the foregoing restrictions on free choice of governing law. It is also worth noting that the discretion afforded to the forum judge by Article 7(2) of the Rome Convention does not relate to the 'case-by-case' derogation of Article 3(4) of the E-Commerce Directive. For practical purposes and without prejudice to the systemic differences between the two concepts, the 'case-by-case' derogation is solely available to courts and administrative authorities in respect of legal material being otherwise within the scope of the principle of country of origin, whereas the powers recognized by Article 7(2) refer to legal provisions governing contractual obligations which are almost never within the scope of the country of origin rule – unless they refer to non-consumer contracts where the parties have not chosen the applicable law.

---

[81] See BGH RIW 1997, 875; A. Nuyts, 'L'Application des Lois de Police dans L'Espace' (1999) 88 RCDIP 31.
[82] See Roy Goode (ed.), *Consumer Credit Law and Practice* (London: Butterworths, 1999), para. 49 (86).
[83] See BGH ZIP 1999, 103.

# Conclusions

The technological advances in information and communication technology over recent decades have transformed the way businesses are operating, and have resulted in changes in the patterns of global trade in goods and services.[1] The increased use of processed digital information, computer processing capacity and innovative software, telecommunications and computer networks are rapidly shaping a real knowledge-driven and information-based global economy. Many types of economic activities and transactions, from online reservations to financial services, music downloads, education, professional services and medical advice, consist almost exclusively of digital data circulating over computer networks to which access is affordable, instant and independent of the location of the recipient or the provider of content.

In this global economic landscape, financial institutions and markets are ripe to increase their productivity, lower their costs, enhance customer convenience and develop new products and services. The suitability of financial claims and commitments for being accounted, administered, transferred, performed and settled in the form of digital information elevates network technology into a potential stimulator of beneficial structural reforms in the business of banking and finance. Organized markets, firms, depositors, borrowers, investors and regulators are potential peripheral components of global or regional integrated markets where market entry, sources of funding and opportunities for investment are not disturbed by distance, lack of personal contact and national boundaries.

This book examined the legal aspects of financial integration in Europe and the role of electronic finance in enabling European credit institutions to reach and serve businesses and consumers in other

---

[1] See generally Markus Haacker, 'The ICT Sector and the Global Economy: Counting the Gains' in Soumitra Dutta and Augusto Lopez-Claros (eds.), *Global Information Technology Report 2004–2005* (4th edn, London: Palgrave Macmillan, 2005).

Member States. My research demonstrated that, despite the suitability of the Internet for cross-border services, it has not significantly altered the way in which banking services are provided across borders.[2] One of the tasks of this book was to explain why and propose appropriate remedial policies and legal institutions.

In facilitating financial integration through e-commerce in financial services, legal and regulatory institutions at the EU and national levels have an important role to play. Banking and financial services are heavily regulated products of law. Their structure and economic value are often determined by legal requirements that shape the obligations of the parties. In essence, financial services involve contractual undertakings that a certain sum will be paid in the future in exchange for assets or payment of monetary value at present. This fragile bond relies on trust and reputation that some market participants, whether banks, customers, issuers or organized markets are more reliable than others in keeping their promises.

Trust, reputation and perceptions of creditworthiness are built on shared information, personal relationships and experiences. Insofar as human experiences are associated with individual circumstances and familiar persons, firms and markets, trust is naturally directed to participants in local markets. Distance services are bound to be distrusted unless the financial and operational benefits are convincing and a sound and predictable legal framework implants the confidence that transactions with firms and customers outside the local market will not suffer from failed promises, poor quality and slow, corrupt or inaccessible mechanisms of enforcement if something goes wrong. This fundamental importance of protecting property rights and maintaining quality legal institutions for well-functioning national and international financial markets suffices to demonstrate the hollowness and fallacy of the notion of 'cyberspace', a supposedly new social and economic order where the circulation of digital data for information or commercial purposes is or must be beyond the reach of mechanisms of social and legal control.

To the contrary, the conduct of cross-border electronic banking activities is primarily a new mode of international trade in financial services. It offers distance access for banks and customers to overseas markets and services respectively. The trade perspective signals that in practice it has not been the notion of unregulated cyberspace or the misunderstood

---

[2] See ch. 1.

value of legal institutions which has had to be addressed by lawyers and policy makers but the full might of conflict of laws and regulations and the direct and collateral legal barriers caused by conflicting national laws and mechanisms of control and enforcement.[3]

The growth of cross-border services requires international cooperation and coordination, which should ensure clear, predictable and non-discriminatory legal and regulatory requirements and institutions without discrimination between domestic and local firms and customers. Whatever the form that this coordination might take, its purpose is dual: to remove barriers caused by the multiple sovereign sources of law in the international legal order and their different views on the content of legal and regulatory institutions; and to achieve the efficient regulation and supervision of the market in view of avoiding 'post-integration' risks. The former is a de-regulatory function. The latter amounts to regulation proper where common rules and enforcement cooperation among participating countries aim to achieve efficiency gains, a 'level playing field' and an equivalent level of market and consumer confidence at the national level.

The European internal market is fully concerned with those institutional choices in its own distinctive way. On the basis of quasi-constitutional commitments among sovereign nation states, a single financial market has been slowly but steadily emerging through the many political, economic and legal differences and perspectives of the constituent Member States. The optimal course of action for removing legal barriers and safeguarding systemic and consumer interests, although informed by the intricacies of financial markets and financial regulation, is part of the fundamental political choices and controversies relating to the wider integration process. Policy makers in Europe had no choice but to deal with the micro-detail of regulation in direct discourse with fundamental policy choices about the level of centralization, the allocation of competences among European institutions, the level of judicial review at the European level and the residual national powers, the division of powers among nation States over cross-border affairs and the general direction of the common rules towards more or less intervention in the market.

In view of the increasingly important role of vibrant and efficient financial markets in free democratic societies, the political process

---

[3] See ch. 3.

becomes increasingly interested in the model of governance of the single financial market and brings into play the different choices about how better to reconcile unimpeded cross-border activities with efficient regulation in the light of the institutional debate about the direction of the European project.

At first glance, the provision of services via the Internet does not appear to be a typical stimulator of exciting controversies. On closer inspection, I have been minded to take a different view. The Internet diminishes distance, creates access to markets and may potentially offer choice to consumers, particularly in smaller Member States. This perspective has placed this otherwise indifferent topical debate at the core of the competing policies and interests operating in the single financial market and even further; for it is so different from other models of market entry that the tension between Internet services and established concepts of jurisdiction and market control over cross-border activities has been particularly strong.

In a model of 'imperfect' mutual recognition of national laws and incomplete 'home country' control, Internet services must overcome one or more of the four deadly sins of conflicting laws, namely information costs, uncertainty as to the applicable law, overregulation and mandatory adaptation of services and products to the law of each national market, which destroy the opportunities for simultaneous market access from within a single location at a minimum entry and operational cost.

I also noted the catalytic supremacy of mutual recognition and free choice of law over extensive harmonization in remedying the failure of conflict of laws and conflicting laws, without sacrificing the benefits of decentralization in making laws and policies, regulatory competition and preservation of national choices in rules and institutions.[4] Legal harmonization is a necessary precondition of a well-functioning model of perfect mutual recognition in that it achieves minimum convergence of national laws and thereby implants consumer confidence in the market and a minimum 'level playing field' for competitors. The threshold of the required scope and intensity of harmonization is, however, lower than would have been the case if legal and regulatory diversity were attacked by means of total harmonization.

I demonstrated that the gaps left behind by the 1992 single market programme are rapidly being corrected in implementation of the

---

[4] See ch. 4.

Financial Services Action Plan. Policy makers understood the importance of electronic commerce in the provision of financial services and were keen to promote e-commerce in financial services as an integration mechanism by an array of single market measures, including the E-Commerce Directive,[5] other policies relating to the Information Society, the Distance Marketing Directive[6] and other consumer protection measures which relate to financial services provided at a distance by electronic means.

Recalling the importance of complementing common rules with adequate and trustworthy practices of enforcement, supervision and cooperation, I noted my cautious optimism on the attained level of legal convergence of national laws and supervisory practices and the improvement in international regulatory cooperation as a means of sustaining a model of perfect mutual recognition.[7] It seems that EU law makers are similarly content at the achieved level of legal convergence insofar as one can tell from the gradually expanding scope of mutual recognition of national laws and 'home country' control beyond the realm of prudential banking regulation and supervision. This is clearly demonstrated by the E-Commerce Directive and the principle of country of origin established therein, as well as the Directive on Markets in Financial Instruments[8] and the Directive on Unfair Commercial Practices,[9] which also establish an undiluted model of mutual recognition and 'home country' control for investor protection rules and the law of advertising, competition and financial promotion.[10] Following the recent implementation of the E-Commerce Directive, the provision of banking services via the Internet is now subject to the law and supervision of the country where the bank is established, with the exception of contractual obligations concerning consumer contracts where the traditional principles of private international law will continue to apply. In this respect,

---

[5] EP and Council Directive 2000/31/EC of 8 June 2000 on certain legal aspects of information society services, in particular electronic commerce, in the internal Market, OJ 2000 No. L178/1, 17 July 2000.

[6] EP and Council Directive 2002/65/EC of 23 September 2002 concerning distance marketing of consumer financial services, OJ 2002 No. L271/16, 9 October 2002.

[7] See chs. 5 and 6.

[8] EP and Council Directive 2004/39/EC of 21 April 2004 on markets in financial instruments, OJ 2004 No. L145/1, 30 April 2004.

[9] EP and Council Directive 2005/29/EC concerning unfair business-to-consumer commercial practices in the international market, OJ 2005 No. L149/22, 11 June 2005.

[10] See chs. 6 and 7.

Articles 5(2) and 7(2) of the Rome Convention[11] – in joint forces with the almost inevitable jurisdiction of the courts of the consumer's domicile in consumer contracts under the Brussels Regulation[12] – ensure that it is not unlikely that online banking services at a distance would be subject to mandatory rules of the customer's country of residence, which may relate to consumer protection or other socio-economic policy objectives.[13] This derogation purports to protect consumers by restricting the free choice of governing law and mandating the application of the law of the consumer's country of habitual residence.

The derogation preserves the status quo in relation to the law governing consumer contracts. The service provider will be subject to an open-ended list of mandatory rules of consumer protection and other grounds of public policy of the forum, normally the customer's country of habitual residence. The derogation is effectively an inroad to certainty of governing law and an obstacle to providing services on the basis of similar contract terms simultaneously in different Member States because it allows the application of local consumer protection and other public policy standards in each jurisdiction. While the differences do not appear to reflect genuinely different views on market control, they suffice to disturb cross-border services. Further, the derogation opens the floodgates for the application of national public policy of the forum in circumstances that the forum judge determines unilaterally and brings into play an open-ended list of mandatory rules relating to contractual obligations. The derogation may prevent products formulated under the law of the country of origin from circulating, as they should, in other Member States. It will force overseas service providers to adapt to the law of the market in which services are supplied destroying competitive advantages and consumer choice. It will work to the benefit of those firms originating in jurisdictions where commercial freedom is subject to more stringent restrictions than those applicable elsewhere.

I remain sceptical about the wisdom of that choice. Admittedly it is not clear whether the law of the consumer's place of residence will apply

---

[11] Convention on the Law Applicable to Contractual Obligations (Rome, 19 June 1980); consolidated version at OJ 1998 No. C27/34, 26 January 1998.
[12] Council Regulation 44/2001/EC of 22 December 2000 on jurisdiction and the recognition and enforcement of judgments in civil and commercial matters, OJ 2001 No. L12/1, 16 January 2001.
[13] See chs. 8 and 9.

in the first place.[14] The three-prong test for applying Article 5 of the Rome Convention is full of ambiguities and there is no case law suggesting that online banking activities via the Internet meet the necessary territorial conditions. Despite the lack of consensus among legal commentators and national courts, there are indications that cross-border electronic banking services will be caught. For example, national courts and supervisory authorities in many different sets of circumstances have applied national law and regulation on the basis of services being intentionally addressed at local recipients. This is a derogation inserted after vibrant and concerted political negotiations. I expect that it will be used at the earliest opportunity to extend the long arm of local protective mechanisms against Internet services originating in other jurisdictions.

Technically, the Internet facilitates consumers' access to services and goods offered by foreign firms. It does not create a virtual market in the consumer's country of residence. Article 5(2) of the Rome Convention presupposes the active solicitation of customers in the country of their habitual residence. Offers directed at the general public on the web or the failure to disclaim that services are addressed at a given national market and take measures to avoid being solicited by overseas customers are not special steps to solicit consumers in a given Member State. In the event of ambiguity, the interpretation promoting the free movement of services must take precedence. A less onerous regulatory framework should apply to services provided at a distance than those services provided by suppliers moving permanently or temporarily in the recipient's jurisdiction.

From a policy perspective, the protection of consumers in online financial services through the application of their own consumer protection rules is not helpful. There is no reason to distrust freedom of choice in contractual matters. The harmonization of consumer protection law, particularly following the implementation of the Distance Marketing Directive, will be substantial and the disclosure of information to consumers will be unprecedented. The profile of the average use of Internet banking provides assurances that responsible choices can be made. Competition is strong and it will intensify after the market opens under a model of undiluted 'home country' control.

The mutual recognition of national laws on the basis of 'home country' control is now the way forward. Institutional reforms, however, are

---

[14] See ch. 9.

not sufficient to improve the reality of the single market. National authorities must work laboriously to test and prove the workability of that model. They must build mutual trust and understanding. National authorities in their capacity as 'home state' authorities must cooperate with 'host state' authorities and regard the exercise of 'home state' supervision, for the benefit of domestic as well as overseas customers, as the best way to enhance the credibility and competitiveness of local firms and markets.

The emergency powers of the recipient country to restrict the cross-border provisions of online services, if 'home state' authorities fail, reflect a sound policy choice. They should be exercised with the same rigour and spirit of cooperation as the primary 'home country' duties. Prior consultation and cooperation with the country of origin are of course procedural conditions which must be fulfilled before the country of destination resumes its enforcement jurisdiction against incoming service providers. The first signs of implementation of the emergency mechanism are encouraging: in its recent report on the implementation of the E-Commerce Directive, the Commission indicated that there has been already a case where the authorities of a Member State successfully took action to enforce their law against a service provider established on their territory in response to an official request by the authorities of another Member State.[15] The country of destination invoked the procedure of Article 3(4) and the eventually the 'home country' resolved the problem without the recipient country needing to take any measures against the service provider.

In principle, I do not argue that the mutual recognition of national laws on the basis of 'home country' control will necessarily work. I argue that on certain preconditions, which are by no means easy to fulfil, this model of governance operates appreciably better than alternative realistic models. This view is premised upon the spectacular failure of the previous model of incomplete mutual recognition with residual 'host country' powers and the broader supremacy of mutual recognition as a successful compromise between centralization and decentralization in making policies and laws. It is also driven by my growing suspicion that the voices in favour of outright 'host country' powers reflect an outdated model of consumer and regulatory policy which misinterprets the

---

[15] See European Commission, *First Report on the Application of Directive on Electronic Commerce*, COM(2003) 702 final.

potential value of a genuinely single financial area, the appetite for competition, the properties and added value of Internet services, the dynamics of the market for technology and innovation and the demographics of Internet users.

Law is not a substitute for sensible business choices, commercial appetite and customer demand. A clear, predictable and non-discriminatory legal framework will not automatically increase consumer confidence in the emerging cross-border Internet banking services. It will not suffice to convince firms that market entry at a distance is a sound commercial venture. I do not disregard the significance of information, well-functioning clearing and settlement systems and the standardization of market infrastructure as essential conditions of cross-border Internet banking. But European bankers and customers deserve choice. This is what the single financial market has promised to deliver. The model of complete mutual recognition of national laws on the basis of 'home country' supervisory control as well as unrestricted freedom of choice in contractual matters will offer a clear and predictable framework conducive to the aims of the single market without jeopardizing worthy social and legal interests. A clear and predictable legal framework will remove the legal obstacles and shift the discussion towards the commercial and economic arguments and conditions. How the market will react is another story.

# SELECT BIBLIOGRAPHY

Aboutabit, A. and Lerbret G., *E-Banking Services Proposés et Demande des Utilisateurs* (Dissertation) (Paris: Ecole Nationale Supérieure d'Ingénieurs de Caen, 2001)

Abrams, C., 'The Financial Services and Markets Act and Cross-Border Issues' (2000) JFRC 237

'The Second Banking Directive and the Investment Services Directive: When and How Can the Single European Passport Be Used for Cross-Border Services' (1997) 4 EFSL 248

Ahrens, H. J., 'Das Herkunftslandprinzip in der E-Commerce Richtlinie' (2000) CR 835

Akehurst, M., 'Jurisdiction in International Law' (1974) *British Yearbook of International Law* 145

Allen, F. and others, 'E-Finance: An Introduction' (2002) 22 JFSR 5

Allen, H. and Hawkins, J., 'Electronic Trading in Wholesale Financial Markets: Its Wider Impact and Policy Issues' (2002) *Bank of England Quarterly Bulletin* (March) 50

Alpa, G., 'The Harmonisation of the EC Law of Financial Markets in the Perspective of the Consumer Protection' (2002) EBLR 523

American Bar Association, 'Achieving Legal and Business Order in Cyberspace: A Report on Global Jurisdiction Issues Created by the Internet' (2000) 55 *Business Lawyer* 1801

Andenas, Mads and Roth, W.-H. (eds.), *Services and Free Movement in EU Law* (Oxford: Oxford University Press, 2002)

Antoine, M. and others (eds.), *Le Commerce Electronique Européen sur les Rails?* (Brussels: Bruylant, 2001)

Arora, Anu, *Electronic Banking and the Law* (2nd edn, London: Banking Technology, 1993)

Association Française des Entreprises d'Investissement, *La Fourniture de Services et de Produits Financiers à l'Epreuve d'Internet* (Paris, 2000)

Association Française des Entreprises d'Investissement, *Obligations et Responsabilités Attachées à la Fourniture de Services d'Investissement* (Paris, 1999)

Association Française des Entreprises d'Investissement, *Services d'Investissement et Passport Européen* (Paris, 1998)

August, Ray, 'International Cyber-Jurisdiction: A Comparative Analysis' (2002) 39 *American Business Law Journal* 531

Australian Securities and Investments Commission, *Offers of Securities on the Internet* (Policy Statement 141, 1999)

Azzouni, A., 'Internet Banking and the Law: A Critical Examination of the Legal Controls over Internet Banking in the United Kingdom and their Ability to Frame, Regulate and Secure Banking on the Net' (2003) JIBLR 351

Baele, Lieven and others, *Measuring Financial Integration in the Euro Area* (Frankfurt: European Central Bank, 2004)

BAFIN. *See* Bundesanstalt für Finanzdienstleistungsaufsicht

BAKRED. *See* Bundesaufsichtsamt für das Kreditwesen

Balzer, Peter, 'Aktuelle Rechtsprechung zum Discount Broking' (2001) 1 *Die Bank* 51

'Haftung von Direktbanken bei Nichterreichbarkeit' (2000) ZBB 258

'Legal Aspects in Direct Banks Securities Business. A German Perspective' in N. Horn (ed.), *Legal Issues in Electronic Banking* (The Hague: Kluwer, 2002)

'Rechtsfragen des Effektengeschäfts der Direktbanken' [2001] WM 1533

Bank for International Settlements, *Electronic Finance: A New Perspective and Challenges* (Basel, 2001)

Banking and Finance Commission (Belgium), *Financial Services via the Internet: Prudential Requirements* (Announcement Brussels 2000) http://www.cbf.be/pg_pdf/en_g00/en_g09.pd (15 November 2003)

Banque de France, *Disposition applicables à l'Activité en France des Etablissements de Credit ayants leur Siege Social Dans un Autre Etat de l'EEA* (Paris, 1997)

Banque de France, *Livre Blanc sur la Sécurité des Systèmes d'Information* (Paris, 1997)

Banque de France, *Les Principal Procédures de Financement Entreprises et Ménages* (Paris, 2001)

Banque de France, *Recueil des Textes Relatifs à l'Exercice des Activités Bancaires et Financières* (Paris, 2002)

Banque de France and Commission Bancaire, *Internet: The Prudential Consequences* (Paris, 2000)

Baquero, Cruz J., 'Free Movement and Private Autonomy' [1999] EL Rev 603

Barcelo, J. and others (eds.), *Commerce Électronique: les Temps des Certitudes* (Brussels: Bruylant, 2000)

Barnard, C. and Deakin, S., 'Market Access and Regulatory Competition' in C. Barnard and J. Scott (eds.), *The Law of the Single European Market, Unpacking the Premises* (Oxford: Hart, 2002)

Barth, J., *The Prospects of International Trade in Services* (Bonn: Friedrich Ebert Foundation, 1999)

Barth, J. R., Caprio, G. and Levine, R., *Bank Regulation and Supervision: What Works Best?* (Washington DC: World Bank, 2001)

*The Regulation and Supervision of Banks Around the World* (Washington DC: World Bank, 2001)
Basedow, J., 'The Communitarisation of Conflict of Laws' (2000) 37 CML Rev 687
Basedow, J. and Kono, T. (eds.), *Legal Aspects of Globalization* (The Hague: Kluwer, 2000)
Basel Committee on Banking Supervision, *Core Principles for Effective Banking Supervision* (Basel: BIS, 1997)
Basel Committee on Banking Supervision, 'Cross-Border Electronic Banking Issues for Bank Supervisors' in *Electronic Banking Group Initiatives and White Papers* (Basel: BIS, 2000)
Basel Committee on Banking Supervision, 'Electronic Banking Risk Management Issues for Bank Supervisors', in *Electronic Banking Group Initiatives and White Papers* (Basel: BIS, 2000)
Basel Committee on Banking Supervision, *General Guide to Account Opening and Customer Identification* (Basel: BIS, 2003)
Basel Committee on Banking Supervision, *Information Flows Between Banking Supervisory Authorities* (Basel: BIS, 1990)
Basel Committee on Banking Supervision, *International Convergence of Capital Measurement and Capital Standards: A Revised Framework* (Basel: BIS, 2004)
Basel Committee on Banking Supervision, *Management and Supervision of Cross-Border Electronic Banking Activities* (Basel: BIS, 2003)
Basel Committee on Banking Supervision, *Principles for the Supervision of Banks' Foreign Establishments* (Basel: BIS, 1983)
Basel Committee on Banking Supervision, *Risk Management for Electronic Banking and Electronic Money Activities* (Basel: BIS, 1998)
Basel Committee on Banking Supervision, *Risk Management Principles for Electronic Banking* (Basel: BIS, 2003)
Basel Committee on Banking Supervision, *Risks in Computers and Telecommunications Systems* (Basel: BIS, 1989)
Beatson, Jack, *Anson's Law of Contract* (28th edn, Oxford: Oxford University Press, 2002)
Benjamin, J., *Interests in Securities* (London: Sweet and Maxwell, 2000)
*The Law of Global Custody* (2nd edn, London: Butterworths, 2002)
Benno, J., *Consumer Purchases through Telecommunications in Europe: Application of Private International Law to Cross-Border Contractual Disputes* (Oslo: Complex, 1993)
Benston, G., 'Consumer Protection as Justification for Regulating Financial Services Firms and Products' (2000) 17 *JFSR* 277
Berger, Allen, 'The Economic Effects of Technological Progress: Evidence from the Banking Industry' (2003) 35 *Journal of Money, Credit and Banking* 141
Berger, A. and others, 'Efficiency Barriers to the Consolidation of the European Financial Services Industry' (2000) 7 EFM 117

Berger, Allen and others, 'Globalization of Financial Institutions: Evidence from Cross-Border Banking Performance' (2000) *Brookings-Wharton Papers on Financial Services* 23

Bergsträsser, Susanne, 'Regulatory Implications of an Exchange Merger' in Guido Ferrarini, Klaus J. Hopt and Eddy Wymeersch (eds.), *Capital Markets in the Age of the Euro: Cross-Border Transactions, Listed Companies and Regulation* (London: Kluwer, 2002)

Berman, P., 'The Globalization of Jurisdiction' (2002) 151 *University of Pennsylvania Law Review* 311

Bernard, N., 'La Libre Circulation des Marchandises, des Personnes et des Services dans la Traité Ce Sous L'Angle de la Compétence' (1998) 34 *Cahiers de Droit Européen* 11

Bernardeau, L., 'Droit International Privé et Services Financiers de Détail' (2001–2) *Euredia* 313

Bhala, R., *International Payments and Five Foundations of Wire Transfer Law* (London: London Institute of International Banking, 1996)

Biancheri, C., 'Is the E-Commerce Directive the Best Solution to Achieving an Integrated Internal Market in Financial Services' in Guido Ferrarini, Klaus J. Hopt and Eddy Wymeersch (eds.), *Capital Markets in the Age of the Euro: Cross-Border Transactions, Listed Companies and Regulation* (London: Kluwer, 2002)

Biernaux, J.-F. and Domont-Naert, F., 'La Banque par Internet: pour une Meilleure Protection des Consommateurs' (2000) 4 *Revue de la Banque* 253

Binder, H., 'Financial Markets Regulation in Germany: A New Institutional Framework' (2000–1) *Yearbook of International Financial and Economic Law* 401

Bizer, J., 'Elektronische Signaturen im Rechtsverkehr' in D. Kröger and M. Gimmy, *Handbuch zum Internetrecht* (2nd edn, Berlin: Springer-Verlag, 2002)

Blair, W. and Quest, D., 'Jurisdiction, Conflicts of Law and the Internet' in Guido Ferrarini, Klaus J. Hopt and Eddy Wymeersch (eds.), *Capital Markets in the Age of the Euro: Cross-Border Transactions, Listed Companies and Regulation* (London: Kluwer, 2002)

Bloch, P., 'La Coordination de la Convention de Rome avec d'autres Règles de Conflit' (1993) *Banque et Droit* (June Special Issue) 5

Boele-Woelki, K. and Kessedjian, C. (eds.), *Internet: Which Court Decides?: Which Law Applies?* (The Hague: Kluwer, 1998)

Bonneau, T., 'De l'Inulité du Droit Contractuel pour Assurer le Respect des Règles de Marché' (1999) 52 RTD com 257

Bonneau, T. and Drummond, F., *Droit des Marchés Financiers* (Paris: Economica, 2001)

Boos, K.-H., Fischer R. and Schulte-Mattler, H., *Kreditwesengesetz* (Munich: C. H. Beck, 2000)

Borges, G., 'The Localisation of Electronic Banking Transactions: The German Perspective' in N. Horn (ed.), *Legal Issues in Electronic Banking* (The Hague: Kluwer, 2002)

Bougrault, C., *La Libre Prestation de Services et la Protection du Consommateur dans le Cadre de la Vente à Distance de Services Financiers* (dissertation) (Paris: University of Paris V, René Descartes, 1998)

Bouilhol, H., 'Les Aspects Juridiques de l'E-Banking' (2000) 74 *Banque et Droit* 3

Bourin, P. and Bourin, C., 'L'Ouverture d'un Compte Bancaire par Voie Électronique' (1999) 28 *Bulletin Droit et Banque* 15

Bradley, Chris, 'Competitive Deregulation of Financial Services Activity in Europe After 1992' (1997) 11 OJLS 545

Bradley, Laura and Stewart, Kate, 'A Delphi Study on the Drivers and Inhibitors of Internet Banking' (2002) 20 *International Journal of Bank Marketing* 250

Braithwaite, John and Drahos, Peter, *Global Business Regulation* (Cambridge: Cambridge University Press, 2000)

Breton, Albert, *Competitive Governments: An Economic Theory of Politics and Public Finance* (Cambridge: Cambridge University Press, 1996)

Breton, Albert and Salmon, Pierre, 'External Effects of Domestic Regulations: Comparing Internal and International Barriers to Trade', (2001) 21 *International Review of Law and Economics* 135

Breuer, R., 'Banking in the Electronic Age. A Banker's View' in N. Horn (ed.), *Legal Issues in Electronic Banking* (The Hague: Kluwer, 2002)

Brevoort, Kenneth P. and Hannan, Timothy H., *Commercial Lending and Distance: Evidence from Community Reinvestment Act Data* (Board of Governors of the Federal Reserve System, Finance and Economics Discussion Series 5, 2004)

Buch, C. M., *Distance and International Banking* (Kiel: Institute of World Economics, 2001)

Bülow, P., 'Verbraucherkreditrecht im BGB' (2002) 55 NJW 1145

Bundesamt für Sicherheit in der Informationstechnik, *Security Considerations with Electronic Commerce* (Bonn, 1999)

Bundesanstalt für Finanzdienstleistungsaufsicht (BAFIN), *Annual Report 2002* (Bonn: Bonn, 2003)

Bundesanstalt für Finanzdienstleistungsaufsicht (BAFIN), *Guidelines Concerning Measures to be Taken by Credit Institutions to Combat and Prevent Money Laundering* (Bonn, 1998)

Bundesanstalt für Finanzdienstleistungsaufsicht (BAFIN), *Hinweise zur Erlaubnispflicht nach § 32 Abs. 1 KWG in Verbindung mit § 1 Abs. 1 und Abs. 1a KWG von Grenzüberschreitend Betriebenen Bankgeschäften und/oder Grenzüberschreitend erbrachten Finanzdienstleistungen* (Bonn, 2003)

Bundesaufsichtsamt für das Kreditwesen (BAKRED), *Anzeige gemäss § 24 Abs. I Satz 1 KWG Errichtung einer Zweigniederlassung* (Bonn, 2001)

Bundesaufsichtsamt für das Kreditwesen (BAKRED), *Marketing of Foreign Collective Investment Schemes on the Internet* (Berlin, 1998)

Bundesaufsichtsamt für den Wertpapierhandel (BAWe), *Bekanntmachung zum Wertpapier- Verkaufsprospektgesetz* (Frankfurt, 1999)

Bundesaufsichtsamt für den Wertpapierhandel (BAWe), *Richtlinie zur Konkretisierung der Organizationspflichten von Wertpapierdienstleistungsunternehmen gemäss § 33 Abs. 1 WpHG* (Frankfurt, 1999)

Bundesaufsichtsamt für den Wertpapierhandel (BAWe), *Richtlinie zur Konkretisierung der §§ 31 und 32 WpHG für das Kommissionsgeschäft, den Eigenhandel für andere und das Vermittlungsgeschäft der Wertpapierdienstleistungsunternehmen* (Frankfurt, 2001)

Bundesverband Deutscher Banken, *Banken und Verbraucher das verbraucherpolitische Gesamtkonzept der privaten Banken* (Berlin, 2003)

Bureau, H., *Le Droit de la Consommation Transfrontière* (Paris: Litec, 1999)

Burghof, H.-P. and Rudolph, B., *Bankenaufsicht: Theorie und Praxis der Regulierung* (Wiesbaden: Wiesbaden Gabler Verlag, 1996)

Buxbaum, H., 'Conflict of Economic Laws: From Sovereignty to Substance' (2002) 42 *Virginia Journal of International Law* 931

Cachard, O., *La Régulation Internationale du Marché Électronique* (Paris: Librairie Générale de Droit et de Jurisprudence 2002)

Caffard, C., 'Online Brokers Lead the Way for French Internet Finance' (2001) *International Financial Law Review* (March) 20

Caprioli, E., *Règlement des Litiges Internationaux et Droit Applicable dans le Commerce Électronique* (Paris: Litec, 2002)

Carlson, J. and others, 'Internet Banking: Market Developments and Regulatory Issues' (paper presented at the Office of the Comptroller of the Currency and Society of Government Economists Conference Washington DC, November 2000)

Carty, Hazel, *An Analysis of the Economic Torts* (Oxford: Oxford University Press, 2000)

Cary, William, 'Federalism and Corporate Law: Reflections upon Delaware' (1974) 83 *Yale Law Journal* 63

Cavusgil, T., 'Globalization of Markets and Its Impact on Domestic Institutions' (1993) 1 *Indiana Journal of Global Legal Studies* 83

CECEI. *See* Comité des Etablissments de Crédit et des Entreprises d'Investissement

Centre for the Study of Financial Innovation (CSFI) (ed.), *The New World of European E-Finance* (London, 2002)

Choi, Stephen, 'Assessing Regulatory Responses to Securities Market Globalization' (2001) 2 *Theoretical Inquiries in Law* 613

Christiansen, Hans, *Electronic Finance: Economics and Institutional Factors* (Paris: OECD Financial Affairs Division, 2001)

Claessens, Joris and others, 'On the Security of Today's Online Electronic Banking Systems' (2002) *Computers and Security* 253

Claessens, S., Glaessner, T. and Klingebiel, D., *Electronic Finance: A New Approach to Financial Sector Development* (World Bank Discussion Paper 431, Washington DC, 2002)

Claessens, S. and Jansen, M. (eds.), *The Internationalization of Financial Services: Issues and Lessons for Developing Countries* (Boston: Kluwer, 2000)

Claessens, S. and others, *E-Finance in Emerging Markets: Is Leapfrogging Possible?* (Washington DC: World Bank, 2001)

'Electronic Finance: Reshaping the Financial Landscape Around the World' (2002) 22 JFSR 29

Collins, Hugh, 'European Private Law and the Cultural Identity of States' (1995) 3 *European Review of Private Law* 353

Collins, Lawrence (ed.), *Dicey and Morris on the Conflict of Laws* (13th edn, London: Sweet and Maxwell 2000)

Comité des Etablissements de Crédit et des Entreprises d'Investissement, *The Freedom to Provide Services in the Area of Investment Services* (Paris, 1998)

Conité des Etablissements de Crédit et des Entreprises d'Investissement, *La Libre Prestation de Services en Matière de Services d'Investissement* (Paris, 1998)

Commission Bancaire, *White Paper on the Security of Information Systems within Financial Institutions* (Paris: Bank of France, 1997)

Commission des Operations de Bourse, *Les Courtiers en Ligne* (Bulletin COB No. 348 July/August 2000)

Commission of the European Communities. *See* European Commission

Committee of Wise Men, *Final Report on the Regulation of European Securities Markets* (the 'Lamfalussy Report') (15 February 2001)

Committee on Payment and Settlement Systems, *Clearing and Settlement Arrangements for Retail Payments in Selected Countries* (Basel, 2000)

Committee on Payment and Settlement Systems, *Core Principles for Systematically Important Payments Systems* (Basel, 2001)

Committee on Payment and Settlement Systems, *Recommendations for Securities Settlement Systems* (Basel, 2001)

Committee on the Global Financial System, *The Implications of Electronic Trading in Financial Markets* (Basel: BIS, 2001)

Conseil d'Etat, *Internet et les Réseaux Numériques* (Collection Etudes du Conseil d'Etat), (Paris, 1998)

Conseil des Marchés Financiers, *Note sur l'Applicabilité du Titre III aux Prestataires de Services d'Investissement Intervenant en Libre Etablissement ou en Libre Prestation de Services en France* (Paris, 2003)

Corcoran, A. and Hart, T. L., 'The Regulation of Cross-Border Financial Services in the EU Internal Market' (2001) 8 *Columbia Journal of European Law* 221

Corporation of London, *Creating a Single European Market for Financial Services* (London, 2003)
Crabit, E., 'La Directive sur le Commerce Electronique. Le Projet Méditerranée' (2002) *Revue du Droit de l'Union Européenne* 749
Cranston, Ross, *Principles of Banking Law* (2nd edn, Oxford: Oxford University Press, 2002)
Dalhuisen, J. H., 'Liberalisation and Re-Regulation of Cross-Border Financial Services. The Situation in the EU and WTO/GATS' (1999) EBLR 158
Dassesse, M., 'The Localisation of Electronic Banking Transactions. EU, WTO and Tax Considerations' in N. Horn (ed.), *Legal Issues in Electronic Banking* (The Hague: Kluwer, 2002)
  'The Regulatory Implications of the Location of Financial Services under EU Law' (2001) 16/BJIBFL 473
De Matos, A. M., *Les Contrats Transfrontières Conclus par les Consommateurs au Sein de l'Union Européenne* (Aix-en-Provence, Marseilles: Presses Universitaires d'Aix-Marseille, 2001)
De Vauplane, H. and Bornet, J. P., *Droit des Marchés Financiers* (3rd edn, Paris: Litec, 2001)
Delacourt, J. T., 'The International Impact of Internet Regulation' (1997) 38 *Harvard International Law Journal* 207–35
Dermine, Jean, 'European Banking: Past, Present and Future' (paper presented at the 2nd ECB Central Banking Conference, Frankfurt, October 2002)
Deutsche Bundesbank, 'Electronic Banking from a Prudential Supervisory Perspective', *Monthly Report*, December 2000, 43–58
DeYoung, R., 'The Internet's Place in the Banking Industry' (2001) 163 *Chicago Fed Letter* 1–4
Dickie, J., *Internet and Electronic Commerce Law in the European Union* (Oxford: Hart, 1999)
Director General of Fair Trading, *Vulnerable Consumers and Financial Services* (London, 1999)
Dodge, William, 'Breaking the Public Law Taboo' (2002) 43 *Harvard International Law Journal* 161
Ducoulombier, E., 'La Communication Interprétative de la Commission Européenne Relative à Deuxième Directive Bancaire' (1998) *Revue de la Banque* 147
Easterbrook, Frank E., 'Federalism and European Business Law', (1994) 14 *Int'l Rev L Econ* 125
Eeckhout, P., 'Constitutional Concepts for Free Trade in Services' in G. de Burca and J. Scott (eds.), *The EU and the WTO: Legal and Constitutional Issues* (Oxford: Hart, 2001)
  *The European Internal Market and International Trade in Goods and Services: A Legal Analysis* (Oxford: Clarendon Press, 1994)

Egland, K. L. and others, 'Banking over the Internet' (1998) 17 *Office of the Comptroller of the Currency Quarterly Journal* (4) 25

El-Agraa, Ali M., 'General Introduction' in Ali M. El-Agraa (ed.), *Economic Integration Worldwide* (London: Palgrave Macmillan, 1997)

Ellis-Chadwick, F. and others, 'Online Customer Relationships in the European Financial Services Sector: A Cross-Country Investigation' (2002) 6 *Journal of Financial Services Marketing* 333

European Banking Federation, *Communication on Electronic Commerce and Financial Services* http://www.fbe.be/pdf/y0016aey.pdf (20 November 2003)

European Central Bank, *The Blue Book: Payment and Securities Settlement Systems in the European Union* (Frankfurt, 2001)

European Central Bank, *The Effects of Technology on the EU Banking Systems* (Frankfurt, 1999)

European Central Bank, *Improving Cross-Border Retail Payment Services: The Eurosystem's View* (Frankfurt, 1999)

European Central Bank, *Report on EU Banking Structure* (Frankfurt, 2004)

European Central Bank, *Structural Analysis of the EU Banking Sector: Year 2001* (Frankfurt, 2002)

European Central Bank, *Towards a Single Euro Payments Area: Progress Report* (Frankfurt, 2003)

European Commission, *The Application of Conduct of Business Rules Under Article 11 of the Investment Services Directive*, COM(2000) 722 final

European Commission, *Application to Financial Services of Article 3(4) to (6) of the Electronic Commerce Directive*, COM(2003) 259 final

European Commission, *Completing the Internal Market*, COM(85) 310 final (White Paper)

European Commission, *Consumer Policy Strategy 2002–2006* OJ 2002, No. C137/2

European Commission, *The Conversion of the Rome Convention of 1980 on the Law Applicable to Contractual Obligations into a Community Instrument and its Modernization*, COM(2002) 654 final

European Commission, *E-Commerce and Financial Services*, COM(2001) 66 final Communication to the Council and European Parliament, 9 February 2001

European Commission, *A European Initiative on Electronic Commerce*, COM(97) 157, 15 April 1997

European Commission, *Financial Services: Building a Framework for Action*, COM (98) 625, 28 October 1998

European Commission, *Financial Services Enhancing Consumer Confidence*, COM (97) 309 final

European Commission, *Financial Services: Implementing the Framework for Financial Markets: Action Plan*, COM(99) 232, 11 May 1999

European Commission, *First Report on the Application of Directive on Electronic Commerce*, COM(2003) 702 final

European Commission, *First Report on the Implementation of the Data Protection Directive*, COM(2003) 265 final
European Commission, *Freedom to Provide Services and the Interest of the General Good in the Second Banking Directive*, SEC(97) 1193 final
European Commission, *A Possible Legal Framework for the Single Payment Area in the Internal Market: Non-Resident Accounts*, MARKT/4006/2003, 14 April 2003
European Commission, *Report on the Implementation of Council Directive 93/13/EEC of 5 April 1993 on Unfair Terms in Consumer Contracts*, COM(2000) 248 final
European Commission, *Upgrading the Investment Services Directive*, COM(2000) 729 final
European Committee for Banking Standards, *Electronic Banking* (Brussels, 1999)
European Committee for Banking Standards, *European Electronic Banking Standards Framework* (Brussels, 2001)
European Opinion Research Group, *Public Opinion in Europe: Views on Business-to-Consumer Cross-border Trade* (Brussels, 2002)
European Parliament, *A Single Market in Financial Services: Effects on Growth, Employment and the Real Economy* (Strasburg, 2001)
Fallon, M., 'Les Conflits de Lois et de Jurisdictions dans un Espace Economique Intégré: L'Expérience de la Communauté Européenne' (1995) *Recueil des Cours de l'Académie de Droit International* 9
Fallon, M. and Meeusen, J., 'Le Commerce Electronique, la Directive 2000/31/CE et le Droit International Privé' (2002) 91 RCDIP 435
Federal Banking Supervisory Office, *Annual Report 2000* (Bonn, 2001)
Federal Banking Supervisory Office, *German Banking Supervisors to Perform Security Analyses of E-Banking Platforms*, Press Release (Bonn, 18 January 2001)
Fédération Bancaire Française, *Banque en Ligne: Guide des Bonnes Pratiques* (Paris, 2003)
Fédération Bancaire Française, *Charte Relative aux Conventions de Compte de Dépôt* (Paris, 2003)
Ferrarini, Guido, 'Pan-European Securities Markets: Policy Issues and Regulatory Responses' (2002) 3 EBOL Rev 249
Fezer, K. H. and Koos, S., 'Das Gemeinschaftsrechtliche Herkunfslandprinzip und die E-Commerce Richtlinie' (2000) *IPRax* 349
Financial Law Panel, *Report on Jurisdiction and the Regulation of Financial Services over the Internet* (London, 1998)
FSA. See Financial Services Authority, *Annual Report 2001–2002* (London, 2002)
Financial Services Authority, *The FSA's Approach to the Regulation of E-Commerce* (London, 2001)
Financial Services Authority, *Implementing the E-Commerce Directive* (Consultation Paper 129) (London, 2002)

Fischel, Daniel, 'The "Race to the Bottom" Revisited: Reflections on Recent Developments in Delaware's Corporation Law' (1982) 76 *NWUL Rev* 913

Florian, U., *Rechtsfragen des Wertpapierhandels im Internet* (Munich: C. H. Beck, 2001)

Foot, Michael, 'International Cooperation and Exchange of Information' (paper presented at the Guernsey Financial Service Commission Seminar, June 2003)

Fort, Jean-Louis, *Banking Supervision and the Evolution of Banking Risks*, General Secretary, Commission Bancaire (Speech Delivered on the Occasion of the Bicentennial of the Bank of France, Paris, 25 May 2000)

French Banking Federation, *Five Principles for a Unified Banking and Financial Services Market* (Paris, 2003)

Friedman, Thomas L., *The World Is Flat, A Brief History of the Twenty-First Century* (New York: Farrar, Straus and Giroux, 2005)

Furst, K., Lang, W. W. and Nolle, D. E., *Internet Banking in the US: Landscape, Prospects and Industry Implications* (Washington DC: Office of the Comptroller of the Currency, 2001)

Gautrais, V., *Le Contrat Electronique International: Encadrement Juridique* (2nd edn, Louvain-la-Neuve: Bruylant-Academia, 2002)

Gavalda, C. and Stoufflet, J., *Droit Bancaire* (5th edn, Paris: Litec, 2002)

Gavis, A., 'The Offering and Distribution of Securities in Cyberspace: A Review of Regulatory and Industry Initiatives' (1996) 52 *Business Lawyer* 317

Giovannini Group, *Cross-border Clearing and Settlement Arrangements in the European Union* (Brussels, 2001)

Giovanoli, Mario, 'A New Architecture for the Global Financial Market: Legal Aspects of International Financial Standard Setting' in Mario Giovanoli (ed.), *International Monetary Law: Issues for the New Millennium* (Oxford: Oxford University Press, 2000)

Giuliano, Mario and Lagarde, Paul, *Report on the Convention on the Law Applicable to Contractual Obligations* (the 'Official Report'), OJ 1980, No. C282

Gkoutzinis, Apostolos, 'The Promotion of Financial Services via the Internet – A Comparative Study of the Regulatory Framework' (2002) 17 *BJIBFL* 29–36

Goldring, John, 'Consumer Protection, Globalization and Democracy', (1998) 6 *Cardozo Journal of International and Comparative Law* 1.

Goldsmith, J. L., 'Against Cyberanarchy' (1998) 65 *University of Chicago Law Review* 1199

'The Internet, Conflicts of Regulation and International Harmonisation' in C. Engel and K. Keller (eds.), *Governance of Global Networks in the Light of Differing Local Values* (Baden-Baden: Nomos, 2000)

Goode, Roy (ed.), *Consumer Credit Law and Practice* (London: Butterworths, 1999)

Goodhart, Charles and others, *Financial Regulation, Why, How and Where Now?* (London: Routledge, 1998)

Gralla, Preston, *How the Internet Works* (Indianapolis: Que, 2004)

Granier, T. and Jaffeux, C., *Internet et Transactions Financières* (Paris: Economica, 2002)

Griffin, P. B., 'The Delaware Effect: Keeping the Tiger in its Cage, The European Experience of Mutual Recognition in Financial Services' (2001) *Columbia Journal of European Law* 337

Griggs, L. and Nitschke, P., 'Banking on the Internet – Reformulation of the Old or Adoption of the New?' (1996) 7 *Journal of Law and Information Science* 223

Group of Ten, 'Report of the Working Party on Financial Stability in Emerging Market Economies' (Basel: Bank for International Settlements, 1997)

Group of Thirty, 'Global Clearing and Settlement: A Plan of Action' (Washington DC, 2003)

Grua, F., *Les Contrats de Base de la Pratique Bancaire* (Paris: Litec, 2000)

Grundmann, S., 'Das Internationale Privatrecht der E-Commerce-Richtlinie – was ist kategorial anders im Kollisionsrecht des Binnenmarkts und warum?' (2003) 67 RabelsZ 246

Haacker, Markus, 'The ICT Sector and the Global Economy: Counting the Gains' in Soumitra Dutta and Augusto Lopez-Claros (eds.), *Global Information Technology Report 2004–2005* (4th edn, London: Palgrave Macmillan, 2005)

Hahn, Robert, *Reviving Regulatory Reform: A Global Perspective* (Washington DC: AEI-Brookings Joint Center for Regulatory Studies, 2000)

Hartley, Trevor, 'Mandatory Rules in International Contracts: The Common Law Approach' (1997) 266 *Recueil des Cours de l'Académie de Droit International* 337

Hawke, John D., 'Electronic Banking' (paper presented at the International Monetary Seminar, Paris, February 2001), available at http://www.occ.treas.gov/ftp/release/2001-14a.doc (10 August 2005)

Heinemann, Friedrich and Jopp, Matthias, *The Benefits of a Working European Retail Market for Financial Services* (Report to European Financial Services Round Table, – the 'Gyllenhammer Report') (Berlin: EU Verlag, 2002)

Hellenic Bankers' Association, *E-Banking: New Horizons in Banking Enterprise* (Athens, 2001)

Herrington, T., 'Marketing Funds on the Internet: The Position in Europe' (1997) *International Business Lawyer* 343

Hertig, Gerard and Lee, Ruben, 'Four Predictions about the Future of EU Securities Regulation' (2003) 3 *Journal of Corporate Law Studies* 343

High-Level Group on the Information Society, *Europe and the Global Information Society, Recommendations to the European Council* (the 'Bangemann Recommendations') (Brussels, 1994)

HM Treasury, *Completing a Dynamic Single European Financial Services Market: The UK Strategy* (London, July 2000 and statement by the Chancellor of the Exchequer, Gordon Brown, 17 July 2000) available at http://www.hm-treasury.gov.uk/newsroom_and_speeches/press/2000/press_91_00.cfm

HM Treasury, *Implementation of the Distance Marketing of Consumer Financial Services Directive* (London, 2003)

Hong Kong Monetary Authority, *Authorization of Virtual Banks*, Regulatory Guideline (May 2000) available at http://www.info.gov.hk/hkma/eng/guide/guide_no/20000505e.htm (10 August 2005)

Hopt, K. and Baumbach, A., *Handelsgesetzbuch* (29th edn, Munich: C. H. Beck, 1995)

Horn, C., 'Verbraucherschutz bei Internetgeschäften' (2002) MMR 209

Horn, Norbert. (ed.), *German Banking Law and Practice in International Perspective* (New York: Walter de Gruyter, 1999)

  'Germany' in Ross Cranston (ed.), *European Banking Law – The Banker–Customer Relationship* (London: LLP, 1998)

Huet J., 'Le Droit Applicable dans les Réseaux Numériques' (2002) 129 JDI 737

Hunger, P., *Die Begründung der Geschäftsverbindung im Internet Banking* (Zurich: Schulthess, 2000)

International Chamber of Commerce (ICC), *Report on Jurisdiction and Applicable Law in Electronic Commerce* (Paris, 2001)

International Chamber of Commerce (ICC), *Survey on Jurisdictional Certainty for International Contracts* (Paris: 2001)

International Monetary Fund, *Assessment of the Compliance by France with the 1997 Basel Committee's Core Principles for Effective Banking Supervision* (Washington DC, 2001)

International Organizations of Securities Commissions (IOSCO), *First Report on Securities Activity on the Internet* (Madrid, 1998)

International Organizations of Securities Commissions, *Objectives and Principles for Securities Regulation* (Madrid, 2002)

International Organization of Securities Commissions (IOSCO), *Report on Securities Activities on the Internet III* (Madrid, 2003)

International Organization of Securities Commissions (IOSCO), *Second Report on Securities Activities on the Internet* (Madrid, 2001)

Jackson, Howell E. and Pan Eric, 'Regulatory Competition in International Securities Markets: Evidence from Europe in 1999' (Pt 1) (2001) 56 BusLaw 653

Johnson D. R. and Post, D., 'Law and Borders: The Rise of Law in Cyberspace' (1996) 48 *Stanford Law Review* 1367

Kahler, Miles, 'Trade and Domestic Differences' in Suzanne Berger and Ronald Dore (eds.), *National Diversity and Global Capitalism* (New York: Cornell University Press, 1996)

Kemppainen, Kari, Competition and Regulation in European Retail Payment Systems (Bank of Finland, Discussion Paper 16, Helsinki, 2003)

Kenen, Peter B., *Capital Mobility and Financial Integration: A Survey* (Princeton Studies in International Finance 39, 1976)

Key, Sydney J. and Scott, Hal S., *International Trade in Banking Services: A Conceptual Framework* (Washington DC: Group of Thirty, 1991)

Klauer, Irene, 'General Clauses in European Private Law and "Stricter" National Standards: The Unfair Terms Directive' (2000) 8 *European Review of Private Law* 187

Koch, C. and Maurer, P., 'Rechtsfragen des Online-Vertriebs von Bankprodukten-Behindern Gesetzliche Regelungen den Elektronischen Geschäftsverkehr?' (Pt 1) (2002) 55 WM 2443 and (Pt2) (2002) 55 WM 2481

Kronke, Herbe, 'Applicable Law and Jurisdiction in Electronic Banking Transactions' in Norbert Horn (ed.), *Legal Issues in Electronic Banking* (The Hague: Kluwer, 2002)

Kuhn, T., *The Structure of Scientific Revolutions* (3rd edn, Chicago: University of Chicago Press, 1996)

Kümpel, S., *Bank- und Kapitalmarktrecht* (2nd edn, Cologne: Verlag Dr Otto Schmidt, 2000)

Kunst, D. 'Rechtliche Risiken des Internet-Banking' (2001) MMR 23

Lafitte, M., *Economie Digitale et Services Financiers* (Paris: Banque, 2002)

Lagarde, P., *Le Consommateur en Droit International Privé* (Wien: Manz, 1999)

Lascelles, D., 'Regulating Financial Services on the Internet' (1999–2000) 10 *Central Banking* (2) 67

Lastra, Rosa M., 'The Governance Structure for Financial Regulation and Supervision in Europe' 10 *Columbia Journal of European Law* 41–68

Law Commission, *Electronic Commerce: Formal Requirements in Commercial Transactions* (London: Law Commission of England and Wales, 2001)

Leborgne, A., 'Responsabilité Civile et Opérations sur le Marché Boursier' (1998) 48 RTD com 261

Liao, Z. and Cheung, M. T., 'Internet-Based E-Banking and Consumer Attitudes: An Empirical Study' (2002) *Information and Management* 283

Lindsey, Brink, *Against the Dead Hand: The Uncertain Struggle for Global Capitalism* (New York: Wiley, 2002)

Lomnicka, E., 'The Home Country Control Principle in the Financial Services Directives and the Case-Law' (2000) EBLR 324

Mackenzie Stuart (Lord), *The European Communities and the Rule of Law* (London: Stevens, 1977)

Maduro, Miguel P., *We the Court: The European Court of Justice and the European Economic Constitution* (Oxford: Hart Publishing, 1998)

Magnus, U., *J. von Staudingers Kommentar zum BGB mit EGBGB und Nebengesetzen EGBGB/Internationales Privatrecht* (Berlin: Walter de Grayter, 2002)

Mai, G., 'Wertpapierhandel im Internet' (2002) CR 200

Mankowski, P., 'E-Commerce und Internationales Verbraucherschutzrecht' (2000) MMR 22
  'Das Herkunfslandprinzip als Internationales Privatrecht des E-Commerce Richtlinie' (2001) 100 ZvglRWiss 137
  'Das Internet im Internationalen Vertrags- und Deliktsrecht' (1999) 63 RabelsZ 203
Mayer, P., *Droit International Privé* (Paris: Montchrestien, 2001)
Melzer, W., 'Europe: Cross-Border Financial Services and Mandatory Rules under National Law' 14 (1995) (6) IBFL 66–7
Mestmäcker, E. J., 'Staatliche Souveränität und Offene Mätkte, Konflikte bei des Extraterritorialen Anwendung von Wirtschaftsrecht' (1988) 52 RabelsZ 205
Mitchell, John, 'Response to the Commission Green Paper: Financial Services: Meeting Consumers' Expectations' (1997) *Journal of Consumer Policy* 379
Mogg, J. F., 'Regulating Financial Services in Europe: A New Approach' (2002) *Fordham International Law Journal* 58
Molle, Willem, *The Economics of European Integration: Theory, Practice and Policy* (4th edn, Aldershot: Ashgate, 2001)
Moloney, N., 'Distance Marketing of Financial Services: The Approach Towards Harmonisation Emerges' (2000) *Company Lawyer* 198
Money Laundering Steering Group, *Guidance Notes for the Financial Sector* (London: British Bankers' Association, 2001)
Montesquieu, Charles de, *The Spirit of Laws*, Book I Of Laws in General (Amherst, NY: Prometheus Books, 2002)
Moos, F., 'Entwicklung eines Supra- und Internationalen Rechtsrahmen für das Internet' in D. Kröger and M. Gimmy (eds.), *Handbuch zum Internetrecht* (2nd edn, Heidelberg: Springer, 2002)
Moos, F., 'Unterscheidung der Dienstformen Teledienste, Mediendienste und Rundfunk' in D. Kröger and M. Gimmy (eds.) *Handbuch zum Internetrecht* (2nd edn, Berlin, Springer: 2002)
Morse, C. G. J., 'Choice of Law in Tort: A Comparative Study' (1984) 32 *American Journal of Comparative Law* 51
  'Consumer Contracts, Employment Contracts and the Rome Convention' (1992) 41 ICLQ 1
Müllbert, P., 'Die Auswirkungen des Schuldrechtsmodernisierung im Recht des Bürgerlichen Darlehensvertrags' (2002) 56 WM 465–76
Niglia, Leone, *The Transformation of Contract in Europe* (The Hague: Kluwer, 2003)
Nuyts, A., 'L'Application des Lois de Police dans L'Espace' (1999) 88 RCDIP 31
Nygh, P. E., *Autonomy in International Contracts* (Oxford: Clarendon Press, 1999)
Oddy, Christine, *Report on the Proposal for the E-Commerce Directive*, PE 229.868/fin, (European Parliament), 23 April 1999

OECD. See Organization for Economic Cooperation and Development

Office of New York State Attorney General, Investor Protection and Securities Bureau, *A Report on the Problems and Promise of the Online Brokerage Industry*, November 1999

Ohler, C., 'Aufsichtsrechtliche Fragen des Electronic Banking' 2002 WM 162

Olivei, Giovanni P., 'Consumption Risk-Sharing Across G-7 Countries' 2001 New England Economic Review (March/April) 3

Olson, Mancur, *Power and Prosperity: Outgrowing Communist and Capitalist Dictatorships* (New York: Basic Books, 2000)

Oppenheimer, Wolff & Donnelly LLP, *Study on the Verification of a Common and Coherent Application of the Cross-Border Credit Transfers Directive* (Brussels: Oppenheime, Woff & Donnelly LLP, 2001)

Organization for Economic Cooperation and Development 'A Borderless World: Releasing the Potential of Global Electronic Commerce', (OECD Ministerial Conference, Ottawa, 7–9 October 1998)

Organization for Economic Cooperation and Development, *Guidelines for Consumer Protection in the Context of Electronic Commerce* (Paris, 2000)

Organization for Economic Cooperation and Development, *Measuring the Information Economy* (Paris, 2002)

Organization for Economic Cooperation and Development, Financial Action Task Force on Money Laundering (FATF) *The Forty Recommendations* (Paris, 2003)

Oxelheim, Lars, *International Financial Integration* (New York: Springer, 1990)

Paulik, I., 'La Loi Applicable aux Contrat Internationaux du Commerce Électronique' (2002) 4 *La Semaine Juridique–Cahiers de Droit de l'Entreprise* 23

Pennington, Robert, 'Fraud, Error and System Malfunction' in Roy M. Goode (ed.), *Electronic Banking: The Legal Implications* (London: Institute of Bankers, 1985)

Perritt, Henry, 'The Internet as a Threat to Sovereignty? Thoughts on the Internet's Role in Strengthening National and Global Governance' (1998) 5 *Indiana Journal of Global Legal Studies* 423

Plender, Richard and Wilderspin, Michael, *The European Contracts Convention: The Rome Convention of the Choice of Contracts* (2nd edn, London: Sweet and Maxwell, 2001)

Prioux, R., 'L'Incidence des Lois de Police sur les Contrats Economiques Internationaux' (1994) 10 *Revue de Droit de l'ULB* 129

Radicati di Brozolo, L. G., 'La Loi Applicable aux Contrats Interbancaires selon la Convention de Rome' (1993) *Banque et Droit* (June Special Issue) 32

Reed, Chris, *Electronic Finance Law* (Cambridge: Woodhead-Faulkner, 1991)

*Legal Regulation of Internet Banking: A European Perspective* (London: Centre for Commercial Studies, Queen Mary, University of London, 1996)

Reed, C., 'Managing Regulatory Jurisdiction: Cross-Border Online Financial Services and the European Union Single Market for Information Society Services' (2001) 38 *Houston Law Review* 1003–35

Reed, C., Walden, I. and Edgar, L. (eds.), *Cross-Border Electronic Banking* (2nd edn, London: Lloyd's of London Press, 2000)
Reich, Norbert, *Europäisches Verbraucherschutzrecht* (Baden-Baden: Nomos, 1993)
Reich, Norbert and Helfmeier, Alex, 'Consumer Protection in the Global Village' (2001) 106 *Dickinson Law Review* 111–37
Reserve Bank of India, *Report on Internet Banking* (2001) para. 8.3.4, available at http://www.rbi.org.in/sec21/21595.pdf (10 August 2005)
Romano, Robert, 'Law as a Product: Some Pieces of the Incorporation Puzzle' (1985) *1 JLEcon. &Org.*225
Rossini, C., 'Cross-Border Banking in the EC: Host Country Powers under the Second Banking Directive' (1995) ERPL 571
Rove, M., 'International Jurisdiction over the Internet: A Case Analysis of Yahoo! Inc. v. La Ligue Contre Le Racisme et l'Antisemitisme' (2003) *Temple International and Comparative Law Journal* 261
Ruet, L., 'La Passation des Ordres de Bourse via Internet' (2000) *Revue de Droit Bancaire et Financier* (May/June) 194
Rühl, C., *Rechtswahlfreiheit und Rechtswahlklauseln in Allgemeinen Geschäftsbedingungen* (Baden-Baden: Nomes, 1999)
Sato, S., 'Creating an "E-Finance Friendly" Regulatory and Institutional Framework' (paper presented at the UNCTAD Expert Meeting on Finance and E-Finance, Geneva, October 2001)
Sato, S. and Hawkins, J., 'E-Finance: An Overview of the Issues' in Bank for International Settlements, *Electronic Finance: A New Perspective and Challenges* (Basel: Bank for International Settlements, 2001)
Schaaf, J. and Stobbe, A., 'Online Banking in Germany', *Deutsche Bank Research*, 22 February 2002, 1
Schaechter, A., *Issues in Electronic Banking: An Overview* (Washington DC: International Monetary Fund, 2002)
Schimansky, H., Bunte, H. J. and Lwowski, H. J., *Bankrechts-Handbuch* (2nd edn, Munich: C. H. Beck, 2001)
Schreibauer, M., 'Strafrechtliche Verantwortlichkeit für Delikte im Internet' in D. Kröger and M. Gimmy, *Handbuch zum Internetrecht* (2nd edn, Berlin: Spinger-Verlag, 2002)
Schüler, Martin, 'Integration of the European Market for E-Finance – Evidence from Online Brokerage' in Paolo Cecchini, Friedrich Heinemann and Matthias Jopp (eds.), *The Incomplete European Market for Financial Services* (Heidelberg: Physicaverlay, 2003)
Schüler, Martin and Heinemann, Friedrich, *How Integrated Are the European Retail Financial Markets? A Cointegration Analysis* (ZEW Discussion Papers, Mannheim: ZEW, 2003)
Schulze, Reiner and Schulte-Nölke, Hans (eds.), *Analysis of National Fairness Laws Aimed at Protecting Consumers in Relation to Precontractual Commercial*

*Practices and the Handling of Consumer Complaints by Business* (Brussels: European Commission, 2003)

Schwintowski, H.-P. and Schäfer, F. A., *Bankrecht: Commercial Banking, Investment Banking* (Cologne: Cart Heymanns, 1997)

Securities and Exchange Commission, *Use of Internet Web Sites To Offer Securities, Solicit Securities Transactions, or Advertise Investment Services Offshore* (Release No. 1125, 1998)

Sieg, O., 'Allgemeine Geschäftsbedingungen im Grenzüberschreitenden Geschäftsverkehr' (1997) RIW 811

Smith, G., 'Liability for Computer Errors in Online Banking' (1996) CLSR 277

Snell, Jukka, *Goods and Services in EC Law* (Oxford: Oxford University Press, 2002)

Sonnenhof, Jürgen, 'Änderungen der AGB-Banken zum 1. April 2002' (2002) WM 1269

Souci-Roubi, B., 'La Convention de Rome et la Loi Applicable aux Contrats Bancaires' (1993) *Dalloz Sirey* 183

*Droit Bancaire Européen* (Paris: Dalloz, 1995)

Spindler, G., 'Bankrecht und E-Commerce-Sicherheit im Rechtsverkehr' in W. Hadding, K. Hopt and H. Schimansky (eds.), *Entgeltklauseln in der Kreditwirtschaft und E-Commerce von Kreditinstituten* (Berlin: Walter de Gruyter, 2002)

'Elektronische Finanzmärkte und Internet-Börsen' (2002) 56 WM 1325

Spindler, Gerard, 'Herkunftslandprinzip und Kollisionsrecht-Binnenmarktintegration ohne Harmonisierung?' (2002) 66 RabelsZ 633

Spindler, G. and Fallenböck, M., 'Das Herkunftslandprinzip der E-Commerce-Richtlinie und Seine Umsetzung in Deutschland und Österreich' (2002) ZfRV 214

Starck, B., Roland H. and Boyer, L., *Droit Civil des Obligations: Contrat* (6th edn, Paris: Litec, 1998)

Steck, A. and Landegren, K., 'Cross-Border Services into Germany', (2003) 11 *Journal of Financial Regulation and Compliance* 21

Strub, A. J., *Bankdienstleistungen im Binnenmarkt* (Munich: Beck, 1994)

Sullivan, R., 'How Has the Adoption of Internet Banking Affected Performance and Risk in Banks?' (2000) *Federal Reserve Bank of Kansas City: Financial Industry Perspectives* 1

Sun, Jean-May and Pelkmans, Jacques, 'Regulatory Competition in the Single Market' (1995) 33 JCMS 67

Swiss Federal Banking Commission, *E-Finance*, available at http://www.ebk.admin.ch/e/faq/faq4.html#4P (10 August 2005)

Sykes, Alan, 'The (Limited) Role of Regulatory Harmonization in International Goods and Services Markets' (1999) 2 *Journal of International Economic Law* 49

Tabarot, Michèle, 'Rapport sur le Projet de Loi pour la Confiance dans l'Economie Numérique,' (Assemblée Nationale No. 608, 11 February 2003)
Tetz, Stefanie, 'The German System of Securities and Stock Exchanges' in Norbert Horn (ed.), *German Banking Law and Practice in International Perspective* (Berlin: Walter de Gruyter, 1999)
Tiebout, Charles M., 'A Pure Theory of Local Expenditures' (1956) 64 *Journal of Political Economy* 416
Trachtman, J. P., 'Cyberspace, Sovereignty, Jurisdiction, and Modernism' (1998) 5 *Indiana Journal of Global Legal Studies* 561
  'Trade in Financial Services under GATS, NAFTA and the EC: A Regulatory Jurisdiction Analysis' (1995) 34 *Columbia Journal of Transnational Law* 37
Vallelersundi, Ana P. (Rapporteur), *Recommendation for Second Reading on the Council Common Position for Adopting the Directive on Electronic Commerce*, A5-0106/2000, 12 April 2000
Van den Bergh, Roger, 'Regulatory Competition or Harmonization of Laws? Guidelines for the European Regulator' in Alain Marciano and Jean-Michel Josselin (eds.), *The Economics of Harmonizing European Law* (Cheltenham: Edward Elgar, 2002)
Van Houtte, H. (ed.), *The Law of Cross-Border Securities Transactions* (London: Sweet and Maxwell, 1999)
Walter, I. and Grady, P., 'Protectionism and International Banking: Sectorial Efficiency, Competitive Structure and National Policy' (1983) 7 *Journal of Banking and Finance* 597
Weatherill, Stephen, 'The Commission's Options for Developing EC Consumer Protection and Contract Law: Assessing the Constitutional Basis' (2002) EBLR 497
  'Consumer Policy' in Paul Craig and Grain de Burca (eds.), *The Evolution of EU Law* (Oxford: Oxford University Press, 1999)
  'Recent Case Law Concerning the Free Movement of Goods: Mapping the Frontiers of Market Deregulation' (1999) 36 *CML Rev* 51
Wiegand, W. (ed.), *E-Banking: Rechtliche Grundlagen* (Berne: Verlay Stämpfli, 2002)
Williams, Jody, *The International Campaign to Ban Land Mines – A Model for Disarmament Initiatives* (1997) at www.nobel.se/peace/articles/williams/index.html (6 December 2003)
Wolf, Martin, *Why Globalization Works* (New Haven: Yale University Press, 2004)
Wood, Philip R., *Maps of World Financial Law* (University edn, London: Allen and Overy, 2005)
World Bank and International Monetary Fund, *International Standards: Strengthening Surveillance, Domestic Institutions and International Markets* (Washington, DC: 2003)

Wouters, J., 'Conflict of Laws and the Single Market for Financial Services' (Pt1) [1997] MJ 161 and (Pt2) [1997] MJ 215

Wunsch-Vincent, Sacha and McIntosh, Joanna, *WTO, E-Commerce and Information Technologies* (New York: Markle Foundation, 2005)

Yntema, Hessel, 'The Historic Bases of Private International Law', (1953) 2 *American Journal of Comparative Law* 297

# INDEX

access control, 37
advertising
  consumer contracts, conflict of laws, 299–302
  consumer credit, 205–6
  domestic regulation, 65
  EU legislation, 171
  French law, 173–4
  German law, 176–7
  harmonization, 171–3, 179
  home state rule, 286–7
  host country rules, 256–9
  misleading advertising, 143, 174
  UK law, 174–6
  websites, 300–1
agency, securities trading, 45–6
applicable law. *See* choice of law; conflict of laws
Austria, 271

Bangemann Recommendations, 263
bank accounts
  domestic laws, 30–2
  English law, 30, 188
  French law, 31–2, 188–9
  German law, 31, 188
  harmonization, 200
  IBANs, 203
  opening, 188–90
  UK law, 30, 188
Bank of England, 118
banker–customer relationships
  domestic laws, 29–40, 204, 205
  French law, 204
  German law, 205
  harmonization, 200

party autonomy, 114–17
UK law, 204
banking
  2nd Banking Directive, 101, 237
  accounts. *See* bank accounts
  advertising, French law, 174
  applicable law. *See* conflict of laws
  Bank Identifier Codes (BICs), 203
  Banking Directive, mutual recognition, 237–42, 288
  confidentiality, 133
  consumer protection, 92, 142
  corporate governance, 151, 153
  cross-border. *See* cross-border Internet banking
  deposits. *See* deposits
  domestic bias, 39
  domestic regulation, 65
  electronic banking, meaning, 7–8
  financial risks, 148
  and free movement principle, 89–99
  French prudential regulation, 160–2
  German prudential regulation, 162–4
  legal barriers to international banking, 51–6
  licences, 41, 61, 154, 160, 162
  mutual recognition of services, 89–99, 237–42
  online. *See* online financial services
  prudential regulation, harmonization, 101–2, 141–2, 154–6, 240–1
  public interest exception, 140–8, 242–3

339

banking (cont.)
  standard form contracts, 292–3
  transparency. See transparency
  UK prudential regulation, 156–60
banking licences
  and foreign banks, 61
  France, 160, 162
  Germany, 41
  harmonization, 154
Basel Committee, 66–7, 72, 131, 150, 151, 152
BICs, 203
Braithwaite, John, 118
business names, 154

cancellation, online contracts, 190–1
capital adequacy, 151, 154, 158
centralization
  full decentralization, 105–9
  maximum harmonization, 103–5
choice of law
  See also conflict of laws
  certainty, 183–4, 290, 291
  competition and single financial market, 118–23
  consumer contracts, 296–305
  contract, 183–4, 275
  cross-border contracts, 292–6
  discretion to disregard, 292
  forum selection, 293–4
  freedom of choice, 114–17, 293–4, 296
  and home country rule, 275
  mandatory rules, impact, 305–9
  no choice made, 294–6
  public policy disregards, 292
  standard terms, 292–3
City of London, 104
clearing systems, 38–40, 151
cold calling, 111–12
collective investment schemes, 274
commercial communications, 172, 175
companies, place of incorporation, 154
competence
  boundaries of EU competence, 85
  domestic competences, 102
  subsidiarity, 85, 87, 105

competition
  See also regulatory competition
  cartel law, 263
  free competition principle, 86
  legal protectionism, 15–16
  and single financial market, 118–23
conduct of business rules
  EU investor protection regulation, 217
  financial services, 113
  French investor protection, 221
  German investor protection, 225–6
  UK investor protection, 219
  United Kingdom, 234
confidentiality, 133, 158
conflict of laws
  See also choice of law
  consumer contracts, 275–6, 292, 296–305
  advertising, 299–302
  credit, 297, 299
  impact of mandatory rules, 305, 315–16
  international jurisdiction, 303–5
  services provided in other country, 302–3
  specific invitation, 299–302
  supply of services, 297, 299
  contract, 83
  defamation, 258–9
  domestic financial regulation, 58–63
  French torts, 259–61
  German torts, 259–61
  harmonization of rules, 291
  impact on cross-border services, 312
  international financial contracts, 290–2
  legal uncertainty, 98, 273
  and localization of online services, 244–61
  European Commission's views, 245–6
  French position, 246–8, 251
  German position, 248
  notification requirement, 244–5
  UK position, 248

## INDEX

mandatory rules, impact, 305–9, 315–16
no choice made, 294–6
performance, place, 245–6, 248, 249–51, 253, 294–6
principles, 271–2
*renvoi*, 273
and single market directives, 289–90
territorial principle, 62
torts, 287–8
UK crimes, 257
UK torts, 257–9
consumer confidence
  EU policies, 78
  honesty and integrity, 144
  measures, 127
  quality of regulatory agencies, 129
  and single financial market, 121–2, 311
consumer credit
  advertising, 205–6
  agreements
    domestic laws, 207–9
    EU law, 206
    requirement of writing, 186, 206
  conflict of laws, 297, 299
  Consumer Credit Directive
    implementation, 207–13, 208
    minimum harmonization, 207, 210–13
  and online bank loans, 205–13
  domestic laws, 40–2, 207–13
  early repayments, 209, 210
  information rights, 206–7
  online practice, 23
  overdrafts, 40–1, 210
  party autonomy, 210, 211–12
consumer demand, 63, 117
consumer protection
  average consumer, 146
  banking services, 92, 142
  beneficiaries, 145–8
  conflict of laws, 275–6, 292, 296–305
    advertising, 299–302
    credit, 297, 299
    impact of mandatory rules, 305, 315–17
    international jurisdiction, 303–5
    services, 297, 299
    services provided in other country, 302–3
    specific invitation, 299–302
  Distance Marketing Directive, 80, 168–71
  domestic laws, 62, 65
  EU regulation, 75–6, 134
  financial services, 78
  and free trade agenda, 146–7
  and freedom of contract, 114
  harmonization, 76, 82, 86, 275
  host state regulation, 275–6
  information rights, 143
  international standards, 152
  investment services
    domestic laws, 218–26
    EU law, 214–18
    host country regulation, 254–6
  non-judicial remedies, 134
  public interest exception, 141, 142
  Rome Convention, 116
  vulnerable customers, 116–17
contract
  asymmetrical bargaining power, 116, 120
  choice of law. *See* choice of law
  conflict of laws, 83, 116, 290–2
  consumer contracts. *See* consumer protection
  consumer credit. *See* consumer credit
  *culpa in contrahendo*, 177, 267
  electronic contracts. *See* online contracts
  and financial integration, 183–4, 290–2
  Internet service agreements, 35–7
  party autonomy, 114–17, 183–4, 275, 293–4
  performance, place, 245–6, 248, 249–51, 253, 294–6
  pre-contractual information, 177–9, 184–5
  Rome Convention, 116, 249
  standard forms, 120, 292–3
  unfair terms. *See* unfair contract terms

contract (cont.)
  validity, 267–8
  withdrawal rights, 190–1
cooperation
  Basel Committee, 131
  e-commerce jurisdiction, 284
  EU banking Directive, 154
  exchange of information, 129, 133
  international standard setting, 150
  memoranda of understanding, 133
  national regulators, 128, 134, 314
coordinated fields, 262, 266–78
Cortal, 278
country of origin. *See* home state regulation
credit
  *See also* consumer credit
  credit institutions, meaning, 22, 237
  reference services, 40
  risks, 154
cross-border Internet banking
  advertising and marketing, 256–9
  alternative regulation model, 67–73
  Basel Committee, 72
  benefits, 82
  conflict of laws. *See* conflict of laws
  contracts. *See* online contracts
  country of origin principle. *See* home state regulation
  credit transfers, harmonization, 200
  euro payments, 200, 202–3
  home state regulation
    financial directives, 237–42
    notification of authorities, 241, 244–5
    prudential standards, 237–42, 268
    public interest exception, 242–3
  host state regulation, 117, 243–61
    advertising and marketing, 256–9
    investor protection, 254–6
    non-prudential matters, 243–61
    identification of customers, 190
  impact, 311
  models, 238
  mutual recognition. *See* mutual recognition
  securities trading, 43–4
  self-restraint, 69

  services, 37–40, 253–4
  total harmonization, 103–5
  unpredicted model, 252, 253
  without home state regulation, 232–7
    French regulation, 236–7
    German regulation, 235–6
    UK regulation, 232–5
*culpa in contrahendo*, 177, 267

data protection
  Data Protection Directive, 179–82
  E-Commerce Directive, 263
  harmonization, 152, 179–82
  implementation of Directive, 182
decentralization, full decentralization, 105–9
defamation, conflict of laws, 258–9
'Delaware phenomenon', 109
Denmark, 293
deposits
  deposit guarantee schemes, 139, 141–2
  and E-Commerce Directive, 266
  French regulation, 204
  harmonization, 200
  online practice, 28
  UK regulation, 176, 204
deregulation
  Anglo–American agenda, 104
  delaying tactics, 104
  and domestic technical standards, 96
  and financial integration, 82
  negative integration, 84
  political economy, 99–102
developing countries, 150
digital signatures, 187–8
direct effect of EU law, 85, 89
discrimination, 84, 138
Distance Marketing Directive
  advertising, 172
  French implementation, 170
  generally, 168–71
  German implementation, 170
  information requirements, 251, 180–1
  legal history, 78–81, 105
  national implementation, 170–1

subject matters, 169–70
UK implementation, 170
domestic bias, 39
domestic laws
  banker–customer relationships,
    29–40, 204, 205
  banking contracts, 199,
    200–5
  barriers to single financial market,
    51–6, 58–63
  conflict of laws. *See* conflict of laws
  consumer credit, 207–13
  contract laws, 183–4
  costs, 147
  covert protectionism, 110
  developing countries, 150
  direct barriers, 52–4
  diversity, 54, 58–63
  v. freedom of Internet, 18
  freedom to legislate, 90
  harmonization. *See* harmonization
  indirect barriers, 54–6
  investment services, 65
  investor protection, 218–26
  mutual recognition. *See* mutual
    recognition
  'product rules', 62
  risk-based framework, 228
  securities, 42–7
  uncertainty, 59–60
Drahos, Peter, 118

e-commerce
  alternative international regulatory
    model, 67–73
  contracts. *See* online contracts
  cost reduction, 9
  country of origin principle. *See*
    home state regulation
  Directive. *See* E-Commerce Directive
  'effects test', 58, 65, 67
  EU policies, 76–7
  financial services. *See* online
    financial services
  growth, 14
  harmonization, 165–8
    prohibition of licensing, 166
    subjects, 166–7

  and international financial
    integration, 10–17
  international regulation,
    64, 152
  local targeting, 65, 67, 115
  marketing, 172
  pharmaceutical products, 71–2,
    122–3
  pre-contract information, 177–8
  principles, 71
  territorial connections, 65–6
  UNCITRAL Model Law, 185
E-Commerce Directive
  harmonization instrument, 165–8
  implementation, 106, 167–8, 278–81,
    284–6
    Austria, 271
    France, 168, 281, 286
    Germany, 167–8, 271, 280, 286
    United Kingdom, 167, 186–7,
      278–80, 284–6, 288
  information requirements, 251,
    180–1
  internal market clause
    case-by-case derogations,
      281–6, 309
    coordinated fields, 262, 266
    critique, 269–72
    distance services, 265
    domestic implementation, 278–81
    effect, 314–16
    electronic means, 265–6
    general derogations, 274–6
    individual requests, 266–78
    information society services, 262,
      263, 264–5
    mandatory EU rule, 272–4
    meaning, 262
    normative impact, 286–8
    place of establishment, 276–8
    remunerated services, 263
    restrictions, 262–3
    scope, 262–6
    theories, 268–9
  legal history, 76–7, 79–81
EEA countries, e-commerce with UK,
  279–80, 284–5
'effects doctrine', 58, 65, 67

electronic finance
  advantages, 40
  domestic laws, 40–2
  meaning, 7
  technical risks, 102
electronic means, meaning, 265–6
electronic transfer of funds
  cross-border, 38, 200
  domestic laws, 32–5
  English law, 33–4
  French law, 35
  German law, 33, 34–5
  harmonization, 200
  process, 32–3
errors, online banking, 159
euro
  cross-border payment, 200, 202–3
  impact on financial services, 16
  outside euro zone, 203
European Court of Justice
  activism, 89
  impact of free movement
    jurisprudence, 94–6, 98,
    99–123
  legitimacy of jurisprudence, 96
European Union
  See also Financial Services Action
    Plan
  1992 financial services
    reform, 56–8
  centralized law making, 84
  competence, boundaries, 85
  deregulation. See deregulation
  direct effect of EU law, 85, 89
  directives, and harmonization
    process, 227
  dynamics of integration, 19–20
  European financial supervision
    agency, 113–14
  harmonization. See harmonization
  information society, 76–7
  internal market. See single financial
    market; single market
  Internet banking practice, 20–8
  law-making process, 75
  legal instruments, 85
  online financial services, policies,
    73–81

Proposed Framework for Action
  1998, 57
secondary law, 85, 251
securities trading, 44
supremacy of EU law, 85
exchange controls, 51

FIN-NET, 134
Financial Action Task Force, 150, 151,
  189, 190
financial institutions
  Internet banking providers, 24
  Internet-only banks, 24, 28
  notification of home authorities,
    241, 244–5
  overseas institutions
    French regulation, 236–7
    German regulation, 235–6
    UK regulation, 232–5
  place of establishment, 276–8
financial markets, liberalization, 52
financial reports, 154
financial services
  conduct of business rules, 113
  confidence, consumer confidence
  consumer protection. See consumer
    protection
  cross-border services, 1
  EU policies, 74–5
  European supervisory agency,
    113–14
  honesty and integrity, 144
  intermediaries. See intermediaries
  meaning, 1
  online. See cross-border Internet
    banking; online financial services
  prudential regulation, 141–2
  public interest exception, 137–48
  single market. See single financial
    market
  transparency and disclosure, 142–4
Financial Services Action Plan
  and financial integration, 57
  mutual recognition, 81
  policy reforms, 2
  proposals, 74–5
  recent reforms, 228, 313
  strategic objectives, 79

# INDEX

Financial Services Authority
  *Conduct of Business Sourcebook,* 170
  cooperation, 133
  directory services, 122
  UK banking regulator, 30
Financial Stability Forum, 151
First-e, 26
France
  advertising and marketing
    regulation, 173–4, 259–61
  *Autorité des Marchés Financiers,*
    160, 221
  bank accounts, 31–2, 188–9
  banker–customer relationship, 204
  banking licences, 160, 162
  Banque Cortal, 278
  Banque de France, 160
  conflict of laws
    advertising and marketing, 259–61
    criminal offences, 260
    localization of online services,
      246–8, 251
  consumer contracts, 298
  consumer credit, 42, 208
    advertisements, 260
    agreements, 209
    early repayment, 210
    overdrafts, 41, 210
    party autonomy, 211–12
  contracts
    standard form contracts, 193
    validity of electronic contracts,
      187–9
  credit law, 41–2
  cross-border Internet banking,
    236–7
  electronic transfer of funds, 35
  and harmonization, 104
  home and host state regulation,
    281, 286
  implementation of directives
    Data Protection Directive, 182
    Distance Marketing Directive, 170
    E-Commerce Directive, 168,
      281, 286
    Unfair Contract Terms, 196–9
  investor protection, 220–4
    conduct of business rules, 221

    economic loss, 223
    execution only, 222
    identification of customers, 222
    online services, 221, 222–4
  legal codes, 29
  online banking
    prudential regulation, 160–2
    self-regulation, 37
  securities trading, 45–6
  use of Internet banking, 22, 21
  Yahoo case, 68–9
fraud, online banking, 159
free movement principle
  direct effect, 89
  EC Treaty, 84, 85–6
  economic globalization, 11
  freedom to provide services, 89–94
  margins of discretion, 125–6
  and mutual recognition of banking
    services, 89–99
  obstacles, 14
  overriding principle, 90
  persons, 17
  pharmaceutical products, 71–2,
    122–3
  public interest exception, 91, 92,
    97–8, 137–48
  single market, 11, 94–9
Friedman, Thomas, 12

gambling, 263
general good. *See* public interest
  exception
Germany
  adverse publicity by banking
    regulator, 69
  advertising and marketing, 176–7,
    259–61
  BAKRED, 163
  bank accounts, 31, 188
  banker–customer relationship, 205
  banking business, 31
  banking licences, 41
  *Bundesbank,* 162, 163
  conflict of laws
    advertising and marketing, 259–61
    consumer contracts, 297
    criminal offences, 260

Germany (*cont.*)
  localization of online services, 248
  consumer credit, 41, 208
    agreements, 209
    overdrafts, 210
    party autonomy, 211–12
  contracts
    consumer contracts, 297, 298
    giro contracts, 31, 33
    standard form contracts, 192
    validity of electronic contracts, 187–8
  credit law, 41
  cross-border Internet banking, 235–6
  deposit guarantee schemes, 139, 141–2
  electronic transfer of funds, 33, 34–5
  Federal Financial Supervisory Authority, 162
  Frankfurt Stock Exchange, 133
  and harmonization, 104
  home and host state regulation, e-commerce, 280, 286
  identification of customers, 189–90
  implementation of directives
    Cross-Border Credit Transfers, 202
    Data Protection, 182
    Distance Marketing, 170
    E-Commerce, 167–8, 271, 280, 286
    Unfair Contract Terms, 196–9
  investor protection, 224–6
    Chinese walls, 224
    conduct of business rules, 225–6
    continuity of service, 225
    cross-border services, 255–6
    execution only, 225–6
    information requirements, 225–6
  legal codes, 29
  online banking regulation, 162–4
  online banking security risks, 120
  securities trading, 45
  standard form contracts, 193
  teleservices, 168
  use of Internet banking, 21, 22

globalization, 11, 12
good faith, *culpa in contrahendo*, 177
Greece, 20, 61
Gyllenhammar Report 2002, 26, 57

Hague Conference, 151
harmonization
  advertising online services, 171–3, 179
  banking contracts, 183–205
  centralized supervisory powers, 103–5
  conflict of law rules, 291
  cross-border credit transfers, 200
  data protection, 179–82
  delaying tactics, 104
  Distance Marketing Directive, 79–80, 105, 168–71
  e-commerce, 77, 165–8
  EC Treaty, 85, 86
  or full decentralization, 105–9
  investment business, 214–18
  margins of discretion, 125–6
  marketing, 171–3, 179
  maximum harmonization
    consumer protection, 76, 82, 86, 275
    futility, 103–5, 313
    investment services, 218
  minimum financial harmonization, 56
    Banking Directive, 155
    consumer credit, 207, 210–13
    contents, 124–8
    and home state jurisdiction, 110, 123
  non-EU international initiatives, 150–3
  objective, 88
  online financial services
    advertising, 171–3, 179
    assessment, 226–8
    contracts, 199, 200–5
    investment services, 213–26
    relevant directives, 170
  policy costs, 103
  processes, 226–8

prudential banking regulation,
    154–6
  or regulatory competition, 105–9
  speed, 104, 106
  transparency, 127–8
  and uniform procedures, 128
Hawke, John D., 72
Heinemann, Friedrich, 24
Hertig, Gerard, 104
home banking, meaning, 8
home state regulation
  Banking Directive, 237–42
  and Basel Committee, 67
  benefits, 110, 232
  and conduct of business
    rules, 113
  consensus requirement, 252–3
  and democracy, 111–12
  Distance Marketing Directive, 80
  diversity of regulatory
    quality, 120–1
  e-commerce, 77
    case-by-case derogations,
      281–6, 309
    coordinated fields, 262, 266–78
    critique, 269–72
    domestic implementation,
      278–81, 284–6
    general derogations, 274–6
    normative impact, 286–8
    place of establishment, 276–8
    scope, 262–6
    theories, 268–9
  ECJ jurisprudence, 122–3
  effect, 73, 117, 317–18
  electronic commerce,
    harmonization, 166–7
  EU principle, 56, 75, 81,
    231, 272–4
  imperfect functioning, 82, 313,
    317–18
  investment services, 218, 237–42
  minimum harmonization condition,
    110, 123
  non-duplication, 110
  normative impact, 286–8
  notification of authorities, 241,
    244–5
  online financial services, 77
  prudential rules, 237–42, 268
  public interest exception, 242–3
  recent directives, 314–16
  retention of domestic
    powers, 57
  and single financial market, 98,
    99–123
  theories, 268–9
  trust between national regulators,
    128, 134
host state regulation
  advertising and marketing, 256–9
  consumer protection, 275–6
  e-commerce
    case-by-case, 281–6
    domestic implementation, 284–6
    emergency powers, 284, 317
    general cases, 274–6
    procedural conditions, 283–4
    public policy, 282
    substantive conditions, 282–3
  investor protection, 254–6
  non-prudential matters, 243–61
  outdated model, 317

IBANs, 203
identity of customers, 187,
    189, 222
IMF, 151
India, foreign banks, 60
information
  consumer credit, 206–7
  consumer right, 143
  cross-border credit
    transfers, 201
  Distance Marketing Directive,
    180–1, 251
  E-Commerce Directive, 251,
    180–1
  international regulatory
    cooperation, 129, 133
  investment services, 216–17
  pre-contractual requirements,
    177–9, 184–5
  EU policies, 76–7
information society services, 165,
    262, 263, 264–5

information systems
  errors, 159
  fraud, 159
  interruptions, 159
  misinformation, 159
  security, 159–60, 182
ING Direct (UK), 26
institutions
  See also financial institutions
  mutual recognition principle, 86–99
  single financial market, 84–6
  standard setting, 127
  trust between national regulators, 128, 134
insurance, 274
intermediaries, 12
internal market. See single market
International Accounting Standards Board, 151
international financial integration
  and conflict of contractual laws, 290–2
  consumer demand, 63
  and electronic commerce, 10–17
  EU. See single financial market
  Internet as catalyst, 7–20
  legal barriers. See legal barriers to integration
  meaning of integration, 10–12
  measuring, 26
  non-EU standards, 150–3
international standards
  institutions, 127, 150
  online banking, 150–3
Internet
  catalyst of international financial integration, 7–20
  and cooperation between national regulators, 130–1
  cross-border financial services, 37–40, 253–4
  financial benefits, 15, 313
  minimalist architecture, 17
  political challenges, 17, 20
  popular acceptance, 14
  protocols, 9, 17–18
  romanticism, 64, 67
  and single financial market, 12–17, 77–81
  transmission method, 9
Internet banking. See online financial services
Internet service agreements
  banking, 35–7
  French investor protection, 223
  securities trading, 47
investment services
  conduct of business rules
    domestic rules, 218
    EU regulation, 217
    France, 221
    Germany, 225–6
    United Kingdom, 219
  cross-border services
    French investor protection, 256
    German investor protection, 255–6
    host country rules, 254–6
    mutual recognition, 242
    UK investor protection, 255
  domestic regulation, 65
    France, 221
    Germany, 224–6
    investor protection, 218–26
    United Kingdom, 219–20
  execution only, 219, 222, 225–6
  harmonization, 214–18
  Investment Services Directive 1993
    harmonization effect, 216
    home country rules, 254, 256
    mutual recognition, 237–42
    reform, 256
  Markets in Financial Instruments Directive, 214–18
  mis-selling, 216
  mutual recognition, 218, 237–42
  online. See online investment services
  records, 217
  retail v. professional services, 219
  transparency, 217–18
IOSCO, 66, 150, 151, 213–14
*ius cogens,* 305

Jackson, Howell, 118
jurisdiction. *See* territorial jurisdiction

Kuhn, T., 70

Lamfalussy Report, 57, 75, 105, 228
Lee, Ruben, 104
legal barriers to integration
  1992 EU reforms, 56–8
  administrative quotas, 53
  conflict of laws, 4, 58–63
  deregulation, 82
  direct barriers, 52–4
  domestic contract laws, 183–4
  elimination, 11–12, 82, 312
  futility of total harmonization, 103–5
  hostility, 53
  indirect cost barriers, 54–6
  international banking, 51–6
  legal diversity, 54, 58–63
  and mutual recognition, 87
  and non-legal barriers, 62–3, 116–17, 127
  nuisance measures, 54
  'product rules', 62
  protectionism, 15–16, 104
  restrictions on foreign entry, 53
  structural barriers, 54–6
  uncertainty, 59–60
legal representation, 263
legal uncertainty
  applicable law, 270, 273
  domestic financial regulations, 59–60
  and harmonization of conflict of law rules, 291
  imperfect EU mechanisms, 82
  mandatory conflict rules, 305, 306, 315–17
  mutual recognition practice, 82, 98
liberalism, constitutional principle, 14
licensing. *See* banking licences
Lindsey, Brink, 11
loans. *See* consumer credit; electronic finance

Mackenzie Stuart, Lord, 95
Maduro, Miguel, 96
market economy principle, 86
market failure, 126–7
marketing
  *See also* advertising
  commercial communications, meaning, 172
  cross-border services, host country rules, 256–9
  EU legislation, 171
  French law, 173–4
  German law, 176–7
  harmonization, 171–3, 179
  UK law, 174–6
  unsolicited e-mail, 172–3, 174, 274
  websites, 300–1
member states
  dissimilarities, 99–100
  laws. *See* domestic laws
  national policy objectives, 90
  regulatory independence, 90
  sovereignty, 100, 103
mis-selling, 216
misrepresentation, 177, 258–9
money laundering, 151, 189
Montesquieu, Charles de, 54
mortgages online, 28
mutual recognition
  Banking Directive, 237–42, 288
  banking services and free movement, 89–99
  *Cassis de Dijon*, 90, 143
  concept, 87–8
  coordinated fields, 262, 266–78
  and country of origin. *See* home state regulation
  E-Commerce Directive. *See* E-Commerce Directive
  EU principle, 56, 86–99
  and freedom to provide services, 89–94
  and harmonization process, 227
  imperfect reality, 57, 73, 313, 317–18
  investment services, 218, 237–42
  legal uncertainty, 82, 98
  minimum harmonization prerequisite, 123

mutual recognition (*cont.*)
　model, 79–80, 82
　online financial services, 77
　perfecting, 74, 107, 108
　recent directives, 314–16
　and subsidiarity, 87
　theories, 268–9
　trust between national regulators, 128, 134
　uncoordinated, 106, 107

Niglia, Leone, 196–7
notaries, 263
notification, home state authorities
　EU Commission's view, 245–6
　French position, 246–8
　German position, 248
　requirement, 241, 244–5
　UK position, 248

OECD
　Financial Action Task Force, 150, 189, 190
　international standards, 151
　money laundering recommendations, 189, 190
Olson, Mancur, 19
Ombudsman schemes, 134
online contracts
　banker–customer relationship, 29, 188–9
　choice of law, 292–6
　customers' identity, 187, 189
　digital signatures, 187–8
　and financial integration, 183–4
　harmonization, 183–205, 199, 200–5
　information requirements, 184–5
　and money laundering, 189
　standard forms, 191–3
　　France, 193
　　Germany, 192, 193
　　notice, 193
　　United Kingdom, 192, 193
　Unfair Contract Terms Directive, 194–9
　validity, 185–90, 267–8
　withdrawal rights, 190–1

online financial services
　advertising. *See* advertising
　alternative regulatory model, 67–73
　bank accounts, 30–2
　banker–customer relationships, 7–9, 29–40
　benefits, 17
　categories of activities, 22–4
　causes of incomplete integration, 51–63
　choice and competition, 119
　communication methods, 8
　competition, 119
　and Consumer Credit Directive, 205–13
　contract. *See* contract; online contracts
　cross-border. *See* cross-border Internet banking
　directives, 77–81
　enforcement jurisdiction, 68–9
　EU policies, 73–81
　finance. *See* electronic finance
　financial risks, 148
　framework, 29–47
　freedom v. control, 18
　fund transfers. *See* electronic transfer of funds
　general good concept, 140–8
　harmonization. *See* harmonization
　and international legal framework, 19
　international regulation, 66–7
　Internet-only banks, 24, 28
　internet service agreements, 35–7, 47, 223
　investment. *See* online investment services
　legal uncertainty, 59–60
　marketing, 171–3, 179
　meaning, 8
　measuring impact, 24
　non-financial risks, 149
　practice, 20–8, 21
　pre-contract information, 177–9, 184–5
　providers, 24
　prudential issues and risks, 148–50

prudential regulation, 141–2
  EU harmonization, 154–6
  France, 160–2
  Germany, 162–4
  international standards, 150–3
  United Kingdom, 156–60
retail banking, 27–8
securities. *See* online securities
  trading
security. *See* security
survey of key countries, 22, 26
technical risks, 102
technological neutrality, 148
transparency. *See* transparency
user profiles, 21, 119, 316
online investment services
  cross-border services
    French investor protection, 256
    German investor protection,
      255–6
    home state regulation, 288
    UK investor protection, 255
  domestic laws of investor protection,
    218–26
    France, 221, 222–4
    Germany, 224–6
  harmonization, 213–26
  host country rules, 254–6
  risks, 213–14
  United Kingdom, 220
online securities trading
  agency laws, 45–6
  cross-border trading, 43–4
  domestic laws, 42–7
  execution-only, 43
  French law, 45–6
  German law, 45
  international standards, 66
  Internet service agreements, 47
  practice, 23
  process, 42–3
  UK law, 46
  US jurisdiction, 65–6
overdrafts
  domestic information
    rights, 210
  EU information rights, 206
  French law, 41, 210

Germany, 210
UK law, 40–1, 210

Pan, Eric, 118
Perritt, Henry, 130
pharmaceutical products, 71–2,
  122–3
politics, challenge of Internet, 17, 20
privacy, harmonization, 179–82
'product rules', 62, 128
proportionality, 85, 92, 105, 138
public interest exception
  Banking Directive, 242–3
  conflict of laws, mandatory
    rules, 306
  consumer protection, 142
  financial services, 140–8
  free movement principle, 91, 92,
    97–8
  harmonization of concept, 137–48
  honesty and integrity of services, 144
  host state regulation, 282
  justification, 138, 139, 140
  market for financial services, 137–40
  non-discriminatory application, 138
  proportionality, 138
  prudential safety standards, 141–2
  suitability test, 139–40
  transparency of services, 142–4

Qualisteam, 20

race to the bottom, 108–9, 118
regulatory authorities
  arbitrary actions against foreign
    institutions, 130
  competences, 129
  and consumer confidence, 129
  cooperation, 128, 134
  duty to integrate, 131
  mega-regulators, 129
  notification of home authorities,
    241, 244–5
  professional secrecy, 154
regulatory competition
  appeal, 104
  benefits, 107
  critique, 107

regulatory competition (*cont.*)
  'Delaware phenomenon', 109
  meaning, 106
  race to the bottom, 108–9, 118
  single financial market, 118–23
  unlimited competition, 105–9
remedies, out-of-court
  procedures, 134
*renvoi*, 273
retail banking online, 27–8
Romano, Roberta, 109
romanticism, 64, 67

savings accounts online, 28
Schüler, Martin, 24
securities trading
  agency laws, 45–6
  EU regulation, 44
  French law, 45–6
  German law, 45
  international principles, 151
  Markets in Financial Instruments
    Directive, 214–18
  online. *See* online securities trading
  principles, 213
  UK law, 46
security
  Basel Committee, 152, 153
  errors, 159
  fraud, 159
  French online banking
    regulation, 162
  German online banking regulation,
    163–4
  information systems, 159–60, 182
  international standards, 152
  interruptions, 159
  misinformation, 159
  online access control, 37
  online banking risks, 36–7,
    119–20
  risk management, 152, 153
  UK online banking regulation, 158
services
  consumer services and conflict of
    laws, 297, 299
  for remuneration, 263, 265
  freedom to provide, 89–94

information society. *See* information
  society
single financial market
  1992 reforms, 56–8
  competing objectives, 101–2
  competition and choice, 118–23
  and conflict of laws, 289–90
  consumer confidence, 121–2
  consumer credit, 205
  consumer demand, 63, 117
  deregulation, 82
  duties of regulators, 131
  emergence, 312
  EU policies, 74–5
  and euro, 16
  European supervision agency,
    113–14
  free movement principle, 94–9
  full decentralization model, 105–9
  gaps, 57
  harmonization. *See* harmonization
  home state regulation. *See* home
    state regulation
  incomplete integration of online
    services, 51–63
  institutional foundations, 84–6
  and Internet, 12–17, 77–81
  legal barriers. *See* legal barriers to
    integration
  minimum harmonization model,
    110, 123
  mutual recognition, 56, 57
  political economy, 99–102
  public interest exception, 137–40
  regulatory competition model,
    105–9
  regulatory models, 70–3, 79–80,
    82–4
  supply side, 63
  total harmonization model, 103–5
single market
  1970s political sclerosis, 105
  characteristics, 11
  and e-commerce, 106
  financial. *See* single financial market
  harmonization. *See* harmonization
  institutional foundations, 84–6
  legal and institutional gaps, 51

legal barriers. *See* legal barriers to integration
and less developed EU countries, 86
requirements, 2
values, 83
Spain, Internet banking, 20
spamming, 172–3, 174, 274
spot markets, 19
standards. *See* international standards
state sovereignty, 100, 103
subsidiarity, 85, 87, 105
supremacy of EU law, 85
Switzerland, foreign banks, 60

taxation, 263
telegraphic fund transfer, 7
telephone banking, meaning, 8
territorial jurisdiction
   conflict of laws. *See* conflict of laws
   country of origin. *See* home state regulation
   and cross-border online banking, 244–61
   determination, 58
   'effects doctrine', 58–63, 65, 67
   enforcement jurisdiction, 68–9
   international law principle, 58
   local targeting, 65, 67, 115
   national criteria, 60, 67
   and place of online banking services, 244–61
      EU Commission's views, 245–6
      French position, 246–8, 251
      German view, 248
      UK position, 248
   territorial connection, 65–6
Tiebout, Charles, 106
torts
   conflict of laws, 287–8
   France, 259–61
   Germany, 259–61
   United Kingdom, 257–9
   English economic torts, 174
Trachtman, Joel, 70
transparency
   consumer credit, 205
   financial services, 142–4
   French investor protection, 222

harmonization process, 127–8
investment services, 217–18
online financial services, 177–9
trust. *See* consumer confidence

UNCITRAL, 151, 185
unfair contract terms
   Directive, 194–9, 298
   factors, 195
   implementation of Directive, 196–9, 197
   legal jargon, 198
   lists, 194, 198, 199
   meaning, 194, 196–9
   non-consumer contracts, 195
   scope, 194–5
   UK case law, 298
UNIDROIT, 151
United Kingdom
   advertising and marketing, 174–6, 257
   bank accounts, 30, 188
   banker–customer relationship, 204
   Banking Code, 204
   banking regulator, 30
   capital adequacy, 158
   common law, 29
   conduct on business rules, application, 234
   conflict of laws
      criminal offences, 257
      localization of online banking services, 248
   consumer contracts, 298
   consumer credit, 41, 208
      agreements, 207–9
      early repayments, 209
      overdrafts, 210
      party autonomy, 211–12
   consumer protection, 156
   contracts
      characteristic performance, 296
      standard forms, 192, 193
      validity of electronic contracts, 186–7
   credit law, 40–1
   cross-border Internet banking
      advertising and marketing, 257

United Kingdom (*cont.*)
  investor protection, 255
  national regulation, 232–5
  e-commerce
    EEA countries, 279–80, 284–5
    home and host state regulation,
      278–80, 284–6, 288
    implementation of directives
      Data Protection, 182
      Distance Marketing, 170, 182
      E-Commerce, 167, 186–7, 278–80,
        284–6, 288
      Unfair Contract Terms,
        196–9, 298
  investor protection, 219–20, 255
  London Stock Exchange, 133
  online banking
    prudential regulation, 156–60
    security, 37, 120
    transfer of funds, 33–4
  volume, 21, 22
  regulatory competition, 118
  securities trading, 46
United States
  centralised regulatory powers, 103
  'Delaware phenomenon', 109
  National Commission on Electronic
    Fund Transfers, 149
  online securities trading jurisdiction,
    65–6
  regulatory competition, 118
  regulatory model, 114
user profiles, 21, 119, 316

Voltaire, 54, 56

Williams, Jody, 130
WTO, 2, 101

*Yahoo* case, 68–9

For EU product safety concerns, contact us at Calle de José Abascal, 56–1°,
28003 Madrid, Spain or eugpsr@cambridge.org.

www.ingramcontent.com/pod-product-compliance
Ingram Content Group UK Ltd.
Pitfield, Milton Keynes, MK11 3LW, UK
UKHW011327060825
461487UK00005B/401